This anthology represents the diversity of experiences of social class of University of Michigan undergraduate students. Authored by students during the university's bicentennial year, this volume includes essays by students from a broad range of class backgrounds. Informed by a sociological lens, the writers trace the imprint of larger forces on their individual experiences. The students were guided in the production of the essays by Dr. Dwight Lang. This collection will become part of the historical record.

—Elizabeth Armstrong, University of Michigan, Ann Arbor, author of *Paying for the Party: How College Maintains Inequality*

This is a remarkable project and one we sorely need in the academy. We owe a debt of gratitude to Dwight Lang's students for their honest and heartfelt accounts of growing up and going to college in a society steeped in class inequality. Stories like these can help guide new generations towards healthier and happier social arrangements. They remind us the damages of class run far and deep, for all of us. It is time for a change. Read this book now!

—Allison L. Hurst, Oregon State University, author of *The Burden of Academic Success: Managing Working-Class Identities in College.*

It used to be said that Americans don't think about class. The stories in *Social Class Voices* reveal this is no longer true, if it ever was. Beautifully recounting the slights, shame, confusion, contradictions, surprises, and occasional joys at living in an unequal society, these students show, far from not thinking about social class, our daily encounters do not let us avoid it.

—Jessi Streib, Duke University, author of *The Power of the Past: Understanding Cross-Class Marriages*

Social Class Voices is a timely, honest, and personal reflection into the lives of modern college students across the social class spectrum. Bursting with insights about how to truly make colleges inclusive and welcoming for all.

—Dilip Das, University of Michigan, Ann Arbor, Assistant Vice Provost, Office of the Vice Provost for Equity, Inclusion and Academic Affairs

SOCIAL CLASS VOICES: STUDENT STORIES FROM THE UNIVERSITY OF MICHIGAN BICENTENNIAL

Edited by
Dwight Lang,
University of Michigan, Ann Arbor
and Aubrey Schiavone,
University of Denver

Published in the United States of America by
Michigan Publishing
Manufactured in the United States of America

DOI: dx.doi.org/10.3998/mpub.9895231

ISBN 978-1-60785-433-3 (paper)
ISBN 978-1-60785-434-0 (e-book)

Front cover image: "The Wanderers, The Good People Series" 2012 Oil on Canvas ©
by Laurie Pace, http://lauriepace.com

An imprint of Michigan Publishing, Maize Books serves the publishing needs of
the University of Michigan community by making high-quality scholarship widely
available in print and online. It represents a new model for authors seeking to share
their work within and beyond the academy, offering streamlined selection, production,
and distribution processes. Maize Books is intended as a complement to more formal
modes of publication in a wide range of disciplinary areas.

http://www.maizebooks.org

For Albert and Dorothy Lang

CONTENTS

ACKNOWLEDGMENTS

We would like to acknowledge the support of the Bicentennial Theme Semester Planning Committee at the University of Michigan. The committee made funding available to revise Dwight Lang's winter 2017 semester bicentennial course: The Experience of Social Class in College and the Community (Sociology 295). Funds also supported editorial assistance for student anthology writers.

The University of Michigan Bicentennial Office, College of Literature, Science and Arts Dean's Office, the Department of Sociology, and Sweetland Center for Writing provided additional funding for anthology production. Sweetland Center for Writing peer tutors generously worked with contributors as they revised essay drafts during the 2017 winter semester.

We would like to thank Angel Dillard (Associate Dean for Undergraduate Education, College of Literature, Science and Arts), Gary Krenz (Executive Director, University of Michigan Bicentennial Office), Al Young (Professor and former Chair, Department of Sociology), Elizabeth Armstrong (Professor, Department of Sociology), Howard Kimeldorf (Professor Emeritus, Department of Sociology), Christine Modey (Peer Writing Program Director, Sweetland Center for Writing), Elise Bodei (Student Administrative Manager, Department of Physics), Dilip Das (Assistant Vice Provost for Academic Affairs, Office of Diversity, Equity, and Inclusion), Jessi Streib (Assistant Professor,

Department of Sociology, Duke University), Sylvia Wanner Lang, and Greg Merritt for their interests in supporting explorations of student social class experiences.

During the summer of 2016, LeAnn Fields (Senior Executive Editor, University of Michigan Press) provided initial and useful feedback to Dwight Lang regarding his idea for an anthology examining social class experiences of Michigan undergraduates. Jason Colman (Director, Michigan Publishing Services) was very helpful in planning and production stages. And Amanda Karby (Digital Publishing Coordinator, Michigan Publishing Services) handled important details leading up to the anthology's publication.

Finally, we are grateful to our contributors for their openness and honesty. Social class experiences can be difficult to write about, but everyone was up to the challenge. These Michigan alums and current University of Michigan students make visible what is often hidden. Go Blue!

Introduction: Social Class at Michigan
Dwight Lang

Images

If you turn to the back cover of this anthology, you will see University of Michigan students standing and sitting in front of the Student Union on State Street across from Angell Hall here in Ann Arbor. This photo was taken on a cool, cloudy April 13, 2017. You will see a few students born to working poor families. You will see some students born to the working class. You will see others born to middle-class families. You will see students born to the upper-middle class. And you will see a few students born to upper-class families. Can you determine their class backgrounds? If it is difficult to get a close look at these students' faces, turn to the contributor section to see student photos, as well as their brief biographies. For detailed narratives making more visible the typically invisible phenomena of social class background and identity, turn to the Table of Contents and carefully read their remarkable social class stories—a type of class meditation.

These voices reveal important aspects of the Michigan story.

University of Michigan and Higher Education Stories

Anthologies are products of collective efforts and this anthology is no exception. In these pages we read social class stories carefully crafted by Michigan alumni and current undergraduates at the University of Michigan. They explore important social class experiences in their families, in K–12 education years, in communities where they grew up, and during their time here in Ann Arbor. As students share aspects of their inner and public lives, we also gain insights into how social class is experienced in the wider society. I admire my students' openness and honesty; they help tell important, too often ignored, stories of social class in America.

The anthology emerges from a course I have taught at the University of Michigan since 2007: The Experience of Social Class in College and the Community (Sociology 295). All anthology contributors have taken this course. The course examines how social class differences and inequalities are created and encountered in America—particularly as students study in our schools and eventually live and work in wider communities. For purposes of our course, students and I define "social class" as groupings of people who share similar incomes and wealth, similar occupations, similar levels of education, and similar cultural components (e.g., language, musical/artistic tastes, food, and leisure). We also discuss a variety of factors influencing one's social class background and identity, especially family and educational experiences. Close attention is paid to how individuals experience social class in economically struggling areas and wealthier, more comfortable communities. Ironically, class inequalities thrive in a society publically committed to equality of opportunity for all, but also in the same society unable to achieve its well-intentioned ideals. The course considers this contradiction as well as matters of ethics and social justice. In the early 21st century, we need to move beyond simply analyzing the extent of social class inequality and then making attempts to construct policy solutions. It is time to challenge the morality of America's centuries-old class inequalities and the human suffering they create. Future generations rely on our visions and resolve.

During the winter 2017 semester, students wrote their class stories and located these stories in broader social contexts of social class differences in America. Throughout the semester, I facilitated class discussions and interaction with course readings that asked students to consider a number of questions regarding systems of social class inequality.

Is social justice achievable for all social class groups in America?

Are humans free, given various existing class inequalities?

Why have we been unable and unwilling to achieve our meritocratic ideals for all?

Why do we allow class inequality to exist and persist?

Why do we underfund K–12 education in working- and lower-class areas, thus guaranteeing social class inequality for millions of children? How is this purposeful class stratification shameful, unethical, and immoral?

Why do we expect colleges to solve problems of unequal educational access, given ongoing K–12 inequalities?

Why do most Americans—especially those more economically privileged—claim class inequality is nonexistent? Is inequality necessary and inevitable when some choose to drop out of school? Is it just that millions of children attend run-down, failing K–12 schools?

Why do 16 million American children live in households that struggle to put enough food on the table each day?

How and why does capitalism (our "free market") leave and maintain a certain percentage of the population ("reserve labor") at, slightly above, or below the official poverty line?

How do social class inequalities actually benefit millions of more affluent Americans? Why do more privileged Americans often avoid reflecting on their social class conditions?

What social and economic changes are needed to give all children—regardless of class of birth—authentic equal opportunities?

My winter 2017 Sociology 295 was also designated as a university bicentennial course. I examined how the University of Michigan has addressed social class differences from the early days of 1817 to the second decade of the 21st century. We examined, for example, how and why in 1879 James Angell—the third president of the University of Michigan—envisioned our institution as "The University of the Poor." With various historical and contemporary contexts in mind, students wrote 10- to 15-page essays exploring selected social class experiences from their own personal lives before starting Michigan and during their time on campus. Essays were written, edited, and revised, with feedback from myself and my coeditor Aubrey Schiavone, within time constraints of a four-month semester. I am indebted to Aubrey for her insights regarding the writing process and her commitment to students and this anthology project. Thirty-three (out of 39) students chose to have their essays appear in the anthology, while 12 former Sociology 295 students also composed essays. These 45 essays from individuals from a variety of disciplines provide a fascinating snapshot of undergraduate life at the University of Michigan's Bicentennial.

> Life is just a short walk from the cradle to the grave—and it sure behooves us to be kind to one another along the way.
> —Alice Childress, American playwright

Social Class in the Classroom

As a way to more comfortably discuss social class differences in the college classroom, I acknowledge student lives and experiences at the traditional ages of 18–22. I make it clear that students are not responsible for economic inequalities and related human suffering we will be studying. I also acknowledge that though preceding generations—parents, grandparents, and great-grandparents— have been unable to successfully solve these problems, social class inequality today is a result of complex systems and collective activities rather than the fault of single individuals from any one social class. And someday—as their adulthoods evolve—they will be responsible for finding solutions. They will explain to their children, grandchildren, nieces, and nephews why problems of social class inequality exist, persist, or are being successfully addressed.

Students from economic comfort and privilege should not be guilty, and students born to economic want should not feel shame. We are in Sociology 295 to study and discuss why social class inequality exists, and is created and sustained by an economic system—capitalism—evolving over centuries to the present day. Students should not hold college peers responsible for social class differences or the effects of those differences. This approach gives all students—regardless of their social class background—permission to be honest and open without guilt or shame and more easily talk and think across economic boundaries, both in the classroom and as they write.

Sociological Creative Nonfiction Strategies

These "sociological creative nonfiction" essays explore social forces shaping students' lives and changing identities, as those identities are located in our nation's ongoing social class structure. Student class identities are relatively fresh, not yet fully developed or influenced by realities of marriage, parenthood, career, or geographical mobility. Essays acknowledge how we are not simply products of our personal experiences. How we define ourselves and places in society we have been randomly born into are largely—but not totally—products of shifting class and economic forces beyond our control. Student essays show how we are socially constructed in complicated ways. Using this sociological lens and addressing selected course questions, students write about meaningful personal experiences and histories. By exploring the past and present, they write accounts of American college students and students at the University of Michigan—histories likely to be read in 50 years (2067) and at Michigan's Tricentennial Celebration (2117).

In addition to capturing key social class experiences before and during college, we see how student worlds and identities have changed over time—from earliest years in family to recent and current college experiences. College is a crucial period in life, filled with thoughts of transition from childhood homes to independent, young adulthoods. Students explore how these changes are frequently filled with a variety of emotions. Writing about aspects of one's inner life—as related to social class—allows students to carefully consider connections between the personal and the social. Their college journeys are more complete as they contemplate these essential relationships—a key sociological insight.

In her memoir *Bone Black* bell hooks (1996) describes creative nonfiction as an effort to "recover the past." These undergraduate writers use sociological lenses to explore their past and present social constructions. They help us to better understand the powerful influence of social class whether we are born to poverty or wealth, or whether we are born to the working-, middle-, or upper-middle classes.

George Saunders - in My Writing Eduction (2015) - also considers the positive virtues of good writing. Early in the semester, as current and past students planned their essays, I encouraged them to reflect on Saunders' insight: "A story should be honest, direct, loving, restrained." My students wrote in ways that allow readers to engage, interpret and imagine experiences of social class for themselves. Their essays reflect the writer Margaux Fragoso's (2011) suggestion: "My feeling is that writers should give readers the freedom to think for themselves and form their own opinions."

I give these Michigan students from across America's class spectrum a lot of credit. They honestly reveal aspects of their class heritages at a time when many Americans still have trouble acknowledging the power of social class difference. Perhaps student willingness to disclose is a sign of the times, as more and more Americans recognize economic inequality as a core structural problem facing millions—independent of individual efforts and talents. Perhaps the inclination to write about their lives is a product of our new social media age in which individuals are continually encouraged to reflect on their own experiences and identities. Perhaps their interest in exploring social class is a product of colleges like Michigan stressing race and gender inequalities for the last 50 years, while paradoxically not publicly acknowledging obvious campus class inequalities. Student writing sheds light on what is too often overlooked on and off campus: social class. This type of writing, by its very nature, is also political. In the United States where social class is too often ignored or minimized, openly writing about one's own social class experiences can be controversial—generating degrees of trepidation for both writers and readers.

Hopefully anthologies like these will assist colleges across the country to more effectively address campus social class disparities, thereby helping lower-income, working-, and lower-class students—usually first in their families attending college—to thrive, not merely survive. As we know from empirical research in the field of higher education, diverse learning contexts in colleges enrich learning for all students. As such, public recognition of class differences can likewise help all students, regardless of backgrounds, to reach out and effectively communicate across economic, racial, and other constructed boundaries.

Social Class Voices: Student Stories from the University of Michigan Bicentennial is unique in important ways. First, creative nonfiction work addressing social class differences is usually completed by older writers, graduate students, and/or faculty members (see, for example, Collins et al., 2014; Dews and Law, 1995; hooks, 1996, 2000; Hurst and Nenga, 2016; Ryan and Sackrey, 1995; Welsch, 2004). In this anthology we read about experiences of undergraduates previously or currently enrolled at a selective, large, public university. Second, most writing about class experiences emerges from people born to the working and lower classes. In *Social Class Voices*, we hear from students not only born to the working poor and working class, but also to middle- and upper-middle classes, as well as the upper class. Students raised in economic privilege frequently find it difficult to reflect on their class experiences. In these stories we read about growing up in significant economic comfort and certainty.

Before former and winter semester 2017 Sociology 295 students started writing, I had the opportunity to talk with each person about essay ideas and approaches. We discussed differences between *showing* and *telling* and I encouraged them to use important scenes to share their social class stories. Writing that only *tells* readers about subjects, places, or persons feels remote and misses opportunities to connect with readers in immediate and understandable ways. Students in *Social Class Voices* vividly *show* important people, situations, scenes, and places in action and dialogue. They directly show us how social class influences children, students, and adults in powerful ways—both private and public.

I asked students if they had any regrets, as related to their social class backgrounds. Is this something that might guide their essays? I also encouraged each student to think about how readers might evaluate the kind of person they are. As they have been randomly born to one social class or another, and as they are Michigan undergraduates or alumni of the University of Michigan in the early 21st century, how will readers—across time—assess their characters and intentions?

Finally, I encouraged students to think deeply about how we imagine solutions to inequality. Is the problem of social class inequality simply a matter of America's inability to foster more upward mobility, thus failing to produce an ample supply of middle-class consumers? Or is class inequality a moral issue—separate from the urgencies and complications of economic production and consumption? Does America, as a matter of public policy, sustain social class inequalities? If so, do we need to address the moral implications of maintaining human suffering for millions? I asked students if they are radical thinkers—that is people who seek the roots of social class inequality. Should we merely list and review the countless, cruel effects of ongoing economic differences? Should we challenge existing policy options—often failed—intended to end human misery? If not, then how do we account for social class stratification in American society?

The anthology is organized by what individual students identified as their family's social class status: working poor, working class, middle class, upper-middle class, upper class, and mixed class. While most Michigan students hail from the working-, middle-, and upper-middle classes, we also hear from those whose parents are wealthy or barely surviving on minimum wages. Mixed class students often describe how their families experienced significant downward or upward mobility.

Social Class Measurement

Together, students and I discussed many factors influencing their social class identities, including but not limited to: parents' income, wealth, occupations, and education, as well as students' educational histories before college, and their work experiences before and during college. These varied influences on social class identity are apparent in students' narratives and in personal moments they've chosen to share and describe. However, parents' income featured heavily in our discussions of social class in general and of students' individual social class identities.

For purposes of our course, social class correlates with family/ parental *yearly* income as follows: poor and working poor: less than $29,999; working class: $30,000–$59,999; middle class: $60,000– $99,999; upper-middle class: $100,000–$249,999; and upper class: $250,000 or more. Because students are usually unaware of parental wealth (e.g., stocks, bonds, real estate) I did not ask them to identify these elements of class position.

For purposes of comparison between anthology contributors and Michigan undergraduates, see *Estimated Parental Incomes* provided by 72.3% ($n = 4,846$) of entering first-year students in fall 2016. These income distributions reflect the general social class composition of all undergraduates at the University of Michigan ($n = 28,983$ for 2016/2017) (Student Life, 2016).

Poor and working poor (less than $29,999):	7.4%
Working class ($30,000–$59,999):	7.8%
Middle class ($60,000–$99,999):	13.7%
Upper-middle class ($100,000–$249,999):	37.4%
Upper class I ($250,000–$499,999):	14.3%
Upper class II ($500,000 and above):	10.2%

Equipped with these specific social class income brackets and various characteristics of social class, students composed narrative essays included in this anthology. As emphasized throughout this introduction, social class is a complex phenomenon that is exceedingly challenging to write about. I hope you will encounter these student essays with patience and empathy. I commend student writers who have contributed to this anthology for their creativity, their honesty, their bravery, and their willingness to reflect on such an off-limits, often invisible topic as social class in America. As you read I hope you can do the same.

See Essay Guidelines in the Appendix. I am available to discuss this resource further with anyone interested in assigning a similar essay.

Works Cited

Collins, Chuck, Jennifer Ladd, Maynard Seider, Felice Yeskel (eds). *Class Lives: Stories from across Our Economic Divide.* Cornell University Press, 2014.

Dews, C. L. Barney, and Carolyn Law (eds). *This Fine Place So Far from Home: Stories of Academics from the Working Class.* Temple University Press, 1995.

hooks, bell. *Bone Black: Memories of Girlhood.* Henry Holt and Company, 1996.

hooks, bell. *Where We Stand: Class Matters.* Routledge, 2000.

Hurst, Allison and Sandi Kawecka Nenga (eds). *Working in Class: Recognizing How Social Class Shapes Our Academic Work.* Rowman & Littlefield, 2016.

Fragoso, Margaux. *Tiger, Tiger: A Memoir.* Farrar, Straus, Giroux, 2011.

Ryan, Jake and Charles Sackrey (eds). *Strangers in Paradise: Academics from the Working Class.* University Press of America, 1995.

Saunders, George. "My Writing Education: A Time Line," *The New Yorker*, October, 2015.

Student Life (2016). https://studentlife.umich.edu/research/factbook; University of Michigan.

Welsch, Kathleen, L (ed). *Those Winter Sundays: Female Academics and Their Working Class Parents*. University Press of America, 2004.

Part I

WORKING POOR

FEELING DOWN ON MY WAY UP
VIANNEY FLORES

I like to believe my story is a continuation of my parents' story, so I'll start there. They were both born in Mexico and arrived in Chicago, roughly around 18 years of age. They met soon after working at a factory, married, and had me, and my sister followed two years later. Growing up, my parents worked multiple jobs, often at once, that varied between working in a factory or working in janitorial services. When I was a baby, we would move from basement to basement and had horrible experiences with flooding and rat infestations. For most of my life, however, we lived in an apartment on the first floor in Brighton Park, a predominantly Hispanic neighborhood with not too much gang activity at the time and where parts of houses were rented out as apartments.

I still remember how amazing it felt to live there in the beginning. We had never lived in the first floor of an apartment, much less in one in which the landlord didn't live in! The first time we visited, it felt surreal. There were windows you could look through! There was a backyard with a tree and a deck to which we had direct access to! And we also rented the garage... we had a garage!! The walls were white and clean and the floors wooden and polished. This apartment was so incredible to us; we lived there from my second grade elementary school year until senior year of high school. It wasn't until I left to college that my family bought a house on the south side of Chicago, where we live now. We bought it with damaged doors, stained carpets, creaky floorboards, and unstable flooring, but at least it was ours. Although the neighborhood wasn't the safest, that house was a personal achievement for my family and me. We no longer paid monthly rent to anyone, we could paint the walls whatever color we wanted to, and we could add extra rooms, and choose whether or not to have carpet flooring! It was the first time I've ever had my own room and that initial excitement hasn't worn off yet. You never finish fixing a house, but I can definitely say it looks much better and feels more personalized than when we first bought it.

When we were kids, my parents were not always in well-enough financial standing to afford a babysitter for my sister and me. When they could, we were handed to family members, neighbors, friends, and maybe acquaintances. When they were in a situation where they couldn't find someone to take care of us, they would try to take us to work or leave us at home by ourselves. I still remember cold nights when my sister and I slept in the car outside my parents' workplace while they worked through the night. Sometimes we would take our bikes and my mom would clean a whole factory by herself while my dad supervised us as we happily rode our bikes in the large, empty parking lot. When I was around eight years old, my parents trusted me to take care of my sister and we were often left alone. These were stressful times for my parents. Sometimes they would get calls from my sister and me fighting and crying, neither of us mature enough to back down after stating we were calling mom. But my poor parents could only feel frustration at the fact they were far and were in too much need of money to leave work and handle the situation properly. All they could do was beg me to understand and to stop fighting with my little sister.

One job in particular took over our lives for three years. Both my parents decided to dedicate themselves to delivering newspapers before the sun rose near suburbs of Chicago. For three years, with only days of vacation every year, my parents had horrible sleeping schedules. They would work at night up until morning under stressful and physically demanding circumstances, often with second and third jobs throughout the day. In the summer, my parents paid my sister and me to help roll the hundreds of papers into little colored bags and then help dad deliver them by running up and down the neighborhood and skillfully throw them near front doors and hope they didn't end up behind a bush. It was such an odd job that my cousins would stay with us a couple of days to help us deliver newspaper for fun. I remember bringing my friends to show them what my parents did for a living. My sister and I often complained about having to help them, but I always felt a pang of guilt every day I didn't go because I was given the luxury to choose and my parents didn't have that. Even as a kid I wouldn't ask for much because I experienced firsthand what my parents went through for every dollar they earned. They were working to provide my sister and me with food, clothing, toys, and trips to arcades. I knew how much my parents appreciated my help and how much earlier they finished with an extra person, so if I didn't help, did I have a right to ask for a snack at the store?

Looking back, I can't say I felt embarrassed about my parents having this job. I didn't have friends from extremely well-off families. Everyone I knew struggled in one way or another; otherwise they wouldn't live in our neighborhood and go to my school. Working-class families were all there was in my world. Somewhere in the back of my mind I knew I wasn't in the ideal situation, but I didn't realize just how poor I really was until later in life.

My mother always told us we had it better than most other people. Not only would she refer to starving kids in Africa, but she would also tell us how, as a kid, it was rare for her to get a new outfit in a household with six other siblings and that when she did, she wore it every Sunday to church until it was worn out. She would remind us at Christmas how my dad never got the fancy, expensive toy cars he wanted as a kid because his single mom couldn't afford it. We were very fortunate to get what we did for Christmas. My mom loves to remind us how she used to drown us with toys from the dollar store and we would play with them happily for hours at a time. Yes, I was aware that we couldn't afford to take luxurious vacations, that we didn't own the latest technologies, that if our dog got sick we couldn't afford visits to the vet, that my sister constantly caused a scene in the store when she was denied an expensive toy, and that I wasn't in private school because it was expensive.

Ever since we were little girls, my parents stressed the importance of doing well in school. From experience, they knew that in this country you had to have a degree for most careers. My mom even went back to school to get her GED (General Education Development) test and learn English because she knew it would give her an advantage in the job market to be bilingual and have an educational background in the United States. It wasn't easy at all, and like most working-class students, she took classes at night. No matter how difficult of a situation she was in, she proudly arrived home with 100% on her assignments. "You have no excuse," she would tell us, "you don't have to work, you don't have kids, and you don't even have to cook or clean. All you need to do is focus on school. If I can do it, imagine how far you can go." Being in a Mexican American household often means speaking Spanglish, and my mom says she didn't want her daughters speaking in another language in front of her without her understanding. In reality, however, this has given her a huge advantage in the workplace. She would later go on to become a manager at a clothing store and then at a cleaning company because she was able to read, write, and speak English. It made me realize the impact that even a GED could have in her social class standing. She also made me realize the amazing advantage I was given at being fluent in two languages.

My parents firmly believe we are in the land of opportunity and that it is possible for my sister and me to be upwardly mobile. "Echale ganas a la escuela, mija" ("Work hard in school, sweetie") mom would tell me. "No quieres partirte la madre como nosotros, mejor ve al colegio y buscate una carrera" ("You don't want to work as hard as we do, go to college and find yourself a career") dad would say. It was crucial to my parents that my sister and I took advantage of every possible opportunity to exceed in school. Education was the key to success. It was important for my parents that we live a life where we didn't live paycheck to paycheck and could afford luxuries they never could.

Although they stressed the importance of our education, they didn't know how to help us. Because of where we lived, I went to our neighborhood elementary school from second grade through eighth grade. Overall, I was a bright student. I had the grades, the reputation, and the certificates. However, my mistake was getting an education in the wrong school. My parents had no way of knowing that not every school was equal, and even the neighborhood you can afford to live in determines the quality of education. My school had drama, not only among students, but also among teachers. The teachers used their phones, had us work in our textbooks, or watch a documentary instead of teaching, and they let the drama among themselves affect students' grades. Reflecting on these experiences, I can see how the teachers might have given up, in a sense, to provide a good education when most students ended up dropping out of high school, if they attended at all. I could see how taking us to jail for our eighth grade field trip was a desperate attempt to scare us into avoiding gang-related activities. I can also see why we had oversized uniforms in our sport clubs; who has money left over when the past two principals were trying to steal it the whole time?

My algebra teacher was the only one who taught me anything meaningful. I didn't know that at the time, but when I tried applying to selective high schools I failed the exams so miserably that my only choice was my neighborhood high school: Kelly High School. I was crushed at the realization that I wasn't as smart as I thought, especially in comparison to the rest of the city. However, I was fortunate enough to hear about Noble Street Charter Schools and they completely changed the course of my life. They accepted students based on a lottery system (randomly pulling your name out of a bowl) and I was lucky enough to be accepted to UIC College Preparatory in Chicago. The school had a 100% student acceptance rate to four-year universities and high ACT (American College Testing) averages. I was getting a second opportunity at my future because they didn't take my educational past into account; they were letting me start over. Of course, because of my elementary school background, I was at a disadvantage. Based on my entrance exams performance, I was placed in regular courses as opposed to honors in my first semester. However, I noticed the vast difference in the quality of education I was given at my high school and was given the proper tools to succeed and get into honors courses the very next semester and during the rest of my high school years.

At UIC we had to wear proper uniforms, be on time to everything, hand in excellent work, and maintain an amazing grade point average (GPA). Every teacher was required to have office hours, and we were taught to answer emails within two business days and how to dress formally, and so on. Most students identified as first-generation college students and/or minorities, so the school was prepared for all the questions and assistance we and our families needed. Being a first-generation student myself (someone first in the family to graduate from college), I appreciated having a college seminar class where I learned everything from which college to apply to, to how loans work. I know my parents appreciated parent meetings that had translators for those who spoke Spanish because it allowed them to understand and feel more comfortable asking questions.

Because of the strict rules on uniforms, it was hard to identify which student was part of what social class. We weren't allowed to wear logos or too many accessories, so the only way people could show they were from a certain class was taking opportunities to go abroad that most of us couldn't afford. One student in particular loved to brag about having a mansion on a hill and how his dad was a cop; you could just hear the class privilege in his voice and the respect he demanded because of his family's economic background. Freshman year of high school, I was dating a guy for a couple of weeks, unaware of his social class status. It wasn't until I was introduced to his mom that I saw he lived in a crowded basement with mismatching furniture, random decorations, and a run-down kitchen. I learned he worked with his mom at the local Dunkin Donuts to try to make ends meet. He was incredibly smart, but he never had the time to do his homework and his grades suffered.

He eventually dropped out of school and moved back to Mexico. It was a real scenario that made me appreciate that I was privileged enough not to have to work to survive and I was able to focus on my education.

During my sophomore year, I joined a program called Minds Matter. It was a nonprofit organization that paid for students from low-income families to go to summer college programs. In Minds Matter, I had ACT (American College Testing) prep on the weekends and a mentor with a college degree who assisted me with the application process to summer college programs and then college. Thanks to this program, I was able to go to Skidmore College in Saratoga, New York, the summer of my sophomore year and the University of Maryland the summer of my junior year for five and three weeks consecutively to take college courses and get a feel for what college would be like. During these experiences, I encountered people from social classes vastly different from my own. One friend in particular was always carrying around an umbrella because she didn't want to get tanned, a completely new concept to me. This was the first time I encountered a person who truly believed the whiter you were, the better. I made a point of explaining how tanning can be beautiful too, and after that conversation, she didn't get anxious leaving the dorms without an umbrella. Thankfully, Minds Matter gave me a $150 stipend on top of paying for my flight and pre-college program, so I didn't feel excluded from any events because I had saved so much money from the experience. I felt I could eat out with friends and do activities such as bowling as much as we planned because I had nothing else to spend money on.

My most memorable socioeconomic shocks came when I arrived at the University of Michigan (UM). I wasn't aware of the amount of prestige that surrounded Michigan. Although I felt prepared academically, I was not prepared to see Canada Goose jackets everywhere, UGGs and Bearpaw boots, Timberlands, and Apple watches. To this day, I don't think I've grasped the wealth of students' parents at this university. I know how much these brands cost, but I think I avoid thinking about how much that excess money would have been helpful to people in need—it just makes me sad. I try to focus on the fact that I am sitting in the same classroom as others who attended private schools and most likely had tutors. In the end, we all ended up in the same university receiving a great education.

The summer before starting college, I was in MSTEM. I wasn't invited into the Michigan Summer Bridge Program, which was highly recommended for some students of color and some first-generation students, so I decided to do MSTEM instead. They were both summer programs designed for accepted students to get a head start by getting to know the university before being an official student. Aside from college credit, I gained a diverse group of friends from this program. Spring break that freshman year, I decided to go skiing with these friends. It was my first time ever, but one of my friends, let's call him Daniel, was an expert snowboarder because it was what he usually did for fun. Because it was a long drive up Michigan, my boyfriend and I decided to sleep over at Daniel's house to get an early start. He had a car, so he would be able to drive us the rest of the way.

I remember how upset Daniel was that I got a full ride to UM and he was taking out thousands in loans. I told him I had great financial need, my family makes less than $25,000 a year, and if he didn't get a lot of aid, he may have been able to afford it. But nothing I said would calm him down. He didn't have the money either, he would tell me, and it wasn't fair.

When we first pulled into Daniel's garage, the first thing that struck me was the neighborhood: mowed lawns, houses back to back, no empty lots, no fences, beautiful large houses. And then there was his beautiful home. We went inside this amazing place. It was perfectly painted, spacious, and beautifully decorated, and he had a "man cave" in the basement. I'm talking about four new reclining leather sofas, a mini bar, UM decorations everywhere (and I know from visits to our M Den Store they do *not* come cheap), large TV, and animals on the walls from their father–son hunting trips. Also, they had a sick, blind, old dog. If my dog were to ever get sick that would be it because my parents wouldn't be able to afford visits to the vet. Everything Daniel owned was new, nothing from garage sales or alleys in the suburbs. How, I thought, did he fight me on not being able to afford college when he was living this lifestyle? When he had his own car? When he had the luxury of caring for his sick dog?

I had another encounter with social class difference when I started dating Jon-David, my boyfriend during freshman year. I'm not sure why, but I had assumed he was from a lower social class like me. But when my friend told me he had nannies as a kid and his parents were rich, I was shocked. He didn't appear "bougie" because I didn't exactly see him wearing the latest brands. But all of the sudden I felt guilt and immediate self-awareness. Did I ever make it seem like I was dating him because of the money? After that, I fought him to pay half of every date and would go as far as taking his card away from him to let me pay. I didn't want him to think I wanted to go out because I knew he would pay; I didn't want money being a factor in our relationship, period.

For Easter, he invited me to have dinner with his family in Detroit. His family was Christians and took this holiday seriously, so Jon-David and his brother were getting new suits. I had borrowed a dress from a friend because I didn't have anything formal to wear. When Jon-David's mom found out, she offered to buy me a new dress. I was extremely reluctant to accept, but they insisted. As we looked around the store, I noticed they would offer a dress to me without even looking at the price. I was so used to checking the sale items first or at least checking the price to decide if it was worth trying on in the first place. Thankfully, we didn't find a dress that fit. I didn't want them to think I was eager to have them buy me something, or that I would visit them only for the presents. I was always told to reject anything that was offered to me as a child because we were supposed to enjoy people's company, not what they could offer.

Today, I am still constantly aware of how I present myself. After constant encounters with different social classes, I've been made aware of all the luxuries I never had and can't afford, but try to remember how fortunate I have been despite my social class background. When I go back home, I constantly analyze my behavior. Have I changed the way I talk? Do I dress differently? Am I acting in a way that makes my family believe I'm too good for them? I feel the need to constantly remind my parents that I do, in fact, remember where I come from and how I still appreciate all the sacrifices they continue making for my sister and me. I also have a bit of "survival guilt" when I reunite with old friends from my old neighborhood. Could I have done something to motivate them to go to college? Should I have helped them get into my high school? Do I sound stuck-up when I talk about my college experiences? One friend in particular, Veronica, loves to remind me how I used to slave at my school work and how I've earned every opportunity I now have. I'm glad she feels happy for me, but my heart aches at my inability to pull her on my journey to upward mobility along with me. It makes me wonder how I will be able to move out of my neighborhood while I leave everyone else behind.

Just Another Boy
from the "Hood"
Eduardo Gutierrez

My life had never been easy; I had to work hard to get where I am today. Coming from a city full of ghettos, it was not easy to have a safe childhood. Coming from a city full of crime, it was not easy to prevent being inflicted with crime. Growing up in the city of Detroit was a unique experience that most people would probably not relate to. I am a child of parents who had, within the few months before I was brought into this world, immigrated to the United States from Mexico. Since my parents knew no one in Detroit other than my grandparents and knew very few words in English, they had to begin new lives. Since they had to start from "scratch" at the bottom of the social class totem pole and I was born into poverty, my first 10 years were very hard. My parents have told me stories about how both had jobs to make ends meet while I was always sent to neighbors in the apartment complex since they were away at work. Even though both my parents had jobs, they accumulated just enough for necessities and monthly rent.

I've asked my parents how the living conditions were in the apartment: it only had one bedroom, one bathroom, and a kitchen connected to the living room, and the size was probably about less than 800 square feet. According to my parents, the living conditions were miserable; every time there was a severe storm, we would lose power or rain would leak in through the windows. My parents were tired of the apartment and that's why it seemed our first home was a mansion to my baby eyes. Honestly, I do not remember much about the apartment since I lived there at a young age and I was either with the neighbor in the apartment or at my grandparents' house. Since both parents had jobs and had made just enough money to pay rent and bills, they could not afford to put me in daycare or a nursery or hire a nanny. This is one social class barrier I did not recognize at the time. People who tend to be in the middle or upper class could afford daycare or nannies for their children, especially if both parents have jobs.

Right about the age of three, we had the opportunity move out of the apartment complex and into our first home. At the time, I was excited because I was going to have more room to play with my toys. Moving into our first home was a sign of upward mobility since my parents could pay rent for a house instead of an apartment. Even though we were part of the lower class, I felt we were rich because we had necessities: food, water, and shelter; and we had a safer, bigger home as well as vehicles for transportation. The house was in a great location as well, near an elementary school and several groceries stores. My parents would buy a lot of things for me that I did not consider a privilege then. Since, I was an only child at that time, my parents would buy me all the toys I wanted, if they were at a reasonable price. When my parents and I look back at that time, my father tells me that my mother would nearly spend her whole paycheck on me to buy clothes, shoes, and anything I saw. I could say that I was a spoiled little boy who was spoiled by love from my parents. I did not know my parents were paying rent; I thought this was the house where I was going to create all my childhood memories. But after living there for about two years, my parents purchased our first home that was about seven blocks from where we lived.

When moving into the new house, at the age of five, my mother told me I was going to be a big brother. I was excited that I was going to have someone whom I could play with once he grew up. After buying this house, there was no more moving around; this is the home my family lives in. In coming years I learned a lot of things about life, that the world is not all sunshine and rainbows, including my awareness of social class. One thing that made me think that the world is full of sunshine and rainbows was the love and affection given to me when I was a child. Once when I began playing the role of the big brother, my parents decided my mother was going to be a stay-at-home parent and my father would take over the financial burdens. Having a stay-at-home parent was a sign and privilege of upward mobility; we could have a stay-at-home mom without having a negative effect on family income. Having a mom staying at home was great. I was part of a family that was full of love and affection which is another reason I felt rich; I was part of a functional, loving family. I felt rich because I was given everything I wanted that was reasonable to buy. For example, on my sixth birthday, my parents gave me a PlayStation 2 game console, one that I always wanted at the time. All these things given to me made me conclude we were rich since I felt everything was nearly perfect and I was given everything I asked for.

I realized what social class was when I was eight years old. One day coming back from school, I found my father at home, who was home early from his job, which was weird. I had asked him why he is home so early since he usually arrives in the evening from his blue-collar job. He took me upstairs to my room and I saw that my gaming system was missing. I asked him if he was hiding it from me but he denied it and had told me what had happened. Burglars came into our house, stole our goods, including jewelry and my PlayStation. At the time, I was not worried about when I was going to get a new one. I was mad because I was almost finishing up one of my video games, and I would not be able to finish it. Later, that night, I asked my father when I was going to get another PlayStation and he said it is going to take a while because he did not have any extra money. That's when I was first aware of social class: that we did not have extra money to immediately buy another gaming system or to replace the jewelry. Typically, those who are in a middle or upper class have home insurance in case of any damage to their homes such as a robbery or natural disaster. Families in these social classes don't have to worry about having to pay out of pocket for their stolen or lost goods because they were able to afford insurance.

Another time I became aware of class was when my father took me to his job. Throughout most of my life, he has been a hard-working laborer in a landscaping company. I did not have to go to school as it was a Saturday. I helped with tools and taking out lawn weeds. As he did maintenance of all the shrubs and trees, I realized we were doing work for a mansion. I was amazed how huge the house was and how it had an outdoor pool with a nice patio set in the backyard. The picture of the mansion stuck in my head throughout the whole day, and when we were going back home, all I did was talk to dad about the mansion. He said one day I can own a house that huge if I pursue a college education. Then I asked him why he couldn't buy a house like that, and he responded; "I did not feel like going to school after elementary school in Mexico, so I began to work right about your age. Therefore I did not continue my studies that would have let me become a more successful person. With this job that pays very little, I could not buy a house as big as that one." From that experience, I realized that we were part of the lower class because of where we lived and my parents' education. I could say their education was one reason why they decided to come to the United States, so that their kids could do the things they could not do, which is obtain a college degree and live a successful life.

When I began growing up with my only brother, my parents would tell me that I must be a good kid so I can set an example for my brother. Fast forwarding to the present. I have two brothers, one is 6 and the other is 14. Being upwardly mobile throughout their childhoods, I feel they have it easier than I did when I was about their age. For example, my 14-year-old brother has a biweekly allowance and the other does not have to worry about anything regarding whose house he is sleeping at or what he is going to eat for dinner. Another reason why they might have it easier is their exposure to electronics at an earlier age than me. I had been raised to see electronics as a privilege of social class. For example, I had my own iPod at the age of 12 but my 14-year-old brother had his at 8 and my youngest brother had his own tablet at age 4. In my shoes, it seems that I would be jealous because they have more privileges than I had in my childhood, but all that was given to them was because my family became upwardly mobile and the different generation we currently live in.

My parents have always put through my head that I need to set a great example for my younger brothers so they would look up to me as a role model. What they meant was not doing any mischievous things in the neighborhood such as stealing candy from stores and breaking windows. One thing that was increasing all around Detroit, including my neighborhood, was crime. Crime increased because most of the residents were and still are poor; since a lot of residents were unemployed and in desperate need for cash, crime was their solution. Another problem in my neighborhood when I was a teenager was gang activity. The gangs were probably considered the biggest problem in Southwest Detroit, which is where I grew up. Since the residents are majority Hispanic, some teenagers and young adults would "jump-in" in Hispanics gangs. My parents' biggest fear was me joining any type of illegal street gang. These gangs break families apart with all the killings they do; they also made and distributed drugs. My parents did their best to prevent me from falling under the influence of gangs.

One important thing my parents did was enroll me in after-school programs. Not only did it help with the neighborhood problem, but I benefited from the programs regarding academics. To this day, I know some of my childhood friends that participated in the gangs who are no longer my friends. I feel the difference between me and them is parent involvement in the household. In my early years of life, both my parents had jobs and if this would have continued, I honestly say I could have been raised by the streets since there would not have been anyone at home to look after me. I understand the situation of my some of my former friends; had I been in their shoes at my younger age I also would have been in trouble. Their parents were never home when the kids were growing up because one or both had to work to support the family. In my situation, my parents were very involved with my life and made sure I stayed on the path to success. With my experiences in the neighborhood, I feel that parent involvement is key when keeping kids away from negativity. My family was blessed with the opportunity to afford to have a stay-at-home parent to make sure I and my brothers would not fall under any negativity in the neighborhood.

Another major component that played a big role in my childhood was my love for sports. My parents felt that if I was doing sports, it would keep me busy enough to stay away from gangs. Although I played various sports throughout my life, the one that stuck with me the most was swimming. I loved being on the swim team because it was unique; you would rarely hear about kids in the neighborhood being part of a swim team. It all started when I went to the recreation center near my house and had gone in to swim with my family. I was in the pool chasing a ball in the water and the next thing I know I got too deep in the water and began to drown. After this frightening experience, I wanted to learn how to swim so I would never have to experience that again; after a month of swimming lessons, swimming became my lifestyle. Another reason I enjoyed swimming was the intense feeling among competitors—knowing you could lose a race by as close as one one-hundredth of a second. I continued to swim throughout my childhood because all my coaches told me I had the potential of becoming a great swimmer. I continued swimming through high school and was considered one of Detroit's fastest high school swimmers. I would like to thank my coaches in helping me stay on the path to success because most coaches knew what was going on in the neighborhood. There were fewer teenagers coming to the recreation center—due to gang influence. In high school, our coach made sure we were on track with our academics since we were student-athletes, but academics were always first. Having coaches care about their athletes made me push through in pursuing a college degree; back in the city, it is not the norm to pursue a college degree.

Being a graduate from the Detroit Public School (DPS) system, an underfunded school district, I accomplished a lot in my education, even with all the obstacles in place, to graduate high school. I continued to be a role model for my brothers. Being a former student of DPS, I did not have the best education in comparison to students in well-funded schools such as Bloomfield Hills School District (BHSD)—north of Detroit. BHSD is well funded because most students who go there are from either upper-middle or upper class. Even though I was not given the best education, I did my best to prepare myself for college. In the DPS system, there are only a few students who go to prestigious colleges, including myself. Most students attend community colleges or nearby four-year colleges. Many people I know do not go to any college. In my neighborhood going to college is not the norm after graduating high school. Since I live in a working-class neighborhood, the excuse most give is they can't afford college. But being a high school graduate from the poor/working class automatically qualifies them for financial aid to any public college. For some reason, they want to follow the same footsteps as their blue-collar fathers or mothers. One reason why some former classmates work in blue-collar jobs instead of pursuing a college degree is parent involvement in education. Both my parents were very strict about my grades all throughout K–12 because they wanted me to excel. All throughout high school, my mother would always check up on me with progress reports, and if something was not right with my grades, she would send me to school with a note for the teacher requesting a parent–teacher meeting. Parent involvement is the major reason why I have dedicated myself to pursue a college degree. It is rare to hear people from my neighborhood enrolling in prestigious universities like the University of Michigan.

When I received the news that I was accepted to go to Michigan, I was also given the opportunity to study under the circumstance that I would need to participate in Summer Bridge. Bridge is an eight-week program that introduces accepted students to college culture and expectations; this helps students who are in the program when matriculating in the fall. Honestly, when I first arrived on campus during the summer, I did not know what to expect. Were there going to be people I knew from back home? Move-in day was full of emotions such as being anxious and excited. As I started to roam around the building to see who was in the program, I did see people whom I knew from back home. The first person was my cousin and it was great. I knew things would not be as bad if I had at least a family member around since we had one another for any type of support. Both being first-year students, we were going to have our struggles with academics and possibly fitting in with this upper-middle-class environment.

During Bridge we had to take eight to nine credits to help prepare for the rigorous classes we would take in the fall. I have heard testimonies about Bridge being one of the best summers of the students' lives, and I wanted to live up to that experience. I became social with people around me because I wanted to have a lot of friends, since Bridge is such a small world in comparison to the rest of the university. Since Bridge was composed of mostly minorities, I felt it easier to interact with students there. I felt that it was a bad thing that the environment of the university is an upper-middle-class environment, but Bridge is most a middle- and lower-class environment. I felt this might be a problem in the fall since I could not integrate with the upper-middle-class environment. Coming out of the Bridge Program, I left with a group of friends that I would consider best friends who would stick with me for a long time. I needed this coming out of Bridge, a group of friends to support you whenever you need them.

Over the summer, I began to realize that few things began to change while at Michigan: spending habits and my vocabulary. Coming from the DPS I may not have the best vocabulary, but it improved since being here in the summer. Typically, the vocabulary used in Detroit is not as complex as terminologies applied here at Michigan. Vocabulary is a social class barrier that many people may not know about but does exist. Throughout this essay I've attempted to use an appropriate vocabulary when talking about my stay at Michigan, but I use a more basic vocabulary when back at home, so I use two vocabularies in these two places.

During Bridge, I applied to be part of a Michigan Learning Community since I did not want my college experience to be a typical first-generation student experience. A usual Michigan first-generation experience is when you do not know anyone from your hometown and since you are solitary most of the time, you become segregated from the mainstream, upper-middle-class environment. Often you have the urge, after finishing your first year, to transfer to a college or university near home. I did not want that first-gen experience because people I know who have graduated from college have said that college time is the best years of your life; I wanted to live up to that potential. But for me to have the best years of my life here at the university, it would require me to integrate into the upper-middle-class environment. One step in pursuing this nonacademic goal was to become part of a campus organization: Michigan Community Scholars Program. This group focuses a lot on social justice issues around the university as well as taking the lead in several community service projects all around Ann Arbor.

To this day, I do not regret being part of this program because I have met people whom I am going to stick with for many years to come. I chose this program because I wanted to have a diverse group of friends since most of my hall-mates came from middle- or upper-middle-class families. I felt that interacting with them would be an initiative to integrate into the typical Michigan environment. For example, one of my hall-mates skipped classes for one day to attend Game 7 of the World Series between the Chicago Cubs and the Cleveland Indians. During spring break, there were a few hall-mates who went to Europe for their vacation. Then there's me, a middle-class kid who has watched playoff baseball games on television and must wait for a vacation once a year. Don't get me wrong, I am not repining about my situation, but I am blessed with opportunities to work hard to be where I am, but there are consequential distinctions between social classes here at Michigan. Although throughout the fall and winter semesters, my hall-mates and I grew proximate as a family, class was still an issue. Since most of my hall-mates were moving out into houses or apartments, I would not be able to move with them because of my social class; I could not afford to live in Arbor BLU Apartment on Church Street, where the monthly rent is $1,500. Honestly, I do not let social class intervene with any of my interactions here at the university. Looking back at my freshman year, I do not feel like an outsider. I feel like I am at home and it is sad to hear that many first-generation students are having a rough time integrating into this environment. But is this environment making me fall apart from my working-class roots in Detroit? I fear living a double life and not being able to connect to my roots. I am proud of where I come from and I am proud to tell people where I am from even though there might have been negative things said about Detroit—the city where I am from.

Many people who blend into an upper-middle-class environment ordinarily disconnect or forget where they come from. I do not feel I am disconnecting from my roots; I embrace where I come from. Being a Hispanic or minority at Michigan might be difficult for many first-generation students, but personally, I embrace it and will never forget my roots. There have been instances when people have asked me about Detroit's crime rate. When people ask me about it, I say it is true, but you must stay focused on the path of success. Being at Michigan makes me realize, no matter from what social class you come from and what kind of education you have had, if you work hard, you will be able to succeed, just like the American Dream. This journey is possible with all the support I have had throughout my life: primarily my parents as well as all my coaches. American Dream is the primary reason why my parents immigrated to the United States, for their kids to be successful by pursuing college degrees. Now, me being the oldest of three, I must set an example for my brothers to demonstrate that college is a great place to be, so they won't have to be afraid of not integrating with the college environment.

During my first year here at Michigan, things at home were quite different. The home is more quiet than usual since there are only two boys. When my family comes to visit, my brothers like to walk around campus to look at how nice this campus looks. Once I was talking to my six-year-old brother and out of the blue he said he wanted to come to Michigan and become a doctor. This is the motivation that I want to see from my brothers; following the same footsteps to show that pursuing a college education is the norm in our household and how it should be the norm in our neighborhood. I want people in my neighborhood, including my brothers, to view my life before, during, and after college as motivation.

When returning home, people have a different view of me because I am attending a prestigious university; it carries a stigma such that people look up to you as a genius bookworm. Since it's rare for people in my neighborhood to attend college and since they have seen I am attending Michigan, I hope that high school students in my neighborhood can view me as a role model. Perhaps they can also believe they can pursue a college degree and be viewed as another neighborhood genius! I have made it further than most people I know despite obstacles on my way toward matriculation at Michigan. Instead of being here, I could have been in a community college employed part-time, working a blue-collar job, or, worse, I could have been incarcerated or possibly six feet under. People from my neighborhood may view me as a genius, but I am just another boy who is trying to get out of the "hood."

Just Getting By

Yadah V. Ramirez

The sound of desk chairs screeching across the floor as the cluster of students found their seats resonated in my ears. Each breath filled my nostrils with the stench of combined perfume and lotion scents. I glanced down at the handout on my desk as the professor began to speak. My eyes rested on the income bracket that matched my family's. On the first day of class, I never imagined I'd learn my family had actually been in a lower social class all my life: the working poor.

I was born into a culture of hard work. My father woke up before dawn to work in the fields alongside his *abuelito* as a child. As an adolescent he worked odd jobs, like digging burial holes for the Pilgrim Home Cemetery in Holland, Michigan, earning only $10 for a day's work. My father labored long hours to help support his family and to satisfy his own material needs. Life eventually led him to attain a GED (Graduate Education Development) diploma and struggle to try to attend and graduate from a community college. He never did *graduate*. My mother immigrated to the United States from Mexico as a young adult and worked multiple low-wage jobs to make a life for herself. She took English courses while here—but never managed to further her education. Neither of my parents achieved stable white-collar careers. However, all their sacrifices would make it possible for my sister and me to be more successful in our lifetime.

I grew up in Holland on the west side of Michigan. It is a small city that can be divided into urban, rural, and suburban areas. The rural areas made up most of the northside of the city. This is the part where most of the low-income and minority residents lived; this is where I lived in my childhood. A mobile home in a trailer park is what I called home for the first 13 years of my life. In our trailer, there was only one bedroom and it was shared between my parents, my sister, and me. Positioned in a small lot of land, this trailer was surrounded by others like it. It rested on ground covered in patches of brown grass. Heavy rainfall was the only chance for green grass, as our family could sometimes not even afford a gallon of milk let alone to water the lawn. The trailer park had a playground that became dangerous to visit as gangs started to congregate there. The beauty of the properties and sizes of the houses in the more afflu-ent neighborhoods contrasted this barren and crime-ridden land-scape, especially in winter.

The freshly fallen December snow glistened in the moonlight. It was a Christmas tradition to drive to the "nice" neighborhoods to see the Christmas decorations the residents placed at their houses. Entire scenes of Jesus in the manger and Santa Claus with his rein-deer were immaculately displayed. Extraordinarily ornamented Christmas trees could be seen through oversized windows. As a child, I would ask my father why we could not decorate our home in a simi-lar fashion or have such a beautiful tree. The reply was always that we did not have the money to spend on such things. In the process of my parents' explaining our lack of material goods, the holidays became other ordinary days and the world lost some of its wonder.

Our working-poor status could not afford for me and my sis-ter to believe in common childhood fantasies. Santa Claus was exposed as unreal. This way there would be no expectations and disappointments when we did not receive presents on Christmas morning. The Easter Bunny was revealed as fictive; there would be no Easter eggs waiting to be found. We were told the tooth fairy did not exist. While the other children in Sunday school showed off the crisp $1–$5 bills the tooth fairy left for their teeth, we understood the reason for the vacancy in our pockets.

In addition to lack of money and material goods, differences in life experiences also separated me from my middle- and upper-class peers while growing up. An assignment in my high school Honors American Literature class required the inclusion of photos. Students' hands shot up like lightning all around me. They asked if photos from family or their parents' vacations could be used. The teacher answered "yes." My hands began to feel clammy against my bouncing knee. I was worried those vacation photos would put me at a disadvantage in receiving a good grade on the assignment.

My minimal in-state and out-of-state traveling experiences, usually for family emergencies, did not measure up to my classmates' leisure trips to Costa Rica, Florida, or Niagara Falls. I did not have a camera, let alone a high-quality one to produce the kind of photos I anticipated my classmates had. As my thoughts drifted away to memories that might have been caught on camera, a sinking feeling in my stomach started to form. I began thinking that perhaps I did not belong in this course. The extra effort I put forth by borrowing a camera, spending hours rummaging through old photos, and creating a video with music instead of a PowerPoint landed me a great grade. Although I overcame this challenge, it gave birth to insecurities about how my class background would impact my academic performance relative to my more affluent peers. These insecurities would follow me to college.

* * *

Navigating through the campus environment at the University of Michigan in Ann Arbor proved to be just as difficult as getting there. When I first arrived on campus, I had preconceived notions of what life as a student would be like. Most of these expectations came from media representations and high school teachers' anecdotes as my parents and extended family could not supply them. They also could not directly assist me with the process to get into college. Information about how to fill out the FAFSA (Free Application for Federal

Student Aid) forms was provided to my parents and me by my youth group leaders and high school counselors. My high school teachers told me what classes I should take to strengthen my transcript for college admission. They answered questions about what college would be like based on their experiences. From their accounts, I imagined college to be a lot different than it turned out to be.

I imagined the University of Michigan to be a place of personal and intellectual growth: a place where I could exercise my independence as a new adult; a place where I could engage in discussions of politics, discrimination, legacies of slavery and colonialism, art, and history; a place where I could tailor my schedule to becoming a better and healthier me; and so much more. Although I did get to experience these things in unanticipated ways, I also experienced a lot of what I did not expect. I did not expect: to have multiple courses every day and practically all day to amount to an even longer day than when I was in high school, to have about a hundred pages of reading on a weekly basis among other heavy coursework assignments, to feel like I was drowning trying to balance coursework and job work, to feel isolated because the few hours of the day I had to myself had to be used for sleep most of the time instead of forming new friendships. My busy schedule did not allow me to practice self-care extensively, but I did try to set aside an hour a day, if I could, to watch the Ellen DeGeneres talk show. The stories of people that Ellen shared inspired and motivated me to persevere through my own struggles and it was a time for me to just laugh and de-stress from the hardships of the day. It really got me through some tough times and continues to do so.

My college experience started with Michigan's 2013 Summer Bridge Program. The first few weeks were filled with workshop activities of some sort. One of them was a financial aid 101 informational workshop. Our class was ushered into a lecture hall. Shoulders brushed and passed me as people hurried to sit next to their friends. I sat in an empty row toward the back. All were a silent audience until the workshop presenter began to talk about refunds issued by the university. She said at the beginning of each semester a refund would be issued by the university if there were funds in the student's account that were not used. We were warned to only use the refund money to care for our needs. She said the financial aid department does not care if we need to spend it to support our family, but we would not be awarded any additional funds. At this statement, whispering erupted among the students around me. It was not what the speaker said, but how she said it. Her tone of voice was flat, matter of fact. She lacked compassion when describing the situations that actually occurred with previous students she listed as examples. Some students had spent the money to help their family with mortgage payments, funeral arrangements, rent, groceries, medical expenses, and other bills. It all seemed contradictory. Bridge program was supposed to help some students, with a low-income, first-generation status that tended to have this type of family background, acclimate into college life. Yet, here was a person who seemed to be saying she did not care about our family struggles. The experience was unsettling. What did I want her to say? Well to speak with compassion, to convey a sense of understanding. She should have provided students with resources within the university or the city of Ann Arbor that could possibly help us if our families were experiencing the situations she described or to disclose there were no such resources—unfortunately. This moment made me think that perhaps the University of Michigan was not the best place for a student from an underprivileged, low-income background.

Differences in educational levels tend to exist between social classes. However, while I was at Bridge I learned that some may even exist within a single social class. I was surrounded by students with similar social class or cultural backgrounds. This resembled my high school and hometown environment. Most everybody, if not all, had taken an Advanced Placement (AP) English course in high school along with other AP courses. I was the only one from the West side of the state in my Bridge English 125 course. The rest of my classmates were from the Detroit, East Lansing, Michigan, or even out of state areas. Many of them had been in the top 10 of their graduating class just like me and made many achievements in their lives to be proud of. Despite these similarities, grade distributions in our course divided us. To my knowledge, based on discussions regarding grades amongst ourselves, I received better grades on all my English 125 course papers than my peers. Certain classmates would question, in a teasing kind of way, why I received a better grade than they did on a paper. One particular time another classmate jumped in and said to stop giving me a hard time; that I deserved that grade. The student questioning me replied: "Yes, you know you're right. All she ever does is spend her time in the Morgue (a study area) so I guess she does deserve it." This statement was true. I did spend every free minute of the day in that study lounge located in Mosher-Jordan Hall on campus. Though I do not think it was intentional, the comment did sting a little. It suggested that the price of my good grades was the sacrifice of social interaction and that in that way the grade did not mean as much somehow. While discussing one of the papers I had written during office hours, our English professor gave me some words of encouragement. Some dealt with my coursework. He said that based on my paper grades, setting the curves for the exams, and my overall work in the course that it was clear to him I was ahead of my classmates. He told me to never let anyone say I do not belong here at Michigan.

I started to think how much of my success was due to long hours of studying and how much was due to the quality of my high school education. I say this because the paper assignments for the course were very similar to paper assignments I completed in the AP Language and Composition course, the AP Literature course, and the writing component of a program through LAUP (Latin Americans United for Progress) when I was in high school. They did not seem that hard to me for this reason. A few of the other students would occasionally make comments about the paper assignments being too difficult and not having done something like them before. The high school I went to was sometimes referred as ghetto. It is considered to be located in an underserved community and has on average a low academic performance rating in terms of state examinations. Despite all these labels, my high school and community was obviously doing something right to have helped me gain a competitive edge among college peers. The Bridge program made me realize how fortunate I was to have received the level of education that I did at Holland High School and opened my eyes to educational inequalities that exist even within a single social class, perhaps due to geographical location.

I also received a level of exposure to social class differences through roommate interactions. I had two apartment suitemates my freshman year and it became clear early on that I was the odd one out in terms of social class background. One of my suitemates was Japanese and from Japan, but had studied in a private school in Brazil because her parents believed the English language courses were better there. My other suitemate was Caucasian, from Farmington Hills, Michigan, whose parents were on their way to Europe with some of their pets as passengers instead of cargo.

Later, I had another roommate whom I would describe as average middle class. She lived in a house in a "nice" neighborhood. Though I did not ever find out the value of her house, I do know that on average the value of houses in that neighborhood ranged from $200,000 to a little over $500,000 at the time. So her parents were pretty well-off. She started working at The Victors—an Ann Arbor store—only to quit within less than a month. I asked her the reason. She said because the shifts that were available to take before class were too early for her and it would require for her to open the store and she did not want to do that. The shifts that were later in the day required her to wash cooking ware and she did not want to do that. To sum it all up she said that basically she just did not like working there so she stopped. I wished I had the luxury to not have to work if I did not like the type of work. One day while she was apologizing for her most recent episode of unjustifiable moodiness, I caught a glimpse of the kind of problems that someone from this social class background might experience. She explained that she had been in such a foul mood since her return from visiting home because of the events that took place. Her mother had made her a big pot of one of her favorite soups. My roommate dropped her bowl on the floor. She was apparently too devastated to get another bowl and serve herself more soup. She went to Taco Bell for food next time. They ran out of the particular meat she wanted and again devastated. All this amounted to a series of slamming doors shut, minimal snap responses, to no communication at all, and anger radiating from her that I could feel whenever she sat in a room with me. I accepted her apology all the while thinking: *I recently found out that my credit card information was stolen and maxed out and I may be liable for paying all the money back, that I just lost my health insurance, and that a doctor discovered an unidentifiable mass in my father that the doctor said is most likely cancerous. If someone from her kind of background gets so wound up over not getting something to eat, I hate to think how they would react if they had to go through what I was going through.* Yes, I definitely found out that not everyone's problems revolved around what I define as more major life-altering matters.

The first time I heard upper-class students openly expressing opinions about working- and lower-class students was in a social psychology lecture. The two-hour lecture reached its first hour mark. Room 1800 in the Chemistry Building is vast in size, perfect to engage in conversations without getting caught by the professor. Two female students who sat in front of me began to make plans for spring break. They decided whose driver would pick them up at the airport, what stores they would visit in New York City, and whose penthouse they would use for the duration of break. They moved on to whom they would invite to accompany them. One of the girls offered the first suggestion. The other girl shot down the suggested saying: "Oh no, we can't invite her, she's a scholarship student. Not really worth our time." It struck me that I could be the topic of one of these conversations someday. This unsettling conversation did not make me ashamed of being a scholarship student. It brought into perspective the type of social class self-segregating that takes place at Michigan.

The more time I spent living on campus, the more social class social markers I encountered. I saw it in obvious ways sometimes: attire and accessories, for example. Usually, these observations tended to be influenced by gender as I paid more attention to what female students wore. Girls carried Coach and Michael Kors bags. In the winter it's Nordstrom parkas all the way. I started to look up the prices online of the apparel that I kept seeing so many female students wear. They seemed to range between approximately $200 and $1,000. Whenever it rained, Hunter brand knee-high boots could be seen splashing through puddles. These sell for $150 to $200 online. One pair of these boots could feed my family for over a month. These girls even paid excessive amounts of money to smell nice, sporting scents by Chanel. Other signs of upper-class status showed themselves in their behavior and activities.

Frequent bar hopping, partying at frat houses, or spending a ridiculous amount of money eating at high-end restaurants were activities that higher-income students tended to partake in. Other activities were not as frivolous or costly. The more well-off students could also be found participating in certain student organizations on campus. What did all these activities have in common if it was not just money? *Time.* Students from higher-income families tended to have more time to do whatever they pleased as their financial needs were being met by someone other than themselves. These students had time to take an unpaid internship or be involved in an organization that would benefit their career goals, the time to take the minimum amount of credits that may prolong graduating but would make their grade point average (GPA) look great, and time to go abroad even if the trip would have nothing to do with their degree program. I did not have that kind of time to spend, and the time I did have I spent differently. I wanted to be sure I graduated on time so I took the maximum amount of credit hours permitted, 18. The standard of living in Ann Arbor seemed higher than that of Holland. It was clear that I would need to acquire a job to buy all the things that my scholarships did not cover and to have enough money to send home. I juggled work and schoolwork. Working 35 to 40 hours a week while taking a maximum amount of credit hours left little room for anything else.

College has not been easy for me. I had trouble adjusting to life on campus. I found it difficult to find and interact with students who had similar backgrounds to mine. College was the first time in my life when I experienced the full force of the intersection of class and race. It was no longer a given for someone who identified as Hispanic to also share the same social class and cultural experiences as me. I joined a few nonethnic specific student organizations like K-Grams, Circle K, Miscellania, The Red Shoe Crew, and Northwood III Community Council to improve my chances for meeting students whom I could relate to. I did meet one of my best friends this way. We bonded through our low-income identities rather than our ethnic ones. I quickly had to stop my involvement in these groups as work and study took up most of my time. However, it was not as bad of a trade-off as I initially thought. I tended to relate more to fellow students in the places of my employment anyway.

I worked multiple jobs during my college years. I have worked at Meijer, McDonald's, University of Michigan Catering, Bursley Dining Hall, and JavaBlu (a coffee shop) in the East Quadrangle dormitory. I also worked as a research assistant. Out of all these jobs I maintained steady employment at two. One of them was at Bursley Dining and the other was JavaBlu. My coworkers at both locations were for the most part low income or middle class, first generation, or of a minority status or a mixture of these and they knew the value of hard work. We spoke passionately about course topics, national politics, and global issues with each other. We also shared frustrations about work and class schedules, poor experiences at University Health Services (UHS) or at Counseling and Psychological Services (CAPS), instances of discrimination, and experiences with social class and sexism on campus. Many of us had at least one story of a wrong diagnosis by UHS. For me, UHS had concluded once that I did not have an illness. They called me two days later to say I actually did have the illness and I needed to pick up the antibiotics prescription right away since it was a severe case. Other cases of inadequate health services were related to mental health.

Mental health issues are steadily increasing among college students. I would argue that they are more pronounced in college students from a low-income and/or minority background. My own struggle with mental health issues has largely been due to the excessive amount of hours I work, and the responsibility of financially supporting myself and my family. I decided to seek help for my anxiety and depression after my freshman year. This was a big moment for me to admit that I needed mental health assistance because growing up in a Mexican American culture meant mental illnesses were rarely discussed. Culturally, I was brought up to stay strong and tough it out. If things did become overwhelming, you could turn to family members for support or to God. It would be an anomaly to see a doctor for an emotionally related problem. If you were feeling down, you were not depressed, just sad and you would eventually get over it. Depression then was described as being a white and/or rich person problem. I know now that mental illness is not dependent upon race/ethnicity, gender, or social class though it can be influenced by these identities at times.

The appointment in which I disclosed my struggle with my mental health did not go as expected. After I informed the doctor of my situation and how I thought working was a major contributor to my poor mental health, the doctor asked: "Well, if you know working is making your depression worse, why don't you just stop working so much?" I thought of possible snappy responses I could give like: *Oh, it's because I have this weird habit; I like to eat and not be homeless.* I settled on saying that it was not an option for me because of my low-income background that I had previously mentioned at the start of the appointment. My coworkers had received similar remarks from UHS doctors or counselors at CAPS. The minimizing of our struggles by acting as though there was an easy solution to them deterred us from getting the help we needed: our academics and personal lives suffered as a consequence.

CAPS apparently releases an annual report of the "accomplishments in the wide scope of services and programs that are offered for students, staff, faculty and others throughout the campus community." Although the 2015–2016 report states that 92% of clients having received services feel that they received quality care, 92% of clients would return to CAPS, and 95% of clients would recommend CAPS, I would urge CAPS to deconstruct their statistics in order to better measure the success of their services. They should look at the social class and ethnic background of clients responding to these survey questions. Are these clients saying they would return to CAPS or recommend it because they received quality care or because it is the only convenient and free resource available?

The annual report of 2014–2015 includes a breakdown of clients who received services through CAPS by race and ethnicity. Clients that identified as Caucasian/white were 63%, Asian American/Asian 17%, African American/ black 6%, Hispanic/Latina(o) 5%, multiracial 4%, self-identify 3%, and no response 2%. Based on these statistics, it would appear that students of an ethnic minority status do not turn to CAPS for mental health services. There are a number of arguments that could be made to explain these results. One is that there is simply not a significant ethnic minority presence on campus in comparison to the white majority. I would argue though that, since race and class tend to intersect, these low percentages have something to do with the kind of experiences that my coworkers and I have had when seeking mental health assistance. I am not saying CAPS or UHS are not successful at all. I am saying though that they need to make more of an effort to not further alienate communities that have historically been marginalized. I think the first step is to understand that people experience depression differently and that these differences can be influenced by social class. It is important that when a person shares his or her struggles with mental health, the person on the receiving side should not only hear what the other person had to say, but *listen* so that those experiences are validated and language is used to avoid minimizing their struggle.

I enrolled in a number of courses that included topics of social class in their course description. It was not until Sociology 295 though that we discussed it in such detail. I found myself disagreeing with a few perspectives given by readings or by classmates. Most of the literature assigned for reading regarding first-generation, low-income student experiences on campus at a university shared similar themes. That's fine except that I cannot help but feel as though it leads to the stereotypical image of how people perceive these students. It also shifts the blame on them when things go wrong academically. For instance, most of the literature stated that one of the biggest challenges for first-generation college students is asking for help—whether this be asking for help in regard to health, academics, acclimating to college life—because they are too proud or afraid of sounding ignorant. Well in my case and for dozens of workers at all of my employment places, past and current, along with my friends, that is not the case. It is not that we are too proud to ask for help or that we are afraid of sounding ignorant. Rather, it is because we have asked for help before and we did not get the help we needed and we were not treated with the level of respect we deserve as I mentioned earlier in dealings with UHS and CAPS. I think that it would be beneficial to have differing perspectives more openly recognized regarding low-income, first-generation, minority student experiences to try to avoid the creation of harmful stereotype representations.

Our family never had much, but we made do. So it was constantly surprising to see the ease at which some students spent their parents' money. There was a regular stream of student customers who came into JavaBlu. The credit card machine at our store had a delayed processing transaction time. It was during this waiting time that customers would converse with their friends and we as workers would get a glimpse into their lives. One particular customer's debit card was declined. I handed back the card and asked for another form of payment. The customer began to complain to her friend that this is probably all a part of her father's plan to make her get a job. They both agreed this was the most horrible thing that could happen, especially considering it would be the first time she ever worked in her life.

* * *

I started working when I was 14 years old to help with my family's financial situation and to save money for college. The jobs I acquired during my high school years were not labor intensive. I was lucky to be able to get paid internships over the summer. I was not allowed to work during the school year. My parents wanted me to focus on my schoolwork because excelling in academics enough to get scholarships would be the only way I could attend college. Most of the internships were in areas that could become careers: film making and laboratory research, for example. There were times though when office spaces at an internship location needed cleaning and I took the additional opportunity to make extra money. My parents were not particularly happy when I took such cleaning jobs on the side. They wanted something better for me and my sister. Despite their unhappiness with the situation, they respected my decisions and efforts I made to alleviate some of our financial burden. No matter how much money I seemed to make, it was never enough.

*   *   *

My sophomore year of college was the hardest. In addition to schoolwork and paid work, I dealt with a lot of family problems. My father's already detrimental health issues worsened. He incurred medical bills that could not be paid in full. I started working longer hours between my two jobs on campus. In the end, my family lost our apartment: we were homeless for a second time. That whole summer was spent searching for a new place to call home. In the last week of classes, almost everybody was talking about their plans for the summer. I remembered others' plans for personal trips to Europe or the Caribbean as I stared out the McDonald's drive-thru window. After my shift was over I walked to the van I had bought for my family to live in, thinking how unfair it was for some people to have enough money to take luxury trips when I could not even afford to replace my shoes that had holes in them.

Everything worked out in the end for us. We have either lived in a trailer or apartment all my life. Now, we have our first house. It's a family effort to pay the mortgage, continue to pay my father's medical bills, and other household expenses. We do everything we can to save money where we can. My family lives on a diet of eggs, beans, rice, and tortillas for the most part. I work enough in a given day so I can collect on the free meal policies at Bursley Dining and JavBlu so to save money on groceries. I am hopeful for our situation to improve once I graduate and settle into a job that has the potential to become a long-term career.

Life experiences of class consciousness and studying social class at college have taught me valuable lessons. It is not an easy climb up the ladder to upward social mobility. However, it is possible for some people to make it to the top in their lifetime. I hope that I am one of those people and something tells me my chances are pretty good. I have never been ashamed of my social class. It never made me think less of myself when I did not have brand name attire and the people around me did. I will always be proud of my roots and dream of one day when my family and I won't just be getting by.

Why Is My Cheese Immortal?

Sean Smith

I am 5'8", maybe 150 pounds, soak n' wet. At 21 years old, a doctor told me I was prehypertension. I had no idea what that implied.

"What's that supposed to mean? Can you explain that in layman's terms?"

"It means that if you don't change your diet you might have a heart attack one day."

"So basically, I'll die if I don't make changes?"

Damn.

I thought about my cousin Sabrina: she died. She left behind two kids in the summer of 2002, including belongings, romance, and dreams unfulfilled. She died. She never had the chance to see her grandkids, a black First Lady, the Cubs end their championship drought, or her daughters finishing high school: because she died. She died in her early 30s.

"What are your suggestions? How do I avoid something like that?"

"You should monitor the amount of sodium you consume"

"Salt?"

"Sodium. Sodium is in salt. Try to cut back on processed food, read the back of products, see how much sodium is in what you're eating, and drink more water."

No one had ever explained it to me that way. I only monitored the amount of salt I added to my food, I never considered the amount of sodium that was already present. I didn't question what I ate: I ate what I knew. As a child there were nights when I had water and saltine crackers for dinner. My objective was to shush a growl to a whisper.

Growing up I watched mom work full time, babysit and braid hair to make ends meet. No matter how hard she worked, our living situation remained in jeopardy: we always seemed on the precipice of eviction. We often came home to utility shut-off notices posted on the front door.

It wasn't out of the ordinary to use candles in place of lights.

I remember using an extension cord to get electricity from the apartment across from us. It was in the thick of winter and we were without gas. My brothers and I huddled around a space heater and stretched toward its red glow. The temperature was in the teens, there wasn't any snow, but the cold had bite. I went to bed hearing wind whisking through corners of doors. I cocooned in my blanket the best I could, but the draft still crept in, crawling up my legs, slowly, until it had me by the neck. I squirmed back and forth, to create friction, to foster warmth, to no avail.

The next morning mom scraped up enough money to pay the gas bill, but not without going into her grocery budget. This was usually the first thing to get cut whenever we were in a pinch. In the absence of excess groceries, mom often relied on her uncanny ability to make full course meals out of fundamental ingredients. There was a church or liquor store on every other corner in my community. We often kept our heads on a swivel for churches clearing their pantries. Every once in a while we got fresh fruit, but the majority of time we only had nonperishable items to sift through.

When the food trucks came, it was a rare chance to conveniently get groceries and the whole neighborhood would stock up. The majority of households did not own a car and no one on my block owned two. There was only one grocery store—Food Town—on the corner of Madison Avenue & Hall Street, so access to fresh produce was either limited or in compromised conditions.

Most of us had no choice, but to do our shopping at liquor stores. The merchants knew our alternatives were limited, so they gladly overcharged us.

Prices were almost never visible on grocery items at liquor stores.

"How much is this?"

"$4.99"

"What about this?"

"$3.88"

"How much are these?"

"$7.72"

Prices seemed completely arbitrary.

One week pancake mix would be $2.75, two days later it would be $3.33, and then $3.50. There were many instances where mom scraped up pennies hoping to have just enough to get this or that item, only for me to come back empty handed, because I was a few cents short.

Some customers disputed prices, but this rarely went over well. Price debates were usually followed by a barrage of expletives and epithets between merchants and patrons.

"Get the fuck out of my store!"

"I'll air this muthafucka out!"

"I'll call the police!"

"I'll beat your ass until they get here!"

"Get out of my store!"

"You lucky you behind that glass! Otherwise I would snatch you from behind that counter and drag you through this muthafucka."

It wasn't unusual for merchants to be veiled by bulletproof glass. Since being black and poor is framed synonymously with being untrustworthy, we were usually given customer surveillance, instead of customer service.

"I come in here and spend money with ya'll damn near every day and this how ya'll repay me? I ain't gotta steal!"

Price debates and being accused of stealing usually led to cursing matches, and sometimes violence.

A merchant once hit a woman in the head, with a lead pipe, so hard it required her to get staples. She had asked for a refund after being unhappy with a slice of pizza, and the situation escalated from there. A few community leaders staged a boycott for a few weeks, but it eventually lost steam.

We were in a food desert and our options were limited. People needed groceries, bus lines were limited, and we didn't have cars.

I didn't realize the impact these limitations had on me until I transferred from Grand Rapids Community College to the University of Michigan, Ann Arbor, in the fall of 2014. The university setting was my first sustained interaction with middle- and upper-middle-class people. Back home, those living in poverty were heavily concentrated in one area of the city. Our mobility was limited by housing policies, section 8, and lack of transportation. Police patrols further ensured our community remained isolated from the well-to-do. The lack of social class diversity in my neighborhood led me to believe there was a universal black experience. When I came to Michigan I met children of black professionals and realized their black experiences were vastly different from my own. Living in Ann Arbor forced me to branch out and stretch beyond my class comfort zone. Prior to moving here I thought there was an assumed camaraderie among all black people, but I learned that I couldn't always rest on that assumption.

Whenever I entered a predominantly white space, I always opted to establish a connection with the nearest black person in the room. Often times we would both spot each other from a distance, almost communicating telepathically. Our messages to each other would be something along the lines: "Damn, I'm so glad you're in here; I thought I was going to be by myself again." or "Bruh, dafuq? I thought they said they valued diversity?" I also noticed telepathic connections weren't always in service. Many middle-class blacks were already accustomed to navigating white spaces, so they didn't need to establish a relationship with me. Some didn't even acknowledge I was there. It's as if they felt their token membership would be in jeopardy if they associated with me. When it was time to pick partners for group presentations, they would look elsewhere, even if I was right next to them.

The legacy of white supremacy is so entrenched in America's collective conscience that not even more affluent black people are exempt from harboring negative sentiments toward working- and lower-class blacks. Classism is pervasive. Those of marginalized identities in collusion with those who hold privilege contribute to the preservation of the status quo.

A combination of racist housing policies and black middle-class reluctance to intermingle with "po' folks" left and leaves my home community insulated as a remote island. When we hear about a brain drain we tend to think of migration from abroad to America, but seldom do we observe the brain drain taking place from America's inner cities. When some talented poor and minority students leave for college, where do they feel comfortable? Can they ever really go back?

I've been thinking about this lately: a lot has changed since I moved to Ann Arbor. When I left Grand Rapids, nothing stood still. My friends are now a few years older, some have families, and they've settled into their working-class lives. Their kids either don't know me or I have to reintroduce myself to them. Just as I've moved on, so has everyone else. Everyone down their own path.

One of my brothers has been in and out of jail for the past six years: he says he's not going back. His girlfriend has a baby on the way. "I'm done with that shit bro! My seed on the way, I gotta boss up now!" He's been home a couple months. I have faith in him.

I talked to Julius a few weeks ago—I told this childhood friend we would go to Real Food Cafe, on Alger Street, and get some vanilla battered French toast. He said he planned on transferring from Grand Rapids Community College to Howard University. I was so proud. He was killed two days later. He was 25.

Ronald and his fiancé are finally getting married after being together a few years. I remember when he first mentioned her. We were at the Raider Grille, eating buffalo chicken sandwiches, in between classes. "Aye, I think I got me one man, she's everything. I can't see myself with nobody else." I guess he meant what he said.

Gaby and her husband just had their second kid a few months ago: he's so chubby. I can't decide whether he looks more like Shontae or Gaby.

My best friend's daughter just turned three and I still haven't met her yet. They live in Texas. We've been friends so long we don't even remember how we met: our moms have been best friends since they were 14. When we were younger, we used to play under the streetlights, and talk about how our kids were going to be best friends, too. He has two kids. I have none so far.

Chaka is moving to North Carolina soon. I texted her and asked her to pray for me for my first day of community college: that was in 2011. I was so nervous. We laugh about that now.

These were thoughts and memories that came to me while my family tried to decide where to go for lunch on my graduation day from the University of Michigan in April 2017. They went back and forth a good 10 minutes:

"Let's go to Panera Bread!"

"Panera bread is for vegetarians and white people."

"Aye, where the corner store at? I need a black & mild, some hot cheetos and a Brisk."

"Look man, all I want is some chicken nuggets and fries."

I found it interesting how I was trying to introduce my family to something new, but they wanted no part of it. They wanted what was familiar and their requests were simple. The dialogue reminded me how my food preferences have changed since moving to Ann Arbor. I traded in my $1 Arizona Iced Teas for $4 Chai Latte's and I started eating organic whenever I could. I stopped knowingly eating processed food and I rarely ate anything fried. Very few of these dietary changes were intentional. Ann Arbor just had *different* options.

I often wonder why I decided to change and extend out to a wider social landscape. I think back to growing up in Grand Rapids, starting college there, and landing in Ann Arbor. I was not content and wanted something else. The journey is not complete and I am hoping for resolution.

Part II

WORKING CLASS

WORK BOOTS AND BOOKS
NATHANAEL BOORSMA

Ham and cheese or peanut butter and jelly? This is my important choice of every school and workday. I spread a thick layer of peanut butter on my whole wheat bread. It has to be crunchy peanut butter, of course. And no better way to complement this than with mom's homemade raspberry jams. I throw a ripe banana, bag of chips, and an ice pack into my Igloo lunchbox. I hope it is enough to keep me full until 6:30 p.m.

Before heading out the door to my first class at college, I grab work boots and a fresh work uniform. Every day it is a new pair of brown, pleated pants and a button-down, short-sleeve shirt, carefully pressed and folded by the uniform company so that my embroidered name stares back at me. After class I trade my notebooks and pens for the uniform, work boots, and a trusty, black-to-brown faded Carhartt sweatshirt. Since it is fall, daylight is getting shorter, and that means my 30-minute commute to Grand Rapids Community College (GRCC) in Michigan is in the dark. During fall months, I schedule my classes early in the morning, and rush off to my landscaping job in the afternoon. It is strategic scheduling on my part. Sitting in a warm classroom is much nicer than shivering outside each brisk, fall morning. I could join up with my landscape team later when the sun melts the frost, making the job of cleaning up customers' fallen leaves much easier.

Since I was 16, I have held manual labor jobs, usually involving the outdoors. Working overtime leading up to starting community college in the fall of 2013 and part-time during semesters allowed me to pay for my first car and my community college tuition. It was only natural for the boys from Plymouth Christian High School to find a job where you got a little dirt on your hands and sweat on your brow. I wanted to work hard too. Dad, my school, and community all taught the importance of a work ethic and its role in my future success. If I was not hustling with the wheelbarrows of landscape mulch or digging holes fast enough, I would hear about it from my coworkers. We all took great pride in the quality of our work because that is what sets your work apart and above the competition. This was directly linked to integrity, character, and, ultimately, affluence. However, it was not until recently that I discovered there is a difference between working hard and working your life away. That lesson was taught as a function of my social class background.

I was on my way to Argentina: Argentina, of all places, for six weeks. The very thought was foreign, knowing I would soon be on a 14-hour flight away from family and my country home; in a different continent, on the flipside of the world. The study abroad and scholarship opportunity was too good to pass up and I figured I would likely not be able to travel to Argentina again in my lifetime. I could finish the University of Michigan's foreign language requirement quickly and graduate on time. The May 2016 afternoon before I left for the Grand Rapids airport, dad called me during his lunch hour asking me to search for a small envelope in his wooden cubby next to his favorite spot on the couch. Every night for the past 17 years you could find him there, sprawled out, reading a *4-Wheel and Off-Road Magazine* or snoring away, with a pair of dollar-store reading glasses clinging to the end of his nose. With him still on the phone, I opened the envelope to find $400. He said it was a gift to use during my trip. I told him there was no way I could accept the money. After haggling for several minutes, he told me in his usual calm, deep voice that I needed to take it. He wanted me to have it. He also asked that I did not let mom know that he was giving me the money. I accepted, thanking him as much as one can over the phone. With that, I grabbed my luggage and sped off to the airport with mom.

As they asked, I called my parents as soon as I landed in Atlanta for my connecting flight. This was my last taste of American culture before being thrown into something completely foreign. When I called, mom and I said our final goodbyes. She said dad wanted to talk to me. Over the phone, I could hear him tinkering away in the background on my '97 Volkswagen Jetta. My $1,500 car had held together since high school, even until today, thanks to dad's mechanical knowledge. He asked me a few questions about what seemed to be wrong with my car before I left. I do not remember what the issue was, likely something trivial. We concluded the conversation, and I again mentioned he did not have to give me the money. Then it came. Over the phone, dad started pouring out feelings that had no doubt been accumulating. His trembling voice immediately drove me to tears. I collapsed into the nearest chair. I had never heard such emotion from my dad, a man of few words. He was always the quietest one in the room—preferring to listen and observe. In so many ways, I am just like him. Earlier that year, dad had a scare with prostate cancer. During that time, I know he and mom had many long conversations; he probably did a lot of reflecting throughout his treatment. He likely considered how valuable his time was and evaluated how he wanted to spend the rest of his life. Those thoughts and feelings all came out that afternoon.

He said how special it was that I was being given an opportunity he never had. Immediately after high school, he and mom got married and had my two brothers and two sisters. He worked tirelessly every day to afford to send us to a private school and move out from congested city home, out to the Michigan countryside. I remember one ordinary evening in particular; my family was sitting around the dinner table as usual. I started asking questions about what life was like when he and mom first got married. He recounted how he spent long hours, sometimes 60 or 70 hours a week, working in a bakery and at his grandpa's grocery store. He did it so he could create a better life for his wife and children. For him, it was the American Dream in action, alive and well.

Now as I flew to South America, he wanted me to enjoy the irreplaceable moments. He wanted me to take advantage of every unforgettable experience Argentina had to offer. I realized he envisioned something different for me. I was his first and youngest son to take on a completely different pathway through life. I was going to college. To him, I represented someone he could live through; I was his legacy, and he wanted me to take advantage of every opportunity set before me. He envisioned me as someone who applied himself every day to the best of his ability to achieve a greater goal. After all, is that not what every honorable dad dreams of giving his children? That was why he gave me the $400. It might have well been a gold mine. No, more than that, it was priceless. It was affirmation of his love for me. I think that's why it hit me so hard. It was never so real to me on that May day at Atlanta airport in 2017 that he loved me. I sat there crying, thanking him and telling him I loved him. I know some people reading might think giving a son $400 is a shallow way to express love, but for me, growing up working class, it meant everything. It was the meaning behind it and whom it came from that made it so special.

One year before my trip, I was making the life-defining decision of where to transfer after graduating from GRCC. My first two years of college were finished and I had to decide where to go for my bachelor's. As a first-generation college student, I participated in TRIO, a federal outreach and student services program. TRIO is specifically for first-generation and low-income college students, and, as it would happen, I fit that first category. I asked my mentor about my options for transferring and she suggested I was qualified to transfer to the University of Michigan in Ann Arbor—a name only used in conversations about football. My brothers, my friends, and I have always been Michigan fans, but we never considered it as a place to get an education. I was staunchly opposed to even applying; my academic self-concept did not extend to huge, public, prestigious four-year universities and there were so many other reasons that deterred me.

First off, it was a huge university and I would be living away from home. I was already a 21st-century pioneer in my community's eyes, departing from the traditional ways of my family, and exploring a new dimension of opportunity. Attending Michigan would only exacerbate my feeling of guilt I was not contributing to the manual labor force as much as my community. How was I supposed to cope with living as a white-collar student from a blue-collar community? There was a level of distrust of "suits" in my blue-collar community. Multiple times the photos showed up on my Facebook feed, shared and liked by my community: "This country was built by men in denim and will be destroyed by men in suits." How was I going to cope with progressing toward being one of them?

My family and my community are close. This speaks to the values I learned in early childhood that would be challenged to a much greater degree at Michigan. This was mom's main concern with me moving away to Ann Arbor. She always heard stories of sons and daughters moving from their Christian homes and communities to attend college. At the end of the four years, they rejected most beliefs learned as kids. The day I got my acceptance letter to Michigan, she was immediately concerned, though not vocalized. I could easily feel it. Even today she encourages me to come home as often as possible. During the week, she sends me daily devotions and reminders. Despite her initial reluctance, she is now comfortable with me living away from home. She understands the opportunities I have today would not have been possible if I did not decide to come to Michigan. I am thankful she has been able to cope with my extended absence—absence that is rare for working-class families.

Finally, the biggest factor influencing my decision to apply to Michigan was finances. I had been able to pay for my community college tuition in cash, but the cost of Michigan's tuition and rent was staggering. The thought of accumulating debt was terrifying to me and my parents. Recruiters and continuing-generation students, those who had four-year college-educated parents, always mentioned how the return of a degree was worth the investment, but at that time, the risk seemed too great. After dedicating 20+ years to a company, dad began to make a decent living, meaning I was not eligible for federal aid or need-based scholarships. Also, as a result of my parents paying for elementary and secondary private education for their five children, they did not save money for our college attendance. With all this in mind, I knew it was solely up to me to pay for college. Thankfully, my TRIO mentor advised me I would never know what my financial aid package would look like if I never applied. If I did not like what I saw—which I was sure would happen—then I could transfer elsewhere. A few months later, I was proved wrong in the best possible way. I was given enough scholarships to cover all of my tuition. A weight had been lifted off my parents' backs and I could now attend Michigan.

Throughout my first year, I recognized that I grew up aspiring to a simpler template for happiness than most students around me. I realized how many different directions I could go in life, adding new, complex additions to my template. Returning home, I was surrounded by those who are still pursuing the simple lifestyle, the modest yet fulfilling goals, the traditional family—their version of the American Dream. At times I wish they could see the world from my perspective and understand how much there is to learn and explore. However, I know this is a selfish and demonizing way to look at family and friends—the ones I love most. They have done what they have known to be everything in their power to develop and provide the best for themselves, their families, and their community. How could anyone criticize that? With my simple template, I pressed on to Michigan, bringing my social-class background and its culture with me.

The first challenge I faced as a first-generation, transfer student was finding housing in Ann Arbor. I understood outright I would not be living in the dorms on campus because they were too expensive.

However, apartments and housing rentals also came with a steep price tag. I eventually found a room, off campus but within walking distance of my classes, that was within my price range. The home was owned and occupied by an elderly man and a middle-aged woman. It was certainly a nontraditional living arrangement, but it worked. I had my own private space: a place to call "home" for the next nine months. During my first year, I managed to build friendships with people from different states, countries, and cultures. I would have never had opportunity back in rural Grand Rapids. The 2015–2016 academic year was not without its social class struggles, however.

In November 2015, as students were finishing their work before traveling back home for Thanksgiving, my car's old, original brake lines had rusted completely through. For weeks, I was immobile. I could not crawl under my car and replace the lines due to lack of clearance. My family has never once called a tow truck or required professional car service. We understood those services were too expensive to not do ourselves, so dad taught us how to work on our vehicles. Homesick, I made the bold decision to make the two-and-a-half-hour drive back to Grand Rapids, despite the obvious danger. I justified my decision with the thought I could simply downshift the gears on the manual transmission to slow down, if needed. I made it home safe for Thanksgiving.

At the beginning of each new semester, every student expects the first class to be laid back and light on course content. Icebreakers are inevitable. Many students give generic responses to their hobbies or interests. Coming from a rural community, I was always excited to share something different. I would proudly tell classmates my hobbies included off-roading and riding quads or dirtbikes, and my interesting fact was that I raised pigs for five years. I see how quickly I could be labeled the class redneck. I feel sorry for those who have only gotten to experience playing sports or an instrument. The feeling of cruising unoccupied land and being outdoors is a natural high. Few understand the mesmerizing serenity of watching a sunset, from your four-wheeler's seat, paint the sky every shade of orange, pink, and yellow. Each rolling hill for miles displays another farmer's corn or soybean field. Frogs croak in the background and birds make their way back to their nests. I can read every book, read every poem, and write a paper describing the scene, but I could only experience it in the hillsides surrounding my home.

Growing up in a Christian home meant I would face many challenges at Michigan. Explaining those beliefs to new people I meet is an easy way to be ostracized and labeled a religious nut. Beliefs such as traditional marriage, not performing work on Sunday, or cursing are constantly challenged every single day, in and out of the classroom. Michigan has pushed me to educate myself on various topics and approach people's contrasting beliefs in respectful manners even when they might not respect me. I found suppressing my religious background to appease professors and make new friends is damaging. However, in the college environment where the need to belong is so powerful, suppression of one's beliefs becomes common place for many students.

The moments in which my social class background is most apparent are when I hear of my friends' or other students' parents paying for their tuition. This was never an option for me. Having to stay within a limited budget and prioritize all purchases restricts my freedom to do many things they have the privilege of doing. Of course, I could get a private loan, but I had to be wise about my purchases. I could not justify getting full meal plans while living off campus, nor could I live in expensive apartment complexes near campus. However, I do not begrudge those who have this privilege, nor should I be jealous of them. Since I am responsible for covering all my college tuition, I have had the opportunity to practice fiscal responsibility and live on a budget, unlike many other students. If applied wisely, I know these skills will help me in the future. Someday, I hope I can pay for my children's college tuition while teaching them those same lessons. My hope is that they can take advantage of college experiences without a dark cloud of financial anxiety hanging over them. Additionally, there is a sense of pride I have in paying for my entire college experience, with no help from my parents. Few other students can claim those bragging rights. I am proud I will be able to say I earned my degree in its entirety. Of course, my parents and faculty mentors have provided practical and emotional support that has allowed me to persist. Through merit and need-based scholarships, Michigan has supported my experience and allowed me opportunities to learn abroad and during the summers.

Ultimately, I am proud of my social class background, the culture it nurtured, and the habits, values, and beliefs I derived. I hope to pass on the same mind-set to my children. Mom and dad emphasized personal responsibility, empathy and respect for others, and work ethic as key values I needed to practice each day. No matter the circumstances, they knew if I had those values, I would be successful. Today, I am thankful they demonstrated those characteristics. I am thankful those values were taught in our Christian home. I am thankful they were applied in my rural, Michigan home. Because, each night when I lie down, whether in the starless sky of Ann Arbor or in the calm countryside of Byron Center, they were right.

What Do You Do in Ann Arbor?
Candyce Hill

"How are you going to get around without a car?"

My stepdad Tom's face was a mixture of bewilderment and concern as he asked me this very simple question. We were discussing my upcoming move to Ann Arbor for the fall 2008 and plans to start my freshman year at the University of Michigan. While Tom thought I would drive my old 1995 Geo Tracker to campus, I had plans to sell the car. The fact that the car was a lovely shade of neon green that would never be appreciated in Wolverine territory was not my only reason for wanting to sell it quickly. I hoped a few hundred dollars would help me pay some of my expenses once I got to campus.

My response to Tom's concern was full of more confidence than I actually felt at the time:

> "I don't like driving and I won't need a car on campus. Freshmen aren't supposed to have them in Ann Arbor anyway. I will be fine without one."

In the end I sold the car. Tom even helped me find a buyer and shook his head as I handed over the keys.

* * *

Cars are important in my family. My great-grandparents, grandparents, and parents have worked for the auto industry in and around Detroit in one capacity or another. I have family members with work experience on the assembly line, a grandma who drove a forklift at Ford until she retired at age 64, a grandfather who made the small pieces of metal that would later be used to build the cars. Then there's Tom who works with diesel engines and learned how to be a mechanic while serving in the army during the Gulf War. He loves engines and spends most of his free time outside of work tinkering with projects. Every time my old Geo Tracker broke down, Tom came to the rescue and managed to get it working again.

My biological father, who worked at a body shop in Ohio, bought the Geo Tracker from a customer who decided it was not worth repairing. Dad got the initial body work done and gave me the car as a present for my 16th birthday with the understanding that I would pay for the insurance, gas, and repairs. Of course, I'd also be responsible for driving my younger sister to school. It was an incredibly generous gift and I happily worked part-time jobs throughout high school to pay for the privilege of owning my own car. And every time the car needed an oil change or air in the tires, Tom was there to help.

By the time I was ready to sell the Geo Tracker, Tom had probably spent just as much time with the car as me. While I drove my shiny green car to and from school and work, Tom was the one who spent time making sure it was running well and fiddling with it while it was parked near the house. He gave it just as much care as the vehicles he and my mom drove. Perhaps that's part of the reason he was so frustrated at my decision to sell the car. This was a machine he put effort into with the hope that it would last as long as possible and there I was ready to sell. I imagine another part of his frustration came from not understanding what kind of space I would be entering when I started college. How would I possibly be able to get by without reliable transportation? Didn't I understand how difficult it was to manage public transportation?

I am a first-generation college student. My great-grandparents, grandparents, and parents never completed college degrees. Instead everyone worked. With well-paying jobs in the auto industry and the benefits gained from collective bargaining through the

United Auto Workers Union, we enjoyed a comfortable lifestyle. Our family always had access to health care, groceries, and any number of benefits that come from earning a decent living wage. However, I was the first one to decide to go away to college. My family and I were excited about my decision to attend the University of Michigan, but none of us really knew what to expect.

* * *

"Everything you're bringing with you has to be in the truck tonight!"

Tom was adamant with his reminder that I must be fully packed and ready to leave that morning of August 2008. Tomorrow was move-in day for first-year students living in the residence hall I had been assigned to and he didn't want us to be late. We stuffed the bed of his truck with all of the things I planned to take with me. Clothes, books, toiletries, towels, and bedding with extra-long twin-size sheets (a size no one had ever heard of before and one which mom at first insisted did not exist) filled in every inch. When we finally left, there was just enough space to fit Tom, mom, and me inside the truck's cab.

Once we arrived in Ann Arbor, Tom parked his truck in front of Helen Newberry residence hall. A beautiful building, on Maynard Street, that would end up being my campus home for the next four years. As we began moving everything up to my new dorm room on the second floor, I noticed how Tom was not taking advantage of any of the student volunteers who were offering to help move things inside. Instead he insisted on carrying all the items, with some help from mom and me.

* * *

Tom, like so many of the people in my family, is very good at working with his hands. Not only does he know how to fix cars; he once installed a second bathroom in our house, and is always around with his truck to help when someone needs to haul a heavy piece of equipment. Growing up, I do not ever remember my family calling a repairman. Fixing things and working with their hands are skills many members of my family have and they take pride in a job well done. It should not have surprised me at all to see Tom insist on doing the full move into the residence hall on our own without assistance.

That first move into Helen Newberry was far from the last. After freshman year, I was able to secure a job as an orientation leader, one that I held for three summers. Tom helped me move from Newberry to a summer residence hall and back again for four years. Every time we went through the same routine. Have everything packed the night before, load up the truck as soon as he came to campus, and move boxes into the new space as quickly and efficiently as possible. By our third move Tom was familiar with the layout of Ann Arbor. He knew which one-way streets to avoid and where to find parking. We built up a familiar routine and in some ways this helped make the college environment seem less uncertain for my parents. However, there were parts of the campus my family had not seen and plenty parts of my new life in Ann Arbor that remained a mystery.

* * *

"What classes are you taking? Why those classes?"

Tom's questions about my coursework initially felt like an interrogation. I had to stop and listen to the tone of his voice to realize he was asking with genuine curiosity. My family knew I had every intention of majoring in history, but by junior year, I added a second major, Judaic Studies, and there was some confusion. In addition to the variety of history classes I usually enrolled in, I was now in classes focused on everything from women in the Bible to intermediate Yiddish language skills. I began taking Yiddish my freshman year and while I think my family thought it was an interesting choice, the idea of a second major in Judaic Studies seemed odd. What would I do with these majors? What was my plan after I finished school? I was funding my own college experience with a combination of scholarships, grants, and loans. My parents were

not concerned about getting a return on their financial investment in my education. They had not made an investment and did
not believe it was their responsibility. They would be supportive
of my choice to attend the University of Michigan, but they did not
have the financial resources to pay for such an expensive institution. The financial burden for school was my responsibility and my
parents' concern for what future career I would have with a double
major in history and Judaic Studies came from their concern for
how I would pay back my student loans.

My conversation with Tom that day eventually ended with me
justifying my majors by saying there were "lots of things" I could
do with my two majors. I was building broad skills, rather than
technical expertise I could use in a specific field. From Tom's working-class perspective this did not at first make sense. The skills you
learned after high school were meant to help you get a job. Just as
the mechanical skills he gained in the army helped him learn how to
fix engines, my major should somehow relate to my future career.
The idea that I was spending so much time learning how to read
critically and write reflectively in hopes of getting a job someday
in a field I had not yet determined was completely foreign. Tom,
like the rest of my family, was supportive, even with his many questions, and I am so grateful for how much he trusted me, even when
he was very unsure about what exactly I was studying and why.

* * *

During my four years at Michigan, my family constantly asked questions about my experiences in Ann Arbor. Beyond what I was studying, they wanted to know whom I was making friends with and what
I did with my time on campus. I only went to class 16 hours a week
and worked for about eight hours. What was I doing with all of my
extra time and who was I meeting? There were many details during those four years I did not feel like sharing. I told my family that
I had two best friends and we spent most of our free time together,
but I did not tell them about how when visiting one friend's house

I discovered her family hired a maid to clean for them a few times a week. I told my family about my classes and the interesting professors who spoke so passionately about the subjects they researched, but I never mentioned how my instructor who taught on the history of ancient Rome asked people to raise their hands if they had ever been to different parts of Italy. I told my family that I spent my free time studying, but rarely brought up how much of my time was spent simply enjoying different activities and clubs.

I loved my experience in college and many of my happiest memories took place in Ann Arbor. But along with the wonderful feelings those great memories bring are reminders about the differences I started to realize would separate my family and me. I was encountering a world where people paid someone else to work with their hands and clean up after them, where trips to Europe were common, and where people in their late teens and early twenties were encouraged to spend their time on whatever activities they found most interesting. While my parents worked and my sisters started their families, I enjoyed what felt at times like an extended adolescence. I studied often so I would do well in my classes and stayed involved in many activities on campus, but I always knew this was an incredible privilege.

*　*　*

"I was thinking of wearing this for graduation. Will it work?"

Tom pointed out the red polo shirt and khaki pants he planned to wear to one of the graduation celebrations later that week in April 2012. This particular celebration was for first-generation college students and their families. I knew there would be many other working-class families at this celebration and I wondered if some of my peers were having similar conversations. To be honest, I was surprised Tom owned a polo shirt. Other than dress shirts worn at weddings or funerals, I don't think I have ever seen him wear a shirt with a collar. I assured him the polo and khakis would be fine and later had a similar conversation with mom about how the black and white dress she was planning to wear would work perfectly. Even after four years of coming down from Howell, Michigan, to visit me, Ann Arbor was still a relatively unfamiliar place where dress codes were uncertain. Even with this uncertainty, we were all excited for graduation. This was a chance to celebrate the last four years and everyone wanted the celebration to go well.

Based on the conversations we had during the events and the following weeks, I know my family enjoyed graduation. From meeting my fellow first-generation students at our graduation celebration in the Michigan Student Union to watching the crowds of graduates in Michigan Stadium—"The Big House"—it was an incredibly meaningful experience for everyone. The whole family attended all the events and in many ways it felt as if there was a shared sense of success. I took the classes, wrote the papers, and passed the tests that allowed me to earn the degree. My family offered the support and encouragement it took to graduate. They were the ones who helped me move in and out of so many residence halls and they were the ones who let me tell them about campus little by little, without pushing me to share every detail. When I received my diploma in the mail a few weeks later, I knew from the looks on Tom's and mom's faces that they were very proud of me.

As I'm sure is true for many Wolverines, leaving Ann Arbor after four amazing years was difficult. When I left, I did not go back home. Instead, I moved to Tulsa, Oklahoma, to work with Teach for America and teach Pre-K at a Title 1 elementary school. The low-income families and students I worked with were incredible. College was a long way off for the four- and five-year-olds in my classroom, but if any of them decided to attend college in the future, they would also be the first in their families. My hope as a teacher was to provide them with strong academic foundations. This would be needed if they chose to become first-generation college students and pursue paths different from the ones their families had traveled.

SEEKING STABILITY
RYANN OOMEN

Mom and dad met in high school, at a local restaurant/skating rink called Johnny's in Custer, Michigan—where everyone hung out in the 1980s. This was a classic high school sweetheart story; they fell in love, were married, moved away after graduating, found jobs, and bought a two-bedroom trailer in Elkhart, Indiana, where I was born. They worked jobs that didn't require college degrees; mom at a medical clinic and dad at the local factory making city bus parts. Things seemed to be okay. But mom moved out when I was three and they divorced by late 2002, after I turned five. I was so young when all this happened that I don't even think of it as a big deal; it's just always been the norm for me.

Growing up, I always tried to divide time between mom and dad and both sides of the family as best as I could. I lived with mom more often than dad since she resided in the school district I attended. But my heart was always divided between them. After their divorce, both began seeing and living with other people. Mom sort of moved up a social class after the divorce. We lived in a two-story house with a decent amount of land in a small town—Edwardsburg—in southwest Michigan, with her new boyfriend who had a degree from Ohio State University; he worked as an automotive engineer.

Dad stayed in the trailer and eventually his new girlfriend and her son moved in. When I spent time with my dad, I always remembered us having the best of times. We would eat cereal for breakfast (and lunch and dinner) and mac and cheese for lunch (and dinner sometimes too), and I could not have been happier. I didn't know, but later found out that dad and his girlfriend spent a lot on credit cards and loans. The excessive spending on top of other financial stressors of being in the working class led to dad's bankruptcy in 2005. I was eight years old.

I was happy during childhood despite my parents being divorced and living separate lives. It took me awhile to realize their divorce and social class even had an impact on me. I never questioned why mom was always gone at work and why I was the only person in my friends group who had to ride the bus to and from school every day. Mom worked two jobs most of my life and that was normal for me. I didn't realize she had to be away a lot so that she could take care of me and put food on the table. As a little girl I just kind of thought that's what adults did.

The only time when my mom didn't work two jobs was when she was diagnosed with breast cancer. I was in the third grade when we found out. Of course, I didn't really know what this meant, but I knew she was sick and it could potentially take her life. I was petrified. I spent hours and hours alone every week waiting for mom to get back from doctor's appointments and chemo treatments, always worrying about what would happen next.

The Christmas when she had breast cancer was especially difficult for us. On the night of Christmas Eve, I remember sitting on the couch and watching her pull out the last strand of hair on her head. All I knew about cancer at the time was that it made you bald, really tired, and very sick. But I realized it wasn't just my mom's health the cancer impacted. That Christmas, the hospital where mom worked and still works (also the one where I was born) decided to "adopt" our family. I remember it being simultaneously one of my best and worst Christmases. It was the best because I got all the presents on my list; including the Bratz spa and limousine I had been wanting all year. I thought mom's work bought all these presents because she was too sick to go Christmas shopping. I never realized the overwhelming amount of medical bills from her sickness were a big reason why my family was actually "adopted" that holiday season.

Thankfully, mom got better with treatments and she slowly regained her health. Not long after her fight with cancer she decided it was time to have her tubes tied. The doctors told her she would never be able to have kids again, due to all the chemicals and radiation from the cancer treatments. She figured it was time. To her surprise, the doctor politely informed her they could not tie her tubes because she was pregnant!! Nine months later on March 24, 2006 (five days before my ninth birthday), we were blessed with my beautiful little sister, Allyx Jolene—Mommy's little miracle.

After Allyx was born I became what you'd call the "built-in babysitter." Mom went back to working two jobs, which meant, when I wasn't at school, I was helping watch my sister. Babysitting her was a lot of responsibility at age nine, but I knew it helped mom, so she could be at work. Although it was frustrating at times, like when I just wanted to go outside and play with my friends, I knew mom needed me to be strong for her.

*　*　*

From the very beginning I loved school; it was my refuge. In kinder-garten I had AM and PM classes, unlike most of my friends. Then after school ended, I would have to spend extra hours at the after-school daycare program and wait for mom to pick me up. I spent long days at school throughout my entire childhood, but I liked it better that way. School made me feel happy and secure.

The idea of going to college was in my head from a very young age despite the fact neither of my parents had graduated from college. Mom, dad, and most of the family have always been University of Michigan (UM) fans, so football Saturdays were a huge part of my childhood. At age six, mom bought me a Michigan cheerleading uniform and blue pom-poms from the M Den Store so I could wear and use them for Halloween. At that age, my aspirations were to be a UM cheerleader on Saturdays at the Big House. What an exciting place to be. Back then I had no clue what college really meant, but I always assumed I was going to Michigan when I grew up.

* * *

Toward the beginning of high school, I started realizing if I really did want to attend Michigan I would have to bust my ass all four years and apply for every possible scholarship. When it came time to applying to colleges I worried if I could even afford to pay the application fee; UM's is $75, in case you're wondering. Thankfully, since I was a student receiving free lunch at high school, my application fees were waived. After I sent my application I thought about it every single day. I doubted myself just as much if not more than those around me. I constantly compared myself to other UM applicants who I assumed were smarter than me despite the fact I was Valedictorian at my high school. I knew I had the disadvantage of being a low-income student from a graduating class of 30 coming from a rural town that probably wasn't even on the UM's map.

I watched Wolverine Access religiously for weeks while I awaited the application decision. I remember checking my email one day in late December 2014 and there was a message from Michigan. I was afraid to open it; this might be the moment of truth. The feeling that rushed over me when I read the words "Congratulations, you're in!" is something that can only be understood when you feel it yourself. My parents could not have been prouder. Michigan had always been my dream and I never looked back for a second after that day. I turned down opportunities for two $50,000 scholarships at Western Michigan University, and other scholarship offers from schools like Eastern Michigan University and Ball State University in Indiana. But as soon as I was accepted, I forgot there would be an attached bill. I didn't care. I knew it would all work out and be worth it; I knew I couldn't turn down this opportunity. Due to hard work and perseverance, I managed to earn enough scholarship and financial aid money to pay for the majority of my first-year expenses. If it wasn't for long hours I put in throughout school years, I know I wouldn't have been able to take advantage of my Michigan education.

* * *

The road to that acceptance letter wasn't an easy one by any means. After I finished middle school, I went through some major changes. To start with, I was beginning my teenage years and high school; which are scary enough when you're 14 years old. On top of that, I had decided to move north with dad, three hours from Edwardsburg to Custer where my family is from. Mom wasn't happy about the move, but she knew it would make me the happiest.

For my freshman year at Mason County Eastern High School, dad and I lived in Aunt Jenny and Uncle Joe's basement: dad's sister and brother-in-law. I liked it better this way because Aunt Jenny's house always had a full fridge, a pantry, and Wi-Fi. Dad didn't feel the same. He always wanted to do more for me, so we could have our own place. I understood that it wasn't easy and I was content with the way things were even if it meant having to register at my school as a "homeless student," since we lived with relatives.

* * *

In high school, getting your license and driving to and from school was a really big deal. When my 16th birthday came around, I didn't even bother going to the secretary of state for my license because I knew I wouldn't have my own car. I didn't actually get my license until the summer of 2013 when dad finally got a little beater car—a gray Ford Taurus—to drive to work, so I could drive his truck. Even though it wasn't much, I couldn't have been more grateful. I drove his 1999 tan Chevrolet pickup truck to school with pride, even during times when the driver's seat window had to be held up with duct tape and the heater didn't work. I knew he was working hard for me to be able to have something. I always wanted more, but I tried not to ask for much. Dad told me how much he hated saying no when

I asked for something, so I started asking less and less. Instead of having my parents buy me things, I would just save up all of my birthday and Christmas money. I used that stash whenever I had expenses I didn't want to stress my parents out about.

* * *

I always knew what social class was about in my own little ways while growing up. I knew I had fewer things than other kids; I didn't have a pool in my backyard or a tutor to prepare me for college. But I definitely didn't really understand until I started college. Social class hit me like a brick within the first few days. I met so many new people from all over the country, many more people from places like New York, New Jersey, or Los Angeles than from places like Custer. I felt out of place right away as I began to realize there weren't many people like me on campus. I struggled to make friends and most of the girls in my hall rushed sororities, another subject I had no clue about. I spent much of my freshman year just trying to get by socially. For the first time in my life, I felt so different from everyone else around me and I started understanding how social class trumps other factors like race and ethnicity.

I worried' I would never find my place among the flocks of Canada Geese. For those of you wondering, Canada Goose is a winter jacket costing more than what I pay for rent each month, even here in downtown Ann Arbor, a notably pricey housing market. I never even heard about this brand until my first winter (2016) when I began seeing the same jacket on almost every girl who walked by. *What is that Canada Goose emblem on their coats?* I thought. Since I didn't have many friends at the time, I asked my boyfriend what they were. I could barely even believe what he told me. *What? A large portion of the student body has enough money to spend a thousand dollars on a winter jacket? Where am I??* From the start I knew I would have to find my own place here if I was ever going to survive.

For the second semester of my freshman year (winter 2016), I enrolled in Sociology 295: The Experience of Social Class in

College and the Community; the course that led me to writing for this anthology. I didn't really know what to expect, but it sounded interesting. I wanted to learn more about this giant, ever-present beast that is social class. As I sat in the classroom and looked around, I noticed the room was pretty ethnically diverse; there were students of many different backgrounds. I sat in the back corner, alone of course. I didn't speak up much because I was too nervous, but I always listened. The course covered material that stirred emotions I had never completely felt before: anger, fear, frustration, and doubt. I enjoyed hearing and reading about student perspectives from different social class and racial backgrounds; it was so eye-opening. I found myself able to relate better to students in my social class from Detroit Public Schools than those who grew up in Bloomfield Hills, Michigan, and other predominantly wealthier, white suburban areas. During the winter of 2016, I truly realized the complexities of social class.

*   *   *

My junior year has started: it has all happened so fast. As I look forward to the future I'm faced with many uncertainties, as always. What will I do after I graduate? Where will I live? Whom will I live with? Will I be able to afford living on my own? Will my parents be able to help me if I can't afford everything? All of these questions constantly fill my head with worry and stress.

As of now, my intention is to pursue a law degree after graduating in 2019. But with law school comes even more stress: financially and mentally. I know that if I work hard I can make it, but sometimes when I think about the journey it is difficult to stay hopeful and motivated. Would I even be able to fund and eventually pay for a legal education? What happens if I'm not successful after law school? How will I ever be able to repay my student loan debts? When I look to the future, I'm confronted by countless questions and few answers. In thinking about the coming years, I worry if I will ever find stability. Throughout childhood I always looked to school for security and satisfaction. School was and still is my sanctuary—my home away from home. What will my life be like when I'm no longer living on and walking around a college campus? What will I do without the stability education has given me?

Despite this questioning and uncertain phase of my life, I continue to tackle new challenges with optimism and hope, and with the goal of making my family proud.

BETWEEN TWO WORLDS OR: HOW I LEARNED TO STOP WORRYING AND LOVE THE WORKING CLASS

LAUREN SCHANDEVEL

My parents fought a lot when I was a kid. In summers, they would do it with the windows open over the steady hum of our neighbor's lawnmower. More often than not, their little black checkbook was mere inches from the scene, its insides stamped with numbers that never quite added up. My dad purchased a TV. My mom went over budget at the grocery store. Let's just refinance the house again; we might as well stay another 30 years.

I guess my story really begins with their stories. My mom grew up on a farm in the rural Michigan town of Peck, the youngest of eight. As of 2010, Peck had a population of 632 people and one traffic light. In high school, she worked four jobs to pay for two years of technical school, where she received her associate's degree in secretarial science. When she moved closer to Detroit for work, she wound up in the same apartment complex as my dad.

In hindsight, it's a wonder the two were compatible at all. My mom was a reserved, small-town girl who had pioneered her way to a desk job in the city. My dad, on the other hand, dropped out of his first year of community college and was hanging around his hometown, trying to make ends meet. Working as a waiter and part-time disk jockey, he loved punk music, old cartoons, and cocaine (on special occasions).

They lived in a mobile home park for a while after getting married, but when my mom became pregnant with me in 1996, they decided to take the plunge into home ownership. Eventually, they settled on a three-bedroom, one-and-a-half-bath ranch-style house in the city of Warren, complete with a big backyard and an unfinished basement. Optimistic and saddled with debt, they made a home for me there, and my brother joined the mix couple of years later to fill the third bedroom.

Over time, we wove in and out of the working class, never quite secure in any position. Money was always a point of tension, as there was never enough of it. As our parents lost and found jobs periodically, my brother and I were firsthand witnesses to the kind of fear and uncertainty that comes with living paycheck to paycheck.

However, I didn't become attuned to these financial struggles until much later. My childhood was all luscious grass, scraped knees, and calloused hands. Our street was a two-block stretch adjacent to the highway, characterized by the sound of vehicles rushing past like meteors hurtling through space. I remember riding my bike with the neighborhood boys, blasting Metallica and playing cards with garage doors open to usher in summer breezes. The world was much smaller back then—confined to a grid of factories, junkyards, and 7-Elevens.

What felt like a rustic paradise came with downsides. Even before I became aware of my working-class status, there were still subtle hints at my family's economic instability embedded in my day-to-day life. They were present when my brother and I accompanied my mom on trips to thrift stores for clothes and church pantries for food. They were more obvious when her job became another casualty in the 2008 recession and my parents' conversations about the future grew more heated as they struggled to pay bills with just my dad's salary. Facing increased turbulence at home, I turned to my education for consistency.

In school, I was considered weird, shy, and painfully awkward. Teachers labeled me as "advanced" early on, and over time, I developed habits that set me apart from my peers—copying pages out of the encyclopedia, writing short stories on computer printer paper, and checking out library books 10 at a time. At age 10, I wrote a four-page essay on Theodore Roosevelt just for the hell of it. The following year, I stood in line with my mom to purchase the final *Harry Potter* book and read it cover to cover in one day.

My parents fanned the flames of curiosity when they could, saving money each year for a coveted Smithsonian lab kit and driving my brother and me to Detroit for museum visits. They understood the importance of a good education and tried to emulate middle-class habits to the best of their ability. Unfortunately, their efforts were never enough to keep me fully engaged.

Frequently chastised for being smart, I learned eventually to despise school and began purposely skipping classes, acting out, and failing tests to fit in. In sixth grade, when teachers urged me to move up two grades in math, I felt so embarrassed that I spent the next year shoving my algebra textbook deep into my backpack where peers couldn't see it.

No one informed me that education would one day be my ticket to upward mobility, and there were very few people around who were qualified to lead by example. Most older peers dropped out of high school, went to community college, or started families before they turned 20. My parents never attended a four-year institution either, and while they planted the idea of college in my head early on, it was more of a vague notion than a fully formed plan.

A turning point in my education came in middle school during a conversation with my friend, whose brother was a student at the local community college.

"Is that where everyone is supposed to go after high school?" I asked her.

"I think so," she replied.

In that moment, I saw what limited aspirations I had dissipate before my eyes. I imagined living in the same neighborhood, shopping at the same stores, and running into the same people with whom I had grown up for the rest of my life. I was terrified.

Later, I tried to disclose this new insight to my mom while bawling my eyes out. I told her I didn't want to spend four years living at home post–high school, and she assured me that it wasn't how it always worked out. She promised I could go straight to college in another city after I graduated if my grades were good and if I chose to do so.

So the summer before I entered high school in 2011, I decided it was time to get my act together. Slowly, I began the lonely process of cutting ties with wayward friends and redirecting my focus to schoolwork. By the end of freshman year, I was depressed, burnt out, and ready for a drastic change. I begged my parents to let me attend an objectively better school in the wealthier suburb of Berkley, and they reluctantly obliged. We spent the next few months scrambling to submit my request to transfer (the district didn't allow school of choice) and arrange transportation for the commute. Finally, with a clear plan in place and a fresh start ahead of me, I began my journey into class consciousness.

Despite being a mere 15 minutes away, my new school felt like another world. Immediately, I was greeted with the exciting challenge of Advanced Placement (AP) classes, ambitious peers, and devoted teachers. It felt like home right out of the gate and, gradually, I made friends who offered me a firsthand look at class differences in action.

"Do you want to come inside?"

The poorer of them had granite countertops, patterned throw pillows, and family photos with brushed silver frames. The richer of them had antique vases, smooth marble fireplaces, and floor-to-ceiling bookshelves.

While my new environment socialized me to enjoy reading, writing, and learning again, it also instilled middle-class values and interests in me without my knowledge. On weekends, I went to coffee shops, brunch restaurants, and art markets with friends, and learned to appreciate their taste in music, literature, and films. Despite how foreign and new it all felt, I never had to pretend I was enjoying myself when I adopted their hobbies as my own—I adored their lifestyle so much, I almost felt like it was mine.

This immersion in their world made me ashamed of my own modest upbringing. I took special pains not to bring friends home with me, afraid they would judge me for my family's shag carpets and floral patterned couch. When asked about my hometown, I would dismiss it as "just a white trash suburb" and the conversation ended there. I put a lot of distance between myself and my hometown in those three years, so much so that I stopped identifying with neighbors and former classmates, and even found myself occasionally lambasting them for their decisions.

"Another one of my friends from home just had a kid," I would say to friends at my new school. They would laugh along with me and ask, "How many is that now?"

Witticisms about my hometown always sounded colder and more detached coming from them than they did from me. In a way, I felt like my peers sometimes viewed me as "one of the good ones"—a girl from the working class who hadn't gotten pregnant before her 18th birthday, to whom they could relate without making much effort to adjust their assumptions. It wasn't until I began reflecting on these interactions in college that I realized just how much I resented feeling like an outsider, how their comments made me feel like I would never be one of them, no matter how much we had in common.

Before I knew it, it was time to apply to college—a process for which I had the mentality of a rich legacy student and the resources of a working-class kid. In addition to being deterred by the price of applying (around $70 per submission), I hadn't the slightest idea what selective schools were looking for in an applicant. This was obvious in my application to Columbia University, in which I gushed about their journalism school, totally oblivious to the fact that it was a graduate program. (Frankly, I didn't even know what a graduate program was, and no one close to me had the authority or knowledge to correct me.) When I was promptly rejected, it served as a painful reminder of my place in the class hierarchy. If I didn't even have the institutional knowledge to distinguish graduate school from undergraduate, then how did I expect to thrive in the Ivy League? What was I thinking?

After coming to terms with my lack of social capital, I followed many of my peers and accepted a place at the University of

Michigan for fall 2015—a dream come true for my parents and a respectable decision in the eyes of the middle class. That spring, my hard work reached its culmination when I graduated summa cum laude from a high school I had gone out of my way to attend. When I walked across that stage, I felt like I was finally rewarded for all of those daily commutes (which could take up to three hours in heavy traffic), tough AP classes, and countless unforeseeable expenses with a future that seemed to promise upward mobility and financial security for me and my family.

The summer before college was the last time I remember having my feet planted firmly in the working-class world. I spent those few anxious months attending graduation parties with catered food and elaborate decorations, and chatting up with parents who had attended either Michigan or elite private colleges. They seemed grateful and relieved that their children had survived the grueling application process and were now seemingly on a path to success, and I couldn't help but think about my own parents and how they must have been swelling with the same sense of pride. For me, it was comforting to know that, regardless of how often I compared myself to my friends, we were all headed to Ann Arbor to live out our undergraduate years. The only difference was that this sort of trajectory was expected of them; for me, it was just short of a miracle. I kept this in mind as I pocketed food from their buffets.

Eventually, when it came time for college orientation, I got my first taste of life as a low-income student at the University of Michigan. As I introduced myself to my roommate, she began complaining about her trip from New York City to Michigan.

"I lost my iPhone in a cab," she griped, "so my mom bought me this shitty replacement."

She held up an exact model of my phone, and I felt my face turn bright red.

"Wow, that sucks," I replied sheepishly, moving my phone out of her line of sight.

Once school started, I quickly learned that these kinds of interactions were pretty typical at elite colleges all over the country.

This has only become more of a problem for Michigan in recent years as both tuition and the population of out-of-state students with wealthier parents have increased.

However, despite having to fend off the occasional classist remark, my middle-class training paid off and I was able to fit in with relative ease. In my first year, I joined the political scene on campus, biding my time between the College Democrats and the school newspaper. I made friends who were passionate about social change and took informed, progressive stances on issues like education, health care, and the economy. I found myself becoming swept up in the theories of professors and colleagues who seemed to know a lot more than I did about social inequality and its origins.

Meanwhile, I used writing to analyze my own story. In a bi-weekly column in *The Michigan Daily*, I explored my childhood, hometown, and experiences being a low-income, first-generation college student. As I reflected on this journey, I began to piece together just how much social class played a role in shaping my path to higher education. I realized my new high school far surpassed my old one because it served so many middle- and upper-middle-class students, whose parents were privy to their children's academic needs. I understood the outcomes of my former classmates were results of their circumstances and opportunities more than bad decisions. Perhaps most importantly, I developed a newfound appreciation of my parents.

These epiphanies emerged from hardships, as well. When my dad lost his job of 18 years during my first year of college, my family lost half of their annual income. The phone call during which he broke the news to me was the first time I had ever felt completely removed from their situation. That night, sitting on my bed in a state-of-the-art residence hall, watching the Michigan Stadium lights blaze in the distance from my dorm window, I cried *for* him, not *with* him. I told him it would be okay, knowing that I would be fine no matter what, so long as the university continued giving me financial aid. I had my other foot in a different world from that point on.

Though my dad got his job back around Christmas time in 2015, the feeling never really left. I still straddle the line that separates my life in college from my life at home—and it entails more than just being far away from family. There is something fundamentally different about me and the way I see the world now. I'm studying topics my parents can't pronounce and I'm interested in subfields they don't completely understand. Internships and office hours aren't conversations that make their way to the dinner table. Sometimes it feels like we're speaking completely different languages, reconnecting only when I give brief summaries of my schoolwork before reverting back to acting as though I never left. That doesn't mean they're not proud of me—they are. They just don't know how to navigate aspects of my life of which they're not actively a part, and I haven't figured out how to let them in without being alienating.

Now, as my sophomore year comes to a close, I feel like I've almost got the balancing act down. I'll soon have to relay all this information to my brother, who received his acceptance from the University of Michigan in December. Because he stayed in my old school district for high school, he's never traversed class boundaries before. He doesn't know the right books to read or the right clothes to wear, and I don't think I'm going to tell him, because I don't want him to feel like he has to assimilate the way I did. So many lower-income students are led to believe that all of their experiences before college were inadequate, or that they're somehow inherently deficient and must work twice as hard to catch up to everyone else. I want my brother to know the skills he gained from his school in our hometown are valuable in their own way— that being working class is strength to admire rather than a flaw to remediate.

Every day, I embrace my upbringing and identity to make up for the time I spent concealing it. I continue to write and openly talk about my frustrations with higher education, from the cost of textbooks to the impracticality of unpaid internships, with the hope students in similar positions will feel some sense of solidarity.

Recently, I formed the organization Collaborative Learning across Socioeconomic Statuses (CLASS) to coordinate events on campus centered on raising class consciousness. My team is also in the process of working with administrators to develop the first academic minor in the country that focuses explicitly on the topic of social class.

Ironically, as it turns out, my working-class background didn't hinder my experience in higher education: it enhanced it. I incorporate my perspective into all of my work—specifically as a student at the Gerald R. Ford School of Public Policy—and I'm often made to feel appreciated for the insight I bring to the table. As I immerse myself deeper into the political sphere, I try to make a point of always looking out and speaking up for the little guy. I see institutional barriers that are frequently overlooked and do my best to create policies that are both inclusive and empathetic. If I could trade in my family's financial situation for Ivy Leaguer parents and a boarding school education, I wouldn't dream of it. The compassion and awareness that come from being a low-income student at an elite university is easily more valuable to me than the luxury of monetary security. I can only hope these values are retained as I continue to ascend the economic ladder in years to come.

Suppers and *Weared Its*

Zachary Tingley

The first time I returned home freshman year was toward the end of October 2015—two months after starting college in Ann Arbor. During that time, I dropped a math class, spent too much money on books, learned to use chopsticks, attended too many student mass meetings, and didn't call home enough. It was a rough time in many ways, but I found the necessary friends who helped me find my way. Many people consider the process of going from high school to college a transition. My process was more like assimilation.

After starting college at the University of Michigan, it was troubling to understand how my experiences and class background would shape interactions and friendships. I exploited the life I had before college, yet still carried a sense of elitism that comes with attending a selective university. The first time I went back to my Ohio hometown, I began understanding these feelings. At my old high school for my sister's choir concert, I was surrounded by people whom I had grown up with. For the first 18 years of life, I believed everyone was just like the occupants of my hometown, but 60 days in Ann Arbor proved me wrong. My mind was spinning with this new world. These feelings pitted my old world against a new one.

Knowing most of my new college peers weren't from the working class, I imagined the different ways my classmates would be experiencing a younger sibling's concert and then dinner at the local Italian restaurant: cashmere sweaters and fathers in ties. Running late from work, staying late with a client. But they made it, pulling up late in a new Mercedes, Audi, Cadillac. With a presence of envy, despair, and a posture of elitism, I squeezed through the warm, obese bodies, worn-out sweatshirts, and tired eyes to get to a seat next to my parents. After sitting down, I observed what was happening around me. There were kids crying with snot running down their noses. Most of the fathers in the room, including mine, had been up since 4:00 a.m. to get to the factory, working a 10-hour day. It was 7:00 p.m. now and they didn't seem to want to be at this concert. They would be up at the same time tomorrow morning. Some of them recorded the children singing with an off-brand Android phone. I'm sure I scoffed to myself and thought about how everyone at college would probably be filming with an iPhone or their own AV equipment, even though I didn't own an iPhone at the time. Displeased with the inhabitants of my hometown, I was excited to get back to the richness of Ann Arbor, the sophistication of my peers, and the ability to hold an *actual* conversation.

Looking back now, I realize my social class has always held a strong presence in my life—a presence I haven't always had the words to describe or language to understand. Since the flood of feelings I experienced during my first visit back home, perceptions on my class have changed. It's something I've thought about a lot, as it is an integral part of me. Not only did I mentally categorize members of my hometown as *other* or *those people*, but I also didn't allow myself to appreciate the fact that this was where I came from. My father was one of the fathers in that room, and if it wasn't for my college attendance, one of my children might be up on that stage someday.

I first began noticing disparities in my education during the process of applying to college. My dad never went to college and my mom only went for one semester. Because of the homogeneity of my small town, this was the norm and never distanced me from peers. My parents never had any grand expectations for me to attend a prestigious college, but still pushed me to do the best in high school. Their support provided the freedom to hope, dream, and imagine.

Because of this, I have always known college was where I wanted to end up. I figured any path I was going to take was going to involve more education than the resources my hometown offered. Looking back now, I am surprised I could be so optimistic. A lot of kids from my area didn't go to big four-year colleges and most didn't go to college at all. Statistically, I am surprised I have already begun to break away from the cyclical process most members of the working class experience. Some kids I graduated with are already engaged with physical labor, buying houses, having kids, and getting ready to live the same lives their parents are living. Class inequalities are self-perpetuating and systemic.

My parents' support allowed me to dream big. By my sophomore year of high school, I was already looking at colleges and universities across the country. I wanted to go to a big school—prestigious and selective—with academic buildings that looked like they came from Europe with a diverse crowd that would add to the experience. My closeted self still didn't feel comfortable in rural Ohio. While the barns, cornfields, and small-town atmosphere were nice, I still dreamed of someplace more open minded and in touch with the world.

When your parents didn't go to college, Google can answer college-related questions and the online forums provide information not always heard at the dinner table. I frequented College Confidential discussions, memorized the acceptance statistics needed to get into selective schools, and after months of doing my own research discovered I was in a bubble. My isolated rural high school offered nothing in comparison to the high schools of the forum members. After realizing students interested in attending the same selective universities had so many more educational opportunities and resources, I was pissed. I had been ripped off. Kids across the country had been taking three Advanced Placement (AP) classes a semester and I only had taken one my entire high school career. Their flourishing extracurricular participation and ability to do research made me feel like I had no chance. I felt like I was already 10 paces behind before I even had the chance to apply. With my newfound disadvantage, I was furious with my school, the administration, America's educational system, everything.

Yearning to attend a prestigious school close enough to home that would allow my parents to pick me up, I applied to the University of Michigan in Ann Arbor. Ambitiousness led me in the application process and optimism allowed me to believe I had a chance of actually being admitted and affording the $60,000 annual out-of-state tuition. Knowing the price tag was so high, an acceptance e-mail didn't guarantee my attendance. But before I knew it, I was standing in front of a crowd of hometown people who were applauding a large scholarship and my decision to attend Michigan. On the same stage that my sister's choir concert would be held nearly six months later, the graduating class's scholarship numbers were announced. My financial aid package alone nearly tripled the total amount of my class's awards. Part of this is because not many students were attending college, but also because Michigan gave me a financial package that allowed me to attend. When standing on the stage in front of everyone, I felt proud, yet ashamed. This wasn't a merit-based scholarship. Did these people realize I had only gotten so much money because my parents make so little? I wasn't going to tell them. I felt like I had been doing a systemic dance, avoiding these questions. A dance I had been doing all my life would continue in college. These mixed feelings still didn't matter. I had gotten in and was planning to attend the perfect college—Eurocentric architecture and all.

Little did I know that I would be attending a school where kids from online forums who had taken three AP classes a semester would also attend. Soon, the disadvantages came back to complicate the optimism I felt when getting into Michigan, and I began to notice large divides between me and my peers' perspectives on social class.

"You know, I'm surprised that someone like you is going to Michigan. Normally when you think about first-generation students, they go to like community colleges or something like that. And then their kids are the ones that go to schools like Michigan."

My classmate in my political theory class responded to my essay about being a first-generation student on peer review day. While he was unable to understand the process I was going through, the girl sitting next to me related to my paper. She was a first-generation student too. It was one of the first times I was able to connect with someone on that level. She shared that even though she went to Michigan, her parents weren't supportive of her choice to go to college, and like me, her small rural high school hadn't prepared her in all the right ways to succeed at Michigan.

The summer after my freshman year I worked alongside my dad in a factory. While some of my Michigan friends were *vacationing* in Europe, interning in bigger cities, or just relaxing for the summer, I worked more than 40 hours a week helping build countertops. Although my days started at 4:00 a.m., the pay was incredible, and by the time summer was over I had saved up enough cash to ensure a financially stable school year *and* afford a vacation out west to Seattle and Los Angeles; my first trip in an airplane. Two weeks of relaxation and sightseeing. My college friend from the upper-middle class accompanied me. When planning the trip, I saw an online advertisement for an underground tour of Seattle, remembering my grandparents had once suggested it. But when I proposed the idea to my friend, she wasn't very interested.

"I have *literally* been in the catacombs of Paris," she exclaimed. "I don't know. I think we could just find something cooler than that!" My lack of travel experience was subpar compared to hers.

The first portion of this trip was in Seattle, Washington. My freshman year had begun to prepare me for social mobility, but I hadn't picked up on enough cues that allowed me to feel at ease with my friend's upper-middle class family. I felt my working-class manners leaking into many of these interactions. One morning after waking up, bloody mucous had leaked from my nose all over the pristine, white pillowcases I had been using in the guest bedroom. It's never great to be sick on vacation, but it's even worse waking up to a situation like this. I stared out the window, past the badminton court in the backyard, and watched golfers zooming by in their golf carts, getting in their morning rounds. I needed to figure out some way to tell my friend and her aunt about this situation. Her aunt was one of those people who made sure shoes were off before coming into the house, and when we brought our luggage upstairs, we needed to make sure not to drag it across the carpet. I felt out of place and I couldn't do anything right. Everything turned out fine that morning; thanks to my friend's quick thinking, we were able to fix my issue with minimal confrontation.

I was excited to try the Pacific Northwest's selection of seafood. As a Midwesterner, I had little interactions with oysters and clams, but the trip changed that. My lack of understanding on how to consume an oyster was acceptable, but one night my friend's aunt took us out for dinner at a nice restaurant. As the appetizers were brought out, I looked around the table and wondered where everyone's napkins had gone. The other dinner guests had put their napkins on their lap. Mine was still folded neatly next to my plate. After noticing the mistake, I quickly pulled the black cloth off the table and draped it over my legs, hoping my inexperience with the seafood had masked my mistake. I made sure to put the napkin in the right place during the next meal. Growing up, these manners were never discussed or needed, but it wasn't too late for me to discover them during my west coast trip. Full assimilation.

The culture around food has always been interesting to me. When visiting the University of Michigan after getting admitted in spring of 2015, my parents and I were impressed with the wide variety of food in the dining halls. I later came to the realization that this food was prepared in such a way that appealed to the tastes of the wealthier students. "Risotto with garlic basil tofu." "Basmati rice, curried lentils, and naan bread." "Stuffed quinoa peppers." While some of the components of food are more cultural than class-related, my class background didn't give me any preparation to understand what dining halls served. Many times, I was the odd one out at the dinner table, trying new cuisine out of sheer curiosity. One instance sticks out. It was dinner time with my two closest friends, and I'm sure I was eating some dish that I couldn't even pronounce.

"I've never ate this before," I said, picking at the new meal in front of me.

My friends looked at each other and laughed.

"What is it this time?" I asked, conscious that I made another grammar mistake. It happened enough. I was corrected and then told that I "say it this way all the time." I was informed that when I speak, I often have trouble using the correct grammatical tenses. Who else noticed this? I wondered what types of assumptions peers made when I slipped up. After that incident, I worked on using proper grammar that didn't reveal unsophistication or indicate any working-class roots. Full assimilation. I was becoming one of them. I didn't know how to feel.

A recent trip home reminded me my entire life has been filled with the same grammar my college friends have criticized. "She has weared them for a while now," my dad told me, referencing a pair of my basketball shorts my sister had somehow stolen. Realizing this speech had surrounded me since I was born made me feel much less guilty about slipping up every once in a while around my friends back in Ann Arbor.

Sometimes I still and ask my friends what time they are planning to get *supper*, not dinner. An outdated word apparently, that appears solely in 19th-century literature. *Supper* is indicative of my working-class, rural roots. I have been told: "You're such a farm boy." and "It's so cute!" While I don't mind being called cute occasionally, being called cute for something that feels normal isn't what I want. Knowing that this word choice may result in criticism in more professional or academic settings doesn't help. I've gotten better at not letting my "suppers" and "weared its" out, but the truth is, it's quite possible I inadvertently say or do things in ways that display my working-class heritage. Until I hear subtle, friendly criticism from friends or peers, I won't be able to fix them.

Recently I've been trying to understand what all of this means. I'm lucky being able to attend a great university that allows me to think about these things. If I had gone somewhere else, many of these worries wouldn't be relevant. While my future or any career

I'll hold is uncertain, I know I'm currently in some type of transition upward. My attendance at Michigan has given me the chance to reach the middle class. It's important to know what this means and how I can interact with others on the way up, keeping in mind the things I have experienced. I'll never forget what it's like feeling the need to memorize my dad's pay period. The biweekly period coincided with his stress level, the food we ate, even how much we were able to drive. There was a temporary relief every spring that came in the form of a tax return, and in midsummer when our insurance deductible was met and we could finally feel some wiggle room. I have experienced firsthand the type of financial stress a family can experience, and I don't want to go back.

During freshman year of college these ideas sat, swirling around in the back of my brain. I didn't have the vocabulary or terminology to describe what I was feeling. I had known that my first-generation status and unchallenging high school curriculum had complicated my transition to college, but it took a while to realize there were so many other social forces contributing to what I had been feeling. When Donald Trump was elected president, I started to fully understand these feelings. We heard the white working class took the blame for this one. Who were these people? Well, they were my people; my parents, my hometown, the tired eyes, worn-out sweatshirt-wearing folks of America. In postelection discourse, there was talk of an abandonment of the white working class. This wasn't a lie. I've seen how economic stress shapes the minds of so many people who have misplaced their concerns.

In a Facebook feed full of articles dissecting the results of the election, a friend and fellow Michigan student wrote an article identifying the classism pouring out of Left circles in postelection conversations. I didn't know the author, but was instantly in support of what she had to say. I messaged her asking if she wanted to discuss *social class*. There it was. The word I had been in search of for such a long time. The elections results jolted me into a realization; my being occupies two social spaces. I've grown up in a working-class family, but I'm now in the affluent, culturally rich city of

Ann Arbor. I can understand the abandoned portion of the country many academics and wealthier Michigan students can't. After fully realizing this, I decided to do something. Since the fall of 2016 here at Michigan, I've been working hard with other students attempting to establish an academic concentration studying social class as an identity and the way it affects people. I hope many students at Michigan from all social classes will benefit from coursework that will highlight complications of the American Dream.

NOT MY BIRD: CROSS CLASS OR NO CLASS?

RYAN VENNARD

I am pressed against a screen door. The metal door is cool against my naked body. The screen is missing and I clutch the door tightly. My brothers lean on either side of me. We pose, framed by a doorway of gray metal, offset by the dirty whitewashed boards that compose the exterior of our home. We are looking out at my mother and the film camera she's pointing at us. She presses her finger down, and we are immortalized in film, stereotypes of Appalachian poverty. I look out at a yard littered with dirty toys and rusty equipment. The lawn is not manicured by any metric. Crabgrass sprouts in patches amongst an unkempt yard of varying shades of yellow and green. This is home; this is where I have spent the first four years of my childhood.

I was born in 1996 and in my 20 years on this Earth, I have spent time in almost every socioeconomic class. When I was little, my family lived on the right side of the poverty line. We have been climbing the ladder since then; a textbook example of the American Dream. My parents are simple folks with working-class origins. They grew up in the backwood valleys of rural New York State, Appalachian to the core. My grandpa was a truck driver before he retired, and my grandma was a stay-at-home mother for most of her life. After all of her children moved out, she worked a pink-collar job in the payroll office of a utensil-making company. My parents were different. Through hard work and lots of familial support, both managed to be the first in our family to attend college. After spending seven years to get a bachelor's degree in forensic chemistry, my dad broke us out of the working class into the middle class, starting my family's trek up the social ladder. My family has continuously moved up the class hierarchy since then, stopping just short of "upper" middle class.

Despite being upwardly mobile, my parents never assimilated into middle-class ideology. This is one reason we never made it to the next level of America's social hierarchy. We did not fit in with middle-class wheel-and-deal culture and my parents made conscious decisions to not become a part of "higher society." As a second-generation college student, I am trying to continue my parents' path. This trek up is not sunshine and rainbows. I am irrevocably tied to my childhood community of rural Ohio, a small village called West Alexandria, and I feel the burden of being the one "who got out." This creates pressures, whether external or internal, that I still struggle with today. As I move ever closer to graduating college, I have two identities to choose from. The first is the one my parents gave me through their blood, sweat, and tears: middle class and stretching upward toward the upper-middle class. The second I absorbed from where I grew up: a small town boy who made it to the middle class. Is that as far as I am going to get? These conflicting identities put me at odds with upper-middle-class peers I interact with on a daily basis here at the University of Michigan.

It is an early summer evening. The weather is fantastic, sunny, and warm. I am eating supper with my family in our dining room. The dining room used to be a closed porch or sunroom. The walls are made of a redneck mixture of glass and clear plastic (reminders of childhood games gone wrong). As we devour the meal in front of us there is a knock at the door. The knocking is unique for a few reasons. First, it's suppertime; there should not be any salesmen or neighbors coming around at this time. Second, the knocking is not coming from the front door, but from the side door. This door opens to the fenced in backyard; certainly no place for an unexpected visitor to be. Third, and most bemusing, the knocking is delicate and soft, yet boisterous. Too soft for a man and too energetic for a woman. Dad stands up and goes to answer. We all make a beeline after him, interested in who could possibly be calling at such an unexpected hour. Dad opens the door and is greeted by a young girl with an expression on her face somewhere between a smile and a scowl. Her exact age is indeterminable due to the level of dirt and filth that covers her; a rough estimate puts her between ages 5 and 10. It is clear that she has not bathed in several days. This level of grime is not what makes her interesting; I see that level of personal hygiene in school every day. No, what sets her apart is the chicken she is casually holding. Presumably the source of the girl's scowl is no small hen. It is about as large as the girl's torso, making her appear tiny. She looks up at my dad with wide eyes and asks: "Is this your chicken?" She speaks in the accent of the area: a mix of peasant southerner and rural Midwestern. The accent, along with her natural childish inflection, makes the question sound more like: "Iz this yar chick'n?" My father is speechless for a moment, caught off guard by the absurdity of the situation. Eventually, he replies that it is not our chicken. The girl ponders this fact for a moment, her scowl deepening as she thinks. "Ya shur?" she asks, "I caught 'em ousside en da street." My father responds, politely but firmly, that no, we do not have any chickens. This back and forth continues for another 10 minutes or so, with the girl asking if dad is sure the chicken doesn't belong to us and him confirming that it definitely is not our bird. Throughout the whole process, the chicken in question is not taking being held upside down very well. Every couple of minutes it starts to flap wildly, trying to peck at the girl's hand. Every time this happens, the girl starts shaking the bird up and down until it stops trying to escape. Finally, the girl gives up trying to convince dad the chicken is ours and after a quick "Alright, if ya shur sir, g'd'night" she skips out of our backyard and into the street. At this point, the chicken finally frees itself and escapes. The girl starts the chase, as we return to our now room-temperature supper.

This event stands out as the epitome of where I grew up. When happening it was a funny interaction, an odd reprieve from rural monotony. After living in wealthier communities and developing a sense of class consciousness, I look back with a certain level of wonder. Why was this girl so dirty? Why wasn't she eating supper with her family? Why was she unsupervised, playing in the middle of the street with a chicken? This wonder extends to me and my family. Why didn't we invite her inside for supper? Or even just a glass of juice? We just let her disappear. Were we being classist because she was small and dirty?

I grew up in what I used to think was a "reasonably" diverse community, due to the different social classes and "varied" Christian religious sects. While my family was lower-middle class, there was plenty of rural poverty to go around. The factories and farms that once provided jobs and resources were either gone (in the case of the factories) or mechanized (in the case of the farms). Money was on everyone's mind. Even the wealthiest people in the community (white-collar workers like my father) went paycheck to paycheck. My family (and everyone around us) was always one accident away from poverty, one mistake away from failing the American Dream. Many people, especially young adults who blew in from one of the plethora of crumbling villages, turned to making and selling drugs. It was mostly meth, heroin, and crack, brewed in one of the semi-abandoned barns outside town and brought next door for distribution. That's not exaggeration! My house was on a street corner, and both houses on the other sides of both streets were "drug houses." The air outside these houses smelled of a confusing mixture of urine (meth) and dirty chemicals (crack). Sometimes they would smell sweet in an indescribably muted way. I know now this is the scent given off by heroin.

Frequently, the neighbors would throw huge, loud parties lasting all night. On one occasion they fired fireworks into our house. Since the police would never do anything (even when my parents called multiple times in a night), one summer dad installed a security camera pointing into the street to record the issues we were experiencing. That camera lasted one night. The morning after dad put it up, someone had stolen it. Growing up, I had complicated feelings for these people. They were immoral according to my religion and my familial ethics, but crime was just how people survived. When work is gone and the church cannot support you, families have few options. If it were down to the wire, I too would enter the underground or illegal economy to support my family.

The one way out for most of my friends was the military. From a young age, we were educated that military men represented the peak of masculinity. Growing up we played war with sticks and fake plastic guns. It was expected and encouraged that boys would play fight. Some of my fondest memories are of my friend and me, along with our siblings, hunting each other in the woods. We would end the game covered in bruises, cuts, and dirt. In a strict patriarchal society, we should emulate the emotions, physique, and morals of men in the armed forces. Now as adults, the military is sometimes the only possibility for escape or to provide for your family. You serve your country, become a real man, and then return home. The logical leap we were never shown is how one finds a job after returning. My best friend from childhood recently told me he is no longer attending classes at the local community college. He is considering joining the military as a last ditch effort to climb up the social ladder. I am terrified what could happen to him. Not only could he die or lose a limb or two, but I have seen how active duty changes people. And it is not always change for the better. War, in my opinion, is insidious by nature, and falls on sons and daughters of the working and lower classes to serve as fodder for that sinister beast. Serving in the armed forces can open doors for people stuck at the bottom, but those opportunities come with a heavy price tag.

I am simultaneously pissed off and nervous. I have been torn from the only community I have known. My family is relocating from rural, rust belt Ohio to an upper-middle-class community in Southwest Michigan. No one is safe from shifting job markets, not even white-collar workers like dad. He has found a new job in the nearby city of Battle Creek, Michigan. At this point, however, I am over the pain and teen angst of being uprooted in the middle of high school. My emotions stem from my current situation: I am touring my new school for the first time. I am accompanied by mom, who has yet to see the whole school herself. This school is huge compared to the community I came from. It is also much

nicer than my previous school: a foyer with comfy loungers, bright nat-
ural light filtering through an overhead skylight, two whole floors! I am
overwhelmed by the building, let alone the throng of students flowing by
on their way to their next classes. After the hallways settle down, a stu-
dent approaches me. He is dressed in stereotypical 'white-boy' fashion:
khaki shorts and a gray T-shirt. He oozes a buttery confidence that before
I had only seen in lawyers in the movies. He introduces himself, quite
politely. As he does so, he looks me over. I am wearing an outfit that took
me hours to put together. At 14, all I want is to fit in and make friends.
I'm wearing blue polo shirt, white plaid shorts, and my favorite shoes—
black Walmart brand Converse All Stars. I believe I am dressed as a mid-
dle-class kid; these are my best clothes. As he analyzes me, his eyes end
on my shoes. Looking up at me he says: "You're going to want to get new
shoes. Those are fag shoes; you don't want to wear those here." In that
second, my world came crashing down. I tried so hard to look upper or
middle class. I do not want to be viewed as a hick or redneck. I want to fit
in and in one second this student, who does not know anything about me,
immediately noticed I am a fraud. The rest of the tour goes smoothly, the
student is friendly and helpful, but his ability to so easily see through the
façade I spent hours creating shakes me to the core. In this moment I do
not think I will ever fit into this part of society.

Due to my exposure to rural poverty from an early age, I gained
a sense of class consciousness early on. However, it was not until
I left my rust belt community and moved to a more affluent area
in Michigan that I fully came to understand how class truly oper-
ates. Before this interaction, I had always thought of social class
as only wealth and income. Growing up I had friends across class
lines. Everyone had the same values, the same tastes in what was
"hip" and what was not. After moving, I learned class goes beyond
just money. Your class dictates what you wear, who your friends
are, and even how you perceive the world. I also learned that as
you move up the socioeconomic ladder, the more segregated you
become. I did not, and was socially expected to not, interact with
popular rich kids. By rich, I mean that their parents likely made
$200,000 or (probably) more. My father didn't make close to

that much, and, despite our middle-class income, my family still went paycheck to paycheck. These were the kids who lived in huge McMansions on Gull Lake. They maintained their own table during lunch, and segregated themselves in classrooms. They went on expensive outings: skiing, Mexico for spring breaks, etc. Of course, there were fakers: kids who pretended they were wealthy by dressing a certain way. Khaki shorts (or pants if it was below zero degrees Fahrenheit), solid color T-shirt (normally gray or white), a school or sports-related jacket, and Jordan's or boat shoes to finish the outfit off. In this community, the way you dressed was a statement of your social class. Everyone, from working-class kids to the offspring of the über-rich used clothes to signify their class positions. Clothing was how you identified yourself. How you looked was of paramount importance.

Because of class segregation, the class groups at my high school existed in an odd dichotomy. The upper-middle-class and wealthy students pretended to be wealthier than they actually were both in dress and in how they acted. They carried themselves as stereotypes of how rich kids should act. The working- and lower-middle-class students did the exact opposite; they were in a race to the bottom, pretending to be stereotypes of the "redneck" or "hick." I found most of the members of this group to be phonies. Wearing hunting camo when you're a professed vegan is phony. When your entire family has lived in Michigan going back five generations and you have a huge confederate flag on your 2010 four-door truck, that's being phony. Stereotypes were appropriated and turned into reality, both for the upper and the lower classes. Who you were was based on appearance. How you looked determined who you were.

This was the hardest adjustment I had to make when moving to my new community. I had been raised to believe that what you did determined who you were. Here, who you were was what stereotype you looked like. I have found this to be a trait of the middle classes. They have disposable income to create different personas. Not only is beauty only skin deep, but one's "you-ness" is completely superficial. I was caught between worlds: not rich enough to run with the wealthy popular kids and unwilling to adopt a stereotype of the working-class community I grew up in.

I hated the hierarchy of Richland, Michigan. I hated the phoniness of my high school. Everything was politicized around what you looked like and whose group you belonged to. Although I graduated from Gull Lake High School and although my family still lives there, I do not consider Richland my home. When peers here at the University of Michigan ask where I am from, I identify West Alexandria, Ohio, as my hometown. I thought class segregation was unique to my high school and surrounding community. Coming to the University of Michigan showed me how naïve that hope was.

Another Friday night and I am alone in my dorm room. My roommate is out, either getting high or with his girlfriend. I have been at Michigan for seven months and my freshman year (2015–2016) is drawing to a close. I have yet to make any friends beyond peers to study with and I am bored out of my mind. I think about texting my girlfriend, but realize I would only annoy her. She is out with her friends at a frat party. I know I may get a call from her later, asking if I can come find her and bring her back to her room. I turn back to my computer and restart the calculus video I have been watching. I still do not understand anything on the final next week, but at this point I do not really care. Was coming to Michigan the right choice? The people I know are from a different culture. Everyone and everything have money and time. Meanwhile, I am stressing trying to figure out if I will able to pay for college in the fall. Between academic pressures and social requirements, I have only started part-time work last month. Money, friends, and grades threaten to send me spiraling into yet another bout of anxiety and sadness. I feel inadequate in every part of my life. I feel as if I do not fit in anywhere at Michigan. The thought of quitting crosses my mind. I bury it deep down and return to my computer. I am going to make it. I am not going to waste the opportunity my parents gave me.

My first year and a half at Michigan was an eye-opening experience. I applied on a lark. I did not want to go there, but my parents made me apply because it was relatively inexpensive and had competitive rankings. My dream university was Valparaiso University, a small private institution in northeastern Indiana. I was crushed when I realized I could never afford to go there. Michigan was a compromise for me. I would be able to get out of the area where I graduated high school, but I would not be destroying my financial future with an obscene amount in loans. My freshman year was rough, academically and socially. I failed a couple of classes and dropped a couple more, realizing what I planned on doing my whole life was not going to happen. I never went out, and my relationship with my then girlfriend crumbled. The student organizations I was a part of were almost exclusively upper-middle-class students. I did not have money to go out on Friday nights or to spend on drugs and parties. I was an outsider within the communities I was supposedly a part of. I considered transferring to Western Michigan University in Kalamazoo, near where my parents live. I thought about moving back in with them, working full time at a minimum-wage job, and taking classes in the evenings.

After spending almost two years in Ann Arbor, it is clear the University of Michigan is deeply segregated based on social class. It took me an entire year to find students from working-class origins. Most students in my student organizations are "continuing-generation" students (students with parents or grandparents who finished four years of college) on the fast track to law or medical school. They go abroad for spring breaks, go out to team dinners, and live a lifestyle I thought only existed in books or movies.

I lucked into being able to attend Michigan, gathering enough grants and loans to barely pay tuition. Money is always on my mind; I have to pinch every penny. I cannot afford to go abroad for the summer or even for a week over spring break. I cannot afford to go out on Friday nights, or most nights for that matter. If I go out, it is the product of weeks of financial planning, cutting back spending, and placing strict limits on how much I can spend. It has been life changing to meet working-class students and finding students like me who have diverse class backgrounds. These are students like me, who must work to continue to go to school. We have the same ideals and we all share a common culture that is often at odds with our wealthier counterparts.

This has not been an easy essay to write. I hold a lot of resentment and confusion on how class status has shaped my life. My family has always been climbing up the social class ladder, but coming to Michigan has shown me something important. There is a gap in the ladder; a series of rungs missing in the ladder proposed by the American Dream. This gap is cultural, one rooted in social capital. Unlike the glass ceiling present in gender inequality, the social class divide is more akin to a ceiling made out of tar. Even if you manage to fight your way through the layers of tar, you are marked and stained by the tar. You will always be dirty and separate from those who never fought through the tar. For me, even if I fake being upper-middle class, even if I forget where I came from and assimilate to a new class culture, I will never belong. Here at Michigan, I never felt comfortable talking about class. Class discussion was and is taboo.

I have just finished giving a tour to prospective University of Michigan students. One female student and her father hang back. She tells me this school is her dream. She is from the working class, and goes to a small town school. I am struck by how much of myself I see in her. I can see the excitement and culture shock swirling in her eyes. Her father explains their school does not offer Advance Placement or college prep classes, and they are worried she will not have a competitive application. I give a stock answer, explaining the admissions team takes "strength" of high school into account. After debating the merits of community college instead of high school, the conversation turns to financial aid. Money is a concern for both of them, her father putting on a tight smile as he dances around the issue. I encourage them to talk to a financial aid advisor and show them where the financial aid office is located. As they head off to talk money, I watch them. The daughter is excited, practically skipping. The father's posture is different. He is stiff, shuffling forward. I think he knows, as well as I do, what is in store for his daughter. Even if she gets in, they will still have to scrounge up enough money to attend. If by some miracle they manage to find enough financial resources to attend, she will face years of a culture that is not her own. College will take her hand and change her, dividing her from her working-class origins. College will make her part of the middle- or upper-middle class on the surface. She will be like so many working-class college kids. Like my parents and me she will be classless, and in many ways alone. Her kids will grow up the way I did: at odds with the social class they grew up in. The cycle will continue—one family after another, cogs in a never ending machine. I clock out, grab my bag, and walk briskly out of the building. I have a lecture in 10 minutes, and I cannot be late. Work is a relaxing break, but it's time for this cog to start turning again.

The Places I've Been and the Places I'll Never Go

Rebecca Wren

> You will come to a place where the streets are not marked.
> Some windows are lighted. But mostly they're darked.
> A place you could sprain both your elbow and chin!
> Do you dare to stay out? Do you dare to go in?
> How much can you lose? How much can you win?
> —Dr. Seuss, Oh, the Places You'll Go!

When I graduated third in my high school class, my sister gave me a copy of Dr. Seuss's book, *Oh, the Places You'll Go*. Everyone in my family signed it and wrote me a message. I was the youngest sibling, but the first to be accepted into a four-year university and the first in my immediate family to attend college. From their point of view, it looked like I would be able to go anyplace I dreamed. From my high school's point of view, being one of a hand full of students to be admitted into a college like the University of Michigan in Ann Arbor, it looked like I would be able to go beyond all my dreams. From my point of view fresh out of high school, the world seemed like a big place, full of opportunities. If you had asked me what my favorite line by Dr. Seuss was from that perspective, I would have said:

> You have brains in your head.
> You have feet in your shoes.
> You can steer yourself

any direction you choose.
You're on your own. And you know what you know.
And YOU are the guy [sic] who'll decide where to go.

In high school it was easy for me to think individualistically. I was born into a white, working-class family that lived in a mixed social class neighborhood. It was easy to buy into the "everyone is middle class" ideology of America. I earned good grades, I graduated, and I was accepted into all three of the colleges I applied to. There was no reason for me to think I would not continue to achieve.

College has opened my eyes to many different things—academically and socially. It wasn't until getting onto a college campus that I realized I was a first-generation college student (first in my family to attend college) or that there was a term for it. Through my classes I learned I was working class and that intersections of race, class, and gender, among other things, play powerful roles in how I experience the world. Hearing stories from other students I realized not everybody had grown up eating Ramen noodles or drinking pop (some people call it soda!). Some students could buy winter jackets and snow boots costing more than a month's rent and had their parents' credit cards always available to use. I didn't even know about the tricks to building credit. Honestly, I still don't understand the premise of building credit, but I know I'm not off to a great start.

There's a first for everything, *they* say. Surely there is, but that fact does not make it any easier to do that first thing. I am a first-generation college student and I've spent college studying what else *they* say who *they* are. I am getting a bachelor in arts in sociology with a sub-plan in law, justice and social change, and a minor in statistics. Studying *they* is a playful way of saying I practice viewing society at a larger level, trying to understand what is normal and how we want people to conform to larger social systems that have the power to make, define, and impact members of society. America's individualistic ideology crumbled pretty quickly after my first sociology class. Unintentionally, the social institution I have focused on most is social class.

Attending college as a working-class student, who studies social class, feels like both living in a snow globe and holding that snow globe watching me inside. If the snow globe is social class, I will always be living in it. This system has been set up before me and I am permanently affected by the class I was born in. As the first to attend college in my family, I am on an upwardly mobile path (supposedly), but not without hardship, conflict, and afflictions toward my working-class roots and family. To be a rising scholar of this personal aspect is both eye-opening and disassociating. This allows me to look back critically on my life before attending college and since starting. I have an understanding now of what is inside and outside the snow globe.

There were moments in my K–12 education when I realized things were different in my family compared to others, but I did not have the words to name those experiences and feelings. My parents worked long hours and tried to hide money problems from my two siblings and me, or at least as the youngest one, that's how I experienced it. In their defense, explaining capitalism to your children isn't easy. My sister, 12 years older than me, can't seem to let me forget the time she had run out of her own money babysitting me when I was four years old.

"Well let's go get more!" I demanded.
"Money doesn't grow on trees," she said.
"No, but it grows at the restaurant!"

My parents owned a restaurant when I was growing up. Dad had been a cook there for a long time and eventually became the owner, and mom was a waitress. That's where they met. It's weird how we could be living two versions of the same reality. For me, the restaurant was a playground. I would spend hours there organizing the jelly and creamers, telling customers things I shouldn't, and sometimes sneak eggs home thinking they would hatch into chickens. For my parents, it was a stress of trying to make ends meet. Eventually, they lost the restaurant and had to go work elsewhere.

Dad has been cooking his whole life. Mom has mostly been in the food service industry as well, occasionally holding other jobs. Neither of them went to college and both easily averaged working over 50 or 60 hours a week. I didn't understand what social class was, or where my family's positioning was, but when in fifth grade I noticed a different structure in my family compared to my best friend's family. Her mom didn't have a job and would make dinners for them to eat together as a family. I sometimes joke that my older brother and sister raised me. I remember summers spent with my brother, six years older than me, playing video games. We were responsible for making dinner for ourselves. The worst time was when we made instant mashed potatoes that came out the consistency of play doe. You'd think that kids whose parents cooked and served food would have some natural talent.

The hard part about realizing you're from a working-class family is seeing how this is part of a larger system keeping people in their class. I've listened to mom and dad blame themselves for not being able to do more and it breaks my heart. Being working class means there's no backup, no safety net when something happens. A car breaking down, a medical emergency, or dips in the economy can set you back in a blink of an eye. We lost our house in 2008 when the housing market crashed. My parents told us we were moving, but they didn't tell us why. It wasn't until I learned about the economic crash in college that those difficult family times made sense. Even when we had insurance that covered medical problems, the days off from work were hard to recover from. There have been times when we haven't had health insurance at all.

I've seen my siblings struggle to overcome the social disadvantages we were born to. My sister tried a couple of times to enroll in local schools to become a medical professional, but she's also working in the service industry and the hours are not flexible, nor are the wages significant. My brother didn't like high school and is now cooking like dad. I knew how and when to apply to college because I had teachers in high school who really believed in me. I don't know if my siblings had that support. But I don't think everyone should have to get a college degree to make enough money for things they need or want, especially when the cost of getting a degree is not affordable for everyone.

My parents and siblings did not have the language to make me aware of social class oppression let alone different class statuses. Being from a certain social class doesn't just mean the amount of money available for family use. My class has shaped how I think about money, how I spend it, what I value, and where I want to be in the future.

My social class has shaped my college experiences in subtle ways. My first friends were students I worked with on campus. They were relatable and approachable in ways other students weren't: we all *had* to work. The friends I made later were mostly similar to me in this way too, but often I discovered that after we were friends. Some friendships did not last because of class differences. One person in my dorm hall freshman year complained her mom would not buy her a pair of $80 boots because she already had six other pairs. There was no way for me to connect with fellow students like that; we weren't thinking or worrying about the same things.

And it's not that I haven't made cross-class friendships. I've had roommates whose parents pay for their rent and groceries, go on spring break trips, and don't stress about making enough money after graduation for themselves and their family. I understand and don't resent them. If my parents could support me, I know they would. I know when I visit home, mom throws my clothes in the washer and has a large Tupperware bowl of my favorite family recipe (chicken and rice). This is her way of giving what she can. And if I had to choose between mom's chicken and rice and being born wealthy, I'd choose the rice—every time.

I'll be the first one that is supposed to achieve the Dream in my family. I think about this a lot: what am I supposed to want? How am I supposed to think about success? What am I supposed to value? There's tension in wanting to be an academic from a working-class background, where reading, thinking, and challenging ideas are considered luxuries by members of my family who experience the physical demands and time constraints of working with their hands. There is a tension in pursuing a PhD when you cherish working-class values absorbed over the years, learning to appreciate simple moments and experiences. I don't want to forget where I come from. My time at the University of Michigan has allowed me to develop academically, but it has also made me very class conscious. I don't value the same things many students do and I'm not sure I ever will. I can't rely on my family to help me succeed, but I don't want to leave them behind either.

The American Dream is about working hard, earning more, and succeeding. But this doesn't come true for many people. I've watched my parents work hard, and I still watch my 70-year-old grandma struggle. Her hands are swollen and stiff with arthritis from working in a factory with inside temperatures of 100 degrees in summers. Dad's knees ache working 10–12 hours a day since he was a kid, doing hard farm work and chores for his family. Mom has worked long days, nights, and years too, and still cooked dinners and cleaned the house. To this day, I don't know where she finds the time.

For the first two years at Michigan, I was too excited and academically stimulated to feel conflicted. I had always been good in school and my parents knew I would go to college even if that wasn't the path of my older siblings. I once cried in seventh grade because mom accidently threw away a progress report I was supposed to have signed and taken back. She wrote my teacher a note explaining it had been her mistake and she knew my grades were good. These memories of emotional investment in my education made me feel college was the right path when I started in the fall of 2013. Michigan was a new, expanded world to explore and a place to challenge myself and my assumptions. I embraced that.

But as a first-generation, working-class college student I often felt I was dreaming too big or too late. In high school I did not know enough about colleges to understand the elitism, that where you went to college had implications for how your degree would be viewed or matter. My limited exposure to how to apply to college came from teachers and counselors in high school who knew I had potential. Everything else I figured out on my own.

I only applied to three colleges: Grand Valley State here in Michigan, the University of Michigan, Dearborn, and the University of Michigan, Ann Arbor. I knew Dearborn's campus would be easiest because it was less selective, closer to home, and less expensive. I had only been to Ann Arbor's campus once on a 2010 field trip during high school. I remember being in Michigan's Undergraduate Science building with huge windows and artwork on the walls. It contrasted my only experience on Dearborn's campus: playing a volleyball game in a gym where the walls were painted dark blue. There were no windows. I decided Ann Arbor would be my top choice. The large windows and light seemed to symbolize windows of opportunities: moving out, being independent, and attending one of the best schools in the state of Michigan. This last-minute dream of going to Ann Arbor's campus came true on Christmas Eve 2012 while lying in bed. An e-mail said I was admitted. I cried myself to sleep, because I didn't think I would be accepted.

Now at the end of my college career, I am still dreaming big. I want to continue my education, pursue a PhD in sociology, and have an academic career. I know that if I want to be a professor, where I get my PhD matters. I applied to six of the best sociology programs. But again, I'm a late dreamer. I scrambled to put together my application materials while also managing research for my senior thesis, fall 2016 semester finals, and two part-time jobs. I was rejected from all six of the schools. I'm not that surprised since I was warned about high rejection rates of top programs, but I can't help but calculate the financial and emotional costs. My ego will recover from feeling unqualified, but it will take a few months of credit card payments to recover from the $400 I invested to receive those rejection letters.

Higher education is often more accessible and easier to navigate by certain types of students, especially those who are white and wealthy, and come from college-educated families. Many college degrees are about status rather than knowledge or innovation. Not without problems and challenges, I still want to be a part of higher education. My conflict arises from wanting to be a part of this problematic, competitive institution, but my choice to continue in higher education is also political. I have strong beliefs in the power of education because it is the avenue through which I have learned about systems of inequality that I seek to help change. Through writing a senior honors thesis for sociology, I have been able to interview other low-income, first-gen Michigan students and hear their experiences. I appreciate sociology because it doesn't avoid difficult questions about inequality. Sociology doesn't make me feel like I am competing with other students or that my success depends on their failure. I am thankful for that experience. This is juxtaposed with other majors where I've heard about "weeder" courses designed to "weed out" students. Education should serve everyone.

The conflict of being educated in a capitalist society is seeing flaws in the way we structure society and the economy that primarily benefits some at the cost of others, but feeling too small to fix the flaws. I share my education with my parents and siblings so they can understand what racism, sexism, and classism are and their role in contributing to and internalizing them. The education my family has been able to access did not provide them with a good understanding of these things and challenging their beliefs hasn't been easy for them or me. I have been privileged as a white student. My race has allowed me to fit in on a largely white campus and other students usually don't assume I have a working-class history. As a working-class student, I have struggled with being a full-time student with multiple jobs surrounded by many students who have their parents' credit cards. Both privileges and challenges I have faced make me committed to anti-racism, anti-sexism, and anti-classism. This means I have a commitment to continue educating myself, even informally and outside the educational system.

It has been a constant effort to do well in my classes, maintain a close relationship with my family, and support myself financially. I've had to work 20–30 hours a week to afford living in Ann Arbor while completing my degree. Attending to my health and well-being was an added challenge since the university doesn't accept my Medicaid insurance at its Health Services. I sometimes had to miss classes to pick up extra shifts at my campus jobs and often help my parents with computer-based projects for the restaurant they now own. I do that for free because I know they need the help. My dreams and achievements seem limited and shaped by numerous worries. I also have a lot to lose as first in my family to attend college. My brother and sister are caught working like my parents, making enough to get by, but never enough to get ahead. My parents still work and do all they can to help their kids.

Four years ago, college was an unmarked area for me, but I decided to take a chance. I have gained a lot from the experience. My future is uncertain and I have a lot to win and lose. I am going to re-apply to graduate school and hopefully become first in my family with a PhD. I'll be first "doctor," even though I'll have to explain to my parents that it's not the same thing as a medical doctor.

So what's the new Dr. Seuss quote resonating the most with me these days?

> You will come to a place where the streets are not marked.
> Some windows are lighted. But mostly they're darkened.
> A place you could sprain both your elbow and chin!
> Do you dare to stay out? Do you dare to go in?
> How much can you lose? How much can you win?

Part III

MIDDLE CLASS

Keeping Scores: Personal Prose about Social Class Experiences through Popular Poetry

Stefan Bergman

> Then I'll hang my boots to rest when I'm impressed
> So I triple knot 'em and forgot 'em
> His origami dream is beautiful
> But man, those wings will never leave the ground
> Without a feather and a lottery ticket, now settle down.
> —Aesop Rock, "Daylight"

I just call it as I see it. I have my entire life. My mother, Karen, loves reminding me I was the little terror in the grocery store who would announce "Fat!" or "Short!" at unsuspecting shoppers who happened to fit descriptions I was learning. I can't imagine the embarrassment she was subjected to, but I'm sure I couldn't have been prouder of myself in the moment. My parents were always quick to do their best to correct this kind of behavior, especially in public. Growing up in the town of Harleysville, Pennsylvania, is, as my father, Keith, likes to say, "a lot like growing up in Mayberry." It's a small suburban town outside of Philadelphia, home to almost 10,000 mostly middle and middle-upper-class families. Lansdale, the last interstate highway exit before heading toward center city, is a borough that is historically Mennonite with strong ties to the Pennsylvania Dutch and Amish communities that concentrate further northwest in Lancaster. In Harleysville, there are actually still several bakeries, bars, and restaurants that supply local favorites and Pennsylvania Dutch-inspired dishes. It's a funny thing though, when you're young and your hometown is the only place you know. I feel like most people, to some degree or another, assume that what they're experiencing as their childhood is very similar to everyone else in the world. This perception, for me, was shattered at an early age when I realized my favorite molasses-infused Amish treat, Shoo-Fly Pie, was not in fact available at every grocery store in America. In many ways, my early upbringing was damn near ideal. I understand how much of a privilege it was growing up in one middle-class home with two responsible and supportive parents. This appreciation was only strengthened as some of my closest friends, teammates, and schoolmates lived in divided families and low-income housing. These experiences have helped me shape my own perceptions of what's truly important about being in a family and how valuable unwavering support and dedication from your loved ones should never be taken for granted.

> For what's money without happiness?
> Or hard times without the people you love?
> Though I'm not sure what's 'bout to happen next
> I asked for strength from the Lord up above
> Cause I've been strong so far
> But I can feel my grip loosening
> Quick, do something before you lose it for good
> Get it back and use it for good
> And touch the people how you did like before
> I'm tired of living with demons cause they always inviting more
> Think being broke was better.
>
> —J. Cole, "Love Yourz"

I always found the commentary that J. Cole makes in this song to be particularly provoking. In a capitalist society where financial motivations drive most of our day-to-day interactions, how could anyone take the last line, "being broke was better" seriously? In the same song, he later comments on his own phrasing by stating that he means no disrespect to those living in poverty. I think it was important for him to include that distinction in his message, but the lyrics came to resonate with me personally as my own life has humbled me repeatedly, reminding me that my interpersonal relationships, particularly with my family, are all I've ever needed to fall back on, even when everything else seemed to be going wrong.

Most of my educational career has been defined by transition and adaptation. Oak Ridge Elementary School provided me with a five-year foundation in elementary school, but between fifth grade and my arrival at the University of Michigan, I also attended two different middle schools as well as two different high schools. While my change from Indian Valley Middle School to Indian Crest Junior High School was the result of a public school system shifting student populations to accommodate the newly constructed Souderton Area High School, my transition from Germantown Academy to LaSalle College High School was very much an intentional relocation as a result of my own personal experiences. I still lived in the same home through these transitions, but my perspectives on topics such as social class were significantly influenced by the interactions and occurrences—from different schools that I attended, as well as the associated extracurricular activities.

Indian Valley Middle School was where I would meet some of the people in my life whom, today, I'm not sure I'd be the same without. The pandemonium that sets in for an eager fifth-grader over the summer, the anxiety, the anxiousness, it felt overwhelming at the time. Between waiting to find out which of the four class "teams" I would be on and not knowing whom I was going to sit with at lunch, along with the thought of six elementary populations all heading to the same building, I almost intentionally missed my bus for the first day. As it turns out, missing the bus would've been a terrible mistake because our first day was when we were assigned our seats. Fortunately, I was able to muster up the courage to lock down a spot in the back of the bus with my friend Holden Kudla from a neighborhood over. This was a tremendous relief at the time as Holden and I had attended Oak Ridge Elementary School together and he actually introduced me to the sport of lacrosse that same year. While I didn't realize it at the time, my infatuation with lacrosse would later evolve into my primary vehicle for planning and navigating my college experience. The back of the bus became our brief haven where we were able to attempt to rationalize what we were about to head into, where we realized that everyone else heading into this foreign building was just as anxious and nervous as we were. It was at this point, when I really started to get into middle school, I realized that I wanted to make athletics a more predominant part of my day-to-day life. Fortunately, the school district travel basketball team tryouts coincided with the beginning of school. My mother, heavy physical therapist bias in tow, was always quick to shut down motions toward football or ice hockey as a result of the injury and concussion rates among youth athletes. I'm not sure if it was more of a personal vendetta, or an effort to find more utility in my athletic ability, but I was hell-bent on trying every sport that I could get my parents to sign off on. Over the years, I had experienced the most success in basketball and lacrosse, so I ultimately began putting more of a year-round emphasis on these two sports by discontinuing my involvement in others such as baseball and soccer. Staying after school to basketball tryouts was how I met my best friends Austin Murphy, Jarrett Reinhard, Troy Johnson, and Alexander Kamaratos.

While it would've been tremendous to be the starting five or the five superstars, we ended up bonding together more just because we enjoyed each other's company and were always heading to the same school, sport, and social events. We also bonded over personal interests outside of basketball such as hip-hop and rap music. We came from different racial, class, and, to an extent, socioeconomic backgrounds, but the organic development of our clique was indifferent to these factors. Some of my favorite memories took place in a basement, attic, or, most often, the backseat of a car where we'd put on an instrumental and just take turns trying to rap lyrics off of the top of our head, or freestyling, as it's known in the hip-hop community. The stories we share together will leave us bonded permanently, of that I'm sure. Our appreciation for the music and artistry of the craft was what made enjoying rap together such a positive experience. As we all made our transition to Indian Crest Junior High School for eighth grade, we started referring to our group as "The Fam." It was a pretty cheesy thing at first, but like any senseless inside joke, the more that it got referenced, the more we found ourselves saying it. By the time we were headed to high school, we had become universally known as "The Fam" by a lot of our peers and other groups of friends that we hung out with. I'll be honest, we loved it.

> We made a right, then made a left, then made a right
> Then made a left, we was just circling life
> My mama called—"Hello? What you doin'?" "Kicking it"
> I should've told her I'm probably 'bout to catch my first offense
>   with the homies
> …*Cop Sirens*
> But they made a right, they made a left then made a right
> Then another right
> One lucky night with the homies.
>   —Kendrick Lamar, "The Art of Peer Pressure"

Sometimes I look back and wonder how I never ended up with criminal RAP sheet as long as some of my favorite rappers—just hear me out. While I certainly didn't grow up in any sort of environment comparable to the Compton streets that Kendrick Lamar walks, I believe it's foolish to think that any adolescent population can be steered away from all illicit activity simply by where they grew up. In fact, I would absolutely maintain that it is actually significantly easier to get away with particular criminal acts when you're a white male in a primarily white, affluent suburbia. I often reflect about a lot of scenarios that either I myself or my peers have been in that, simply put, it would have been irrefutably more consequential for someone else to face, someone living a less-privileged life in a less-privileged community. These feelings are consistently reaffirmed in poetic form when I listen to some of my favorite rappers talk about the plight that their communities face. I empathize with rappers like Kendrick Lamar and I don't personally believe that you have to come from a disadvantaged community to appreciate the perspective that their art illuminates. I feel strongly that the artists themselves intentionally construct particular works with this universal accessibility in mind in order to provide listeners like myself with a range of relatable, layered components to convey their perspective. Rappers such as Nas, Tupac, J. Cole, Joey Badass, Vince Staples, Andre 3000, Anderson Paak, Guru, Mac Miller, and Isaiah Rashad were particularly influential for me in this way, if I were to only name a few.

When it came time to head to Souderton Area High School, I found myself at a personal crossroads where my athletics, social life, and, most importantly, education were all up in the air. While basketball was going really well, and I had a bright future on the varsity team at Souderton with my closest friends, I had also begun to view lacrosse differently. What had started out as simply interest in another contact sport that my parents would actually allow me to play had started to form into a sport that was becoming more of a vehicle for my older friends and teammates who were enrolling in supremely prestigious universities. These opportunities seemed available for any youth league players who had the resources and utility to fully engage in the summer club circuit that fuels the NCAA (National Collegiate Athletic Association) lacrosse recruiting machine. It seemed like the sport had such a unique availability, but only for players who had access to all of the successive echelons that pave the way to scholarships from the nation's top universities.

Why didn't I see that with basketball? While attending the Souderton Area School District, it was well known which high school athletes were committed to, and/or receiving scholarships from, damn near any football or basketball program, regardless of which division they happened to be headed to. However, when I was visiting and learning about different private schools, hearing recruiting guides rattle off the near full roster of students graduating to continue playing lacrosse at Division I athletic institutions, it was like I had access to an entirely different selection of top-tier universities depending on how hard I wanted to pursue the sport as my parents were prepared to support me in any way they could to make sure I was able to gather the funding to subsidize all the developmental camps, equipment, and club team memberships to attend premier college recruiting events year-round. The commitment my family made to fuel these adventures cannot be understated—recognize those who have given you more than you could ask for and understand that each is a blessing. Both my family and the Fam helped me keep my head on straight as I've never had to weather any of the storms in my life alone.

Conflict arose as I enjoyed playing basketball with my childhood friends, but I knew that Souderton was not going to attract the kind of college recruiting exposure that I was becoming increasingly interested in. Souderton Area Public Schools didn't have the experience, athletic reputation, or history that the surrounding private college preparatory schools boasted. Regardless of how true it may or may not have been, I also believed I had both the ability and toughness to compete with peers who had attended private schools their whole lives and that my public school upbringing enhanced some additional mental fortitude or form a "real chip on my shoulder," as the saying goes.

My family was also doing very well financially at the time, arguably beginning to establish a more upper-middle-class lifestyle. My father was experiencing, from what I could perceive through factors that were observable to me (e.g., new cars, addition of an outdoor pool at our home), favorable advancement in his career through successive employment with multiple civil engineering associations and forensics investigation firms. On multiple occasions over the years, I was able to further explore conversations about the possibility of transferring schools with my parents, prompted by my own interest in joining a number of club teammates at Germantown Academy (GA) in Fort Washington, Pennsylvania. My parents unanimously agreed that it would likely benefit my future academic and athletic ambitions as it had both a prestigious and historic educational reputation and a competitive men's lacrosse team. Was it finally time for me to sever ties with the nucleus of my social networking in Harleysville to begin familiarizing myself with the members and communities previously only defined as my affluent lacrosse teammates from neighboring communities?

I knew two things: enough of my club teammates were heading into ninth grade and also enrolling in GA that I would feel comfortable transitioning from a public school system but, unfortunately, I resented that the personal ties that I had with my hometown friends wouldn't have been enough to ultimately keep us close for long. I was wrong on both accounts.

> If my homies don't f*ck wit' you, I don't f*ck wit' you
> That's just a code in my hood, don't let these guns hit you
> Be a man of your word, don't ever let 'em play you
> Stand up for your sh*t, make sure these haters pay you
> Can't nothing stop a room full of real homies
> I got some bad rich chicks, they my real homies.
> . . .
> If y'all fell out over some chips that ain't your real homie
> If y'all fell out over a chick that ain't your real homie.
> —Kid Cudi ft. King Chip, "Brothers"

I felt like it was appropriate to censor the lyrics, but the unadulterated content above that introduces the song "Brothers" includes multiple components that all contributed to how I personally valued the relationships with my "public school friends." While I was spending all of my daytime hours away from my closest peers while they continued to share in each other's daily lives, our reunions at night or on the weekend were my reminders that I could still depend on my closest companions and that no matter how physically severed we may have been throughout our upbringing, the bond of the Fam was unbreakable. That was something that felt so real and authentic to me. That was something I needed to be able to depend on. The lyrics, when broken down, describe how invincible we felt in any setting. They describe our group process in terms of adapting to our environment and if one of us didn't vibe with something or someone new, none of us did. We had other friends whom we knew, we had other circles that we were in, but the Fam valued such a connectivity and commitment to each other that falling out over squabbles that ultimately came down to simple frustrations, such as those pertaining to cash or miscellaneous relations with women, as the last two bars mention, were always resolved by the greater calling for companionship that, at end of the day, we knew we all universally depended on. I don't know if I can really put into words the types of situations that our bond as a group have pulled us beyond, but by the time we got to high school, the Fam was forever. In ways I could never fully explain in this particular composition, my relationship with Aust, Jare, Triz, and Alex has literally saved my life. I'm forever thankful for the friendship and trust that they maintained in me; despite my desire to pursue athletic and academic aspirations that would introduce extended geographic divides, I never once in my life felt like the lost member of the Fam, and I spent every opportunity that I could along the way trying to prove, explain, or make that up to them. From what I could tell, they were just proud of my ambition, unaware of my internal conflict that was lingering inside. These few, that crew, our squad—we are Brothers.

Germantown Academy (GA), as I came to know immediately upon visitation, is "America's oldest nonsectarian day school." The K–12 college preparatory school enrolls about a fifth of the students that my pubic high school does, and I was instantly identified as one of the new transfers that hadn't actually been enrolled at the academy since infancy. While I was under the impression that I had experienced all varieties of social class across almost any existing spectrum, it wasn't until I spent my freshman year at GA that I was exposed to, and engaged by, some of the most truly affluent people in the Greater Philadelphia area. While I was always excited for how successful my dad had been doing and thoroughly enjoyed the recent vacations that his company had been able to afford to take us on, for the first couple of months at GA it truly pained me to think about telling him that I wasn't assimilating or enjoying my time there at all.

Anyone who is familiar with GA, or most any of the other Inter-AC schools, is likely well aware of the hefty tuition that accompanies enrollment. With prices per year ranging between $25,000 and $35,000 at the time, how would I ever tell my parents that I didn't believe that I could successfully utilize all that they were sacrificing to provide for me? My father had worked so hard for so long to achieve the position that he was in. My mother had continually kept my sister, Chelsea, and I focused on pursuing what we were passionate about. Both refused to allow either of us children to lazily idle at any point in our lives. I could tell by the way that my parents interacted with other lacrosse families and those affiliated with GA and other local private schools that they were definitely taking quiet pride in being able to afford enrolling their son in such a prestigious school, but everything about my existence at the academy became more intolerable with each daily 45-minute commute that I took to escape and return to it.

> Whether you broke or rich you gotta get biz
> Having money's not everything, not having it is
> I was splurgin' on trizz
> But when I get my card back activated
> I'm back to Vegas 'cause
> I always had a passion for flashing before I had it
> I close my eyes and imagine, the good life.
> —Kanye West, "Good Life"

My father used to seize all kinds of opportunities to teach me financial lessons, starting as early as I can remember. As a first-gen and the only college-educated member of his family, he, similar to my mother, had to work a full-time job all throughout his academic journey as a necessary source of funding. Students whom I would encounter and begin to engage with at GA, in my opinion, had been raised by adults who either failed or didn't care to transfer the same overwhelming sense of appreciation for the objects and opportunities that they were provided. Not to say make blanket statements toward my former classmates, labeling them as "spoiled" or "pretentious," but when I realized that no one at the entire school worked any jobs in the summer that weren't either in their parent's office or on a golf course, it really made me question what I was doing pretending to be able to relate my daily life to this audience?

I worked construction in the summer. Lower Salford Public Works department had been kind enough to allow me to work with its road crew for several summers throughout high school. It was always amusing to me when I explained this to any of my classmates at the time. "What do you mean you help pave roads and mix concrete all summer? Isn't that just like, pretty much already having a blue-collar career?" Man, if they could only meet some of the truly rugged, salt of the earth people whom I got to work with each summer. It might have even made it a little easier to tolerate their mannerisms if I had known they at least had a general respect for working-class professionals and the circumstances that some face, factors outside of their control that impact their lifestyles in ways that you would never be able to tell without meeting them. That was the beginning of my misidentification with the upper-middle- and upper classes.

It started off with the seemingly smallest of annoyances—pet peeves that any non-upper-class student would experience. Watching classmates get dropped off in the morning in a car that likely cost more than the mortgage on the house in which my family lived was especially memorable for me. By the end of the year, cars that I had only seen in magazines or on TV were now being handed out as "Sweet 16" gifts for my newly licensed peers to drive themselves in. Any previous experiences I had labeled in my mind as influential for my understanding of social class, as well as the dynamics of the society that I was becoming aware of, seemed less and less significant. I could feel it affecting how I perceived the world around me.

I didn't like it at all. I wondered at what point I went from thinking of myself as "fortunate enough to not have to buy my own car" to "one of the unfortunate few driving a used Honda." Even as I look back in retrospect, there's an allure. The allure of a mentality that sees comparative privilege and decides that what exists simply isn't as good if someone else is decidedly experiencing better. And it goes way deeper than automobiles.

Ultimately, the "name of the game" for college preparatory schools is to facilitate the process of preparing and sending students forth to whichever college they desire to attend. Some of those whom I met and became acquainted with that year actually went on to graduate and attend the University of Michigan, a prestigious Midwestern institution with a rich and celebrated history, much like that of GA. As my freshman year came to a close, I began making recruiting visits to different colleges in the Philadelphia area; schools that had shown interest at different club lacrosse tournaments were now eager to obtain verbal commitments from prospective high school players. The only out-of-state scholarship offer that I had received would end up being the only out-of-state university that I visited. As the summer came to an end, I was certain of two things: I was no longer going to be attending GA and I was committed to attending Michigan.

When I decided that I wanted to transfer to LaSalle College High School for my sophomore year, and consequently the rest of my high school career, my parents were extremely supportive. My transition to LaSalle had ultimately been a successful one. LaSalle, as I would come to know it, had a reputation similar to that of my own. Playing lacrosse for the institution gave me firsthand experience of this. When we were able to play schools such as GA, we took on the perception of the scrappy, underprivileged kids. When we went into our Philadelphia Catholic League games and played Archbishop Ryan on a football field riddled with empty dime bags and rusted syringes, we were the preppy rich kids. After I started to feel more comfortable as the years went on, my father understood why I made the decision to transfer, and while he warned me that my experience at the University of Michigan might be similar to my experiences at GA, something just felt different about Ann Arbor, and each time that I visited, I was reassured that this is where I wanted to go to college.

> You stayed around the block from me
> Back then it was a very long walk for me
> And we all getting farther away
> From the place that our momma's stay
> ...
> And we all back home
> Grab your bikes
> And we'll ride through the city like kings tonight
> 'Cuz we all getting farther away
> From the place that our momma's stay.
> —Sam Lachow ft. Ariana Deboo, "Brand New Bike"

Moving on from being able to see the Fam every day or every other weekend was difficult. They were so excited for me to be able to play lacrosse at Michigan (which is how they would refer to the university after I snapped at their initial "Michigan State" announcement blunders). But I'd be a damn liar if I said that it wasn't right back to square one with the Fam each time I returned home. While they remained closer to home, they all attended colleges similar to most of their public school classmates. The Fam would always jokingly remind me that they'd beat me senseless if I ever came back home and acted like "I forgot where I came from." I made sure that I would do my best to remind them each time I returned.

While assimilating into any new group or community is instantly made easier when you have 14 lacrosse recruits to do it with, coming in as a large freshman class on what was already a new Division I team was not an easy transition. Our roster was split between upperclassmen who had played club lacrosse for Michigan for a couple of years and the underclassmen who were part of the first classes to be officially recruited. The demographics and characteristics of the players on the team were changing dramatically. What had once been a team with handfuls of Ross Business School students and in-state private school graduates was now an entity primarily constructed of players from out of state, hailing from public and private schools alike. While I certainly felt like, at times, there were similarities that I could draw between my experiences at GA and how I thought that I was perceived by some of the upperclassman, there's something contextually different about being in a college setting that allows for extended opportunity to establish and adjust your perceptions of others. The personas that would show up to class could act so radically different when they returned as their characters in the late hours of the night. It made you wonder if they were really even the same people. For example, I had met a student during orientation and was excited to find out that we had many similar interests and a lot in common. He had also played lacrosse in high school, so that immediately became a source of common ground that we used to help extend both of our social networks throughout the first several weeks.

After the initial hysteria of September, a lot of social groups and campus communities are well into recruiting of their own; among them is Greek Life. Joining a fraternity or sorority, as someone who has no personal experience in doing so, is likely an exciting and also potentially anxious thrill. Without getting overly detailed about the mission statement of most Greek organizations, all I knew during freshman year was that as soon as people started dividing into different fraternities and sororities, interactions that took place around the entire campus began to change. The student whom I had occasional friendly interactions with during orientation had become more like a stranger at the bus stop than someone who still lived in the same dorm as me. I had come to find out that he had joined one of the "top tier fraternities" and spent a majority of his time running errands and doing chores for older fraternity members. When I was able to speak to him, he was usually exhausted, explaining that the pledging process was miserable for everyone. I wrote it off as another anomaly of freshman year and an aspect of college that I would understand some time in the future.

While I cannot say that I have any better understanding on why most prospective members of Greek Life must endure forms of annoying, painful, or embarrassing tasks in order to fully earn their membership, I can absolutely say that I have a better understanding on why processes like these are so socially acceptable. I can draw these comparisons between my social interactions at GA and at those which I began to encounter at the University of Michigan. From my own personal observations and experiences, social class is an underlying bond, an engrained part of the human experience that encourages us as humans to associate primarily with those most similar to ourselves. In my mind, as class attempts to make sense of all the compiled experiences and encounters I'd had, there exists only slim, if any, distinctions to be made between those who flaunted jewelry and exquisite cars and those who proudly don their "top tier" Greek symbols, gather in loud flocks on the front lawns of giant houses, and vacation on the same foreign islands when on break from school. I believe the implications of social class are more profound than most people would assume, but I also believe that the pandemonium that leads some to use social class as the sole determination for their place in the world rely upon a faulty lens as their tool for comparison. I believe that my time spent at the University of Michigan was great preparation for the world beyond college. My social class experiences with GA, and later with aspects of college Greek Life, had found their place within my constantly adjusting perception of what it means to be a healthy and functioning adult. I look at each of my experiences as running observations that I've been able to apply to my own understanding of what social class means. Ultimately, it feels like, through my own observations and insight, that this composition is an essay I've been subconsciously writing for most of my life. I believe that my experiences, some athletic, some academic, some miscellaneous, have been not only positive, but essential for my own personal evolution into the person I've become.

As I look back on the path that led to where I am currently, I wouldn't change anything. I realize the gravity of a statement like that and I confidently stand by it as my unapologetic self. While I'm certainly grateful to be able to state such an evaluation of my own personal circumstance, I challenge anyone who feels they cannot say the same to ask themselves why, and what they feel regret or longing for. If the last four years have truly taught me anything, it would likely pertain to the importance of perspective as it relates to personal proactivity and taking responsibility for my own actions. In a nutshell, if you want/feel/need something to change, do something about it. I'm not going to boisterously exclaim that the University of Michigan was the only place for me to continue some of the most recent steps toward making meaning of my life that I've lived thus far or the social class experiences I've had. I think Michigan was the perfect place for me; just callin' it as I see it.

> All I ever wanted was to pick apart the day
> and put the pieces back together my way.
> —Aesop Rock, "Daylight"

WHAT'S THE DAMAGE?
JOHN CARVILL

If I had to describe my class experience, it would be one without need. I had no need to worry about how much money my parents had to spend. I had no need to worry about from where my next meal would come. I had no need to worry about my education. These affairs were taken care of outside of my consideration and I have no memories of them being discussed when I was nearby. On the other hand, I gained plenty of experience with want. I would save my allowance so I could buy a toy that I wanted. I would be picky and could choose to eat what I wanted. I would pursue my fleeting interests as I wanted. These memories allow me to now understand that I had a middle-class background.

Because of this fertile background, I have never needed to be passionate. I merely had to want to do something. This grants perspective on how I have grown as a person, and how I have germinated. I am the produce of cultivation on the part of my parents and myself. I followed an interest and allowed my parents to prune any unnecessary habits. This wild growth was readily apparent in my middle schooling, as I did chess, band, theater, gymnastics, karate, boy scouts, and Science Olympiad. I initially pursued each of these activities due to some small interest, for chess and band, following my siblings' paths, for theater and boy scouts, to get some exercise, for karate and gymnastics, or some other expectation, imagined or otherwise.

This cultivation prepared me for adult life, even if I did not realize its impact until later, or even think that it affected the course of my life. As a result of this spread of experiences, I developed a wide range of skills, putting down roots in a variety of topics. From theater and forensics, I learned how to properly give a speech, how to project my voice, and how my tone affects meaning. From scouts, I learned the basics of leadership, the clothes to pack, and the meals to cook. From band, I learned how practice affects outcome, how to breathe between beats, and how to keep time despite distractions. These explicit lessons developed my abilities, even if they lacked impact, just as much as the implicit lessons. From chess, I learned how to give a firm handshake and the customary ending to a game. From scouts, I learned how to interview, as I rose through the ranks. From Science Olympiad, I practiced working under stress, because the timer is always ticking. So I grew, ignorant of my achievements and lessons, just living my life and having some fun.

I introduce this cultivation to reveal my definition of want and how I interpret the statement of wanting something. I find myself reflecting on cost when thinking about want, despite cost never acting as a barrier to my growth. Practically, I have been given whatever I wanted when it was desired for my development, and encouraged to use my own allowance for whatever I wanted for pleasure. I have always had the proper uniform and books needed for school. I have always had a winter jacket and hat. I have never needed to go hungry. However, I am finding there is more to want, than this simple fulfillment of physical and emotional needs.

Since I was able to try a variety of different activities without meaningful payment, I lacked attachment to the result of these activities, regardless of struggles they presented. During my time in high school, I participated in forensics in the impromptu category. Despite doing forensics for several years, I never really felt a connection to it. Even as I improved, I struggled to point out any one thing that I was doing better. It was kind of just a way for me to fulfill an extracurricular. This was because my cultivation lacked personal tribulation and so I am detached from achievements I earn.

As such, I feel like a bonsai, something fully grown and carefully sculpted, but that is so much less than its full potential, through no work of its own.

This feeling of detachment is compounded by the knowledge that I am safe. I spend only what cash I carry on my person, limiting my ability to make an error of judgment. I save my money in light of this safety net, in case it should fail. Even then, a second net exists, in the form of my parents. Even now in college, I know that if I ask for support they will be there, and if the request is reasonable, they will help shoulder the burden it presents.

As a result of this sheltering, the first time I thought about circulating money was in the eighth grade. We were assigned the task of picking a pretend job and creating a monthly budget for the salary we had chosen. While I had saved and spent money before, the assignment we were given was the first time I had to think about balancing a budget and taking steps to pay off debts or account for expenses. In a display of naivety, I found a job similar to my father's and built the budget around a $50,000 salary and set about paying off the assigned purchases of a car, rent, and food. I remember questioning how some of my classmates could spend money less responsibly, and my teacher suggesting for the purpose of the project to take a vacation instead of hoarding money, as I saved whatever I didn't spend, and spent on the necessities. Heck, my budget lacked buying a mattress; instead I planned on using a sleeping bag. I made these purchases because they fulfilled my needs, and anything more would simply be something I wanted. I knew from experience that I could comfortably sleep in a bag, so why would I buy a mattress for more money. I knew that I could borrow books from a library, so why would I buy a TV. Part of this strategy could be tied back to my allowance. Since I received about $14 every month, I would save it as there was nothing to buy with just $14. In turn my budget focused on buying the minimum comforts I thought I would need and saved money in case it would be of use later. I probably should have realized something was off when for the follow-up assignment of living on unemployment the only real change to my budget was finding a roommate for a $900 a month apartment. However, this assignment did not have an impact on me. It did not open my eyes to the wider world. It was simply an assignment over the course of a week that made me briefly think about what it meant to earn money, and about what it meant to have money.

The next time that I had to think about accounting for expenses was in my sophomore year of high school. We were assigned to first make a budget to live off of minimum wage, and later asked to design a budget with a partner, while having the same constraint. I will freely admit that I approached both assignments without understanding what living either the lifestyle or the work would require of me. After all, I had never worked for more than the 12 odd hours of service my school required over the course of the year or needed to sacrifice pleasure for work. For the first assignment, I crafted a budget that would provide sufficient income, provided I worked 80 hours a week. I remember approaching the assignment as more of a "challenge accepted," as the teacher implied it should not be feasible to construct such a budget, rather than as a serious reflection on the cost of life, whether that be monetary or physical. It brought about some doublethink in that I understood that an 80-hour workweek would suck, but I didn't get why. So, I just focused on having a balanced budget, that would have me working 80 hours a week, living basically off of straight nutrients, not buying a car due to budget constraints, and having three hours of free time a day. Basically, I was building my vision of the American Dream, even if it was more of a nightmare. I was going to be self-sufficient if it would kill me. I could deal with the idea of lacking comforts, probably because I didn't realize how many I actually had at the time. In hindsight, I think that while I may have been able to survive such a lifestyle, it would not be one I would enjoy living, or one that would be sustainable if I had more dependents. It was a travesty—the delusions of an upper-middle-class boy who was naïve to the grinding of the world.

The second half of the assignment demonstrated a similar naivety, but a powerful cruelty. This is because having a partner not only revealed how insane such a plan was, but we somehow made it worse. The plan was similar to above but included stealing soap from bathrooms, and having no electricity or heating, despite the theoretical increase in income that came with having a partner. It was a comedy of ignorance. I say this to juxtapose this experience against my changed understanding since then. I say this to reveal my understanding of how I have been shaped by class. I say this to grow and understand. As a student, I had all I needed and most of what I wanted. As a student, I was schooled in a private Catholic school and encouraged to pursue service. As a student, I projected my perspective, that of comfort, to my assignment. I lacked the perspective to understand the burden of work rather than the call to service. Work is done day after day. Work is done month after month. Work is done year after year. Years and years of work are different than a day of service.

It is after all a very different experience to go and work in a soup kitchen for six hours, knowing that it is service and that the experience will repeat only voluntarily and another to spend 40 hours a week working behind a counter with all of the responsibilities that a job entails. Even when approached with the same attitude, an actual job has more weight to it than volunteering, especially on a high school level. A job requires preparation for the next day whether that be stocking or cleaning or bagging. Volunteering on the other hand gives me a sense of finality. It ends. Any cleaning is done to restore rather than prepare. Any cooking is done, as is the event. Any bagging is of trash, to be carted away as the sun sets. Thus, the assignment demonstrated the ability to save money, but not an awareness of why that preparation would be necessary.

In turn, I do not think of myself as a thrifty person. This is because of the safety nets I have financially and because of how it affects my purchases. I find myself in a curious position of deciding to make a purchase on impulse, but then delaying the purchase indefinitely should the opportunity to make the purchase simply be off my beaten path. A good example of this happened in my senior year of high school.

I was working toward earning my Eagle Scout award. I was quickly approaching the point of no return, as I had roughly four months left to propose, complete, and submit my project. This was a bit of a crunch as common advice held to schedule six months of time to account for any issues that might—would inevitably—arise. Understanding that without a deadline I would not accomplish anything in a timely manner, I made up a schedule and assigned rewards for milestones, such as having my proposal accepted, finishing the work, and acing the board of review. After a few weeks passed, I completed that first milestone and was on my way to actually completing the project, so I decided to use some money and buy a new game. However, upon purchasing the game, I realized that my family lacked the system to actually play it. Therefore, I simply decided to make the actual system an incentive for completing the project as a whole, as earning Eagle is a time- and effort-consuming accomplishment. However, even once the project was complete, the board of review successful, and the award actually presented, around seven months' total time, with four of those between the completion and the presentation, I still had not purchased the system. This was not due to limited finances or some other obstacle in my path. I simply did not buy the system for four months. It was just outside of my normal routine to go out and buy something even if I had decided that I could and would make the purchase. In the end, it was more due to stubbornness than anything else that resulted in my purchase.

I relate this story to demonstrate how I perceive wanting something. I adopt the mind-set that nothing is really out of reach, but I defer gratification so long as the object is out of sight. This mind-set has persisted for the past several years and is at the root of why I think that I am not a thrifty person. I can wait to make a purchase, but I tend to decide quickly whether or not the purchase will happen in the first place. Looking back, I think this might have been because I had an allowance and I knew that I would receive that allowance every month. This meant that if I wanted to buy something the only limiting factor was time, whether that meant waiting until my birthday in early January or I had the money required. This source of income meant I never needed to worry about budgeting my money. The only place I could spend it was in either small increments at school or a single big ticket item once a year.

I do think that it is a privilege to think this way, but it makes me irresponsible and ill prepared for the world after college. It is probably for the best that I have the opportunity to attend college, because it gives me time to grow out of this mind-set. Part of the privilege I needed to acknowledge was my sense of entitlement. I would like to think that I am not an entitled person, though upon reflection this is simply not true. It tends to appear in subtle ways that complement my quiet nature. Naturally, there is a bias to this observation, but the point remains that I expect things to work out in general. Perhaps the grandest example I can give was my acceptance to college. A momentous occasion which should be celebrated and acknowledged, particularly since I was accepted to my college of choice: the University of Michigan (UM). I noticed the e-mail while I was on break at work, so I shot my parents a text along the lines of "I just got in," and then proceeded to finish my shift not really thinking about the acceptance. When I got home my parents seemed more excited than I did, because of course, it is supposed to be a big deal to be accepted to Michigan. I kinda just went to sleep, because it was late, I was tired, and well, it was just another acceptance in the end. I didn't think much of it because it was expected of me to get into college. My life until then basically discounted any chance of not going to college in some way shape or form. My schooling and peers radiated the idea that college was the natural course. I was cultivated to be a well-rounded individual so I could attend college. I did not feel personally ready to enter the workforce without college, both in preparation of a career or as a means to grow more as a person. So, if college was the next step, why would I be surprised to be accepted? I don't even remember bringing it up to friends, partially due to apathy, and partially to avoid sounding like I was bragging.

I would like to point out how vague the scene is in this case: how it lacks the time I was on break, what day of the week it was, or other such details. It is because that day had little impact on me. I expected to get into every college to which I applied, and deliberately chose not to have a reach school.

Earlier, I mentioned a safety net, how I felt that I lacked a chance to fail. This is my grand realization of those feelings, my eureka, my epiphany, my revelation. Even "expect" is too strong a word to describe how I felt about the college application process. It implies thought and deliberation. "Accepted" would be a better word in this case, as though my acceptance into college was inevitable.

Part of the growing that I would need to do was to begin to observe. One of the interesting things about high school was the dress code. It was pretty basic, just khakis and a uniform polo, but it still felt like those that wore the straight uniform were the minority. Part of this may have been due to being able to wear any sweatshirt or hoodie, provided it had the school's name, but by my senior year it felt like there was a clear division among the students despite the increasing attempts to fix the broken code. It certainly made for a colorful minority when the violations ranged from people dressing above dress code to people in hoodies to one kid who wore a tracksuit. But all of this just goes back to hiding with clothes in the end.

Of course, I paid no attention to hiding in clothes or even how to hide. After all, I attended private schools for my entire career before college, and didn't need to dress fashionably given the uniform. Outside of school, my main activities had either uniforms or required grubbier clothes, whether that is scouting and karate or camping and gymnastics. I had no reason to attempt to fit anyone's standards and so dressed how I pleased.

I have now learned that it is easy to hide behind clothes. My experience with forensics has taught me that a third of any presentation is attire, another third is body language, and the last third is content, with a tenth of laughs thrown in for good measure. High school forensics can be pretty homogeneous for a guy. A tournament is essentially a sea of suits, especially in the more serious events. In rounds this can have the effect of bringing more attention to the presentation since everyone looks alike. How does a person sound? How does a person move? What are the presenters content? Are they on script? These details are made apparent, particularly since it is a competition.

Of course, these nuances were lost on my younger self, and I focused instead on improving myself and building my repertoire and lexicon. Nonetheless, looking back it makes a good metaphor for social class issues. There are those who can blend in with a different class, but there are errors in their piece. While in this case it would be due to a lack of skill or practice, in the real world, lines are blurred as to what the goal ought to be.

One of the best parts of my college experience has been the perspective it grants and how to notice these nuances. I come from five different states, three of which I remember, meaning a lack of deep roots. I come from 18 years of introversion and retreating into myself, meaning that the roots I made did not spread far. I come from 12 years of private Catholic schooling, meaning a homogeneous background. College combats these constants. College is just a new move, a new place to start. College removes my roots, allowing new ones to take hold. College is varied, a mixture of cultures and classes and ideas. I still lacked the perspective to know what to look for in this new environment though.

One piece of advice I received about perspective is to look at a person's shoes. This makes sense to me. After all, people wear shoes every day. People wear the same shoes every day. It follows then that a worn shoe indicates a certain lack of resources, in the same way that the wrong shoe indicates a lack of decorum. Shoes send a message, because they are easily ignored. It is rude to stare at a person's feet when talking to them, and so more emphasis on appearance is placed on the face or chest.

It's funny how obvious a shoe that does not fit a situation stands out, but a shoe worn for a year that has been worn down is almost invisible. It makes a good analogy for social class. Owning a number of shoes easily indicates wealth, but owning appropriate shoes indicate class. I think that the number of shoes I own is the best indicator that I am middle- to upper-middle class. I own one pair of shoes for every scenario I might encounter, and no more. I have a pair of black dress shoes, brown dress shoes, snow boots, tennis shoes, flip-flops, slippers, lawn-mowing shoes, and hiking boots. I am not limited by a lack of appropriate options, nor am I burdened by an abundance of choice. I have a pair for every level of society I might encounter and if I have spares they go unworn. I wear my shoes for a year, so long as they fit, discarding them before they become worn. My feet remain dry and appropriate for every occasion.

To go to college is to move. Moving in turn elicits change: changing scenery, living in a new place, changing home, adapting to new conditions, changing personality, growing as a human. In coming to college I took deliberate steps to better prepare myself for life after my education was finished. A small part of this was establishing a budget, for food and leisure. This was because I knew from past experience that I would fritter away the money I had if steps were not taken to limit and control my spending, and creating a budget was a concrete way of doing that. Granted, I tend to cycle between droughts and floods, though still within budget it is not a stable system. Upon reflection, I find it odd that I never budgeted until college. Which probably owed more to not needing to budget than any effort to avoid learning how to budget. Even when I had to make up a budget using my actual income for a project, my only documented expenses were gas and snacks, coming out to about $50 a week out of a $200 income. Or when I planned my Eagle project and the fund-raising amounted to the money already in my scout account. I had access to money so I ignored the actual amount, for good and for ill.

Having a budget helps me to give substance to my funds. It forces me to be aware of what I have, when I save, and how I spend. Even buying my text books was an exercise in feeling the weight of money. This was because buying my text books was the first time that I acted independently to obtain my own school supplies. This gave me the chance to shop and plan the trip accordingly, rather than simply go and purchase as I had when buying a game or gas. So of course, I walked into the nearest bookstore thinking that it would be a quick trip and proceeded to spend the next hour waiting in line to rent my books, because of course a college bookstore would be busy the week classes start. It probably would have been better to see if I could borrow the text from a more senior student as well, but that too was a lesson to be had.

Nonetheless, these were lessons that I had need to learn. This required trip marked another step into awareness of the world. It ensured that I had the texts needed for class. It ensured that I had the money I needed to purchase the texts. It ensured that I learned that I could no longer just assume that things would go my way.

Altogether, it was time which was budgeted and accounted poorly, but spent well from an existing abundance which permitted a gradient in perspective that I had come to college to enjoy.

Having now presented my definition of need and how it has colored my world, I would like to now address my experiences with need and how I define it at the present. Honestly, I do not understand what it means to need something. I bear the knowledge of having a need. I grasp the necessity of certain ideas and substances. I struggle with applying these concepts to my own being. It frightens me that I am entering a community, an environment, a world, which I am unprepared to confront, due to having a lack of experience. However, I am learning, which of course raises more questions on what defines need.

Beginning in early November 2016, I began to encounter some issues with my health. These issues persist today, and will likely remain with me of my entire life. Now I have little experience navigating the world of health care, which may or may not be a common experience among young adults of any social class. However, my background allows me certain flexibility. I am able to ignore the costs my care incurs due to being under my parents' insurance. I am able to take time and discuss with my parents how to go about making appointments. My parents are able to take time away from their work to help me get to and from appointments. This flexibility means that even though I am responsible for my care, I am not worried. I am not worried about making the money to pay for my care. I am not worried about my inexperience preventing care. I am not worried about my family suffering for my own inability.

It probably says something that I think nothing of this. That I give no thought to the possibility of a threat to my health not being addressed. It makes perfect sense to me, but I now realize this might not be a common scenario for all people. People come from different social classes. Class may mean they lack opportunities to find treatment due to a lack of means. Means that might be held in excess, find a quicker solution of diagnosis. Diagnosis would be the same for me as any other person. I just now know how I am sick, while others might not, and others might already be treated.

If I had to describe my social class experience, it would be one full of want. Not necessarily a life spoiled for want nor a famine of want, rather enough for it to be known, but little more than that. It is interesting to look back and think about the wants I ignored, along with what I was given against what I had. It juxtaposes my ignorance well against my experience, and demonstrates that while I grew without knowing need, there are more ways to need than just fulfilling the physical.

LAUGH AND LEARN
CHRIS CROWDER

Comedian Brooks Wheelan, a former actor on Saturday Night Live, was walking around Times Square in New York a few years ago with some friends when one of them decided on a whim that they should go to Red Lobster for lunch.

"What's the occasion? I have shorts on. I can't be wearing shorts at the RL!"

Wheelan grew up middle class in Iowa and deemed restaurants such as Red Lobster fancy while others scoffed at it. But never before had a joke been so relatable to me. I heard Wheelan opening a comedy show for John Oliver, a show my girlfriend graciously gave me as a Christmas present.

I grew up middle class, thinking Red Lobster and Olive Garden were fancy and for special occasions. Bottomless breadsticks or biscuits with an entrée sounded like heaven to my palate whenever I earned good grades, which I always strived for. When I attended college and went to legitimately fancy places in Ann Arbor, Michigan, I didn't know about wine menus or which forks and spoons were for soups or salads. "Wait, now there are two sets of silverware?" I looked at places like these in awe. The check had a number I hadn't seen associated with a small serving. I thought my middle class was normal, and it is. But coming to Ann Arbor made me realize how different my life was compared to more affluent peers.

*   *   *

I grew up in Flint, Michigan, yes, the one home to the Flint water crisis. My city always had a bad reputation for being one of the most violent per capita. The water issue brought in even more bad press. I live on the city limit, mainly shielded from it all. I recently looked at a map where lead entered the water supply and my house is literally a block away. My family and I are lucky our pipes are new. My subdivision is very safe; it's mostly just older people and I didn't have any neighbor kids to play with growing up. There was one shooting in my subdivision, but my cousin was shot and killed in Flint's inner city when I was in the fourth grade. Two houses have accidentally burned down on either side of our place and the lots are now vacant. These experiences broke my heart, but now three years into college, they're like distant memories. That's probably because they didn't hit me incredibly close to home. However, I have never felt unsafe in my neighborhood. I only mention these unfortunate things to give myself a little street cred, which is kind of sad.

Flint was hit especially hard by the 2008 and ongoing recession because the city's economy was cemented in the automotive industry. Multiple factories closed and thousands lost their jobs. My family was fortunate enough because dad didn't work in a factory like many others. Still, with tough times he chose to take a part-time job as a Transportation Security Administration (TSA) agent at our local airport in addition to his primary job working at a center for disadvantaged children. Even though I had no idea how much money my parents earned (my mom is a second-grade teacher), this was the first time I became conscious of how money came into play in my middle-class life. They never mentioned it and I didn't have much of a reason to ask. I felt comfortable with our money situation. My parents told me when we couldn't afford things and I understood. I made Christmas lists while consciously adding up prices. I made pro and con lists to ponder intently on wants versus needs. I didn't ask for much and felt guilty about asking for money to go on activities like class trips because I didn't want to inconvenience my family. To my knowledge, not having enough money to spend wasn't a problem.

That guilt extends to college. I hate asking my parents for money because I want to be increasingly independent and can imagine the strain my parents experience as they work hard to help me pay rent and my sister's tuition at Grand Valley State University in Allendale, Michigan. They work their butts off. They motivate me and my sister. Dad is now a full-time supervisor for TSA and my mom still teaches second grade in Holly, Michigan. She also has works at Macy's as well as in an old time village tourist attraction on some weekends and in the summer. Meanwhile, Michigan's governor Rick Snyder has held thousands of dollars of mom's in a dispute with state of Michigan teachers. It's her money and she needs it now! The fact my parents have sacrificed so much keeps me motivated so that I can someday spoil them with bundles of cash I'll hopefully gain from my University of Michigan degree and future career. But for now, I stay frugal.

On the other hand, I've seen a lot of fellow students at the University of Michigan with tight pockets and those who spend freely. The first thing I noticed during my freshman year was how frequently peers shopped during lectures. While I was taking notes, several were zoning in on their next purchase. All over MacBook screens were shoes costing over $200, plane tickets, fancy dresses, and suits bought with clicks of a button and glances at credit cards. I even overheard a girl talking to a friend about riding on a private jet. I had been on a plane just once. People talked about yearly trips to the Mediterranean and expensive tropical places I had only dreamed of visiting. I hadn't been to another country until I traveled to Toronto, Canada, in 2017. I also became aware of what others were wearing. What the hell are Vinyard Vines, Patagonia, and Canada Goose? I didn't understand why students—or their parents—could spend almost a grand on a coat when I've had the same one for seven years and it still keeps me warm. In America, there's an overwhelming sense of materialism and brand loyalty, causing people to spend more than they need to. I've always had the mentality of eating leftovers instead of making a new dish, wearing the same shoes if they're not falling apart before buying new ones, and driving a car with multiple problems because it still runs instead of taking it to the shop so that it's in peak condition.

There is no point in keeping up with the Joneses at Michigan. I can't afford to. I also don't have a desire to fit in since I was born to stand out. You see, I'm mixed: half black and half white. I'm viewed as a racial minority. College is different from my K–12 days. At the University of Michigan, the black population is about 4% and I rarely have classes with someone who shares my races. I'm not threatened or particularly angry, but I notice all the time. Any time race comes up, I feel vulnerable and awkward.

But back in Flint, half my school was black and the rest was white, with some Arabic. My high school was and is one of the most diverse in Michigan, but it's not viewed as one of the most academically prestigious. Browsing through Facebook one day, my Michigan friends talked about how a website ranked the top high schools in Michigan. While their schools were the top two, mine didn't crack the top 150. I thought the ranking was absurd because I had received a high-quality education but at the same time I was one of only two kids from my class to start college at Michigan while some high schools sent dozens. Though my school was racially, economically, and religiously diverse, our class standings seemed to be the same, so we all had relatable common grounds. We didn't discuss specifics of social class difference, but nobody was overly materialistic either. We rarely went on vacations, our houses were worth less based on perceptions of our city, and a lot of fellow students worked after school. We hated our rival school 20 minutes away because its students were richer and had everything handed to them. They, of course, deemed us inferior, and whenever we interacted with preconceived notions, we thought they were snobby and elitist.

When I met kids who went to that rival high school here at Michigan, I encountered kind-hearted and hard-working people. The perceptions I attached to all upper-middle-class and rich people of being stuck up and rude were false. They simply had been born into a situation where they could also benefit from their parents' hard work. I didn't resent an imaginary rich person anymore. I respected a real one. Just like me, they deserved to be here and had parents who raised them up right. I'm fortunate enough to have highly educated and intelligent parents who provided examples for me. Some of my peers aren't so lucky.

I didn't experience the reality of poverty until I went on a 2011 high school mission trip to Kokomo, Indiana, with my church's youth group. Kokomo is very similar to Flint in that both are dependent on the auto industry and have social class diversity. We heard stories of how kids would bring home extra napkins from school to split into thirds to stand in as toilet paper for their siblings. And families in poverty were actually hurt financially when they obtained a job because they didn't receive additional government funding. Parents' salaries weren't enough to support their families in a country where the minimum wage doesn't equate to a living wage. We met 16-year-old mothers and former drug users trying to get on the right paths. Six-year-olds directed their younger siblings like seasoned parents. As we went through a poverty simulation, I felt horrible after not eating for one day. I was lost, isolated, confused, and vulnerable to what could go wrong. I couldn't imagine how I would feel if that was my life. We met people at a soup kitchen who had lived in poverty for years. Some were upbeat and open about their experiences, while others kept to themselves.

As a child, I was afraid of people I didn't know. Some still are wary of talking to people from a different class. I've witnessed people different than me who are just like me in many ways. They have feelings and dreams and stories. That's why I'm so impassioned to become a storyteller—because not everyone listens to what the unheard have to say.

We went back to Kokomo the next year, enamored by a pastor who left a very wealthy church and parsonage in a Chicago suburb to come back to help his hometown and its citizens get back on their feet. I'm conflicted on whether I want to do the same someday. I want to help Flint, but at the same time, I have a burning desire to leave. But I guess that doesn't mean I can't serve wherever I live in the future. This pastor lived steps away from government-subsidized housing and hosted weekly picnics in the summer to feed families. Some of the children were foul-mouthed and dirty, a lot different from the way kids behaved when I was in elementary school. And as we learned more about how this poverty was generational, I couldn't help but think how terrible it was that there were so many wasted minds. Who knows, the cure of cancer or an incredible math theorem may be developed by a child in Kokomo. But without education, that intelligence and potential will never be unlocked.

In elementary school, I was one of the smart kids. I kept to myself, remained modest, and pretty much only spoke when spoken to. I was put in an extra class with a handful of other students called highly abled learners. As the only black male in the class, I heard that I acted white (actually middle-class white) throughout my primary education because of the ways I spoke and presented myself. There was also a difference between being deemed "smart" and black and smart. If a white student excelled, it was viewed as normal. But at the same time, I realized there were structural disadvantages for working- and lower-class blacks in school systems, hindering their success. So I'm blessed and lucky to be where I am today. Back then I tried to compensate for my stigmatized intelligence by playing basketball at recess and brushing waves in my hair to seem more like what others expected of me. On the court I felt simultaneously safe and out of place. We were all kids who didn't have a lot of money and didn't act like we were better than anybody else. I didn't talk or walk like my friends: I didn't like the same things. However, with pride in our hometown, there was a mutual respect across class boundaries.

I first realized that Flint was different on my sixth birthday. The party was at Chuck E. Cheese and everything was going just fine. I had pizza and got plenty of tokens so it was a good day. When my party was ending, a dispute developed nearby between two women and the police were called. Pepper spray filled the building and everyone scrambled out. But experiences like this were far from the norm in my area of Flint.

This experience may paint a bad picture, but I'm also proud to boast of our surging downtown area, exceptional arts district, and one of the best farmers' markets in the country. I wish more effort would be put into nearby ghettos and abandoned areas. It always bothers me when people deem places "bad neighborhoods" or "not nice areas" because of what a few parts of my town look like. I know people see a liquor store and a couple of left-behind businesses and freak out, but nobody is going to get hurt. My grandmother used to live in what people called the "hood," but we were always safe when visiting. My great uncle has a large garden in his backyard complete with corn stalks, potatoes, and green produce. The majority of people aren't bad and rundown buildings aren't necessarily a reflection of citizens' actions and characters. There are just a few bad apples, like in every city, that tarnish the overall perception.

Some people who live in Flint suburbs judge the area and its residents (we're called Flintstones) based on what they've heard in the media and from others. Granted, the news calls attention to inner-city crime and shootings, but it is often implied all Flintstones are less educated, poor, and dangerous. And some of those distinctions may be true, but discrimination based on assumptions is wrong. Years ago at a high school baseball game, our opponents' fans and parents called my teammate a nigger. Racism wasn't and isn't dead. Some are still ignorant and stupid in their ways, but we still must love them to make progress in changing hearts. We're still far from overcoming race and social class discrimination. This is possible, but the more hate and lack of acceptance in news and social media prevents a shared vision of a more united country. But I still have hope. No matter someone's race, religion, or class status, I intend to treat him or her with the utmost respect as I see in all God's children. John 13:34–35 says: "A new commandment I give to you, that you love one another: just as I have loved you, you also are to love one another. By this all people will know that you are my disciples, if you have love for one another."

For the overwhelming majority of my time here at the University of Michigan, I have been respected and accepted by peers in regard to my race and social class background. But during one of my first weeks, I had a contrasting experience. One day I wore a blue hat coming out of my dorm room and my neighbor asked: "Do you work in the dining hall?" My hat and the dining hall workers hats were both navy blue. I politely said no and didn't think anything of it, but my other neighbors who saw and heard the interaction thought his question was racist since he asked me, a black person. I thought it more saddening that my peers insinuated working at the dining hall was a job for lower-income people and associated blackness with that work. There's nothing wrong with being black and there's nothing wrong with working at the dining hall. Nine dollars an hour is a hell of a wage for college kids, no matter their race, their class, or how much money they're getting from parents. But my peers didn't have to work in college like I do. Perhaps they do now. But I wonder about their thinking three years later as we've all matured and learned exponentially more about how the world works, how other people live, and how they think.

The summer after my freshman year, I worked for the university cleaning bathrooms and painting dorm rooms in Alice Lloyd Hall. Not only did I work with friends, but also with the same people I saw cleaning dorms while attending school in the 2014–2015 school year. I have always cleaned up after myself and said hello to the custodian who worked on my floor. But actually doing the work gave me the opportunity to know some of the workers better and have a greater appreciation for what they do. They were normal, quick-talking, and hardworking people. I was astounded by how many students didn't have them in mind when they left behind trashed rooms and horrible messes. And through working with the staff who were from the working class, I saw they weren't any different from me. I wondered if other Michigan students agreed. But I'm afraid many students saw these jobs as inferior, less prestigious and sophisticated. But every job has a learning curve, and without these people, the dorms wouldn't be able to function. You can't live in a dorm when no one takes out the trash, cleans the showers, or fixes broken light fixtures. And I doubt everyone wouldn't be game to clean toilets all summer like I did. I miss the housing facility workers and their camaraderie, as well as their jokes and kind hearts. I'm pleased to have met them and gotten to know them on a personal level.

There have been times during my time at Michigan when I wished for a more career-advancing opportunity or internships like my more affluent peers. I'll admit that having money is great in this capitalist country. Along with more money, there is also the aspect of social capital. In a competitive career market, it isn't always about what you know, but about whom you know. Some people, along with their merit, may be able to get certain jobs by way of community or parental connections. And connections come with the territory of wealth. I may know a mechanic I can go to with my background, but I don't know who can help with obtaining a job or internship. I wish the University of Michigan could better facilitate career connections for those from less affluent backgrounds.

All in all, I'm very fortunate to have had the chance to study at Michigan. I'm blessed to have earned scholarships that help pay for educational expenses. I'm lucky to have parents to guide me when I'm in need of direction. I may be a racial and social class minority on campus, but based on my family's income and my race, I have always felt welcome and safe. I can only speak for myself, but I'm glad to have chosen the University of Michigan despite the sometimes acute competitiveness and stressors here in Ann Arbor. Social class hasn't been that much of an issue, as my scholarships and side jobs help out a lot. And, of course, my parents are able to generously help when I ask.

I began this essay with a joke because sometimes humor can be a very effective way to strike a nerve or relate to people. From my perspective, middle-class people like myself are privileged enough to laugh at minor misfortunes and pain. We're fortunate to have basic needs met for the majority of our days. Some communities and families aren't as lucky. Class struggles, differences, and suffering aren't funny; trying to laugh is a sort of middle-class self-schadenfreude (a way to take a little pleasure in minor pain the comfortable middle-class experiences). One of my family's favorite TV shows is *The Middle*. It's about a middle-class Midwestern family that hilariously and heartwarmingly struggles through family relations, expenses, and what discomfort they must endure. My family relates by laughing about the broken wheel bearings and metal squeals of our car, the leaky dishwasher, and how many times we've replaced the bathroom tub's cold handle on the right side with a pair of pliers. We laugh about it, live, keep working, and get along just fine.

Learning by Interacting
Charlotte Feldman

I am one of those people who learns by doing. Even more than that, I learn from others; by observing, befriending, and even dating other people. These relationships have had the power to make me aware of what I have as well as what I am able to give because of privileges I have. My life has been an exchange of knowledge from one person to each other. This is about that exchange.

I grew up in a town right outside of Boston that was commonly called "Jewton" because of the high population of Jewish families. We had bat mitzvahs every weekend in seventh grade. My parents divorced when I was a little older than four years; my mom is Catholic while my dad is Jewish. Since I kept my dad's last name, Feldman, people immediately assumed that I was as Jewish as well. I still am unsure what I am or want to be, but I like to think of myself as both. Orthodox Jews would say that I was not really Jewish because only dad is Jewish, but other than that, in my town, I thought I fit in with everyone: the Jewish people, the Christian people, and then people who had no idea whatsoever. I am not saying I am perfect and everyone loved me, but it worked. That was what I was good at, fitting into different bubbles inside our larger bubble. I also fit into the category of relating to all divorced children, but since both my parents remarried I also fit into the category of having happy parents. Even though I didn't always realize it, I was lucky.

Mom grew up in a little town on the tip of Cape Cod called Provincetown, Massachusetts, and then moved around a lot before landing in Connecticut. She had minimal money and from a young age learned how to manage it and take care of herself. She put herself through college and I will forever respect that. Dad on the other hand grew up in Westchester, New York, in the house my grandparents still live in to this day. They met the last week of college at Brown University and they still live in the same town. They married people who were more similar to them from my eyes. Dad married my stepmom who is originally from a higher class and mom married my stepdad who was not as well-off. I do not see either parent as better or worse because of how they were raised, but I do think that it is interesting how they both ended up with someone who had the same norms growing up. Each parent raised me in different ways, with different approaches to spending money and buying new things. That comparison of looking at the differences between my families embedded a seed in me to look for differences in other people and learn from them. Now if I had to categorize my social class, it would be middle class, which is a very broad category; I go on vacations to warm places over school breaks and have had what I've wanted and more. I am, however, able to do more because there are four sources of income supporting me instead of only two.

In addition to learning about social class from my family situations, I also learned a lot about class through my experiences in middle school. When I got to middle school, I was ready to make new friends and build new relationships. I had a few from elementary school, but I wanted to meet new people. My best friend quickly became a girl named Anna, and she already had her group of friends. Moms sat on the sidelines of soccer game after soccer game and watched their daughters play and then brought over unhealthy snacks at halftime until that was deemed not healthy: the orange slices were delicious. These girls were friends because they had gone to preschool together, then elementary school, and because all the moms were friends. I am not devaluing their friendship and this does not diminish the girl's friendships, but it is a common pattern of how a lot of the friend groups formed in my town. We were all middle class and upper-middle class and there were very few differences.

Middle school was hard for me. Mom started as a substitute teacher there because as she now says: "I heard you were hanging out with the wrong crowd." She would be in my school two to three times a week and often in my classes. She probably sent each of my guy friends to the principal over 10 times. They still call her Mrs. Feldman when they come over to my house. I got bullied like every other middle-school girl because at one point or another everyone does, and my mom knew about it seconds after it happened.

In class, my mom would always pay attention to the same kids, and I couldn't understand why. None of the other teachers paid attention to them because they had given up on them. Everyone called them the METCO (Metropolitan Council for Educational Opportunity) kids. Not all of them were rowdy or bad kids and some became good friends. But they were grouped together because they were bussed in from an underprivileged area in Boston to attend Newton Public Schools. They were loud in class and always late, and I couldn't understand why my mom was rewarding them for their bad behavior by helping them with their work and calling on them every time that they raised their hand. Even if they weren't loud or tardy, they stood out because they were Hispanic or African American. Most of the time these are stereotypes of underprivileged kids but in this case it sadly fell true. They didn't have nice backpacks, and didn't get a cell phone when everyone started to get them in sixth grade. In a way, I was jealous because I felt like they slid by. Mom would tell me to smile at them and sometimes even pair me with them for projects, and I couldn't understand why. It was my first experience where I realized that people were being treated differently because of their social class. Now I realize my mom was being altruistic, wanted to believe in these kids, and saw past what other people may have been unable to.

As I went through my three years of middle school, I began to notice a pattern in teachers who called on the METCO kids and the teachers who didn't. There were teachers who seemed to really care about teaching. They cared about more than just most kids getting good grades, and they were able to adapt activities for METCO kids who did not have a computer at home or were unable to do their homework. In eighth grade, I got to know a couple of kids because they played sports with friends, so they would come and hang out with us. Embarrassingly, I don't think I would have been friends with them otherwise. On weekends, they would switch off sleeping at different guy friends' houses so that they could hang out with us at night and didn't have to go home late at night. I started realizing how people in different social classes lived in different places and just simply had more things to think about like how to get home after school.

Traveling abroad has also heavily influenced my understanding of social class. Sophomore year of high school I stayed with a host family in Costa Rica for two weeks while doing community service. To say thank you, I decided to cook them dinner on the last night. My mom had always cooked me pesto and I knew the recipe was only five ingredients so how hard could it be. I went to the grocery store and looked everywhere for basil, and then finally turned on my cell phone data to Google basil in Spanish, Albahaca. A kind worker understood my butchered version of the word that sounded very similar to alpaca and led me to the spice aisle. Reaching up onto the shelf he grabbed a glass jar of Albahaca and handed it to me and I stared at it realizing my mistake. This wasn't Newton. There wasn't fresh basil shipped in from Hawaii or California. Not knowing what else to make I grabbed the rest of the ingredients I needed and walked back through town and up the winding road back to the place I had called home for the last two weeks. Somehow dinner turned out to be relatively appetizing; I think we were just happy to be in each other's company.

The dinner conversation soon turned to what my house looked like back home.

"What your house look like at home Carlota," my Costa Rican mom asked me. "Well I have three—" I said before stopping myself and realizing what they must think of this American girl with three houses. Knowing I had started and couldn't stop, I continued slowly hoping they would understand "one is my mom's, and one is my dad's, and then my dad has another house in Vermont where we spend a lot of the summer." She smiled at me warmly and I wasn't really sure if she had understood what I said and I asked: "Have you ever been to America?" The smile gone from her face she replied: "no never." Immediately I asked the question I find myself asking anyone who lives in a warm place: "Have you ever seen snow?" The daughter replied: "No y probalamente nosotros nunca veremos"— meaning they will never see snow. My face fell, I got red, and the table became quiet.

Dinner finished quickly after that and the atmosphere around the house was sullen. I wanted to show them what snow was, but more than that I felt like they had given me a new perspective on the world and I needed to show them some of mine. I cut out paper snowflake after paper snowflake and hung them up around the kitchen and living room. In the morning I went down to the kitchen and was greeted by my host mother holding breakfast for me and smiling at the snowflakes. Even though I felt my dinner and snowflakes were not even close to enough to thanking them for graciously hosting me, my host mother still felt she needed to also thank me in return. She didn't know but she taught me more than just her words, but by her actions. It opened my eyes to the real poverty occurring around the world. For me in the places I went in Costa Rica, most people were either lower class or in severe poverty, but that meant very different things for them than it seemed to mean in America.

Over the next couple years, I wondered what became of my host family. At first my host sister and I wrote letters telling each other what was happening in our lives. A couple years later I was scrolling through my Facebook news feed and discovered my host sister was married and pregnant. I always had this hope that she was going to be the one to come to see snow or that I would go back and visit her but I never have. I now realize they would never have my privileges and I couldn't change their culture and pattern of life.

When I came back from Costa Rica I saw things differently and thought I finally understood social class as if it was something understandable. But, after dating a boy from another class, I realized I had no idea what was going on. His name was Griffin, and we met through mutual friends. He went to the other high school in my town, and I didn't know much about him. The first time we met we went on a double date, with the couple who introduced us, to my favorite noodle restaurant: Number One Noodle House. Griffin kindly paid for me and I made sure to thank him. After the date, he asked me if he could see me again, and I decided that would be nice. He picked me up at my home a couple days later and we started driving to his home. He got on the highway and then took Exit 93S to Boston. He told me his house was farther away, but I assumed on the other side of Newton, not in Boston. We took Exit 11B for Dorchester Avenue and I started to get scared. I had never been outside of "safe Boston" before, and everyone had stereotyped it as being unsafe and sketchy. Eventually, when we became more serious, he started taking the back way to his house because on the highway he had to pay the toll, and his mom would get mad at him for wasting money. Whenever I drove by myself, I always took the highway.

Dad would say things to me like: "Wow it is so good that you're getting this other class experience" or "I hope this is opening your eyes." My dad was proud of me for dating someone in another class. He didn't mean it in a bad way, but you could tell there was something about people who would just assume Griffin and I weren't going to get married or stay together for very long. People treated him like he was my charity case, the privileged girl from Newton dating the underprivileged kid from Dorchester or Dot as he called it. I slowly stopped bringing him around my friends and even my parents, making a subconscious point to only be around him and his friends. In his world, I started to pay for more things for him purely because I felt guilty that he was spending all his parents' hard earned money on me. I didn't want to be why another bill was added to the pile on their kitchen table. When I started applying to colleges I would sit with him while he applied because I felt like

I needed to. I was lucky enough to have an ACT (American College Testing) tutor and a college application tutor, and so I wanted to be his. Eventually we both went off to college, him on partial scholarship, and me not even having to apply for financial aid; suddenly we didn't have anything in common. That isn't to say that interclass relationships don't ever work, but when the source of income is your parents, it becomes harder to control.

Another person who really had an effect on me was Anna. Anna was different because she just didn't care. She dressed differently than everyone else, she made her own clothes, and people thought that was cool; I thought that was cool. She shopped at vintage stores and secondhand stores, and I thought that was especially cool. It was not because her family could not afford to buy her clothes, but simply because she wanted to. I was in awe of this mentality, but unable to recreate it in myself because I wanted to fit in with other friends. In high school I wanted to have the newest things, but I was surrounded by people who knew my parents and what my houses looked like. It would have been hard to hide my parents' relative income. Then I went to college, and I wanted to fit in there too. I begged dad to buy me a nice jacket because that's what people told me I just had to have. I looked online for fake jewelry that I could pass off as my own, hoping that nobody would know I might not have as much money as them. Then over the summer of my freshman year of college, I brought a couple of my school friends home for the first time. I was nervous that my cover would be blown and they would realize that I wasn't as well-off as them. That I didn't have my own pool or my TV was too small. Dad's house is a two-family place, but you can't tell if you enter from the garage; so I had them pull into the driveway so that I could let them in that way. I knew I had nothing to be embarrassed of, but for the first time in my life, I was uncomfortable because I assumed my friends would judge me just as I had judged other people. I found myself watching their eyes as I gave them the house tour, and I wished that I didn't care, but I did. Finally, my friend broke my incessant blabbering and asked if we could watch TV, and just like that I relaxed. I realized that it was all in my head and my friends were not my friends because they assumed I had money; they truly wanted to be my friend.

Staying within your social class is something I have found extends past relationships, marriage, and who your friends are. When I came to the University of Michigan (UM), I found myself surrounded by so many different types of people and I wanted to find people who were raised how I was and therefore liked to do the same things. So I joined a sorority. There is a stereotype that joining Greek Life is paying for your friends, but I never saw it like that. Greek Life just happens to be where the people are whom I had a lot in common with. That is not to say that I do not have friends outside of my sorority or Greek Life, but they are the people whom I find myself drawn to because we share similar upbringings. I do not come close to loving everyone in my sorority, but I have met my best friends there. It is almost like a bubble of wealth I am lucky to see through, as well as lucky to be a part of. I do not see my friends with price tags above their heads. That isn't to say there are no benefits to Greek Life. Parents' weekend brunches are like networking sessions but it is a reciprocal system because all of the parents want their kids to be as successful as their friends. I feel comfortable with my friends because I don't feel they are looking down on me for something I am wearing. I don't feel like I should be ashamed of owning a nice jacket or owning multiple pairs of shoes, but when I am not surrounded by my peers, I often feel judged or looked down upon. I don't think I should have to hide my social class any more than the next person.

I am in the Art School at the UM and I have come to realize that it is an entirely different culture than the campus, than Greek Life, than almost anything else I have gotten to know. People in the art school are mostly those I would never have gone out of my way to be friends with in high school or in college because I did not think I would have had anything in common with them; at times I still feel like I don't. Many of my art school peers need to support themselves through school because their parents will not support them because they see art school as a waste of money. My parents, on the other hand, are completely supportive of me. I personally chose to pursue a bachelor of arts, which enables me to take a variety UM classes, but my parents would have supported me no matter what. Besides Michigan being expensive, the Art School is additionally expensive. Even though I do not need as many expensive textbooks, we are expected to purchase all our own materials for projects as well as buy the biggest most expensive version of the MAC computer, which costs up to $3,000 with all of the mandatory software. There are some grants, as well as financial aid, but my class background enables me to not have to worry about making my projects out of the cheapest material when others might look better. While one of my peers might be forced to use cardboard, I can use wood. The materials you use and how much you spend on projects are not taken to account when it is being graded. The appearance and the message of a project are what matters. Just like how you dress, art is a superficial career because people are always judging each other by their appearances.

My sophomore review in winter 2017 was a 20-minute presentation given to two faculty members of all of your artistic work leading up to that point. Passing or failing determined if I was able to continue with my major. The centerpiece of the presentation was a work of art that you spend the second semester of your sophomore year working on in a studio class. To help us to best prepare ourselves, my teacher brought in a professional artist to look at how our pieces were progressing. One of my friends presented his project in our whole class critique. It was obvious he was proud of it, but as soon as the visiting artist spoke, I could see it going downhill. His first critique was the project was made out of cardboard that made it look sloppy. My friend's face fell and I could almost hear him thinking: "What? Are you going to buy me a better material to use?" Even though money and the individual cost of things is something that consumes everyone's thoughts, from my experience it isn't always something looked at by people in the art world. I will not be following the path to become a fine artist, but if I wanted to, my parents would be able to pay for all of the materials needed to get me started. That is not to say that I am building art with gold bars or hundred-dollar bills, but I am blessed with the opportunity to create what I have in mind. The good news is that I did pass my sophomore review and will be continuing on to my bachelors of arts in the Stamps School for Art and Design.

I have been blessed with the ability to make my own choices based on what I want to do in life, not based on a lack of money. I will be forever grateful to my parents for working hard to give me a leg up in the world. I am proud to be graduating college in two years debt-free, and able to use the money I have saved up to start my own life. I know I will work just as hard to provide for my children and grandchildren because I was lucky enough to have others help me along the way; I look forward to it. I am excited to someday share everything I have learned with the man I am going to marry. Will he have the same drive and motivation to provide for our family? Will the amount of money that his family has influence my decision? Will we manage money in the same way or will it be a point of tension? As I have moved through my life, I have gained the most through my relationships with other people especially how they have enabled me to have a different and hopefully less naïve perspective on social class.

THE HIDDEN INFLUENCE

BENJAMIN FREY

Growing up I certainly wouldn't have called myself rich, nor was I poor. While a bit reductionist in nature, such labels are hard to avoid, especially when you're young. Having second-hand clothes, sometimes even the same clothes over several years, sometimes made me feel a bit separated from many of my class-mates. Even then I was never sure how to think of myself in regard to social class. We may not have been wealthy in money or status, but we were established and connected in ways that would greatly help me. When young, I cannot say I thought about money, status, or assets. I did not know what those words meant, but I had other things to think about.

When I was four years old in 1998 I collapsed while playing on the beach. While I don't remember the incident, I apparently did not walk for several days. My family had been visiting our cottage on the coast just outside of Manistee, Michigan. The three-bed-room cottage with a great big deck and a winding staircase to the beach was perched on top of the grassy dune overlooking Lake Michigan. My grandfather had gotten an excellent deal in the late 1980s because the water level was rising and the previous owners were faced with the tough decision of shelling out money to move the house back 200 feet or sell cheap to avoid being swallowed up by rising waves.

A common activity was to walk down the beach or wade in the water to "blood creek," a small stream running through the dunes to the lakefront. It always had a dark red tint, no doubt sediment and tannin runoff from surrounding hills. We spent our time sneaking along the bank trying to catch unsuspecting frogs that lounged in patches of sunlight shining through the canopy above. Our time at the cottage was always an amazing experience. Whether it meant roaming blood creek, playing Frisbee, swimming in the frigid lake waters, or reading a book while listening to waves lap the shore, it was a place to rejoice and relax.

After I collapsed, however, we had to take care of some shit.

When we returned from vacation, mom, who worked in the hospital system, was able to get me an appointment in orthopedics straight away. Her previous employment in the department meant we didn't have to wait several months. The doctors informed us that I had Perthes Disease, which meant at some point during development my left hip had not received enough blood flow; the ball of my hip joint had fractured inside the socket. Of four levels of severity, my case was categorized a four.

I would now need tons of physical therapy, weekly doctor's visits, and more X-rays than I care to count. Getting one morning a week off school meant spending time in the University of Michigan (UM) hospital in Ann Arbor. A favorite part of each visit was measuring myself against the statue of big bird between the orthopedic and radiology departments. Truth be told, I received excellent care. And it was almost entirely due to the excellent benefits mom received through UM hospital. Despite hating her job for as long as I can remember, she always appreciated the excellent insurance and the stability it provided. In addition to my illness, she had her own chronic condition, Type 1 diabetes.

Over the years she worked in a variety of departments, from orthopedics to obstetrics and gynecology doing patient intake, checkout, and scheduling. It didn't pay exceptionally well, but it had great benefits. Dad began his own business before I was born, and when I was young he was doing just about all he could to keep afloat. I learned later he was dealing with a significant amount of debt, which weighed heavily on their marriage. When I was about eight years old, they sat my brother and I, ages 13 and 8, respectively, down on our green couch with wooden arm rests and told us they were getting a divorce. I was certainly in shock, but would eventually recognize it was best for all of us.

There was no doubt this was a challenge for our family. At the time we lived in a two-story home in a neighborhood a few blocks from downtown Ann Arbor. After their divorce, mom and dad found new places to live, away from my childhood neighborhood. Mom lived in low-income housing on Ann Arbor's north side, despite having a financial advisor tell her there was no way she could afford to live in Ann Arbor. As she tells it, she refused to live outside Ann Arbor because it would disrupt my and my brother's lives. After meeting his new partner, Lisa, dad moved to Ann Arbor's wealthier upper west side. My brother and I lived one week on, one week off at each house. This provided an interesting cross-section of social class, not to mention race. When with mom, we were some of the few white folks in the area. I spent many days playing basketball with the local kids or running around parks and woods surrounding the complex. When with dad I spent more time downtown with some of my school friends, or playing video games in either my or my friends' basements.

When I began high school in fall of 2008, my time with dad also included walking through a wealthy neighborhood to the newly built Skyline High School, where I would be a part of the first graduating class. The facilities were amazing! Brand new everything and magnet courses that meant you could focus your courses on a certain field before graduating. I was really interested in the health and medicine magnet my freshmen year. It seemed fitting because at that time I was undergoing my second surgery. This time my left femur was to be lengthened to reduce the discrepancy in the length of my legs and to protect my spine and back muscles from misalignment and chronic injury. The first surgery had been a reconstruction of my hip joint. Once again I was thankful for mom's insurance, as total of $80,000 in medical expenses were accrued from these two operations. My family was only marginally responsible for these expenses and it became a running joke that my surgeries were luxury items I would never be getting—a new car for the first and a new boat for the second.

After recovering for most of my freshmen year, I sank into the world of academics and athletics with renewed vigor. I played soccer the fall season of my sophomore year despite only being out of physical therapy for less than a month. I was sincerely out of shape and contributing in a meaningful way was difficult. That winter, I began to find my community when I joined the rowing team. The program had begun that school year which meant I wasn't far behind the average athlete. The sport was nonimpact and still required a great deal of strength that assisted in the remainder of my recovery. I still believe I owe my level of mobility to my time on Crew.

At the same time, I was exploring the academic world. I took accelerated mathematics and Spanish, while also in Advanced Placement (AP) United States history. I solidified a strong mentality of working hard, despite this not always being the best for my body. Late nights and early mornings were common and as a result I was perpetually tired. I was convinced I had mono, but then realized that to have mono one had to get more than three hours of sleep per night, and still be extremely tired. Despite the exhaustion, I pushed myself throughout the duration of high school. I continued to row on the Skyline Crew team, which required as much as 2–3 hours a day of practice, plus three-day weekend competitions. I took more advanced classes: AP English language & composition, English literature, biology, and accelerated math.

By no means am I trying to argue this is a positive philosophy. In fact, I believe this type of anxious overachievement is a result of deeply instilled family and societal conditioning. From a very young age, we are exposed to experiences and messages saying productivity should be cherished and praised, and something to strive for. Perhaps, even one's significance as a person depends on work and academic achievements. Since my school was new, with beautiful facilities and new accelerated classes every year, without recognizing it at the time, I was being set up for a great many accomplishments, simply through my middle-class communities.

These messages were compounded with the fact I had the Michigan Educational Trust (MET) to financially prepare me for college. When I was about a year old, my grandparents and parents contributed $9,000 to MET. The account matured over the years and eventually would pay for 120 credits at any Michigan public college. If I decided to attend a private or out-of-state college, MET would pay the average semester tuition of public colleges in Michigan for every semester I attended. Not only was I driven because I liked to be challenged, but also I began to understand the gravity of my financial situation was dependent upon my performance in high school and my ability to get into a good college.

When it came time to apply, I had a lot to include in my applications. Combined with good scores, some heavily reworked essays, and a little luck, I made it into several colleges. Two leaders of the pack were the University of Michigan, Ann Arbor, and Kalamazoo College, in Kalamazoo, Michigan. I couldn't even begin to figure out how to think about where I might go. Kalamazoo, a small, liberal arts college, had fewer students than my high school. It was a private school, which meant I would be responsible for a greater amount of educational debt. This was juxtaposed with Michigan with more than 40,000 students, but still with many of the same opportunities at Kalamazoo. More importantly it was a public college. So the smart decision nearly two decades before meant my family's MET investment would mean I would be in less or no debt as I graduated from college. The acute distrust of debt I grew up with would not be a major problem.

This fit with some major lessons from my youth: making use of what I have, being resourceful, and keeping costs low. These were not always outright family statements, but I learned from watching. Mom bought secondhand, only purchasing new clothes if she could not find anything suitable. Even then, she shopped for deals and her black leather bound coupon book was always full. She never owned a new car; she bought them used and did not pass them on until the wheel wells were thoroughly rusted. Dad had a similar mentality and his work around the house contributed to this feeling. He was always very handy. He finished our basement before I was born and throughout my childhood he began to finish the upstairs bathroom. His actions reinforced those messages: Why pay someone when we have the skillset, or can develop the skillset, to do it ourselves?

These messages arrived verbally when mom shared childhood stories; little anecdotes would usually accompany some sort of lesson. When she was in first grade, my grandma made her a dress for school. It had strawberry print all over it—her "strawberry dress"—and she wore it every single day. One morning, it was not in her closet. When she asked her mom where it was, she said that she did not know and that she would have to wear something else. Mom later realized that her mother had thrown it away because she didn't want people thinking the family was poor.

Something my mother recalls fondly were the butter and honey sandwiches my grandmother would make. My mom always looked at these as a treat and loved the way the honey soaked into the bread and crystallized during the day. Years later, mom discussed this with a friend of her mother's. She discovered her mother had secretly been using food stamps throughout much of her childhood, and not even my grandfather was aware of this supplement. Even though mom fondly remembers those sandwiches, this new context made her realize these were the condiments my grandmother had left at the end of the week. Instead of her mother giving her a treat, it became her mother's way of getting by.

These experiences mom shared fell into what she called "depression era residue": this included saving incessantly and struggling to let go of things. She hung on to articles of clothing, shoes, or even Altoid tins because they "could be used for something." This mentality not only gave me ideas of what I should save, but also provided ideas about how I should spend money. I still remember, every time my mother and I would go to the shoe store, she would tell me: "Ben, you always spend money on your feet, teeth, and eyes. We only get one set and we have to take care of them." Even though this meant I inherited some idiosyncratic tendencies, such as being concerned about whether or not to save an insulated plastic bag (I mean, it could be used for something!), it also instilled a strong sense of not being wasteful, and taking care of my belongings. This was made stronger considering that dad cofounded a consulting company—Resource Recycling Systems—that assists with how to set up or improve recycling initiatives at city, state, or national levels.

With all of these ideas in tow, I decided to attend the University of Michigan; it would be less expensive. However, there were also many other reasons. I would be attending the alma mater of both my grandfathers, who had received engineering degrees, and as an Ann Arbor local I was already familiar with the city. I wouldn't have to acclimate to a new place and my family would be close to support me. I was very excited to start my college experience in fall of 2012 and I had a few friends who made the same decision. The first weeks in the dorms were very odd. One of the big changes was keeping track of my own money. Even though my financial stability was based almost entirely on my parents, I wasted no time looking for work directly after graduation from Skyline.

Starting college I was selling kitchen knives with a national marketing company. Between classes and homework I made sales appointments and handed out recruiting business cards on Diag less than 10 feet from the Michigan's famous block M. I eventually became disenchanted by individuals I worked with. They focused on money and material gain. Occasionally, the regional manager held an event at his house for the sales staff. His place was complete with a gorgeous kitchen, a cigar room, and multiple luxury cars, including a bright orange Porche. He wanted to show these off to the fresh-out-of-high-school sales folk. Being a college student and having less time to devote to the organization did not interest my managers. After all, they were paid based upon what I sold. Once they started asking me to miss classes, and I discovered many of the higher-ups had dropped out of college, I realized their priorities were not my priorities. There was too much selfishness and materialism to float my boat.

This was a major factor in my mind as I continued my college career. My courses peaked my interest and I gravitated toward careers that were fulfilling first, with money as background noise. I volunteered for multiple social justice education and advocacy groups such as the Sexual Assault Prevention and Awareness Center (SAPAC) and the program on Intergroup Relations (IGR). Beginning my sophomore year, I started work as a rowing coach on my former high school team. If I break my pay into hourly wage, I earned well less than minimum wage there, but coaching is first and foremost a labor of love. I could work with first-year high school students and help mold them into young adults, assisting them through triumphant steps and heartbreaking challenges. This was the payment I found valuable. Perhaps it did not go extensively toward paying for groceries, but it meant I could make an impact on young peoples' lives. After all, I was getting most of my meals from university dining halls, courtesy of dad's dime.

I eventually moved in with several hall-mates from my first year at Michigan. One was a fairly secluded fellow, from north of Detroit. I knew his family was well-off based on some purchases he talked about along with some of his habits. He would throw away glasses or other dishes. Disposable dishes and silverware were also frequents of his life. This drastically contrasted with my other roommate, Jonathan, a PitE (Program in the Environment) major. He and I got along very well and we would remain roommates for the rest of college.

One of the major things Jonathan and I discussed was money. At no point did I know the details of his finances, but he shared that he had taken out student loans in order to pay for school and this echoed through many of his behaviors. He would always pack a lunch, sometimes the leftover dinner he cooked himself the previous night. Rarely did he spend money on extras and when he did, he was celebrating.

Nicholas and I were the only ones—out of nine—to share a room; we split the largest room to live more affordably. What he and I shared most was a certain social class mentality. He came from a less affluent background. While I did not have to go into student debt like he had to, we were raised with similar traditions of money and wealth. That "depression era residue" mom always talked about is ultimately a careful attention to money and resources. I maintained a frugal attitude because I was raised to watch my money, while Nicholas maintained a frugal attitude out of necessity. Had it not been for MET or mom's health benefits, would I have been in a similar place as Nicholas, fighting to minimize an ever-growing set of student loans?

Between my sophomore and junior years, I was lucky enough to study abroad. I applied to a six-week summer excursion through the university's study abroad program and was accepted to go to Spain. I was so nervous; if I had not gone to Canadian Nationals through my coaching position, it would have been the first time I was out of the country! Travel when I was younger was never focused on other countries. Those trips were always too expensive. Now I would be spending the bulk of my time in Salamanca, Spain, taking classes at La Universidad de Salamanca and we could travel as much as we wanted during the weekends.

Many aspects of this trip were very difficult for me. While dad helped out with close to $7,000—I have never been comfortable accepting large sums of money—I was responsible for the money I wanted to spend. This was something I was more than happy to do. I did have a job and had saved money mom had given me. Despite this, I struggled to spend money in Spain and it took a couple of anxiety-filled Skype conversations with friends and family, especially with dad, to allow myself to spend some money I had saved. I consistently aimed for less expensive trips. I always traveled train, as this was the cheaper option, and I carried my familiar frugal money habits across the Atlantic Ocean. I was willing to spend a few dollars on snacks or experiences, but not willing to spend the kind of money I saw some of the others spending.

This was one of the most shocking parts about studying abroad, how openly my peers spent their money. The program consisted of 30 other University of Michigan students. Everyone else was in the Romance Language & Literature department and was getting course credit. Many of them are dear friends, and all are exceptional people. However, taking a 30-person sample of the university community does not provide a drastic range of social class experiences, especially when you take into account these students are those who could easily afford to study abroad.

One of my most uncomfortable social class experiences came from getting to know a good friend, Tom. We bonded over the fun of being in another country and taking in all the experiences. We played soccer with the locals and had coffee after the afternoon siesta. We drank until the sun came up, as is the culture in Spain, and bartered to get ahold a little marijuana. However, this did not shelter Tom from his class status and the blindness it brought to the table. I cannot pretend to know anything about his finances or his family's financial position. However, I did know he had already spent a semester studying abroad in Asia and, the following academic year, spent another semester in Argentina. Clearly he did not have the same financial limitations that were a large part of my life.

He talked about the yoga classes he was taking or the juice cleanse he was currently undergoing. These were subjects I was happy to talk about, but ones I could not really relate to because they were expensive. During the year after our study abroad, he suggested we room together for our senior years. I was excited about the prospect as it would be amazing to live with the friend I had made abroad! The plan was for the two of us and two other friends to find a place. I was extremely busy at the time so he said he would set up a few apartment viewings.

As the time of our viewing approached, I typed in the address he sent me into my phone's map system. It was a sunny, cool day in early October and the breeze was brisk. Before long, I realized where I was walking. I was in one of Ann Arbor's expensive high-rise apartment areas near campus. Immediately, I knew this was going to be an uncomfortable, if not borderline laughable, experience.

The amenities provided were expansive: laundry and cleaning services, 24-hour fitness center, rooftop and computer lounges, yoga rooms, and free underground parking. I didn't even have a car.

Throughout the tour I was giggling under my breath. I couldn't imagine not having personal responsibility for my laundry and having a rooftop lounge seemed more like something from a movie. Moreover, the pamphlet I held said I could have all this for the meager price of $1,250/month. Keep in mind that wasn't the entire price, but was what a single room in the apartment would cost. This was more than three times what I paid for my shared room with Jonathan.

After leaving, I called dad to vent about this ridiculous experience. He made sure I understood he wouldn't be helping me with rent. I struggled to know how to react. I went through a period of being angry with Tom and realized I was jealous of him. How could he afford such an extravagant environment? How could he afford to go on 30-day juice cleanses: juices bought from the high-priced grocery store next door to the apartment building we had visited. How could he afford to study abroad three times during his undergraduate career, while I had so much anxiety about spending money for just one overseas experience? Above all else, I was jealous about how carefree he could be all the time, how untroubled he could be about money, his career, and classes. More than anything though, I was sad I wouldn't be able to live with my friend, and embarrassed I would have to explain to him that I could not afford it.

It is hard to write about social class partially because we cannot tell our own stories in unbiased ways. We tend to emphasize our challenges and minimize our advantages. It's always easier to talk about instances where we were bullied, teased, or made uncomfortable by our class disadvantage than it is to acknowledge when and where we hold social class privilege. In both cases, the reflection is on a situation we did not deserve. However, frustration at perceived injustices against oneself feels more righteous than admitting you did not have to work as hard as someone else. For these reasons, I struggled to know what to include in this essay. *What do I have to share that is of any value about class experiences?* I asked myself: *Are the main struggles of my life not related to class?* Herein lays the evasiveness of social class and class experiences. So often, it is not the main focus of life. Instead, class is the background noise muddling sounds of experience; rarely on the main stage, yet providing the set and lighting through which the main protagonist walks.

This is, in fact, the main value of these stories. We are bringing attention to what is not discussed, which holds great insecurity, and is too often dismissed as personal struggle everyone has and everyone must navigate. We think of the benefits of wealth and the limitations of poverty, as opposed to the differences in standpoints created by various social class positions. As other class commentaries acknowledge, those among the lower class tend to develop resourcefulness created by the instability of their financial situations. Folks on the opposite end of the spectrum, to whom financial struggle is a foreign idea, become paralyzed by drastic change or system breakdown; their anxiety is caused by the stability their financial station creates for them. Through discussion of this elusive concept and exposure to its insidiousness, there are valuable lessons to be gained from perspectives of people living differently than us. It is through this understanding that we can gain a more holistic view of the world. The end goal being that through greater understanding, there is enough opportunity for the alleviation of class inequality and struggle.

What can I say? I have had a relatively easy time with money. There have certainly been times when money was tight, and there have been times when I have had to worry less. I have been incredibly lucky to grow up with a family that instilled hard work, resourcefulness, and an ability to get by with less. Moreover, I am lucky they have placed such a high value on my education and have been able to support me financially through school and other struggles. Having had jobs where money is the priority, as well as jobs where value lies in the service to others, I am coming to realize I need a healthy balance between the two. Being able to make this decision is a privilege and my family has put me in a position to seek out such a balance.

Being a little more than a year out from college graduation, I still find myself in somewhat of a conundrum with directions I would like to pursue. Wherever I go, I will maintain class consciousness as a part of my life. An integral lesson the hidden nature of social class differences has taught me is everyone I meet is fighting an invisible battle I know little about. I am dedicated to being kind, considerate, and understanding. Always.

Resiliency

Mya Haynes

Growing up, it never really occurred to me what social class was. Perhaps this is because I lived in a Chicago neighborhood (commonly known as the "Low End") with people who looked like me, talked like me, and dressed like me. I remember going out to play in the backyard with my older brother and friends who lived in our apartment. Freeze tag, jump rope, and gate-climbing were staple activities we found entertaining. As I grew older, the "games" we played became a bit more risky.

I remember one night we all decided to throw small rocks at the building next door—an open restaurant. A man came out yelling, telling us to stop throwing rocks, and we would all run away and hide until he went back inside. Then we began throwing them once more. Tired of our shenanigans, the man called the police. We all ran once we saw the roaring red and blue lights as the Chicago Police Department vehicle parked on the other side of the gate. I remember my heart beating uncontrollably as I hid outside the basement with my brother, crouched behind a staircase. We stayed quiet and I guess the police didn't see any reason to hop the gate or take any additional steps to find us—the rock-throwing culprits.

All the kids in our apartment had parents who worked during the day. Even when we were told to stay in the house, my brother and I would sneak out to play with everyone else. I was a bit of a tomboy, so I found myself picking fights with a girl my age who lived above me. I remember attempting to climb the gate and falling down, hurting my hand so badly that I had deeply cut the crease in the palm of my hand. As a chubby kid whose weight and health were often questioned by my doctor and family members on dad's side, this was as far as my tomboy characteristics went. I never could play sports; but I do have a permanent scar across my nose from a Double Dutch rope that slapped me in the face when I tried to jump in.

I often wonder what my life would have been like had I stayed in this neighborhood. I lived there from the time I was in kindergarten starting in 2000 until about third or fourth grade. I was unaware of the fact there was an abandoned building down the street, or that some nights our meals consisted of noodles and hot dogs, or baked beans and hot dogs. I ate these meals as if they were prime rib, relishing in the processed goodness that filled my stomach.

My family—which consisted of mom, my brother, and me—moved quite often throughout childhood. We always lived on the south side of Chicago, but scattered around neighborhoods as we slowly crawled up the class ladder. Mom had become a house developer, and we ended up moving into one of her first buildings. Built from the ground up, this was the first home where I lived. There was an upstairs, downstairs, and basement, and when we first moved in the neighborhood the house seemed nice. Soon after we settled, we learned the block was where two prominent gangs intersected.

When New Year's Eve and the Fourth of July came around, it was often difficult to differentiate between the fireworks and gunshots. The island in our kitchen became a shield for the battle ground where we resided. We would duck behind the island until the roaring gunshots and firework concoctions subsided.

There weren't any kids in the neighborhood for me to play with anymore. As my brother grew older and attended high school, he often faced problems with other students and gang members. After being jumped, he began hanging around the wrong crowds in search of safety. I watched from a distance as I noticed my brother and I slowly drift off into separate worlds, even though we lived under the same roof.

When dad remembered to pick us up, my brother and I would go to his house on the weekends, but we had to stay up until 2:00 a.m., when he got off work at Rose Packing, a meat factory. Despite his job, dad lived well with his new wife and her two children, bouncing back and forth between Plainfield and Naperville, Illinois. There was a clear distinction between my time there versus being at home. Dad and his wife had a trampoline in the backyard, and there was always a pool somewhere in the cul-de-sac. They were often one of the only black families in his neighborhood. I was the youngest of five (now the second youngest of six) children, all on dad's side—all girls besides my older brother. Dad was always frugal—so asking for money was a hassle and created the most arguments between him and mom.

The elementary school I attended for the longest period of time was Andrew Jackson Language Academy (AJLA), a high-ranking public school located near downtown Chicago. This was the first time I had truly been exposed to individuals of ethnic backgrounds different from my own. My closest friends were Filipino, Mexican, and Italian. The melting pot of racial backgrounds provided my first real experience of what society actually looked like. Rather than studying Spanish, as I had in previous schools, I began taking Japanese courses. The other kids had been learning languages since kindergarten, so when I transferred to AJLA in fifth grade (fall 2007) I had a lot to catch up on. Nevertheless, after a few bumps in the road as a result of adjusting to a more academically rigorous school, I was able to succeed and excel.

Everything seemed to be going well. Mom had been able to sell her newly built homes, and she was considering relocating us all to a safer neighborhood. It amazes me how quickly life can change.

At the age of 12 I was robbed. And no, I don't mean someone taking my bike or some materialistic object. I was robbed temporarily of my sanity. My family and I were permanently robbed of our sense of safety and security. I was robbed of being able to stay in Chicago, go to a nearby high school, and be with my close friends whom I had known since the fifth grade. I was robbed of my childhood. I was robbed of feeling normal. I was robbed, but even more than me I would say my brother was stripped. He was stripped of his best friend, who died on a warm summery day in August 2009. He was stripped of an opportunity to be able to attend college three days later, after working so hard to graduate from high school with honors.

My brother and his best friend were robbed and shot in broad daylight. His best friend was shot twice, and died during surgery before his mother was able to see him. I remember this day as if it were yesterday, the day that made me look at the world differently. I stepped into the intensive care unit (ICU) and stared at my brother surrounded by machines and cords. I couldn't eat or sleep that night. My brother was literally labeled John Doe in ICU and security vigilantly roamed the hospital floor. The robbery-turned-homicide was in the newspaper the next day and somehow our home address ended up in the story instead of my brother's best friend's address. The hospital treated my brother as if he were a gangbanger on the street who had been through this kind of thing before, instead of the college-bound, kindhearted young man I knew him to be. Rather than asking if he had medical insurance (spoiler alert: he did), a social worker arrived, holding a clipboard with information on how to apply. Somehow the color of his skin and the nature of the situation formed an easy equation that translated into "uninsured."

Because our address was in the newspaper, we feared for our safety. The suspects remained at large, and they knew there was a surviving victim. Rather than going home when my brother was discharged from the hospital we stayed in a hotel for a few days, hoping things would calm down. Once we finally went home, mom and I were taking our German Shepherd/Pit Bull outside for a walk. We were fearful as we watched a car with tinted windows drive down the street, slowly passing our building as if preparing to make a complete stop. We tried to act normal, watching our dog, but we were terrified. The car continued driving, and we went back inside.

That summer, my brother and I moved in with my uncle while mom worked on finding us a new home. For the first time in my life, I felt like I was the older sibling. As someone who wanted to be a doctor, I took full advantage of the opportunity. I made sure my brother took his pain medicine, helped him walk around until he grew strong enough to walk on his own again, and woke him up when he was having nightmares to tell him that everything was okay. My mother canceled the deal that she had in progress for her dream home, and instead found a home about an hour and a half away from the city, hoping that our new home would give my family safety.

As life finally began to settle down, my family and I were smacked in the face with another unfortunate event. On Valentine's Day in 2010, there was an apartment building fire, which killed seven inhabitants. Five of them were my cousins, the youngest being just a few days old. My aunt was devastated to have lost her children and newborn grandchild: she lost everything in the fire. My mother, her heart pure and filled with the gift of giving, paid for my surviving aunt and cousin to have new clothes and a place to stay as they worked to get back on their feet. After a few months, things finally seemed to calm down.

Later that year, my brother became ill on mom's birthday. We took him to the hospital, only to find he had a hole in his intestine from the initial surgery. The bowel had been leaking into his stomach for almost a year, and he required immediate surgery. At one point, a doctor told us it would take a miracle for him to survive. Mom looked at him, an older white man who could never understand our story, and without hesitation told him we believed in miracles. I don't know if it's because our family didn't look like we had enough money to pay medical bills or that my brother had been a gunshot victim, but he was discharged sooner than we expected. After slapping a colostomy bag on his side and telling us that he would need to have one for about a year, my brother was sent home.

At age 13, I watched him have a seizure right before my eyes because the colostomy bag was improperly placed, and he had lost nutrients he had been obtaining from normal eating and drinking. Having no clue what a seizure was until this occurrence, I was traumatized. I couldn't even stand to see someone shiver without getting anxious. After sending my brother to multiple hospitals to find someone who specialized in his condition, we were told that he never needed a colostomy bag to begin with. Four months and seven surgeries later, the colostomy bag was taken off.

I remember crying for no reason in particular; just knowing my life was so different from people I interacted with on a day-to-day basis. So different, in fact, that I never bothered to tell them what happened the summer before I turned 13 years old. I wondered if they could see it on my face or if they could look into my eyes and see everything that my family and I had been through. After a while, though, things began to go back to normal—whatever that meant. When I graduated from elementary school in 2011, my brother was in college and my family had moved into a new apartment building.

I didn't feel comfortable at the suburban high school I went to my freshman year. All the kids knew one another, and I was often the only black student in my honors classes. I noticed covert forms of racism taking place and soon realized I didn't want to go back. Because this was a suburban district, there were no other schools I could attend, so mom paid for me to take classes with a nationally accredited online home school.

We ended up moving back to Chicago the summer before my sophomore year of high school so mom would be closer to her job. This time, we made sure the neighborhood was quiet enough for my brother to feel safe when he came home from school. We lived around the corner from the University of Chicago, and I was able to attend a public school even though none of my friends from elementary school went there. The Hyde Park neighborhood seemed like a completely different world, and I couldn't believe it was just a few minutes away from the Low End. We lived in a high-rise condo with a doorman, and our neighbors consisted of doctors and lawyers.

Mom began a nonprofit organization called the Community Recovery Network. It enabled high school students from disadvantaged backgrounds to attend free college tours. The following year, she started the World's Largest Trunk Party—an event that ultimately provided over 3,000 students with free "trunks" filled with college essentials. A large sum of this money came from mom's pocket and it was a tribute to give back for all of the blessings we had received over the years. I volunteered with these organizations and loved seeing smiles on people's faces who came from a familiar background.

During my high school junior year, my world came crashing down once again—mom got sick and had a heart attack. She could not work, which meant our family didn't have a steady source of income. I began to realize we were living in a community that no longer belonged to us. A family who had just spent thousands of dollars was now placed on the receiving end as we asked for money from our close friends and family members. When prom season came around senior year, I told my family I didn't want to go because I knew we didn't have the money. However, mom didn't want me to miss out on the experience. My uncle and a few close friends paid for me to have a dress custom-made by a Chicago designer, as well as a makeup artist. These same individuals paid for my school fees as well. All played a large role in my ability to graduate.

I was accepted into the University of Michigan in Ann Arbor on a cold wintery day in December 2014. I could not have been happier. After receiving an additional letter stating that I had received a generous scholarship, I knew I was ready to be a Wolverine. I had been admitted into the Summer Bridge Program, so I began college in June 2015—just a few weeks after graduating from high school. I never forgot one of the first things said to all students during our orientation: "Don't send your refund check money back home." It would be tempting, but we needed to keep that money to pay for books and not have to worry about financial circumstances.

I looked at the speaker in shock. Did he know me? Would he be able to tell if my money didn't go toward school supplies? As a first-generation college student, I honestly didn't understand the concept of refund checks. If the money is in my account now, how could they possibly see what I'm doing with it? Long story short, I disobeyed the recommendation of the associate director of the

Summer Bridge Program. After all mom had done for me, how could I not?

The Summer Bridge Program was a great experience. My roommate became my best friend, and I felt like most of the students came from similar social class backgrounds. Once the fall semester began, I realized just how large the Michigan student population really was and just how underrepresented African Americans were on campus. I struggled with academics but kept problems to myself, as I quickly realized most of the students had parents with college degrees and came from financial backgrounds so extensive their parents could pay their full tuition and fees directly out of pocket. I hid my own struggles very well. My refund check and help from friends and family back home allowed me to feel financially secure so that I wouldn't have to worry about getting a job my first semester. Financial aid covered everything—what wasn't covered by my scholarship was taken care of with grants and a very small loan. I felt blessed to be in college, almost debt-free, and with clothes on my back despite my current financial situation.

I didn't know what the top 1% earners actually looked like until I began to see students who closely resembled what became my personal interpretation. The first things I noticed during my first large lecture class, Introduction to Women's Studies, were the sleek MacBooks everyone seemed to have except me. Had I missed the MacBook memo from the dean? I carried around a bulky, three-year-old 16-inch laptop. A device I relied so heavily on began to make me feel like an outsider, even though I was probably the only person who actually noticed. As I participated in research studies to have extra money in my pocket, students simply called home or reached into their likely trust funds to grab large sums without hesitation. I began noticing little things—how classmates wore expensive Michigan gear despite not being athletes, how an out-of-state student subtly raised her hand and mentioned her parents could afford to pay off all her school fees without hesitation because they made well over six figures. During winter 2017, for example, I noticed red and blue logos on almost everyone's jacket. I later learned these jackets were from the Canada Goose brand and usually cost anywhere from $500 to $1,000. It seemed like I was the only person surprised by these things, so I never bothered to question my observations out loud.

During winter 2016 semester, I decided to apply for another job because the psychology studies were getting out of hand—simple computer tasks and interviews turned into extensive time commitments handling hair, skin, and/or blood samples. I took a position as a front desk receptionist at a hotel located within the University of Michigan's hospital. I felt very accomplished, but a few weeks later my manager called to say she had misunderstood me during my interview. Because I wasn't planning to work during the spring/summer term, I would need to come to pick up my last check. So I was back to square one, searching for low-risk studies to participate in since it was too late in the semester to find a new job.

On the day of one of final exams in April 2016, we had been evicted from our home in Chicago. I dreaded going back and seeing the reality my family lived in. Luckily, mom owned both the unit we lived in and another unit on the floor above us that had not been sold. As I finished my exams at Michigan, my family worked tirelessly, moving all of our belongings from one unit to another.

The summer of 2016 I applied for jobs, but the rush of college students at home and my lacking prior work experience prevented me from getting any callbacks. We continued to live in our economic pitfall as mom struggled with getting a closing. Her increased stress of not being able to provide for her family and her cardiac condition landed her back in the hospital. I spent the night with her in the hospital, and the next day we received a phone call—we had been evicted from the other unit as well. We became officially homeless, all of our belongings remained inside but we were unable to have access. We had gone from going on a cruise for my 16th birthday and a trip to Puerto Rico during spring break to having nothing but the clothes on our backs. We hit rock bottom.

The association at the condo gave us less than an hour to gather some of our belongings out of the unit, and we moved into my aunt's apartment. Although we were technically homeless, I cannot say I know what that truly feels like. I was never outside on the corner, like the lady I passed each day when I walked to class in the morning before she died my senior year of high school. I never missed a meal, even during the times we didn't eat anything except loaves of bread, eggs, and hot dogs in meals that were transformed into breakfast, lunch, and dinner. When it was time for me to go back to college in Ann Arbor for the fall of 2016, I had to buy everything a second time, except for clothes I had piled into a contractor bag when we were allowed to grab a "few" things. Our loved ones continued to provide, making sure our cell phones stayed on, even when we had to switch to the free Android track phones at Boost Mobile.

My sophomore year of college (2016–2017) has been amazing, to say the least. I declared my major in sociology, became a peer advisor, became a paid research assistant, and am now a peer facilitator in the Barger Leadership Institute. I have been able to balance these jobs with classes and a social life, finally. Mom was recently able to close on a home, so we received our first real income. This was enough to foster hope and a newfound sense of comfort.

I have not told any of my friends at Michigan about my financial situation because I never had to—I always had money the few times I went out to party or went out to eat at a restaurant. When I went on the Alternative Spring Break trip to Texas freshman year, I had enough money to pay for food and a few Texas souvenirs. Mom always made sure I had everything I needed, and she never made me question whether or not we would make it through the next day, even though I knew there were times when her level of stress could have ended her life.

The resilience I developed throughout the years has made me a stronger person. I am sharing my story with the world hoping to inspire others to push through whatever life throws at them. Through it all, it is important to keep faith and hope alive.

Looking Both Ways: Reflections from the Middle Class

Michele Laarman

As any of the 1,000 students who live there will tell you, the basement of the South Quad dorm here at the University of Michigan (UM) has dozens of obscure nooks and crannies. I was perched in one such secluded booth with Caitlin, another first-year student who was becoming one of my closest friends on campus, reading articles for class in an effort to start the winter semester off right. As the clock approached 4:00 a.m.—a late night even by our standards—Caitlin announced that she was going to order a transcript for an application and then go to bed. A moment later she frowned, puzzled, and showed me the screen on her laptop. *Error*, it read. *There is a hold on your account.*

That could only mean one thing. Gently, I asked if she had paid her tuition for this semester. She quickly checked her account balance and sure enough, out-of-state tuition and housing charges upward of $50,000 stared back at us, overdue by a few weeks now.

"It will be okay. I'm sure this happens all the time. First thing tomorrow morning, go down to the financial aid office and ask about a midyear payment plan. They must have a procedure for this sort of thing. Try not to worry too much," I advised, my gaze still captured by the shocking figure on the screen.

Caitlin laughed it off. "I'll just text my mom. She'll pay it in the morning. I can't believe she forgot!"

The next day, I asked Caitlin if the hold on her account had been lifted. She assured me that just as she had anticipated, once her mom was made aware of the unpaid balance, she took care of it immediately. I chuckled with her at the ridiculousness of the situation, but I have a feeling that our laughter came from very different places. I could not wrap my mind around the idea that $50,000 had simply been forgotten, overlooked during the busy holiday season—but no matter, it could be paid overnight!

Though such wealth astonished me, I have a lot of privilege myself. I am the fourth child of two nurses. My dad has a bachelor's in nursing science from Grand Valley State University here in Michigan, and around the time I was born my mom began the eight years of night classes by which she advanced from a certificate of nursing to a bachelor's as well. I grew up solidly middle class. As my siblings got married and started households of their own, my parents continued to advance in their careers, and now the three of us reside at the cusp of the upper-middle class.

My parents raised my siblings and me with an interesting mix of class behaviors. My mother continues to clip coupons religiously and prefers to buy generic brands and sale items. Yet my parents signed me up for summer camp and in later years planned road trips to places like the Grand Canyon and Niagara Falls. In my sociology classes, I learned that middle-class parents tend to overschedule their children's time and spend the day hauling them from soccer practice to Chinese tutoring to flute lessons. I did enjoy a variety of private classes over the years, but I feel fortunate my childhood was mostly spent playing outside with friends and neighbor kids. I learned as much turning over rocks to look for bugs with the girl next door and challenging the boy down the street to wrestling matches (he claimed no *girl* could beat him) as I did in my ballet or viola lessons.

I lived in the same house from birth until I moved to Ann Arbor for college. The big square building, painted light blue with red shutters, is located at a southeast Grand Rapids (here in Michigan), intersection that borders two quite different neighborhoods. As one coworker bluntly phrased it, I live on the "right side of Burton Street"—the middle-class white side, that is. I certainly feel more comfortable walking on that side of the intersection than I do only five minutes farther north. Residential segregation, of both class and race, is very apparent in my part of town.

School segregation also characterized my early years. I went to a private Christian elementary school 10 or 15 minutes from home, where almost all of the students were also middle class and white. When I was in third grade, we got the news that the administration had run out of funding and the school was shutting down. Families who wanted to stay in the Christian school system had to choose between Millbrook, a wealthier and even more segregated elementary school, and Oakdale, which was less homogenous. I begged my parents to let me go to Millbrook, where many of my friends were headed. My parents, however, enrolled me in Oakdale, where my older sisters had gone years ago. Looking back, I can see that Oakdale was unique in that it was a mostly white, private school headed by a black principal and actively involved in the surrounding working-class, mostly black neighborhood. At the time, however, I resented the fact that I had to leave my modern school building with two playgrounds and a large, grassy field for a Prohibition-era three-story brick building that offered a small playground, a blacktop, and a dirt patch across the street to play in at recess.

Even though Oakdale boasted a wider range of student demographics than Sylvan and Millbrook, it was still a private school, and thus limited to families who had money or knew how to get one of the limited available scholarships. At that point in my life, the closest interclass relationships I had were probably at church. Like Oakdale, my family's church was located in a lower-class black area of town, and saw community involvement as a Christian duty. Sunday school and GEMS (a Christian girls' group) were open to children from the neighborhood. I felt uncomfortable interacting with the kids I perceived as loud, rowdy, and frequently disrespectful toward the leaders, and I often felt relieved when they did not show up to the meetings. With time, I got to know some of the girls who came more regularly. This helped me view them as complex individuals instead of merely stereotypes—and yet I continued to feel an almost tangible difference between us. I did not understand then that my uneasiness toward my peers from the community was borne of classism and racism.

It wasn't until I reached sixth grade that things really got interesting. That year, I left the Christian school system to attend a magnet program offered by Grand Rapids Public Schools. Blandford Environmental Educational Program brought 60 kids together in a trailer-turned-classroom for a year-long "alternative" learning experience. This was my first encounter with the proverbial salad bowl of real diversity. I soon became best friends with Mackenzie, a small girl with long, dark hair and soft features. We hung out before school and at lunch every day. One blustery November afternoon, we snuck inside during our lunch period to take advantage of the hot chocolate mix that was provided daily by our teachers. I was absolutely scandalized when Mackenzie poured the boiling water into a disposable plastic bottle. "What are you doing?" I can still hear myself exclaim. "Don't you know that you can't put hot things in plastic or you'll get cancer?" My parents had taught me about the carcinogens in plastic since I was old enough to use the microwave. I simply couldn't fathom that Mackenzie's parents did not give her the same education, whether because they did not know themselves or because they did not have the time and energy to treat every mundane interaction as a learning opportunity the way my parents did.

I didn't know then that by Christmas, Mackenzie would leave Blandford. She would move around, living with friends and relatives, and change her last name. Within three years she would give birth to a baby boy named Miguel. Mackenzie and I talked from time to time on Facebook, but I only saw her once since Blandford. When we met at the mall, she looked just as I remembered her—slender, with sweet facial features and the same dark brown hair falling down her back. We had fun chatting and catching up, but when we parted ways, I felt strongly that we were living in very different worlds. Everything about our lives seemed to be shaped by where we had been born on the social class spectrum.

At Blandford, I also made friends with people who were wealthier than me. One such friend was Lisa, who lived in East Grand Rapids, an affluent municipality adjacent to "regular" Grand Rapids. When I invited Lisa over to my house, I planned a special treat: walking up to get ice cream at the nearby cone shop. But when I proposed the idea to Lisa, she told me that she didn't think her mom would want her to walk around a neighborhood like mine. Nothing against *me*, of course—safety first, that was all. Maybe I could go to her house next time? I was shocked, because I lived on the south side of Burton Street, where yellow "caution" tape meant a downed power line and not a shooting. But in Lisa's eyes, I lived in a dangerous place where men yelled inappropriate things from across the street and you had to watch for shattered glass on the sidewalk. I started to better understand the relativity inherent to social class, how one's class background provides a lens through which everything else is interpreted.

The more I became aware of social class differences, the more I looked down on people who came from economic privilege. Even as I pitied Mackenzie for her small house, I scorned Lisa for her mansion, and I increasingly pegged wealthy kids as sheltered and oblivious to what life was like in the real world. Yet I was also very conscious of my own privileged upbringing. This led me to develop a sense of shame around my social class, and I tried to deemphasize my class standing around my friends. I was embarrassed about how much had simply been handed to me throughout my life. Essentially, perhaps, I was worried that I would be judged the same way I constantly judged others.

As my year at Blandford drew to a close, my parents offered me the chance to attend a magnet 7–12 grade public school called City High instead of returning to the Christian school system as originally planned. My parents value racial and socioeconomic diversity and they knew that there was little of either in Grand Rapids Christian Schools. With my parents' and siblings' encouragement, then, I chose to go with my new friends to City High. Middle and high school are formative years, and I consider this to be one of the most influential decisions of my life. As I moved from a school of 60 students to one of about 700, I was exposed to a much greater variety of people, and my awareness of a range of class experiences continued to grow exponentially over the next few years.

City did not have tracking. This had two main effects: each student took about the same number of advanced courses, and with the exception of high school math, students of different levels were mixed together in the same classroom at the same time. City also had a policy of only admitting new students through tenth grade. These factors meant students would inevitably get to know peers from different socioeconomic backgrounds, and would see those classmates as individuals instead of just caricatures. I believe this kind of interaction across social boundaries is one of the most powerful and useful lessons that can be learned in school.

However, social class and racial self-segregation was still a significant issue. From what I can tell, at City there was more interaction among people in different cliques than at many other schools, but the cliques certainly still existed. My closest friends were generally also white and located somewhere in the middle class. Another hugely problematic fact was that the most disadvantaged students are sorted out of City before reaching the upper-grade levels. The demographics of the seventh and eighth grades are much more diverse, both racially and socioeconomically, than the eleventh and twelfth grades. It is true that some advantaged students leave to attend affluent private or suburban schools, but students who are marginalized by class and race experience much higher rates of attrition. Many fail out or choose to leave because of the demanding academics and high workload. Others feel they do not fit in with the school culture and miss their friends at other GRPS (Grand Rapids Public School) schools. Thus even as I met people from many different social class backgrounds, I also became aware of how the education system reflects and perpetuates inequality by providing the best education to kids who already have the resources to succeed academically.

Toward the end of high school, I worked up to 20 hours a week at two jobs. At one, I tutored low-income, mostly Latinx elementary and middle school students a few days a week after school. I really loved working there and forming relationships with the kids. But I knew that like the (white, middle-class) volunteers from a local Christian college who made up most of the other tutors, I did not really understand their world. A little boy named Carlos most clearly illustrated this for me. Before digging into his math problems, Carlos and I would chat as he ate the sack lunch provided by the tutoring program—like the other tutors from outside the community, I always declined mine, able to bypass the shrink-wrapped sandwiches and mushy apples because I had a full fridge at home. One of the last days before winter break, Carlos was fuming. His mom had told him that because he and his three siblings were getting baptized soon, and the clothes for the ceremony were so expensive, they would not get any Christmas presents that year. "Not even one?" he had asked his mom. No, not even one. I pictured the mountain of presents under my own tree and cringed with shame at the comparison.

My other job was at a small grocery store near my house. Every shift there involved cross-class interaction. Strangely, standing at a cash register for 10 hours (no lunch break if the store was busy) for $7.40 an hour didn't seem to appeal to many middle- and upper-class people, so besides by fellow students, most of my coworkers were of the working or lower class. There were a few cases of parents and teenagers working together as coworkers, which was eye-opening for me. Personally, even having unrelated coworkers who were in my parents'—and in some cases, my grandparents'—generation was a significant adjustment.

It was not unusual for employees only to last a few weeks, so over the years I trained a lot of new workers. One such employee was Jasmine. The first thing I noticed upon meeting Jasmine, a single mother of three girls, was that she had JUICY tattooed in large letters across her chest. Jasmine had trouble showing up for work from the start. Without a car, she relied on rides from relatives and friends. She was pregnant and sometimes had to go home because standing for too long was painful. Other times, one of her daughters would get sick and she'd have to leave early or not come in for her shift at all. Jasmine liked working at the store, and she got along well with many of our customers, but she was fired before she even got off training. No one seemed to have much sympathy for her. Instead of a woman fighting many obstacles to provide for her family, she was viewed as a bad worker and a flaky person overall.

Our customer base reflected the socioeconomic range that is represented in and around my neighborhood. Well-to-do young adults, people my mom disparagingly calls "yuppies," came to support local business and avoid the lines at Meijer's. Poorer people came for the fresh food as well, but mostly because it was within walking distance for many. It was at this job that I learned how to show equal respect to soccer moms asking about our organic selection and young women who slowly put back their groceries when they learn we do not accept WIC (Women, Infants and Children). It was also at this job that I was exposed to some of the most overt classism that I've encountered. My managers and many coworkers mocked customers who bought pop and candy with EBT (Electronic Benefit Transfer) and profiled certain patrons based on their appearance and demeanor. I often caught myself behaving in classist ways too, like anticipating who would pay with food stamps or who would probably be walking and thus want their groceries double bagged.

When I put my two weeks' notice in that August, I didn't realize I would come back to work there the next summer relieved to once again be among "real people," who thought nothing of handling hundreds of pounds of vegetables and took smoke breaks and didn't give a damn about whether work experience or education should come first on a resume. I was very unprepared for the upper-class world I was about to enter. I knew that the University of Michigan was a wealthy school, of course—the very name conjures mental images of prestige and privilege. I saw the affluence for myself on my first campus visit. My friend Chrissy borrowed her dad's car and drove us up one sunny day for a tour. During the lunch break, we were sitting alone in the South Quad dining hall when our amiable tour guide brought his lunch over to eat with us. He had noticed that we were the only prospective students who had come solo. "You're so lucky your parents let you come by yourselves!" he declared. "My dad wanted to be by my side every step of the way." Chrissy and I just looked at each other. Really, we were lucky that our parents were working all day and couldn't accompany us? And yet, we did feel freer being on our own, independent among the group of khaki-clad high schoolers and their anxious helicopter parents.

Despite the tour guide's assumptions, however, my parents were involved in my college selection process and took me to visit several other Midwestern universities. It wasn't until late February that I knew for sure I was going to the UM. I had been sorting through the day's mail one afternoon when my attention was immediately captured by a large envelope, the kind that can fit a whole sheet of paper without bending it. I drew in my breath when I saw the address of the UM Office of Financial Aid on the top left corner. I tore the paper open and pulled out a fancy blue folder, which contained a letter congratulating me on receiving the Jean Fairfax scholarship. I let out a whoop and quite literally jumped for joy as I read the magic words: full tuition, all four years.

Because the letter identified the scholarship as merit-based, I assumed it was related to my grades or ACT (American College Testing) score. But the next day at school I found out that about a dozen of my peers—from a class of 78—received the same scholarship. I was excited by the prospect of having familiar faces in college, but I knew something was fishy. Some of my classmates had ACT scores 10 points below mine, and certainly we could not compete with kids who had private tutors or took ACT prep classes. So what "merit" did we demonstrate that marked us worthy of this mysterious full tuition scholarship none of us had heard of or applied to? I did some digging around online, but the only reference I could find on UM's scholarship pages directed students to refer to their individual award letters for information. Finally, I saw it mentioned on a webpage that listed ways UM is seeking to enhance diversity in the wake of the ban on affirmative action. One such work-around, which I believe may apply to the Fairfax, awards scholarships to students from underserved school districts. It clicked—I was receiving this scholarship because I attended GRPS.

I felt a little guilty about receiving the scholarship. My family's income was *only* $45,000 below the median at UM, and I was a white student whose parents both had college degrees. I was one of the most socioeconomically and racially privileged students at the most socioeconomically and racially privileged high school in my district, while my coworkers at the store were raising families on minimum wage. These contexts helped me recognize how incredibly advantaged I am. I struggled with the feeling that going to a diverse school made me somehow better, more socially aware, than my peers in private schools and wealthier districts. I knew this notion was wrong, partially because I shouldn't judge others for the benefits they were born into, but mainly because it was hugely hypocritical for me to criticize them for being sheltered when I live comfortably in my own sphere of privilege.

This was the mind-set I had when I entered college. I had been told by countless admissions brochures, online advertisements, and promotional videos that, at UM, I would have a unique chance to meet people who came from very different backgrounds than my own. This proved to be quite true—for the first time, I was surrounded by people whose family income was in the top 5%. Adjusting to this new social environment was perhaps the most difficult aspect of my first year here. It was also the most unexpected, because while I had been nervous about succeeding in my academic classes, the question of social class hadn't seemed like something to worry much about.

I felt like I could not relate to most of the people I was meeting. I didn't dress like them, talk like them, or—crucially, it seemed—party like them. But to be honest, I made mental efforts to maintain the distance between us. I feared that if I let my guard down, I would start to see the world through an upper-class lens and would lose what small perspective I did have. This has already happened to some extent. I am still afraid that despite my major in sociology, by the time I graduate, I will have little practical understanding of the reality of class in the United States.

My attitude toward money also complicated my ability to form friendships. In any capitalist society, diversion is linked to consumption, but this is especially true on college campuses. When a new acquaintance would invite me to a restaurant or movie, I was afraid that saying no would hinder my chances of becoming friends with them. My strategy of suggesting a free activity instead has gained me a reputation for being stingy. Often I stay behind to save money, and my friends tease me about being antisocial because I rarely venture off campus with them. In dating, too, I fear I will be seen as no fun or as overly frugal if I opt out of dates that cost money. Nor do I want my significant other to pay more than his fair share, in part because I don't want there to be inequality or resentment in the relationship, but mainly because I really do have enough money in my savings account to do these things. I fully deserve to be called a penny-pincher, because my reluctance to spend is a choice and not a necessity. I have money in the bank that I can fall back on, and whenever I do want to buy something or go somewhere, I can.

This is the contradiction of middle-class economics: there's good money in the bank, but it's there because of conscientious saving habits. By what other logic would spending $15 on dinner at a restaurant be okay, but adding a $2.00 drink be an unacceptable splurge? What about being able to afford to travel and stay in hotels overnight, but compulsively hoarding the complimentary soaps and shampoos? As I have come to realize, saving money and planning ahead are themselves classist attributes. My working-class coworkers spent money on snacks throughout the day because they weren't saving for college like me. People poorer than them might not have money to spend on snacks, but nor can they save or plan ahead, since they may barely have enough income to survive day to day.

Despite the challenges that accompany social class difference, I did form a good group of friends at UM. Two, including Caitlin, are wealthy out-of-state students, two are from affluent suburbs of Detroit, and one is a low-income student from out of state named Eva. One afternoon Eva and I were doing homework in my dorm room. She was telling me a story about her dog who had been injured and temporarily couldn't walk.

"She's so cute when she's decapitated," Eva said, pulling up a picture of her dog with a cast on her paw.

"Decapitated?" I repeated with a laugh. "Looks like she has a head to me! Do you mean incapacitated?"

We couldn't stop laughing about the rather significant semantic error. That was the beginning of a running joke among our friends' group about Eva's frequent misuse of the English language. It wasn't until later that I realized how classist laughing at someone's mispronunciations and linguistic mix-ups is, even if Eva herself laughs along.

Now Eva and I live together in a co-op. At $590 a month, including utilities, all meals, and even laundry, the co-op system offers some of the cheapest housing in Ann Arbor. Several of my housemates are wealthy out-of-state students, but they do not flaunt their class status the way that other upper-class students on campus, especially those involved in Greek Life, often do (whether intentionally or not). My fellow co-oppers buy their clothes at Salvation Army, though as much for environmental, anti-capitalist, and aesthetic reasons as for cost-effectiveness.

Clothing is an important aspect of self-expression, but it is also critical to professional success. I had my first taste of business formal earlier this semester when I applied to the Development Summer Internship Program here at UM. I spent a lot of time practicing difficult interview questions and reformatting my resume, but one of the most stressful parts of my preparation was trying to find something to wear. Fortunately, UM offers a service called Career Closet, where students can receive free business clothing that is donated by staff and faculty. With my Career Closet blouse, my (slightly stained) black blazer, and my borrowed skirt and tights, I was almost as well-dressed as the other candidates in my group interview. But they all appeared much more at ease, not just in their tailored suits, but with the environment in general. I suppose they had been in professional settings many times before and knew intuitively how to act. I, on the other hand, have never seen my parents dress, talk, or carry themselves this way. My mom and dad did not cultivate upper-class instincts in my siblings and me. I am generally happy about this, but I do feel like it puts me at a disadvantage when I compete with other UM students for jobs or internships. Even though I could go to the store and buy nicer clothes, there is no way I can consciously learn everything that comes naturally to people raised in the upper class.

Thus I do envy wealthier students in some ways. They are comfortable in the professional world, and they have amazing opportunities to do things like travel. Yet my negative inclination toward them is closer to disdain than jealousy. I still don't fully understand why I tend to look down on upper-class students, and I know that I have absolutely no right to do so. I claim they live in a bubble and do not understand the real world—but I am equally naïve. How can I scoff at them for not having worked in high school, when I did not work during my first year of college so I could focus on my studies? What right do I have to scorn their debit cards linked to their parents' accounts, when my parents paid for my dorm and meal plan my first year? How hypocritical of me is it to speak condescendingly of students who have their own expensive cars on campus, and then ask them for a ride? It's time that I frankly acknowledge how much I have in common with the wealthy students of this campus. Once I can do that, I will be able to more clearly see the individuals behind the "sheltered rich kid" stereotype. After all, Lisa taught me as much as Mackenzie did, and Caitlin is as good a friend as Eva. Every student here has a story that deserves to be heard.

My Class Experience: A Tale of Not Knowing Where I Belong

Brittany Lowell

Here I am, sitting on the porch of the villa that my friend's aunt is renting, listening to the waves of the ocean as they crest onto the beach, enjoying the sun, and realizing how lucky I am to be spending my spring break somewhere other than in the cold, bitter winds currently blowing through Michigan where I live and go to school. This comes with privilege, privilege that I gained through my parents, but also through working four jobs while taking a full course load. What others call privilege, I call a combination of hard work and dedication that functions alongside privileges one is born into, whether monetary or as a characteristic of oneself that outwardly shows. I utilize the coexistence of privilege and hard work to see through the opportunities and experiences I want to have, but I also recognize that without my friend's aunt giving us a place to stay while minimally contributing, I too would be stuck in Michigan like so many others who cannot afford to go away on spring break due to having to choose between somewhere warm or rent/groceries for the next two months. Most spring break excursions cost upward of $500 to go somewhere remotely warm and have a decent amount of activities and experiences to bring back and tell friends about. There are people who experience lower-class backgrounds than me but who are not afforded opportunities because they lack the privilege I unknowingly was given at birth. But with this privilege I had a birth that came at a cost which I would find out about in high school: bankruptcy from debts.

From a very young age, my parents never really talked about money, how bills or groceries were paid for, or where we stood in comparison to those around us. Looking at family pictures, I can tell we were loved and my parents did their best to give us a healthy and productive childhood. I know that from birth to the age of two and a half that myself, my parents, and eventually a younger brother, born when I was almost two, lived in a small two-bedroom apartment along U.S. Highway 127 in a rural area of Michigan. Our little apartment building was a 15-minute drive from the nearest city, St. Johns. The building sat on a decent amount of land, which my mom said was great for me to play in, with a small diner across the street, and surrounding farmland. A few miles further down the highway on one side, there was a cider mill and down the other there was a vast swamp area. From what my father tells me, he was at a lower-paying welding job and my mom had just gotten a job at the state of Michigan in the Treasury Department. All of these details indicate what they have now told me: their combined income put us just on the cusp of the middle class.

Fast forward to when I was two and we moved to a house in a rural city called Laingsburg, Michigan, with a front, back, and side yard totaling over six acres where I would spend the rest of my childhood. Our nearest neighbors were a mile back in the woods and someone across the street that had 10 or more acres of land. Eventually we would use the field space that we called our side yard for planting hay. Growing up, my siblings and I would play outside with the few toys and gifts my parents could afford. For the longest time our only backyard decorations were a lone sandbox and a hand-me-down climbing structure from one of my father's siblings. While we knew a lot of the things that we owned were hand-me-downs, we were never really fazed by it, rather we were thankful. And when we weren't grateful, as we grew older, my parents lectured us that "money doesn't grow on trees." This was the first hint that pointed to a monetary value placed on just what we were able to do and not do as children; it was the basis for the undertones of how I would come to reflect on the social class system. My views are by no means radical; I understand that the class system has injustices and that each person has a place in that system. While I see it as unfair, I also see it as having a purpose and being shaped by the experiences that everyone has, from class at birth to unfortunate circumstances they encounter, with the possibility of mobility.

As I grew, I knew I was lucky to go to the school I attended. Most of the teachers were interested in helping their students achieve the potential they saw within them. While our programs weren't super developed, we were still at a point where we were afforded an art class for part of each school year in elementary school where we got to make and take home clay sculptures and other small paintings. We also had a separate room for all the science classes, and out of the two gyms, one functioned as a lunch room. While we had to use some spaces for multiple purposes, we were able to actually have programs that were being cut elsewhere due to budgets. Looking back now, it really indicates the class level of my school system; most of the families in the area were middle class and that provided the school with art, gym, and a decent science program. But this also impacted my social class confusion; while we did have more programs than some schools, we had significantly less than others making it hard to tell just where in the class structure we were located.

Moving on to a new middle school, since the old one had burned down, each grade was separated into their own pods. The logic behind these pods was that they would go about helping to facilitate growth and the experience would make you closer to your classmates, which wasn't necessarily that hard when each grade consisted of somewhere between 70 and 100 kids. But while they were still able to offer band, they would cut choir and eventually art from the possible extracurricular activities due to not being able to afford them. We also saw budget cuts to the special education program. A couple of years before I entered middle school, a home-economics course was eliminated. These budgets cuts were a clue that while there are programs that really help school children to grow and nurture their talents, they are not available to some and this is a reflection on the social class structure and money available to schools

Middle school was about the time I started realizing there were other people in school who were like me in a way since they did not have the most recent clothing, the popular brands, and their clothes looked worn and used like hand-me-downs I received. But then I began to notice that although we were alike in that aspect they were also different because they were on reduced or free lunch. While going through school I took it upon myself to observe my surroundings and so I knew that most kids would try to hide the fact they were on free or reduced lunch, as if it were something to be ashamed of. But this interaction made me think back to how my mom would freak out every year when the prices of lunch would go up, how she had three kids to pay for lunches eventually, and that there always seemed to be a struggle when it came to that Monday after two weeks of lunch money had run out and another $80 had to be found for lunch for the three of us kids. This subtly was an implication there were others with varying degrees of money troubles and that everyone I encountered didn't have the same amount available to them. But I guess it never really dawned on me fully that this was called social class and that these were the struggles; this realization would come soon though.

There was also a time in middle school when my parents began encouraging and even flat out telling us that if we wanted anything in life, be it a new book or toy, we had to actually work for it; that there was no such thing as a handout. This was about the time I started working on my grandparents' farms during the summer not only to make a little money so that I could get some of the things that I wanted, but also because it was a requirement if we

MIDDLE CLASS | 213

were to go over there. My grandparents by no means were well-off in a monetary sense, but they did show how they worked hard for their money, and so they enjoyed some luxuries my parents didn't have. With my uncle was still living with them, they were able to afford cell phones, cable, and—most important to me at the time—the Internet. This was an escape and even though I had to pick up rocks in the field for hours, learn to drive a tractor to help with planting fields, and do yard-work or chores around the house that were strenuous on my grandparents, I still cherished the life lessons I learned from doing these activities. They taught me the values of hard work, determination, and doing a job thoroughly so that it didn't have to be redone; the work taught me respect, patience, and the appreciation for those who do hard labor.

After a while though, I realized other people my age were doing more with their summers than working for their grandparents, exploring nature, and occasionally going on excursions up north to a relative's cabin. Rather, they were going on extensive vacations outside the state, some even flying to Cancun, Mexico, and other exotic places that were expensive and definitely outside my parents' budget. They would come back with stories of how amazing this or that state was, what their parents just bought them, or how they were going someplace cool again in just a few short months. And not only did they bring back stories, but a lot of them returned to their modern and expensive homes, quite a few of which were located on one of the three lakes that surrounded the town we lived in. They would also say how they spent weeks just going out and being on the water in the summer and how their parents were always taking them jet skiing or tubing. When they would ask what I had done I would just say I had a busy summer and that we were able to go up north a couple times, all the time feeling inadequate and out of place. Looking back, this was probably due to social class anxieties that were present in drastic differences between some of my classmates and me. But this was not yet the catalyst that really made me aware of social class; that was yet to come.

Moving on to high school, it was much of the same as middle school: the consistent feeling of being caught somewhere in the middle of the spectrum of those I attended school with. Still stuck in the same perpetuating cycle of not feeling good enough, but feeling bad when I complained that I didn't have what I wanted. I realize now how petty and grossly mistaken I was thinking that just because I didn't have the newest gadget it was the end of the world. Most of the time my parents had food in the house; they always made sure the heat, light, and mortgage payments were made so we had a place to live; and we never went hungry. Granted a lot of the time they would bring home some form of takeout rather than make a meal, but they didn't let us starve. Looking back, maybe this was also a clue, but I just thought it was due to being too tired at the end of a workday to make dinner. And then there was possibly the moment that changed it all; one word, 10 letters. Bankruptcy.

This word so often brings with it stigma and a sense of failure. The collectors calling every day for my parents and having to tell them that they weren't home and we didn't know when they would be home was probably the first warning sign I was too oblivious to see. The next was that my parents would consistently be getting bills in the mail: multiple envelopes from the same bank or company throughout the month. And finally, whenever it came to asking my parents for money to go to the movies or some activity the answer was always: "We don't have the money right now," or there was just a frustrated sound before they calculated how much they could spare. What I would learn later is that neither of my parents were good with money, that my mom had extensive medical bills—from her hip problems—that were outstanding due to inadequate health-care coverage before working for the state, and that they did not communicate their monetary needs with one another in an effective way that paid the bills and allowed them to save money.

As it was my senior year of high school when this happened, I like to think I was immediately more self- and social class conscious as a result. I started to complain less, tried to work a job to alleviate stress on my parents, and in general started to think about how my going to college would have to rely more than ever on scholarships, grants, and loans. Even though my parents are considered middle class, making around $100,000 a year, they still carried with them the debts of their past when they were part of the working class. I like to think that while the monetary amount assigned to their taxes every year tells one story, their experiences and previous obstacles create another story, one at odds with the new one. The reality of our situation was that whereas our fridge wasn't really stocked in the past, now it was even less so. Extracurricular activities were no longer an option more than once a month, if that. Prom in my senior year of high school was also out of the question. It made me realize that with money comes responsibility and I started to lend my parents money when they couldn't always make ends meet or needed to give us lunch money, but didn't have any. It created a senior year full of stress and worry. As I moved forward with college applications, I began to realize that a lot of the schools I applied to I really could not afford, especially the University of Michigan (UM). And soon after filling out the FAFSA (Free Application for Federal Student Aid), it quickly became apparent that even with bankruptcy on record and my dad receiving wage-garnished checks, my parents were still not poor enough to qualify for financial aid, yet not rich enough to actually afford helping me through school. Where did that leave me? I didn't actually know, I just knew I had to be conscious of the fact that I would continue to be on my own when it came to affording school.

Choosing to come to the University of Michigan, one of the most prestigious public schools in the country, is and was possibly one of the hardest decisions of my entire life. I knew coming here would mean having to take on debt that would accumulate to more money than I had seen in my entire life. If I didn't get a job when I graduated college, I wouldn't know how I was going to pay it back. But despite that, my parents encouraged me to get the best education that was available, and ultimately I decided they were right.

Since coming to Michigan, I have obtained and kept not one but three campus jobs, which include being student manager in dining, a facility supervisor at a recreation center, a field supervisor, and have continued to work at them over the course of four years. I also decided to become a Mary Kay Cosmetic consultant during my senior year, my fourth job and outside of the university. I know these jobs play a large role in how I view the social class dynamics here at the university. Sometimes I can't help but feel out of place on this giant campus. My freshman year I was placed with a roommate who was part of the Summer Bridge Program. Bridge is supposed to be for lower-income students who come from less-privileged backgrounds to have a chance to integrate into campus before actually starting in the fall semester. While I was never quite sure of her social class, my roommate would come home once a week with bags from the mall and stores like Windsor, Abercrombie, and Michael Kors. It frustrated me there was so much she could buy and I was barely scraping by on what I made at my first two jobs; tuition and staying enrolled were more important to me than the latest fashion trends.

When I started my second job halfway through my freshman year, social class became much more evident to me. Most of the other students I talked to were from families that were considered working or middle class, and they needed jobs in order to afford rent, utilities, and groceries that were not included in their loans and grants for tuition. They strived to make ends meet, often living paycheck to paycheck and wishing they could have mom and dad pay off their balances and come out debt-free. I was and continue to be in a similar position; their struggles were very much like mine and I continuously would be appreciative to know that I wasn't alone. People like this offered a community in which I was welcome, found support, and made some friends. Then I would meet the people who made me wonder if being upper-middle class was really what I wanted, the people who perpetuate all of the bad stereotypes about the rich being entitled and only wanting to further themselves. I once heard another student worker who did the minimum that was required of her and always acted like she had better places to be saying the only reason she worked was "because mom and dad didn't give her enough spending money each month." This meant her parents were paying for rent, utilities, and groceries, and also giving her an allotted amount of money to spend; but it wasn't enough. This whole situation baffled me because it wasn't like she needed the job she had, rather she wanted the money for drinking and going out; to have that luxury was an unattainable dream for me. This seemed drastically unfair she would only have a job when it suited her and that she did not care otherwise because at this point I was already paying on my student loans and was lucky if I saw $20 from a paycheck for spending money.

I've also heard people explain over my four years here at Michigan that if it were not for mom or dad pushing them to get a job for the experience, they would not have even considered it. Rather than being at work, they wanted to go party and do fun things with friends, and that really showed; their work ethic was vastly lacking as well as underdeveloped, and their work experience honestly seemed to have no benefit for them. These two interactions gave me a bitter taste for the top 5% upper-middle-class students who seemed to be a major force across campus. While I did find those who were from middle- and working-class backgrounds or who needed to work to afford school, they were lost in a sea of Greek letters, Timberlands, Patagonia, and Michael Kors purses. Essentially those of us who had to work were invisible; there was limited space for us in the ever capitalistic and money-hungry machine that society and the university have become.

Through the course of my four years at the UM, I decided to major in psychology and minor in women's studies, specifically the LGBTQ+ concentration. The classes I have taken and people I have meet have encouraged me to want to pursue a master's degree in social work. One such course is a psychology class where I was placed in a daycare for two days a week, four hours each day—working with 2ffl–3ffl-year-olds. This developmentally focused curriculum helped me realize I want to help children and their development. An interaction with my current best friend who was subjected to the foster care system also spurred my interest in social work. Foster care and systems like them are on the lower part of the class system, and because of that, students who have been in foster care often have less privilege, as well as more adverse life events that make college and other life opportunities not seem realistic. I strive to one day challenge this and help bring opportunities afforded by higher classes to those who are stuck in the lower classes due to no fault of their own. It's not about being upwardly mobile for me, rather realizing and addressing the injustices of our social class system and working as hard as I can to give back and help to brighten the opportunities for people in other, less affluent social classes.

I have graduated from the University of Michigan with over $40,000 of debt, and thinking about adding to that by going to graduate school. Just thinking about this scares and excites me at the same time. By taking Dwight Lang's sociology class on the experiences of social class in college and families in my last semester at Michigan has made me realize just how many people have broken through the barriers and how many people still struggle. It makes me more aware that while I am financially self-sufficient, and that it's terrifying and empowering all at the same time, there are still others out there who are not in the spot I am. I hope one day I can look back and say I've made it and that I am financially able to help those who are still struggling, as I know just how hard it is to come from a background that does not offer much. The caveat to that is I am and always will be inherently privileged and there are others who have overcome more adversity than I have. I come from a middle ground that some may never see in their life, and I can truly say I appreciate all the experiences I've had and how they have shaped my social class consciousness.

HOW DID I GET HERE?

COLINE MICHELUCCI

Attending the University of Michigan, I begin to wonder if I would have attended college had I grown up in the United States of America. The fact is I had never set foot on American land before the fall of 2016. I grew up in a small town of about 7,000 inhabitants in the south of France, near Marseille. We were mostly from the lower-middle to middle classes. There were a few working poor people, but that was about as diverse as it got. Going to America one day had always been my dream.

I watched a lot of American TV growing up and that fed my desire to explore the other side of the Atlantic Ocean. I do not want to say the American Dream exists in the same sense as the self-made man, but, from the outside, America has always had an aura. Going to the United States is considered a privilege in France and affording a plane ticket and the stay is a big deal. When we think of America, we first think about New York or Los Angeles—perhaps among the most expensive cities. I would always daydream about wandering in New York's Central Park or in-between massive buildings we would see in movies. I did not think I would be able to come to the United States before I was at least 40 years old—the age my parents first visited. And here I am in America and I am able to stay for an entire year. As I walk to class across the campus Diag on a cold winter, January day and complain about my work, I sometimes tell myself I am actually living the dream I have had since I was little; my mood constantly changes. I still ask: How did I get here?

In my small town called Saint-Chamas, I grew up with my two parents and my brother who is five years younger. Growing up, I never thought about social class being taboo. My parents often talked about it over dinner. That may have to do with their careers. Before my father became a consultant of workers' rights, he was a fervent union leader. He would always argue with CEOs and organize marches against employers. He argued and continues to argue that workers have to protect their rights against employers and negotiate with companies so that there is equal power. I remember one day, I was maybe 11 or 12, he came home with his head bleeding and his white shirt covered with blood. I asked him what was going on, and he just told me not to worry, that it was no big deal and it often happens in big protests. He explained that policemen had hit him with their baton because his group tried to enter a company by force and he was at the front. I did not even question it because I knew through him and TV news that it could indeed be violent. It had been impressed upon me that they would do this to my dad. Even though he did not go to college, my dad has a small library with Karl Marx's books and other social class–related books. He is convinced of class warfare, often talks about it, and voices his opinion. It caused numerous political debates at family dinners with my uncles and grandparents since a part of my family has more conservative views and align themselves with the far-right wing.

On the other hand, my mom is an English teacher. She spent a year in England and made her way to becoming a teacher through college. She taught at a ZEP middle school for almost 11 years: ZEP is the French acronym for Priority Education Zone. These are target schools that receive more government funding so they can provide individual financial aid to students. These ZEP schools are located in poor neighborhoods and the goal is to reduce social inequalities. My mom liked teaching there because she felt useful trying to interest these kids in a foreign language. It was difficult, but always rewarding. She knew her students grew up in poverty and they often felt rejected by society because they were segregated in neighborhoods. These are mainly kids from Arabic origins, as racism is still significant in France. My parents were living these inequalities in their jobs every day; that is why they often talked about social inequalities at home.

I believe hearing about social inequalities also has something to do with the country's past. In France, we have a long history with communism and socialism, and those are the two political parties that always highlight the social issues and how unjust it is. It might not be the first topic we would talk about; but, as we approach the French presidential elections in April 2017, social issues are important. I always heard about social differences on TV. Evidently, there is no such thing as the French Dream or the "you can make it big no matter what" thinking. Personally, I knew as a kid that I was not rich, but that I was not poor either. We always went on summer vacations as a family somewhere in France, or I often went to summer camps, usually both. We also went skiing in the Alps for a week during ski season almost every winter. I knew some of my friends could not afford all of that. Aside from those differences, there was one moment as a kid that I realized we did not all have the same exact way of living. Before, I thought everyone had the same type of house and approximately the same lifestyle.

In elementary school I made friends with Gwendoline. She was very shy until you got to know her. We were always playing hide and seek and some other games on the playground together. Outside of school, I used to walk in the hills with my grandmother during spring and pick up thyme, rosemary, and asparagus for cooking. That is how I went to Gwendoline's home. She lived near the hill we always went to and would sometimes join us. One time we stopped at her place; she lived in a mobile home. We played the first version of PlayStation in her room, I remember thinking it was a really tiny home, and how cool it would be to live here. It made me think of holidays because sometimes we would go camping and rent a mobile home. Her mother was from the Caribbean Islands and did not work, while her father worked at the town's public dump. We lost contact during middle school because she went to a professional school while I stayed in general school. It was the first time I was confronted to someone who did not have the same social background as me, and while I found living in the hills endearing, I felt lucky to have a house I could call home. I realized social classes were more diverse than I thought.

Later, in high school, I noticed that social inequalities were more pronounced. There was no general high school in my town, so I had to take the bus every day to go to the next town's high school. It was a slightly bigger place with a big Muslim and Arabic population. Even though it wasn't very close to me, I had to go there because it was the high school I was assigned to. This school did not have an outstanding reputation, being located right next to the ZEP middle school my mom taught at. By the time I reached high school, she had changed schools to the one I would be at. Because of all these distinctions, a lot of parents wanted their kids to go to high school in another town, which was more upper class and liberal. They made a special request. Usually kids said they wanted to take an extra class that was not in the first high school such as Chinese and be transferred to another school. I went to the high school I was supposed to attend because my mom believed in the public school system. She said it would only increase inequalities if everyone thought this way. Within my first year of high school, I noticed there were more Arabic people and generally poorer people than in my hometown. I want to stress that even though racism is very present in France, we don't talk about race like we do in the United States. We would never say Arabic French as we say African American in the United States.

There was also the difference between the general high school and professional high school. The latter does not have a good reputation and every parent tries to get his or her child to general high school even if they are best suited for a professional one. Consequently, kids who are doing poorly in middle school but could thrive through a professional school are sent to general high school because, ultimately, it's the parents' decision. Many of them end up failing general high school and do not graduate. With absolutely no diploma, it is very hard to find a job. As for me, I did not know what I wanted to do with my life, so I went into the scientific section to broaden my perspective. As I was looking for college and what branch I wanted to study, I thought about what my grandmother told me. Ever since I was a teenager, she told me over and over that I should be economically independent. When she was young, her father did not want her to go to college and she had to take care of her seven siblings because she was the eldest. She married my grandfather when she was 18 and had my mom at 20. My grandfather was a butcher, and she worked with him. The problem is that they never declared to the state she was working, so she has never "officially" worked. When she divorced my granddad, she had nothing and struggled. Fortunately, she remarried and could have a decent life, but she never found work again. She is retired now and has no pension because she never paid taxes. Now that she is a widow, she is talking about selling her house because it is too big and she could use the money. These are the reasons why she wants for me to be able to decide everything for myself without being tied to someone. Because of her story and her generation, I think women were seen as the ones who take care of the family first doing the domestic chores. Work in society was not their priority and they were a lot more dependent on their partners. When we know that before 1965, women in France had to ask permission from their husbands to work and to open bank accounts, economic independence was out of reach. Gender and social class have always been related.

After going to a prep class in social sciences and literature for a year, which prepares students for different college entrance exams, I finally started my college studies. College in France is free except for schools like mine which are not financed by the government; but it is still nothing compared to Michigan's tuition. I have to pay the equivalent of about $1,000 per year, including social security. Now that I know the American system, I feel lucky not to have to pay much for my education. Sometimes, I wonder if I would have been able to afford going to college had I grown up here. My parents would have probably saved money over the years, and I probably would have had to take out loans. However, I am glad I'll finish my studies in France and be debt-free. My college is a school of political science: Sciences Po. There are several campuses across the country with the campus in Paris being the center of attention. As for me, I live in Aix-en-Provence, which is a rather bourgeois city with a lot of students. Inhabitants are definitely richer than in my hometown. It is about 45 minutes away from my hometown by car.

As I began to attend Sciences Po, I noticed a few changes compared to where I grew up. More people are usually out shopping and grabbing a café en Terrassa. Aix is a student city, so there is always something going on. It really is beautiful, with paved streets, a historic center, and old buildings. I've always felt good living in Aix. The people at my school also changed when I went to college. There are few French students with Arabic origins and most come from the middle class. I am the only one from my high school who attends Sciences Po. Almost no one from my high school knew about Sciences Po and I learned about it in March of my high school senior year when the entrance exam was in May. This might be one of the reasons why I failed the exam the first time. In this institution, almost everyone has the same social class status and I came to realize how education is a reproductive system of class. Even with a free education, class status is still a crucial driver of success, revealing that meritocracy in France is still an ideal that has yet to be realized. I found a small apartment, which was quite expensive; but, as a student, I received some help from the state and I paid for water and electricity while my parents helped me with rent. Furthermore, diversity at my school was limited. It was mainly students with pretty much the same background as me or higher up in the social hierarchy. I lived there for two years. In my program, I had to spend my third year abroad, which led me to Michigan. I am mostly able to come and study here because my school has a partnership with Michigan, and it allows me to get a waiver for tuition. I just have to pay Sciences Po's tuition which is very advantageous for me. I decided to begin a new adventure for the next academic year—2016–2017.

Before leaving everything behind to live in America for one year, I was anxious because of the situation at home. My parents divorced a little over a year ago when I was 19. Dad left the house two weeks after I became aware of the fact they were not doing well in their marriage. It was a big shock for me. They had been together since they were in middle school; if I had to think of an epic love story, I would have thought of my parents. Sadly, life happens, and it was a real hard time for me and my family. I did not realize how lucky I was to have my two parents together. I took it for granted, although I have a lot of friends with divorced parents. It does not get easier when you're older. Now mom is always worried about money because, as is generally the case, dad earns more than her, so her economic situation became worse. On top of that, she's buying his part of our house, so she had to take another loan. It is a stressful change, but I believe in the end we are going to be okay. We are all still adjusting to this new situation. I was afraid of leaving my mom behind in this broken atmosphere, but I think I did the right thing by pursuing my dreams.

Then, for the first time ever, I set foot on American soil. I arrived at the Detroit Metropolitan Airport on August 25, 2016: I knew I was in for a whole new experience. I had never gone too far away from my family and I always saw my parents at least once a week. Yet, I chose the opportunity to live this incredible experience of being in a country where I did not grow up. I wanted to experience another culture. At first I thought: "Well, the US culture does not seem that much different from France." Then I realized it is quite different. There are always some little details that seem odd to me. For example, fashion-wise, I have an Eastpak backpack which is a famous brand in Europe. However, here, most students do not even know the name. Many have a Northface backpack which for me is more for hiking. I am also not used to heavier clothes because, in the south of France, we do not need thicker winter wear. It is difficult comparing French culture with Michigan's. Had I lived here, maybe I would have a Northface backpack and an expensive Canada Goose winter coat, who knows? But I am living here and adapting to this new temporary life. And I am definitely not buying an

$800 coat, which is almost two months of rent. Coming to the University of Michigan, I knew students would likely be more affluent. I mean, I knew it was a well-ranked university and I know that tuition in the United States is absurdly huge, so I expected everyone to have money. I realized later that some people just take out loans and have debts for years. Aside from the clothing, I have found myself wandering through campus here in Ann Arbor. It is huge and exactly what I expected of an American campus: big buildings and symmetric architecture. I always feel lucky to live here and experience American college life. Students are generally nice with international kids. Every time I am upset or in a bad mood I think about how I should not be because I am experiencing a dream and I should be thankful. My mood always lifts up after these thoughts.

I am living in a cooperative house off campus. It was the cheapest option I could find and a friend of mine recommended it to me. The first day I arrived, I was scared. Living with 50 other people seemed to be a challenge and I had never had a roommate before. The place looked messy and empty. However, I remember thinking this is the year to change my routine and try new things. Now I believe that I made the right choice. I have met interesting people and speak mostly English, so I can improve my language skills. It is an international house, which means that although there are 75% Americans, the rest of us come from different countries. I am living with American, French, Indian, Italian, Chinese, Korean, and Brazilian students. Sharing cultures and views of the world is very enriching. My housemates are all unique and almost all are attending UM; however, some of my housemates are struggling financially or have been homeless for a while. We are all so different, yet we live under the same roof and have pleasant times together. Some are working aside from their studies, some do not. I think it is a great way to broaden our minds and meet people we would not meet in our Michigan circle.

During winter break in March 2017, I went to visit a friend in New York City who had spent a semester in my school in France two years ago. She kindly offered to let me stay at her place and

I was so grateful because I know how expensive it is to live in Manhattan. She lives near Wall Street in a "luxury rentals" building. First, I had never seen such big buildings before, and second, I did not know what luxury rentals exactly meant. I entered the building and there were men in suits near a marble desk. They asked me the reason for my visit and I went up in a big elevator. She lived on the 22nd floor. This building was already impressive from the outside, but even more on the inside. I was happy to see my friend and she showed me around her apartment; the view was simply breathtaking. From the windows of the two bedrooms, you could see the Brooklyn Bridge, the Watch Tower on the other side of the Hudson River, and all of those lights that never went off during the night, as well as the sun rising in the morning. Every night and morning I woke up there, I stared outside for 10 minutes. I told my friend this view was amazing more than once and I was so excited to be here. She said: "Oh you're cute. You actually get used to it," but I could not believe my eyes. Coming to New York City was really on my list of things I must do before I die. I used to think how a small-town girl from across the ocean like me could ever go to New York one day. Yet, here I was, in the middle of all of those huge buildings and the vibrant crowd of the biggest city in the country. I remember the night after seeing my first Broadway musical; it was like living a dream. It was exhilarating! I remember feeling like no one could ever dampen my mood that day. What a great way to enter 2017.

In order to be able to afford all the trips to discover more of this country, I worked all four months of the summer of 2016. The day after my last exam, I started working at the town hall of my hometown from Monday to Friday. As I knew I was leaving at the end of August and needed as much money as I could earn, I was also working during the weekends. On Saturdays and Sundays, I became a waitress at a chain restaurant. It was not a job as rewarding as the other one, but it still helped. For two months, I worked two jobs, seven days a week, and I was exhausted. I would finish working on Sunday around midnight and go to the town hall on Monday morning at eight. Eventually, my contract with the town hall ended and

I became a full-time waitress; it was hard. These kinds of summer jobs always remind me of why I'm at college. I have great admiration for those who worked there. I also liked working with some of my colleagues because we joked around a lot during our breaks. Almost everyone kept asking the boss when they would get their pay because they needed money right away. This is the reality of living with a minimum-wage salary. I still remember July 14th, when I worked only in the morning and I had made plans with friends since it is our national holiday. But as I was finishing my shift at 3:00 p.m., my boss asked me to also work the night shift. I wanted to say no. I was tired, I needed time off, and I wanted to see my friends. However, I was new; I knew he could fire me. I tried to argue with him saying it would be nice to have at least a 24-hour notice, but he argued back saying that I knew what this job entailed and that was how it worked. I ended up accepting reluctantly. I was so upset I came home crying. I was upset that, as the newest employee, I had to bend to the boss's wishes. In the end, I learned a lot there, and my boss was not as bad as I thought he was. Although, after this, whenever they called me on my day off and asked me to work in the following hours, I would refuse. One day, I came to work at nine and started wiping the floor for about an hour and my boss stopped me, telling me I could not work today because I couldn't work more than seven days in a row and he had not realized that sooner. He sent me home knowing I lived 30 minutes by car from my workplace. I had just wasted gas and not earned money. I stopped working five days before I was supposed to leave for the United States. I was happy to leave pleased I had saved money. On bad days, I would always think about the money I was making and how I would use it for my travels. It motivated me to keep working hard.

Now at Michigan, I am working at the dining hall. I like how flexible the hours are and it is the perfect student job to make money to help cover most of my expenses. The working environment is really nice and I can save some more for exploring America. I am thankful for this journey that is soon coming to an end. I now understand this country better and I've come to realize that America is not as ideal as I had once imagined. I was only dreaming of the positive sides. However, social issues are important here. For instance, expensive higher education and the lack of social class diversity in colleges can only enhance social reproduction. Moreover, people who have to pay to receive health-care services such as going to the doctor or going to the hospital are not ideal situations for the poor "cannot afford to be sick." Finally, race and social class are closely intertwined in the United States, also laced with history. There are also social issues in France; maybe I just notice them less because I have lived among them my whole life. Now, as I am looking at a society from an exterior point of view, details that may be insignificant to Americans do not go unnoticed by me. I am glad I chose to discover a new country, a new culture, and a new approach to understanding social classes. I will be forever grateful to have been able to experience living in a country that was not mine.

Money, Cars, and Clothes: Things We Place Importance On*
Candice Miller

Prelude

I grew up in the small town of River Rouge, Michigan. It has approximately 7,500 residents, one high school, a post office, and very little of anything else. Most of the time, my family had to travel to nearby cities to grocery shop and make other purchases. My mother tells me it was not always like this, but the lack of access to grocery stores, restaurants, and other stores frustrates me. Every time I return home, I travel through Southwest Detroit to my hometown. Few improvements have been made to Southwest Detroit, and the money being invested in Downtown Detroit has yet to positively affect the residents in Southwest Detroit and River Rouge. While many homes in River Rouge are occupied, the people are a part of the working poor or working class.

Mom grew up in River Rouge, a place where her parents migrated after they left Mississippi. Although mom tells me about the better days she experienced in River Rouge, she also explains how she grew up poor. After moving from Mississippi, my grandfather worked odd jobs to have money for his family. Soon my grandmother and their small children moved too. He eventually obtained a job as a custodian

---

* This essay is dedicated to my parents who taught me to think beyond items society places value on and always strive for the best.

working for the local high school. With this salary, they raised 12 children. My mother was the 11th born. All 12 of my aunts and uncles, now ages 82–62, graduated from River Rouge High School.

After graduating, some my aunts and uncles went directly into the workforce and eventually landed good jobs at the Big Three automotive companies—Chrysler, General Motors, and Ford—where most would end up retiring. Aunt Shirley decided to go directly to college at the University of Michigan where she obtained her bachelor's degree in secondary education. Eventually, some of my other aunts went back to college where they obtained their bachelor's degrees in secondary and elementary education at Wayne State University in Detroit. Mom attributes much of her success to Aunt Shirley. As a first-generation college student, mom had little knowledge of college life. However, my aunt assisted her by suggesting how to apply for grants and scholarships and what classes she might take. Mom has told me she probably would have felt lost if her sister had not attended Michigan before her. Mom eventually graduated with her bachelor's of science in dental hygiene in 1976. Afterward, my mother moved to New York, worked in her field, and modeled for different agencies. Later she moved back to River Rouge and began working in her profession full time with dentists in the Detroit and Downriver areas. Mom did not meet my father until she was in her late thirties. They married when she was 40 and my brother was born that same year in September 1994. I was born two years later. I often wonder why my mother waited so long to get married and have children. Was it because she was so career oriented or did the thought of freedom influence her decisions?

Dad is from Ypsilanti, Michigan, and is the oldest boy of seven children. He was first of his siblings to graduate from Willow Run High School. As a young man, he excelled in basketball and running track and was popular among his friends. He went on to the local junior college, played basketball, and eventually went off to the army. Dad was a paratrooper in 82nd airborne two years later and trained in Louisiana, North Carolina, and Georgia. After discharge dad worked for the state of Michigan and eventually at

General Motors. He has always been a hard worker and has tried to instill this same work ethic in me and my brother. Mom and dad value education and have always taught us that no one can ever take that away. They decided to settle and raise their family in mom's hometown of River Rouge where they purchased my grandfather's old home.

Early 2000s

I hear laughter and giggles from my neighborhood friends as we play outside. We usually play four square, tag, red light green light, and basketball, and hold relay races. I get excited about races because I like to run and I usually win. My neighbors and I typically play in the cul-de-sac where our homes are located on what many people believe is one of the better streets. Many people who own homes on Palmerston Street make an honest living and are dedicated to maintaining their homes. I feel safe as a child and do not worry about much. But there are stark differences between streets in my neighborhood. After leaving Palmerston, the other homes look different. They are usually smaller and some are not as well kept up. However, in the early 2000s, the neighborhood feels like a friendly community and these differences are not a big deal between individuals. However, the social class differences are apparent and I see the differences.

When I was not outside, I usually filled my curiosity with reading or playing with my dolls. At an early age, I showed an interest in reading and my parents let me choose books when we went to the store. Both books and dolls allowed me the opportunity to use my imagination and be a dreamer and thinker. As I grew older, I spent most of my time in school which oddly became a place of both comfort and terror.

In 1999, my mom registered me for a pre-kindergarten program at age three and I have continued in school since then. In kindergarten, I started school at Walter White Elementary in River Rouge. I truly loved what I learned; my teacher promoted a love for reading and even taught me how to count in different languages. My parents loved my teacher as well but they were not fond of my brother's teacher. They wanted me and my brother to get a quality education so they started to look for new schools in our neighborhood that could provide us with a good education.

At first grade they enrolled me in Mark Twain School and Academy, a school with a great curriculum and quality teachers. I was amazed at how much there was to do and learn! I felt like I was in paradise with all the information and skills I was learning. However, a year later, I began to experience trouble with some students. I would soon learn that bullying was a big problem.

One of my first experiences with bullying was in second grade. I sat next to a boy who loved to talk about students' shoes, especially mine. "What are those on your feet?" he said. "What do you mean?" I replied. "Did you go to McDonalds and order biscuits?" "No," I answered. "Yes, you did because those shoes are biscuits." Biscuits were used to describe shoes that did not look good. I quickly responded: "No, they are not!" He continued to laugh and proclaimed loudly that my shoes were biscuits. I resumed reading my book and tried to ignore him. That evening I told my mother the story. "Candice, your shoes are not biscuits. You are a kid and you like to play, so your shoes are not going to be perfect," she said. Since the boy told me my shoes were biscuits, I insisted they were and I needed to change them immediately. That weekend she bought me a black pair of Reebok gym shoes. Little did I know; these shoes would again become the butt of my classmate's jokes too. At school this classmate looked down and said: "Now you have duck shoes!" He continued talking about my Reeboks and I could not do anything to stop him.

I was upset with him and with mom for not buying the latest shoes in fashion. When she shopped for my brother and me, she often went to local department stores such as JCPenney, Sears, and Target. During special holidays, she would even buy me dresses from Macy's. However, because she did not buy name brand clothing popular at that time, such as Baby Phat, Phat Farm, Coogi, Apple

Bottom jeans, Nike's, and Jordan's, it did not matter how decent my clothes or shoes looked because they were not these brands.

Clothing became a salient part of my experience at school. With so many students focusing on clothing, I was under the impression their parents had a lot of money and they lived lavish lifestyles. However, as a young girl, I was deceived about the social class of my peers and I did not recognize that wearing certain clothing brands did not equate to having money or a higher social class. Even though I went to a school that had a dress code, students still found ways to incorporate name brand clothing and shoes into their school attire. If a student wore other brands of shoes besides Nike's or Jordan's, many students made fun of them.

Luckily, I made friends whom I had something in common with, outside of clothing, which made my experience a little bit better. However, by the time I got to sixth grade, I noticed that some of the same students who wore Nike's and Jordan's may not have been as affluent as I once thought they were. I noticed things I did not recognize earlier. At lunch, I was one of the few students who always packed a lunch. Many always ate the school lunch and never had to pay. Some days I wanted to be like other students and eat lunch for free too, but the lunch lady always stopped me and requested that I pay a dollar. I thought it was unfair that they made me pay when many other kids did not have to pay. I did not understand the concept of free or reduced lunch programs which many students qualified for. On Wednesdays, I especially looked forward to lunch because instead of packing one, my mom would buy my brother and me lunch from a restaurant and bring it to school. Receiving lunch from my mom was almost like a double-edged sword at that school. Some of the students showed signs of jealously and even tried to bully me.

2008–2010

Each year Mark Twain became increasingly more unbearable. While teachers were still wonderful and the school still had a pretty decent curriculum, I felt disconnected from many of the students.

Fights were occurring more regularly and classroom supplies were limited. After I completed sixth grade, my parents transferred me to nearby school in Melvindale: Strong Middle School. Although, Strong had a different racial demographic than Mark Twain, I seemed to fit in well and I really enjoyed the people. Many of the students were friendly and there were many more amenities. Strong had a better library and it was filled with books! At Mark Twain, I read most of the interesting books. At Strong, I never came close to finishing them all, and I was even able to join a student book club.

Although Melvindale is not a city with an affluent population, the vast difference between my new and old schools made me think the students and families in Melvindale were middle class. Although many of the families were not middle class, I also recognized that many of the students who went to Mark Twain were living below the poverty line.

Melvindale, mostly a working-class community, offered me the opportunity to be around students who had similar interests. It was easier for different class backgrounds to come together because clothing seemed to be a less salient issue. While attending Strong, I developed friendships with a diverse group of people and participated in sports, which helped me to meet even more like-minded students. Although things seemed to be going well, in the eighth grade, mom informed me I would not be transitioning to Melvindale High School with my peers. I was very upset and disappointed! "Why not mom?" I asked her several times. "I don't think I'm going to like this new school," I complained. I really loved all my friends and they made me feel welcome, loved, accepted, and the teachers were committed to my academic success. I didn't understand why mom wanted this move. "Candice, you will have better educational opportunities at your new school and you will be better prepared for college. You said you wanted to be a doctor, right?"

We sat in the car preparing my applications for the two schools in Detroit she wanted me to attend: Cass Technical High School and Renaissance High School. I thought she was wrong and that I would have the same opportunity to apply for colleges and scholarships after attending Melvindale as I would have at either of these high schools. Well I was wrong! But I would not find this out until four years later when I graduated from Cass Technical High School with an opportunity to attend the University of Michigan, Ann Arbor.

2010–2014

At Cass Tech, I was exposed to students from a variety of social classes. Since it was one of the Detroit magnet schools, people came from diverse class backgrounds: poor, working poor, lower-middle-class, and middle-class families. There were rarely any upper-middle-class students, but there were a few who attended since their parents attended as teenagers. Although, Cass was mostly African Americans and Bengali students, I did not know there could be so much diversity among these two groups. One thing had not changed at Cass Tech and it reminded me of my old school Mark Twain. Students placed a high priority on clothing and the status it provided. I realized that many black students value clothing items for status or social gain. While I enjoyed wearing nice clothing, wearing name brand jeans was not my main priority. Although this was a school with a dress code, students still found ways to dress up their uniforms with expensive pants and shoes. As I got older, mom and I continued to shop at JCPenney and Macy's. However, in high school I did not experience any bullying about my clothing or shoes. I am not sure if this was because I was very involved and excelled academically, or if many students were finally more mature.

Transportation was also another revealing factor of social class. Using public transportation in Detroit is often cumbersome because buses run late and some do not run at all. Public transportation that is supposed to help people was often a burden to many. Although, some things have changed, transportation is still a big issue for people who do not live in Midtown. During high school years this was a key indicator of being in the working- or lower classes. Students thought people with higher incomes did not ride the bus, and would always have a ride to and from school. I always thought this was strange, because normally in big cities many take public transportation to avoid traffic. Instead, in Detroit, many drove their cars to various locations and it was noticeable if a person lacked transportation. While I thought it was no big deal for someone to take the bus, it was sad to see students who were affected by the city's lack of transportation. Until I was 16, my parents arranged for my aunt, who had retired, to pick me up from school. Later I was fortunate enough to receive a car which mitigated many of the issues that some of my less affluent peers experienced.

After having certain materialistic items I realized how deceptive these things can be. While I did have a vehicle, it was not a natural indicator I came from a family with lots of money. In fact, it did not tell the story of how after my parents separated, our household income changed. I went from being in the middle-class to living in a working-class family. My parents separated right before the 2007 recession, so it became extremely hard for my mother to maintain her bills. Despite her struggle with bills, my parents tried to ensure I received the best high school education and experience.

During middle and high school years, I realized my neighborhood shaped how I grew up and what I had access to. There were few resources or grocery stores in River Rouge, and we always drove to get groceries, food, or clothing. The local school system was not great either. School became my haven. Much of my time after school was spent playing on school sports teams. Once home, nights were filled with homework and then my day would repeat. Despite having busy days and evenings, I loved it! I made new friends and formed bonds with peers, especially girls on the track team, which was my favorite high school extracurricular activity. Even though we came from different social class backgrounds, this never made a difference because our love for running prevailed over class differences. Like my teammates, other closest friends also had an interest in learning and were kind and funny. By senior year of high school, we were bonded at the hip.

I discovered my mother was right about Cass Tech offering better opportunities for students. Cass adamantly encouraged students to pursue higher education and apply for scholarships. My counselor also kept students informed about different scholarships offered by local organizations and colleges. Eventually, most of my friends and I applied to and were accepted to our dream schools in Michigan and California. I set off to the University of Michigan in Ann Arbor, to pursue my bachelor's degree in preparation for medical school.

2014–Present

At Michigan I expected to make a diverse set of friends. Since I am a social person, I thought it would be easy to find friends regardless of my background. I did not expect class or race to be issues on campus. I thought once people made it into college, they are accepted for who they are. However, I was wrong. While some students are more open to ideals of diversity, many come with preconceived notions about others, which often turn into overt and covert racism and classism. Some make assumptions about students from Detroit being shot or even attacked on a consistent basis. Once a student even asked me "Have you ever seen anyone shot before?" It was offensive and made me realize the poor judgments many people make as young adults at the University of Michigan.

In my first year during 2014–2015, I made friends quickly. However, I was a little naïve in thinking that issues of race, class, gender, and other social categories were not very important. In fact, college is the very place where conversations about these issues emerge: in- and outside of the classroom. I did not expect to encounter many situations and interactions dealing with social class or race, but especially class. This is because I did not recognize how many wealthy students attend Michigan. Most surprisingly I discovered many wealthy students tried to make light of their social class backgrounds. Some even tried to refer to how their parents or grandparents grew up in a lower social class to make it seem like they were familiar with similar conditions.

Despite attempts to persuade others their families do not have much money, I know many students do not share my social class based on the items they buy and restaurants they chose to eat at on weekends. Before starting college, I had never heard of many of the name brand clothing items some of the students wore, and restaurants on Main Street in Ann Arbor were way too expensive for me. I now understand that many Ann Arbor residents and Michigan students have money but do not like to admit it. While there is nothing wrong with having money, I often question why some upper-middle-class families hide their income and try to relate to working- and lower-class families. I think about my hometown a lot. Many Michigan students do not understand what it is like: to not have decent textbooks, to be in oversized classrooms, and for parents who must search for schools that will help their children excel academically because good public schools are not abundant. These are things I cannot fake or pretend to have not experienced.

In classrooms, I can easily be the only black female from a social class background not representing the dominant social class at Michigan. Despite differences, I see in Ann Arbor similarity to my hometown and have found organizations and communities that make me feel welcome. However, my sophomore year of college brought on new experiences especially when it came to experiencing social class differences. During spring break, I applied to Alternative Spring Break (ASB)—a program allowing students to participate in volunteer work while visiting a city in the United States.

ASB is an enriching and affordable experience. Students pay $200 to travel and stay a whole week; both transportation and lodging are provided. The Ginsberg Center at the University of Michigan offers scholarships to students who cannot afford to pay $200. So, this was one of the most reasonable spring break options that I could find while also giving back to the community. Ten people went on my ASB trip and all were great people. But from some of our interactions I could tell we were from different social class backgrounds. After arriving in St. Louis, many of us settled in and began to bond. The next day brought even more adventures at our volunteer site and while we explored the city.

After a couple of days, many called their parents and family to tell them how things were going. As I was walking into the communal area, I overheard one of the girls talking on the phone. Her older sister was also on spring break, but she and her friends decided to go to Florida where one of their parents had a beach house. Her sister described our ASB as "ghetto" and "cheap" and hoped her sister could join her in Florida the following year for a more appropriate vacation.

I never told the girl that her sister's usage of the word "ghetto" to describe our trip had negative racial and social class undertones. However, since I was the only black girl I decided not to bother with addressing the statement. All that made me think about my hometown again and how many people do not have opportunities to travel, even on a trip like ASB. It also made me think about chances to travel as a young girl. Every year, my parents planned a family trip to an amusement park. Most of our summers consisted of traveling to Ohio to go to Cedar Point or Six Flags, and one year my parents surprised me and my brother with a trip to Disney World. For many, college is the first time they take a major trip in the United States or even abroad. I never brought that conversation up again, but it served as reminder of how uncomfortable someone can feel by just hearing how they others feel about certain programs and neighborhoods.

Since starting college I have thought a lot about my future and how I will fit into a 21st-century society. As a first-year student in 2014, I thought I would major in mathematics and eventually attend medical school. I had many options and was confused by what I should focus on once in college. I liked math but frankly I did not enjoy it enough to make it my major. I began thinking about a degree in African American Studies but eventually shied away from that option. I also thought about going into nursing and how it would give me job security while pursing my medical degree.

However, I thought about how many articles I read about pre-med students who said nursing majors are not favored by medical school admission committees. I finally discovered the major neuroscience and did more research on the subject. I was interested in many of the classes under this program and really enjoyed the information I was learning in related psychology and biology courses.

Most people look at my career choice in medicine as a choice for stability. Early on, I was prompted to think about careers that could potentially provide financial stability, but many told me that it did not matter if I was doing what I loved if I was financially secure. While I began to think about medicine at an early age, I did not consider the risks of pursing medicine. It is truly a time commitment at undergraduate and profession school levels. While the prospect of money can be enticing, I don't believe medicine is something a person can truly pursue with money as the only motive. Fortunately, many of my interests and choices to pursue medicine surpass the thoughts of money I may earn in the future.

I am, however, plagued with the thought of being overcome with debt for my professional education. The thought of finishing medical school with almost triple the debt of the average physician did 30 years ago is scary. While I believe my future profession will truly be rewarding, I also believe many lower-income students have a similar fear of debt. As someone who wants to obtain medical (MD) and Master of Business Administration (MBA) degrees, I have a long road ahead of me.

My choice to obtain an MBA and attend medical school comes from desires to create more businesses within my neighborhood. Growing up in an area where businesses have left, I seek to understand more about business and how I can better serve lower-income communities. I also hope to own my own business and teach others that owning businesses and understanding how to run them can be very beneficial. While I may not be able to change the world in a day or a year, I hope to make positive changes throughout my lifetime. I aim to improve the social class and living conditions in my neighborhood and in the wider society.

LIVING IN LIMBO:
TWO WORLDS COLLIDE
MEGAN TAYLOR

My hands shook with excitement as I nervously waited for the computer to load. As I read the long awaited words—"Congratulations, Megan! You're in!"—I was overwhelmed with excitement. I had been accepted to the University of Michigan and I immediately ran to mom's room to share the joyous news. Michigan was my dream school. The rest of the afternoon floated by in a dreamy daze as I imagined how amazing my life in Ann Arbor would be in the fall of 2013. It wasn't until the next day that thoughts of how I would be able to afford college began creeping into my excitement. I was overwhelmed with worries about how I would pay for college. It just didn't seem fair. Was it wise to turn down an incredible education simply because I couldn't afford it?

My parents were encouraging, reminding me that I had received a full ride scholarship to Saginaw Valley State University here in Michigan, a university closer to home. Each time they reminded me, I resisted. While I was grateful for this scholarship, my dreams did not include Saginaw Valley, and the full scholarship they had offered me loomed as unwanted. Should I go because it was the only affordable option? I couldn't stop thinking about being a Michigan Wolverine.

After receiving my acceptance I spent the next several months anxiously applying to every local scholarship I was eligible for. My parents and I spent hours poring over the complex applications for financial aid. I worried that I couldn't afford my dreams. I heard that Michigan was committed to meeting 100% of need, but it was all so confusing. What did that mean? I waited for my financial aid letter. Four long months passed, and I still heard nothing. I waited anxiously. It wasn't until April of my senior year that the financial aid package was finally arrived. I vividly remember my confusion, which quickly morphed into gratitude and excitement. I scrutinized the numbers in the award letter, trying to make sense of them, to wrap my head around them. I cried with joy as I realized the university would be providing $21,000 for the school year. The rest, approximately $4,000, could be covered in local scholarships. I would have four years of college completely paid for. The potential of graduating from an incredible university debt-free became a reality. I was grateful, but I didn't realize how rare my situation was until I stepped foot on campus four months later in August 2013.

That fall I eagerly settled into college life. I loved every moment. Everything was new and exciting. It was late September when Charlotte and I had only been roommates for a little over a month. I still vividly remember one of our conversations. We were joking around and talking about our expensive dorms. Charlotte whined about having to find decent living for sophomore year. I commented that I was so thankful the university's funding would be covering my housing, even if I lived off campus.

Charlotte just stared at me. "What? How did you get that?"

I stared back, utterly confused. "What do you mean, you *didn't* get that?"

Charlotte's face was etched with pure bewilderment. "I didn't get any financial aid, Meg. I don't qualify for anything."

It was at that moment, a month after arriving on campus, a month after being immersed in the new culture that I started to realize my situation. I, as a self-supporting student on full financial aid, was a minority.

Charlotte and I had become best friends. Inhabiting a 10- by 12-foot box of a dorm room together we were nearly inseparable. But we grew up in what seemed like worlds apart.

"How much aid do you get?" she inquired.

"Char, I'm here on a full financial aid," I answered meekly. "The university is paying for everything."

We both stared at each other bewildered, both not fully understanding the situation. I was shocked she didn't qualify for any financial aid—didn't everybody? Everyone in my high school had filed for financial assistance. Financial aid, scholarships, and the fear of drowning in loans were normal for high school friends and me. Charlotte, on the other hand, was equally confused: How was she so lucky? How did she earn those scholarships? After I shared I was on full financial aid, she nearly fell out her chair, squealing: "What?! You are so lucky! Oh my gosh! How did you even manage that?!" Her response was confusing. I didn't receive aid because of intelligence or because of my grades, but because of my family's financial background. I tried to explain that where I come from, going to college, let alone the University of Michigan, is a big deal and I certainly didn't live up to the label "lucky." But her ears were still ringing with the words: "full financial aid." Anything I said afterward that September afternoon hung visibly and limply in the air between us as we tried to understand one another. I had left my small, rural hometown for a whole new world and I was realizing I had a lot to learn.

It was after this moment that my journey in recognizing the influence of social class began. Throughout the next four years, I found myself enrolling in classes that promised to dig into the effects and realities of social class. With each conversation, I grew more captivated. During these years I reflected back and made sense of the ways social class had shaped my childhood. It was only within the hyper-class privileged Michigan environment that I began to realize my childhood experiences were not the norm of many of my college peers.

I grew up in a modest, middle-class family. I grew up happy with loving and encouraging parents. They were able to provide everything I needed. But divorce can be an odd thing and often has the power to significantly affect the class status of families. It was my freshman year of high school when my parents divorced. Gradually, following the divorce, I began to recognize my parents subtly spending money more strategically and I started realizing the strain on money the divorce created. When I look back now, I am filled with shame as I remember responding to this change in our financial statuses.

After they divorced, mom began looking for a new house. It was a really difficult time financially, as she struggled to find her footing and re-establish herself. When she bought our new house, instead of congratulating her, I was embarrassed to have friends over because of how small it was. When we were unable to afford a washer and dryer, I refused to go with mom to the laundry mat. I was terrified one of my friends from high school might see me. Instead, I rode with mom and went across the street to do my homework at Taco Bell. I desperately wished nobody would recognize me or mom. When I remember these moments, I want to apologize to mom and thank her for how hard she fought for me to continue living a good and happy life. Most of all, I'll thank her for loving me even when I responded so immaturely.

I qualified for free lunch at school back then, and I received high school scholarships to waive the "pay to play" fees required on my school sports teams. When I went to summer camp, I received scholarships from donors at our church. The vast majority of my peers qualified for free or reduced lunch. I was never ashamed for needing scholarships to attend camp or play on sports teams. This was my normal. It was not until I compared my childhood with my peers at Michigan that I finally understood all these childhood and community realities were connected to social class.

My class experiences have always been intertwined with my childhood in a small town. I am from a rural community in Northern Michigan. Houghton Lake is home to the largest inland lake in the state and is the perfect illustration of a summer-time tourist town, full of retirees, cottages, and vacation homes. It also is home to one of higher poverty rates in the state. In the fall of 2015, 69.1% of students from my high school qualified for free or reduced lunch. Similarly, 24.7% of the population lived below the poverty line. Only

13.3% above the age of 25 held a bachelor's degree. Although I grew up with loving parents who always encouraged me to value education, Houghton Lake is my home. It is where I was raised, where I learned the easy lessons like how to drive a car, but it is also home to where I learned the hard lessons. The sad fact is the majority of my classmates would never have the opportunity to attend college and the majority of them didn't want to go.

Throughout childhood, dad always joked that I wasn't allowed to date Houghton Lake boys. I never really understood what he meant: What was wrong with those boys? I thought maybe he was just being a dad and didn't want me to date anyone. It was statements like these that I didn't understand until college. I remember a phone call to mom in in late September of my freshman year of college. I gushed in surprise and confusion: "Mom, all of the boys here dress really nice, I think I like it." She laughed. In my Houghton Lake world, boys wore cutoffs and basketball shorts to school. Dressing up meant there was a big game that night. Little realizations like these marked my journey to class consciousness.

When I began college in Ann Arbor, I was far away from my childhood world. It was strange to hear fellow students, many of whom had become my friends, mocking country music or believing rural communities were trashy. They stared at me in disbelief when I showed them pictures of me and my high school friends dressed in bright orange and camouflage in the student sections of our football games. When I told new friends I had never been to school on November 15th —the opening day of deer hunting season—they were shocked. My school was closed that day because it isn't safe for young children to stand out in the dark woods in the mornings at bus stops. Ironically, we did have school on Martin Luther King Day. They thought I was joking when I told them boys would frequently drive their snowmobiles to school. I constantly felt as if I was balancing two pieces of my identity—Ann Arbor and Houghton Lake: different worlds and worlds apart. How would the two collide?

During my junior year at Michigan, I invited my housemate, Kim, home for Thanksgiving. She is from Los Angeles, and one of my closest friends. I was so excited to share my home with her. I'll never forget the humorous moment of when Kim first walked in the door. One of the first things she said was: "Oh wow!" Confused, I responded: "What?" She politely said: "Oh, I just have never seen a deer on a wall before." I laughed with embarrassment and shock. I hadn't even thought to warn her about it ahead of time. All this was so normal to me and it never occurred to me that for Kim this would be out of the ordinary. I immediately found myself hoping she wasn't offended, and wondered what else may surprise us during the visit. Once again, I marveled at how our worlds were colliding.

Although throughout my childhood I always dreamed of the day I would escape Houghton Lake, yet, it has always felt like an important piece of my identity. It was hard to understand how this part of me was so misunderstood in Ann Arbor. In days following the election of Donald Trump in November 2016, rural communities were often stigmatized as bigoted, racist supporters responsible for the election results. It was hard to hear the cruel stereotypes and assumptions placed on communities like mine. After the election, one of my friends remarked: "These rural communities are ruining democracy. Can't they just f*cking urbanize already?" Those words followed me for weeks. How could I immerse myself in the world of higher education if it meant distancing myself from Houghton Lake?

In my hometown, higher education is viewed as elite and pretentious. So who was I, a small-town girl, going to the University of Michigan? When I finally declared my major—philosophy, politics, and economics—I found myself at a loss for words when trying to describe it to my high school peers. "What career could you qualify for studying philosophy?" they asked. I struggled to explain and justify my choice. So I began lying. I would say: "I'm studying Political Science." It was just easier. The conversations were more comfortable. But, when I was in Ann Arbor, I proudly explained the interdisciplinary complexity of my undergraduate studies. Again, I found my identity split and altered depending on which world I was visiting.

Despite my hometown norms, my parents always encouraged me to value my education and I always knew I would attend college. I remember countless nights of lounging around the house with my parents after school, practicing my spelling words. Fast forward to high school and dad made it a priority to visit college campuses with me, even making certain to take me to his alma matter: Colorado State University. But I was also raised in a world where financial aid was a necessity and applying for scholarships was expected.

Michigan's financial aid package was so lavish that it allowed me to live like my more affluent university peers. Financial aid easily covered my tuition, housing, books, groceries, and sorority dues. I chose to live strategically and frugally. I had roommates all four years, and my friends and I painstakingly searched for housing with lower rent. Similarly, I was employed all four years. In my freshman through junior years, I worked between 10 and 15 hours each week in university work–study jobs. I always loved having a job that gave me a sense of responsibility and commitment. I worked every summer since I was 15. Because my financial aid covered all my expenses, I was able to save all my income—which allowed me to live a comfortable lifestyle.

During senior year, I was privileged to afford to travel to the 2016 Michigan football bowl game in Miami, Florida. Only three weeks later, I traveled for a weekend with friends in Las Vegas, and a month after that I spent my spring break on a cruise in the Caribbean. It felt strange to me to spend so much money on travel and experiences in such a short period of time. I felt guilty my parents or peers from similar class backgrounds could not afford the experiences I had in those months. It felt backward and contradictory. Did I deserve this?

I was in financial aid limbo. I didn't actually have the money in my bank account. I wasn't a legitimate member of the upper-middle class. But, because of the way the university had buffered me, I was able to live without financial concern throughout my college years. This seems similar to the function college plays for so many other first-generation or lower-income students. Higher education has long been recognized as the gateway to the upper-middle class. For so many working- or lower-class students, their college journey will prepare them for upward class mobility. My experience mirrors this phenomenon. The university significantly altered my class status, both through financial aid which affected my college lifestyle and through the academic credentials affecting my future class status after graduation.

Although my social position will change, my passion to fight injustices that originate from rigid class structures has only grown. I have directly experienced this injustice and have witnessed the heartbreaking cycles of generational and systematic poverty. I have focused my years at the University of Michigan studying how policy and social programming can be used most effectively to fight social class inequality in America. I am proud of my four-year journey. I have critically examined how class has shaped my experiences and perspectives and how I can engage in a lifetime of challenging social class inequalities. I am proud of Houghton Lake, and I am proud to graduate from the University of Michigan in 2017. Limbo will be my life. Although it might be difficult to navigate, I am grateful for the unique perspectives I have gained. Two worlds have collided: I value each one and the way they have individually and collectively shaped me into the woman I am today.

THE INVISIBLE PROBLEM
WITHOUT A NAME
KIM TRUONG

My childhood friend was always one of the top-tier students. In third grade (2004–2005), she knew you had to take the average of the middle two numbers to find the median after doing the median number slash dance. Please tell me some of you had teachers who did this. Our teacher didn't even know this, so she had to call another teacher to make sure my friend was right. Even though my friend was so much smarter than me, we were always together. I even gave her the nickname she would use for almost her entire K–12 career, Simba—like the lion! We were in the same classes up until fourth grade. In fifth grade, I kind of ditched her for a super popular friend, but we just kind of pretended that never happened. I'd always go to her nice, large, and clean house and stay over for the nicely portioned meals her dad cooked. It was a nice escape from my boring, messy, and dirty house.

I was so close with Simba and her family that I made a point to call her dad by his first name "Larry," while I called her mom "momma Wong" for as long as I can remember. "Mr. and Mrs. Wong" was something too formal and weird for me. I thought Mr. and Mrs. were titles only for teachers at school, not adults who were my friends' parents.

Whenever I was over at their house, I'd eat fruit with Simba and momma Wong, who lectured us on the health benefits of fruits that she learned from Oprah or Doctor Oz. I'd play with Simba's

Nintendo DS while Larry called her down for 30-minute math lessons. And I was the one to introduce her to the world of online games, which she got kind of sucked into. Larry got mad at both of us for playing so much, and blamed them for making Simba's middle school grades drop half a letter grade.

But even though she got more obsessed with online games than me, Simba was never really in danger. She was so self-disciplined and responsible that she managed her playing and studying time well. And I was too! We were both good about keeping up with our schoolwork, but we approached it in very different ways.

She was always diligent and made sure she understood lessons front and back. She was the type to get started on assignments as soon as they came out. I was almost the opposite of Simba. Maybe that's why we got along so well. I was a chronic procrastinator, but I always got my work done on time at a reasonably high grade. I secretly took pride in my ability to get the same grades as Simba with only a fraction of the effort. I felt more efficient and less of a worrywart. I thought she was working hard but I was working *smart*. I loved being the kid who never studied, but got good grades. I felt super cool compared to Simba, that dork.

Oh, but how the tables turned. Oh, how blind and naïve I was. Of course Simba had to work harder in school! She was put into the advanced track and was getting ahead while I was breezing by in basic track courses. Our slight separation didn't bother me in middle school when this tracking began. Even though we weren't in the same math or English classes, we still had the required science and history classes together. It was fine with me. But when it came to high school, Simba and I were in completely different classes. We started to drift apart because we never got to see each other, even though we went to the same school.

The gap between us grew bigger with each year. Without preparation Simba and I took the ACT (American College Testing) blind together for the first time. She scored an incredible 31 out of 36, while I got a 19. The number of her AP (Advanced Placement) classes grew exponentially each year. So as our academic distance grew, our friendship weakened.

To make things worse, I started to hate the people in my basic track classes. It was filled with the jocks and popular ditzy girls—the cliques I never wanted to talk to. But in Simba's classes, the *cool nerds* were always around. Those were the kids who were smart without trying. These were the people who also bragged about how many AP classes they were taking, extra tennis games and orchestra concerts they were in, how many colleges they were applying to, and how they did on their PSAT (Preliminary Scholastic Aptitude Test—taken junior year of high school).

Honestly, I had no clue what they were talking about. What the heck was a "PSAT"? All I knew was that it sounded important and was something that helped people get into better colleges. It was clear these people were on the track to a successful college career, and I knew that I had to do what they were doing to secure my spot in an elite college.

So I began the "faking game" and worked hard to get to their level. I raised that ACT 19 to 27 without any tutoring. I learned tennis on my own to play with the school team. I funded my own string bass lessons to be able to play a high school senior concerto to show my friends how great I was. I tried to learn how to enjoy science through the school's Science Olympiad club. I tried to jump into their honors and AP classes to get a taste of the great teachers and challenging college-prep courses.

But it was so difficult to truly catch up. I was just a fake and was barely on their level. I got into the varsity girl's tennis team my junior year, but I was just their substitute player who would play for sick or injured teammates only to get crushed by opponents who had years of tennis lessons under their belt. And even though I joined the school's Science Olympiad and specialized in the rocks and minerals test for two years, I was outperformed by our B team when they showed up with no studying beforehand. And when I tried out honors pre-calculus, I got a D– on the first test while the honors-track sophomores thought it was just a refreshing review. Out of pity, my teacher told me "I wasn't a good fit for this class" and advised me to drop back down to the normal track.

I thought back to my sixth grade classes, when the course tracking began. Why wasn't I put in the higher group with Simba when we began to diverge? Why did my teachers separate me and my best friend? Was it because I got a C+ in fifth grade math because I hung out with that popular friend too much? Was it because I turned in my sixth grade poetry packet a few days late? I felt like I was being withheld from a better school within my school. I felt like I was being punished for something I did wrong in my early years—and there was no way that I could take it back or make it right.

Failure even followed me to my summer job. I signed up to be a golf caddie and carry bags for golfers because I wanted to fund myself without burdening my parents with any extra costs. But my first two years of caddying were seasons of anxiety around learning how to act and speak with really rich adults. I hated calling people by their Mr. and Mrs. titles. It was all so strange to me. And almost being the only Asian girl in the entire club made me feel even more self-conscious. I didn't know sports or business enough to make small talk. I didn't know what it was like to spend summers in Northern Michigan. I didn't know I had to research colleges early on. Worst of all, I didn't know how to "suck up" to my bosses and the golfers. But to other caddies, this was just a normal job in communities they grew up in.

I was frustrated with all of these things—not just because I was behind, but because I didn't know why this was happening. But between you and me, would it help if I told you that Larry was an engineer whose job depended on math? And that momma Wong was an accountant? Those daily math lessons helped Simba in ways I didn't notice until she was completely immersed in all advanced classes. And who knows—maybe learning about the health benefits of different fruits helped nurture her scientific mind that would lead her to a future biomedical engineering undergraduate honors degree.

On the other hand, my parents were refugees from the Vietnam War. My mom was the first in her family to go to the United States and almost drowned in a sinking fisherman's boat. After jumping between waitressing and sewing, she finally hit the low-skilled labor jackpot and passed tests to work as a U.S. Postal Service mail organizer. Her job gave about $55,000 per year and cushy health benefits. But from her determination to support her family, she recently brought up that income level up to $65,000 per year by working overtime almost every day in addition to her night shifts. My dad left Vietnam and had to cross many southeast Asian countries to spend a few years in a refugee camp in the Philippines. He tells me he finished high school at the refugee camp, but it didn't really do anything for his dead-end career cooking Chinese takeout food with a lower-than-minimum-wage salary of $13,000 per year.

Because they didn't have the language or educational knowledge to help me and my siblings, my parents were never able to read us bedtime stories or give us school advice. They would ask us to write checks for their bills and do phone calls with the Internet companies. They couldn't come to my orchestra concerts or tennis matches because my mom was sleeping to prepare for the next night shift and my dad was at work all day. It sounds like my parents are neglectful and uninvolved, and some of my friends would get sad when I explained why they were never around. But to me, it was normal. I rarely craved the overflowing words of affection and support that traditional middle-class parents gave their kids.

Up until my junior year, I hadn't really put the pieces together that their immigrant, economic, and racial status affected my education so much. But when I had to explicitly ask their exact income and educational levels to fill out college applications, the light bulb went off. Although it was naïve, I and my parents always believed that if we kept working hard enough, we would overcome any barrier. But even being raised in a great school district wasn't enough to mask the effects of my lower-class, second-generation immigrant status.

Sometimes my parents noticed how late I was staying up each night to cram. They would urge me to go to bed and relax, but I yelled at them to shut up because they didn't understand what it was like to try to go to college. Yeah, I know. My teenage angst was really bad. I wrongfully took my frustration out on my parents—the people whom I owed my safe suburban middle-class life to.

So most of my high school career can be thought of as four years of overworking myself—fueled by jealousy, envy, inferiority, and self-hate I had from these social class–based differences. But in the end, I managed to get the best case scenario that filled me and my parents with pride. I got into University of Michigan early action on a fully covered tuition and housing golf caddie scholarship. I even received a scholarship to study abroad in Finland for the summer before I started college in the fall of 2014.

I felt so great. I made it! I wasn't a fake anymore! I was going to a prestigious school with a full ride scholarship. I finally felt like I was on Simba's level. So of course, I jumped straight into Michigan with a cocky attitude. I signed up for Calculus 2 with dreams to be a math major, thinking that all the suckers who got grades below an A– were dumb, lazy losers. I got a 55% on the first exam because I didn't know there were practice exams. Next semester, I got a C+ in Economics 101. In just one year, I went from the classic "pulling up myself by my bootstraps" success story to a washed up freshman whose grades didn't show how much studying she had done.

It seemed like everyone around me was adjusting just fine because they knew what was going on. When I told my Calculus 2 tablemates that I got a 55% on our first exam, one of them smirked and laughed: "What? *That* low? How is that even possible?" My roommate finished her freshman year with all As and got into the Ross School of Business. Even with college social life, I didn't know what "Greek Life" was and got a rude introduction to it when I moved into my golf caddie scholarship house, which is basically a large wannabe fraternity with about 90% white guys.

I felt like I was dumped straight back to level 0. Just when I was feeling good about the progress I made, the classes and students made me feel incompetent and inadequate. I was like I was trying to reach a finish line that was constantly moving faster than I could keep up with.

I remember in the first week of class, I walked by a huge sign saying: "Are you the first in your family to go to college? Join the First-Generation College Students at Michigan!" I completely ignored it, and even laughed at it a little. Back when I was still riding my high school success-high, I was confident I could do everything on my own, just like how I had gotten into Michigan on a full ride scholarship without any help from rich parents. But after my first semester, I had fallen so behind that I needed someone to tell me they were struggling in the same ways. I needed to know that I wasn't alone.

After going to a few First-Generation College Student meetings, I was blown away by how strongly I identified with the first-gen identity. We were a small group that shared our frustrations and triumphs about being the first in our family to attend college. We built our community by telling our struggles with mismatching class, cultural, and academic levels. We were drastically different from traditional Michigan students whose family incomes were well over six figures.

Their stories were the first stories I heard on campus that truly resonated with me. One girl told us she refused to go to graduate student instructors, professors, or friends for academic help because she had always been doing things on her own. Other first-gens shared they always had to manage their taxes and FAFSAs (federal government student aid forms) on their own, and how parents had to go to *them* for help with their documents. I even bonded with another first-gen who was also a second-generation Asian immigrant who faced similar language and cultural boundaries on top of the typical first-gen struggles.

I did a 180° flip. I stopped worshipping Simba and the rest of the honors/AP class group and paved my own path with Michigan's first-gen group. I eventually became treasurer for the group to get more involved and give back to a community of peers who had helped me build back my self-esteem. After 19 years of trying to fake my way to be something I wasn't, I quickly began to accept my working-class roots as something to take pride in. Thankfully, it also helped me grow away from the teenage angst that made me blame my parents for all my troubles. By my second year in college, my relationship with my parents grew healthier, I found a community where I felt safe and welcomed, and I started to learn how to study for college classes while juggling student organizations, a part-time job, and research.

But even while learning how to be okay with my range of identities, it was hard to keep up with the realities of an elite college like the University of Michigan. Last year I took an Introduction to Public Policy course because I wanted to explore education policy—inspired by my experiences as a lower-middle-class first-gen and my study abroad trip to Finland, where I learned about their amazing education system. I was so excited to be in a space with people who were dedicated to improving the world through large-scale changes and was eager to learn and connect with like-minded students.

But on the second week of class, we took a survey that asked for our household income brackets. Even before I saw the results, I knew what they'd look like. About two-thirds of the students had parents with incomes that were $150,000 per year or more, with half of those students with parental income incomes above $250,000 per year. Only 7% were in my same income bracket. Even though I could literally *see* the students' wealth from the rows of MacBooks, Greek Life tank tops, and expensive name brands like Vineyard Vines and Canada Goose, it hurt to see how isolated I was in a field of study I was so excited to pursue. Even though no one was saying it, I felt like I didn't belong there.

After I learned how rich the families of University of Michigan students were, it was hard to act like it was okay to live with these inequalities. I didn't want to just ignore them and pretend these differences weren't there. After all, my entire high school struggle was essentially a result of highly unequal amounts of class privilege. To dedicate my life to studying and changing these systems of privilege and oppression, I decided to major in sociology with future plans to study education policy. Compared to math classes I took as a freshman, my sociology classes were always applicable and interesting in the context of my own life experiences. I loved being able to talk with my professors about research papers we read, covering topics like how the parenting styles of working-class families affect education outcomes. These were conversations that I felt invested in because I could genuinely contribute to them.

But at the same time, I've learned to accept I'm very privileged within my marginalized identities. My lower-middle-class, second-generation Vietnamese immigrant, and first-generation student identities have the potential to chain me to the same fate as my working-class parents. But thanks to my parents who slave away each day at their jobs, I have the privilege to be upwardly mobile through my success in higher education. I actually didn't pull myself up by my bootstraps on my own. My parents, who came to the America with no English skills and no knowledge of American schools, deliberately placed me in a safe suburb with just enough money and freedom to surround myself with a high-achieving friends group.

As much as I like to take pride in how independent and self-driven I am today, I did not get to where I am by myself. I am indebted to my parents for being patient and fully trusting me to take charge of my own path in life. I am indebted to the support network of the first-generation student group, my professors, and my friends who have helped validate my struggles in community-based and academic settings. But for the future trajectory of my life, I am forever thankful to my friend Simba and the honors/AP class group—the group of people that made me feel inferior and jealous. Even though our differences caused me toxic-filled stress and competition, if they hadn't helped give me tips with my math homework, improved my tennis swing, or gave me direction with my college search, I would not be the college-educated, confident, content, and self-aware person I am today.

As I write this paper and reflect on my K–12 journey with my best friend Simba, I've started to take larger steps toward humanizing groups that hold social class privilege. As I hear and read more perspectives about social class in my sociology classes and being at

Michigan, I've started to accept and acknowledge the vital role that upper-class people have in creating a more equitable world. Moving forward, I am confident the experiences before and during my time at Michigan will prepare me for a lifetime of challenges, diversity, and growth I will face in a career dedicated to education reform. I am excited to get to know my working-class parents better as we get older and let them know how much I appreciate them, even when I was an angsty and angry teen. But above all, I hope to have a future in education policy to break barriers of classist and elitist education by increasing the 7% of lower-income students who were in my public policy class. I plan to create welcoming spaces of learning for all students on our class spectrum.

STUCK IN THE MIDDLE
CAYCEE TURCZYN

I have always asked "why." My parents swear I came out of the womb talking, or, more specifically, asking questions. I constantly strive to look at situations from all angles, refusing to accept surface-level answers. This trait has served me well over the years as I have learned to always dive deeper into an issue to fully understand why and how it is. Since coming to college, I've started asking questions about social class, trying to figure out the "why" and "how" of social class difference.

Early childhood

I originate from a small, rural providence in South Korea called Kyungbuk. I only know this is where I am from because it appears on my birth certificate. The first six months of my life were spent in the care of a foster mom who hosted me until my adoption paperwork was finalized by my parents in the United States. When it was finally time to travel to the United States, I was eagerly received by my parents and three siblings who were also adopted from South Korea.

My adoption was never a secret. Having an Irish mother and Polish father made it obvious my siblings and I were not "their" children, but despite appearance differences, they are my parents. There are pictures in my mother's house from the year my siblings and I became official citizens of the United States. My parents hosted a "citizenship party" with family and friends to celebrate this milestone in our lives. Our ages at the time were 11, 9, 7, and 5 years.

My first encounter with understanding social class came during my first years as a citizen. Although I was probably around eight years old, dad casually explained to me that I was lucky to be living in the United States in comparison to South Korea. In simple terms only an eight-year-old would understand, he would tell me how life in South Korea would have been much different. This means whenever I complained I couldn't get a toy I wanted or that I didn't want to go to soccer practice, he would jokingly remind me that if I was in Korea I wouldn't have these opportunities. He was not saying this to scold me, but to simply open my eyes and appreciate the opportunities the land of the free can and would provide me throughout life. This was a constant reminder throughout the years that kept me humble and appreciative.

It was not until I was 16 when I really learned what my potential life in South Korea could have ended up like if my mother had not given me up for adoption. On Christmas, my family and I gathered together to look through old picture books. In my baby book, I found adoption papers regarding my birth parents with three bullets points under each and a brief paragraph on their relations. In summary, I learned that my mother, a struggling mother of five kids with a seventh-grade education, went to work in a restaurant to help her husband provide for the family. This is where she met my father, listed as an unknown factory worker with a fifth grade education. My birth parents' working-class lifestyle and education level are drastically different than my middle-class parents' college educations and full-time jobs. Mom is a commercial lender and dad is the former director for my hometown's Parks, Recreation and Cemetery. It took eight years to fully realize how life in South Korea would have most likely left me uneducated and struggling.

Youth Sports

Being from a middle-class family in America, I was afforded many privileges that I appreciate immensely now as a junior in college.

Despite having four kids, my parents could afford to put my siblings and me in whatever extracurricular we wanted. Since my dad was the Parks and Recreation manager for the city we grew up in, those activities ended up being mainly sports. To my young self, it seemed extremely normal to be able to go golfing every day or drive with my family to an air-conditioned facility to practice basketball. However, I was blind to the high cost of sports equipment and travel as well as the stress put on my parents to balance four kids' different schedules on top of their own busy work lives.

This was until my middle brother began playing basketball for the Flint Affiliation. We did not live in Flint but resided 20 minutes away in rural Lapeer, Michigan, in a 60-acre home. Most people from our town lived in suburban homes, in the woods, or on farms. As the youngest in the family, I always ended up being with my dad when he drove my brother to practices or was the one to attend weekend games. In other words, I was my sibling's number one fan. Every basketball event that would take place in Flint was hosted in buildings where you had to pass through security guarded metal detectors and the windows were covered by rusting metal pipes. The state of Michigan called these buildings schools, but to my middle-class self, I felt as if I was in a jail from a TV show. My brother's involvement with this Flint basketball team served as another humbling social class experience for me.

Although he traveled to Flint to play, most of his teammates resided in the area. Dad never explicitly told me that living in Flint was different than our hometown, but I could tell by his actions that it was. I was never allowed to walk through the parking lot without him by my side, and if we brought anything of value, we had to put it under our car seats so passersby would not be tempted to break into our car. He also always offered to help with travel for my brother's teammates because often their parents could not get off work to make it to weekend tournaments especially out-of-state ones. There was one time dad hosted all my brother's friends at our house and took them swimming at our city's community center. I can still recall hearing their excitement of having the pool all to themselves. As I watched from the workout room above, my sister and I choose not to swim because it was something available to us whenever we wanted. Despite being aware that the cities we resided in stood in stark contrast to one another, I was always able to talk or joke around with them which in my mind dismissed any thought of there being social class divides.

While basketball taught me about experiences of working-class families from Flint, golfing showed me a whole other world of upper-middle-class and upper-class families. It might be a common stereotype to say poor kids from the city play basketball and rich kids from the suburbs play golf, but these stereotypes turned out to be somewhat true in my own experiences. My father introduced me to golf around the time I could just begin walking. This was mainly because I was the youngest and would be brought to the range with my older siblings. I quickly developed my swing and watched as golf enveloped my life.

Being as young as I was when I began golfing, I never realized how expensive golf clubs, range passes, and country club accesses were because it was always available to me. Luckily, small-town people tend to make relations and my family often received "family" discounts. It made no difference that I was constantly playing the same exact course every single time because I had no idea there was another way. That was until I was 14 and played in my first official golf tournament where I qualified to play in the International Optimist Junior Golf Tournament being hosted in West Palm Beach, Florida. My oblivious self did not realize what was in store.

My family had taken many trips to Florida throughout my childhood so travel was nothing new. However, when we arrived at the beautiful resort and I saw the course my eyes widened in disbelief. Here I was, a small girl from Lapeer, Michigan, being able to play on courses that I watched professionals play on TV. Although it took me the entire trip to grasp the reality of the opportunity, the other girls treated the tournament, fancy hotel rooms, and scenery as if they were second nature. Everything from their ability to have golf pros help them, brand name attire, shiny clubs, and long lists of places they'd travel to play golf revealed the large disparities in our upbringing. Immediately I began to question why I was in Florida because clearly the "golf gods" had made a mistake allowing me to end up here. Dad could sense the discomfort I felt being in this situation and without hesitation reminded me I deserved to be there as much as the next girl. He instilled in me the confidence to "play my own game" which made me proud to be the girl from Lapeer who taught herself how to play golf.

As my golf career continued and I began playing in high school, I tried to remain focused, one swing at a time. I was lucky to begin playing in more tournaments across Michigan that gave me access to exclusive courses such as Warwick Hills. At this time, I began to realize how expensive golf was because I saw the price tag that came along with playing and watched as the dollars climbed at every gas stop along the way. However, my eyes were really opened when I started playing for my school consistently during golf season. I filled the number one spot on my team all throughout high school which paired me with the top golfers from every school. Although I could match or even beat my competition, I still noticed differences between us. For one, if the tournament extended longer than a day I would become riddled with anxiety because I only had one pair of golf shorts. The typical golf conversation during matches usually revolved around normal teenager things which I could talk all day about, but when it came time to start talking about our golf pros, country clubs, etc. I quickly became silent. Again, my dad reminded me: "Keep doing Caycee." As often as I played golf and as good as I was, dad sensed a lack of passion in my game. It was not that I was not passionate; it was that I was fighting my own demons. When the time came to start thinking about a collegiate career in golf I regretfully dismissed the thought because there was no way I was cut out for that. What did I know about golf, how to meet recruiters, or how to be successful in real tournaments? This led me to pull back from golf and shift my focus on the University of Michigan in Ann Arbor and their business school.

Working Life

At an early age dad instilled in me the value of hard work. I am fortunate to have my parents provide me with a phone, car, and almost every other reasonable possession I could ask for. However, my dad did not want me to go through life being a "taker" and so began our exchange of me doing my part to earn the luxuries he provided. That meant doing well in school, practicing my sports, and working as much as possible in my free time. It sounds easy now, but having to tell my friends that I couldn't spend the night because I had to work was the end of the world for my middle-school self. While most of my upper-class friends were sleeping in and spending time at lake houses on the weekends during the year, my dad had set me up with random minimum-wage jobs. The first was running my city's soccer complex's concession stand with my sister every Saturday morning from 7:30 a.m. to 3:00 p.m. The days were spent trying to manage multiple customers' demands, keeping track of money and the dreadful end of the day mopping, sweeping, and cleaning of the hot dog machine. To this day I cannot look at a hot dog without remembering the stench covering me after every Saturday morning shift. In retrospect, I realize I was not the only kid from my hometown working. I am positive some of my peers were working twice as many hours and doing even dirtier work than me, but my middle-class self did not pay attention.

For the most part I didn't mind the hard work because the nice paychecks at the end of the two weeks were a source of gratification. However when dad remarried and moved us in with my stepmom and her boys, the work that came from living in a large house inhabited by eight people was not paid and therefore my least favorite activity of all. The kitchen, my bedroom, and my bathroom were my assigned areas for chores. There was also an unspoken rule to clean up after yourself, but that did not mean my brothers always adhered to it.

Summers were an all-hands-on-deck time. My parents did not care if you had just worked a long shift or had plans with friends, work had to be done and done right. Mowing the lawns, pulling weeds, hand-clipping overhanging branches throughout our property's trails and mulching the flower beds were a few of the routine chores. I recall spending those summers murmuring how unfair it was that I had to do this labor and even asked my parents why they did not just hire someone to do it all. Of course, they would reply with a long speech that typically ended with "you live here so you can contribute to the household." Much to my childhood dismay, I was very fortunate to have humbly experienced working minimum wage and learning household chores all those years as it set me up how to survive in college.

High School

Balancing school, work, and sports was always tricky. I found myself missing many days during the season causing an internal conflict because I highly valued my education. Luckily my grade point average did not suffer which could be because my school was not chalked full of AP (Advanced Placement) or IB (International Baccalaureate) classes like other schools. However, senior year my hometown combined our two high schools and attempted to revamp the curriculum adding several AP classes and dual enrollment. Knowing I wanted to do business in college, specifically the University of at Michigan (UM), I searched for the most rigorous courses to prepare myself. Although new courses had been added, they were lacking in the discipline of business. I worried that I would not be well prepared for college and would not gain entrance into UM.

When it came time to apply to colleges the process of figuring out which to send my transcripts to was limited to three in-state colleges because tuition was reasonable and application costs were high. My choices were the University of Michigan, Ann Arbor; Michigan State University; and Grand Valley State University here in Michigan. To me these colleges were the greatest institutions if only because I was unaware of what else was available. After all, my entire hometown is the type of place where most kids either choose to work after high school or aspire to successful, but smaller state schools. Quite a few of my friends and peers were more than smart enough to apply to UM and beyond, but did not because they could not afford the application or knew they could never pay high tuition bills. Within weeks I was accepted into Grand Valley, but achingly waited to hear back from Michigan.

It was December 18th when I received an e-mail saying I was accepted into the school of Literature, Science and Arts at the University of Michigan. I'd be lying if I said I didn't scream with excitement, and then proceed to cry tears of happiness and relief. I'd also be lying if I said my parents and sister didn't act the same. To some, getting into Michigan may be a no-brainer, but to this small-town girl this was unbelievable. However, my bubble of excitement popped during a senior-only class when we talked about what we were doing the next year. Most had either not heard back yet or did not choose which school to attend. I proudly, but humbly, shared I was off to the UM with the hopes of studying business. This was a mistake because my teacher quickly used me as an example: "Caycee is smart for our school, but she will surely be in the bottom of the group once at Michigan. So think about that when you choose where you are going because Caycee could be the top of a smaller school like UM Flint or Grand Valley State, but will struggle when she gets to Michigan." I began to question my abilities and developed a chip on my shoulder to prove her and everyone else wrong. Going to Michigan was not just beneficial for me, but also my hometown. I thought that if I could do it, then maybe younger students would think they also could do it. When fall came around, four of us packed up and left Lapeer in rearview mirrors.

Freshman Year of College

The transition to college proved to be as difficult as I was warned it would be. I was tasked with making new friends, settling into my dorm, performing well in classes, and finding a job. The people, culture, and actives were nothing I could have anticipated coming from Lapeer. The all-freshman dorm served me well in educating me about the world outside Lapeer. I met students who used summer as a verb, came from families who either owned, worked, or knew someone that had a connection to companies I saw on the news, and ate out for almost every meal despite our costly meal plan. They had all applied to three times as many colleges as me with fancy names like Yale University, Northwestern University, and others I had to Google following our conversation. I spent weekends working at the Hockey Arena serving food, cleaning the stands after games, and closing the building at 3:00 a.m. for time and a half pay, while most of my friends could study and socialize as they pleased.

Everyone wore the clothes and carried the accessories I would dream of one day owning when I was successful and living on my own dime. It caused me great pain when I would see girls using bags I knew cost hundreds of dollars to only carry their old textbooks. They had fancy MacBooks while I had an overheated HP (Hewlett Packard) that I loved in high school, but was ashamed of in college. The most distinct memory I have of realizing the difference between my friends and myself was when winter was approaching and we all began the hunt for a college appropriate coat. I spent weeks looking for deals on long-styled North Face coat and finally came across one that was on sale for $120. Both my parents and I knew it was expensive, but after many discussions we knew it would last over the years making the investment worth it. I was so proud to wear my coat because I felt it made me "fit in." That was until I came to school again and saw people wearing Canada Gooses. After a Google search, I realized they were wearing coats with outrageous price tags of $700 plus. I may pine after expensive things, but I am not wasteful of money. I stopped trying to fit in.

My focus at school quickly became gaining entrance to the Ross School of Business. I joined Preparation Initiative (PI), a learning community designed for students who have demonstrated their potential for outstanding, socially responsible leadership in the business world, but for some reason beyond their control, had pre-college learning situations that left them unprepared to realize that potential through conventional university alternatives. In other words, PI served to bridge the gap between underrepresented, undereducated, and/or low-income-background students and higher education. This community helped me find others who were struggling to fit in to this world where everyone appeared to come from money and privilege. This is not to say I came from struggle because I did not, but in comparison to most my peers I felt poor.

I applied to the business school at the end of my freshman year hoping this would be the next step in my goal of reaching the "top."

The Ross School of Business

With hard work and the support of PI, I was admitted to Ross for the start of my sophomore year. The Ross community is tight-knit. Your graduating class of 625 students is immediately broken into several cohorts of around 80 students, allowing you to really get to know a certain group. While Ross admits a diverse set of students, I once again found myself surrounded by highly privileged individuals. Business is known to be a "who you know" field and my peers surely let me know they "knew" the right people. I immediately felt disadvantaged.

There is a unique grading distribution in Ross where only a certain percentage can receive As. This was created to replicate the competitive nature that comes with being successful in business, but at times can be extremely hard on students because they are pitted against their friends from the beginning. In comparison to my peers who took accounting or had their own business in high school, I started at about zero in terms of business knowledge.

My first semester I enrolled in the required sophomore class: BA (Business Administration) 200. Students work on resumes, explore corporate social responsibility, and attend speaker series. The best part is the access we have to exceptional business professionals across all industries nationwide and beyond. When I found out I would receive credit for attending speakers, I was ecstatic, however, most of my peers griped they had to do this. Maybe it's because I'm from small town Lapeer and do not have a daddy on Wall Street, but my eyes would light up at the opportunity to hear such established professionals from places such as McKinsey or Unilever talk because if it was not for my admission at Ross they would never give me the time of their day.

There is a set timeline that is essentially the formula for success. Students enter as sophomores focusing on classes and narrowing down a career path; junior year there is networking and hopefully interviewing for a summer internship; following that you receive a full-time offer and go into senior year all set. There is an unspoken rule that while Ross helps you get these internships from their brand name, you are still competing against everyone else so recruiting ends up becoming a resume war and a "who you know" game. As early as freshman year even before being admitted into Ross I knew I needed to start filling my resume with leadership roles and fancy summer internships. Since freshman year I have had four internships in both finance and marketing from my connections and hard work. While I am extremely thankful for the opportunities, it's difficult to compare my experiences with some friends who spent their summer working Wall Street internships that they did not have to interview for because their dad set it up.

During winter semester 2017, I was recruited for finance jobs on Wall Street. Almost every day I interacted with employees from firms that I grew up seeing on TV, knowing they play a dominative role in the real world. I had the opportunity to spend spring break visiting Wall Street firms with a group of girls through women in finance initiative. After the trip ended I remember calling dad overly excited and extremely thankful I even had the chance to stand in these buildings. I thanked the employees and the coordinators a thousand times over. I'm sure my social class was showing.

The networking aspect of recruiting is easy because I am a natural socializer. What is not easy is preparation for interviews. The days where interview questions are as simple as "tell me about yourself" have now become "walk me through a DCF" or "if you had one million dollars how would you invest it and why" and you are expected to know DCF is a discounted cash flow and you should invest in emerging markets because of your age and risk level. Lucky for someone like me there are prep books putting me on an even-playing field as my more financially savvy counterparts. However, unfortunately for me these books come at a steep price tag, causing me to call dad asking for help, having to explain how Ross works, and that he is investing in my future.

Hometown

As I continue to be upwardly mobile through my education and experiences, I still find myself being on the outside both at school and at home. I may not have realized it at the time, but Lapeer is a wonderful place to grow up. Although my high school did not have all the classes, resources, or clubs I wanted, I entered college extremely appreciative of everything I was able to do. However, as I continued my education, a distance between some of my childhood friends and I developed. While I know they were extremely proud and supportive of me attending Michigan, it is not easy being greeted with: "Oh look it's Ms. Michigan," or hearing friends say they don't want to visit me because everyone at Michigan is "stuck up." My fascination with markets or my story about hearing Malcolm Gladwell speak is lost on my friends who do not care to have the economy or scholars on their mind.

Despite all of this, I feel the most "comfortable" back in Lapeer, Michigan, surrounded by trucks, and acres of trees, knowing just about everyone's name and dining at the one fancy restaurant in town. There is not a day that goes by where I do not compare what I am currently doing to life in my hometown. I often miss the way people in Lapeer seem not to care about status and money as much as they do here at Michigan. I am thankful to have had the experience of growing up in Lapeer as it has served as constant reminder to stay grounded and remember where I came from.

Conclusion

I spent much of my time reflecting on my purpose behind this essay for the anthology. Like the true inquisitive individual that I am, I wanted to get to the root of my decision for publishing a piece that speaks about an issue—social class—that is so intimate and complex to an individual that is essentially taboo to talk about in social settings. What I discovered after much reflection is I want this piece to be a concrete piece of writing that captures who I am now in my life. I say that because as I continue my college career and pursue a high-paying job in the fields of business and finance, I fear becoming oblivious to social class; I anticipate some shifts in what I value and know about social classes. I want this anthology to show others that it is possible to remain as humble and aware as possible despite advancements in life. While becoming more educated and setting yourself up for success are great, it seems all too often people end up forgetting where they came from with the passing of time. I promise to keep asking why about social class, inequality, and everything in between wherever life takes me.

How Social Class Influenced My Education
Raenell Williams

Elementary

Staring at a half-eaten plate of red beans and rice, broccoli, and chicken, I sat motionless at the kitchen table. I watched dad place the leftovers on my plate as he prepared me for dinner and eventually bed. As he put the last of the food on my plate, I sat motionless attempting to conjure up a way to get out of having to eat dinner. After feeding myself tiny parcels my dad grew tired of me picking at the plate "Why aren't you eating?" he asked. "I'm full." I said without looking up from the table. With a look of disbelief, he peered in my direction and proceeded to ask why I barely ate any food. I knew the real answer but did not want him to know my plan. A few moments earlier, I saw my dad put the last of the food on my plate and knew he intended on going to bed without eating dinner for himself. My plan was to eat enough to not be hungry and save the rest with the hopes he would he eat what was left on my plate. At the young age of 10 I understood he worked very hard to provide for me, yet he sometimes did so at the cost of his own well-being. Many days, my dad would work long shifts and forget to eat. He often worked double and triple shifts and would use his lunch breaks to pick me up from school and after-school activities as opposed to actually taking time for himself. My father never actually ate the food I would pretend to be too full to eat. He would always give it to me for lunch, or I would have the same meal for dinner the following night.

Growing up we were a far cry from rich, however we were not quite poor. There were times we would go out to eat frequently, and I would order all of the food I wanted without a thought about the cost. There were times that I found myself saving meals for the next day because I did not want my dad to have to worry about where my next meal would come from. My dad often spoke pretty candidly with me. He let me in on many conversations that some other adults felt should have been kept amongst the adults. Growing up in a single-parent household was a unique experience: even more so because I was raised by my father. Many people were shocked to find that my father raised me by himself. Shocked by my manners, how I presented myself, and my behavior. There was always some-one skeptical of the fact that my black father was present in my life, and that he raised me as a single parent. My dad and I are extremely close, and many of the ideas that I hold on many issues spring from conversations that he and I shared in our home.

One sunny spring day, my dad and I were in the living room fold-ing clothes and I asked my dad if we were rich or poor. He asked me what I thought the answer was. I thought long and hard, and answered "we are rich, but not as rich as white people!" He then asked me to explain my reasoning, after a few more seconds of thought; I explained that I always had clean clothes, and nice uni-forms. I was comparing myself to my friends and even some of my own family. I had my own room, when I knew many people who had to share a bed with multiple people. My ideas surrounding class were very limited. I thought because our home was always clean and smelled like clean linen that it meant we had a lot of money. I equated wealth to how clean we were. I knew there were houses of family members that I dreaded going to visit because their homes smelled bad or because their rooms were always cluttered and messy. My dad then told me that there were three classes. "One is upper, the next is middle, and the last is lower," my dad explained in the simplest terms possible. "Some people have more money than they can spend, lower class needs more money, and the people in the middle have enough money to buy what they need, but don't have as much spending money as the upper class," my dad responded. Pleased with the answer my dad gave me I spent the next few years of my life believing that my life was as normal as could possibly be. I now realize that based on my dad's income we would be considered middle class. My dad is a police officer, and together we had several memorable experiences that have shown me that class titles do and analyzing someone's income there can be a lot of judgments and assumptions made that do not aptly reflect someone's lived experiences.

Middle

"When we get home it's going to be dark," My dad told me as we pulled out of the driveway of my grandmother's house. "Yeah I know, yesterday we set the clocks forward so it is supposed to get darker sooner than it usually does." My dad let out a slight chuckle and put his head down. He immediately changed the subject and instructed me to charge my phone in the car so it would not be dead in the morning. Before dad picked me up from my grandmother's home he made sure my homework had been completed, I ate dinner, and that I had already had my shower. I remember wondering why my dad looked more stressed than he usually did. When we pulled in the driveway he told me to change into my pajamas and to go straight to sleep. I stepped into our three-bedroom home and instantly felt something different. The sun was just beginning to set so the house was not too dark. I went upstairs and hopped in the bed. A few minutes later my dad came to tuck me in. I was completely unaware that there were so many things going on in my dad's mind. The next morning when I got up for school my room light would not turn on, I thought nothing of it and grabbed my uniform from the hanger and proceeded to go downstairs to the bathroom. My dad was still asleep and the light in the bathroom did not work. I looked around the house and saw the clock on the oven was not lit and that no other digital clocks appeared to be working. I brushed my teeth and waited for what seemed like eternity for the water to get hot. I ended up washing my face with cold water and woke my dad up to tell him that I was dressed and ready for school. He told me we could stop at Burger King for Breakfast and he instructed me to start the car. On the way to school I asked him if there had been a power outage in the neighborhood. He told me that things were going to be different for a while, and that the lights would be back on soon.

I decided to keep the morning's event a secret from my family and friends. We began to spend more and more time at my grandmother's house. My grandmother has lived with my great aunt for as long as I can remember. Gradually, my dad and I lived with them. We would pack clothes for a weekend, and go home and switch out the clothes. My dad stayed home and in the mornings he would pick me up for school from my aunt's home. Through the winter, my dad and I eventually moved in full time. As time passed, we were accustomed to living with two other people. I secretly enjoyed being there. At our old house, sometimes my dad always worked late and I spent a lot of time home alone. There, at my grandmother's, there was almost always someone home. I loved eating dinner together because it reminded me of families that I always saw on television. For almost all of middle school, we stayed with my grandmother and great aunt. We eventually moved back to her home and resumed living back to our regular lives.

High School

Even though my upbringing was one that was the polar opposite of the traditional American way, the way I was raised significantly impacted the goals I have been able to reach thus far. I always had a lot. I was surrounded by a lot of love, I had lots of toys, and I had a ton of family. However, there were some things we never had; Internet and cable just to name a few. When I was in high school I worked hard because I knew everyone expected me to go to college afterward. I had no idea of what college I would be attending, but I knew good grades meant college, and if I was going to college, I would have to have grades good enough for college scholarships. Young and full of zeal, my main goal as a junior in high school was to find a way to stand out on a college application. I realized that having a 4.0 GPA (grade point average) and being a good kid was not enough to be a competitive candidate for colleges. I had heard a lot about the weight of standardized test scores, but I knew that the highest ACT (American College Testing) score in my high school was 24 and my school only encouraged us to reach for a 21, while the average ACT score for admission in the top colleges in Michigan ranged from 29 to 33. Somewhere between ACT prep classes and community program participation, I realized that I was not the only student in the city of Detroit fearing that a mediocre standardized test score would keep me from college. Between soccer, basketball, National Honor Society, debate, martial arts, community service, and ACT prep programs, I did an extracurricular activity seven days a week. Looking back I realize that I was extremely privileged to be able to be afforded the opportunity to participate in so much. Even though my dad worked a lot, he always moved his schedule around to be able to accommodate what was best for me. Even though other parents may have wanted to do that, their jobs probably did not allow for that privilege.

My high school was a Title I school, more than half of the students had free or reduced lunch. This was especially interesting because I never qualified for free or reduced lunch, yet asking for lunch money was something that I never did because I knew that every day he did not have the money. I remember eating pieces of friend's lunch or asking kids who brought their own lunch if I could use their swipe. Looking back I never asked for lunch money from my dad, and eventually just learned to eat less. I took the idea of save more and ask for less with me even after high school. When I got admitted into college, I earned a full tuition scholarship, and applied for and was awarded a five-year room-and-board scholarship. These were blessings, and made college much more affordable but there were still things like books, food, and some school supplies like iClickers and graphing calculators I could not afford but did not tell my dad I needed. Often times there were things that I needed but did not bring up because I felt bad that I was not able to contribute at home while my dad was raising my little sister.

College

Attending college was a huge step for me, I knew I was going, but I never in a million years would have imagined what it would have actually been like on a predominantly white campus. Since the ninth grade I imagined my college experiences taking place at a historically black college or university. My dreams were crushed when a member of my family sat me down and said that going to a predominantly black college would be a waste of money because I have two prestigious universities in the state that I live in. He said the world does not value black college experiences, and I should go with the school that has the most money and prestige. His lesson was that the world is a lot bigger than just the black college experience.

I was saddened by the fact that my dreams of attending Howard University were not going to be a reality. I ultimately ended up choosing the University of Michigan because it was the most affordable. As an aspiring educator I would like to have gone to Michigan State because they have the better education program, but I was indifferent about which school I would end up at because neither one of the schools were an HBCU (historically black colleges and universities). I chose Michigan because it was affordable and that's it. I did not come here to be considered elite or one of the leaders and best. I believed I could get the most out of any college if I applied myself and searched for the best resources. As an aspiring educator, I spent a lot of time in the School of Education and introduced myself to as many people there so that I could get advice on how to get admitted into the school. My own educational experiences have encouraged me to pursue education as a career plan because I want to provide the resources that I felt I missed out on.

One of the most significant college experiences occurred before I was even admitted into college. I participated in Telluride Association Summer Programs (TASP) following my junior year of high school. I was one of the 17 students chosen to live in the Telluride House and participated in a seminar on "Race, and the Limits of Law in America" under the instruction of two university professors. This was the second time that I lived with anyone outside of my family, race, and ethnicity, yet I was still as nervous as it was my first time around. Being accepted into this program meant a lot to me. I knew that I was in for an academic challenge and a life-changing experience.

When I arrived at the Telluride House, I was nervous and anxious. Spending six weeks on Cornell's campus with students whom I felt were academically and economically superior to myself was an intimidating and daunting task. On my very first day students congregated in the basement of the house, played icebreakers, shared our educational backgrounds, and told facts about ourselves. As we shared where we were from, we found that the locations varied greatly. Some TASPers traveled from Beijing, Nepal, Bangladesh, Washington, Taiwan, Michigan, Ithaca, Arkansas, California, and even Tanzania. One of the first observations I made was that majority of the TASPers were students who attended the best boarding and private schools across the country, while I was the only student who came from a Title I charter school in an urban school district. I immediately felt like the least educated person in the room.

The second day of the program we reported to class. After my first day I told my family that I was out of place, and didn't deserve to be there. I was so intimidated that I was afraid to speak in class, and aside from my name and introduction I remained silent. The first week was carried out in the same manner. By the middle of the second week, we discussed topics on education and I eventually learned that no matter how much people knew from reading the works of scholars that they would never be able to discredit my personal experiences. I realized that adding my personal experiences in context of the Socratic discussions was just as valuable as the comments of someone who had read every piece of literature on the subject at hand. I was surprised that other TASPers were actually receptive of my comments and ideas, and people approached me after class telling me that they appreciate my comments in class and that I should share more because my comments made sense and were very inspiring. By the end of the program I learned that my comments were just as valuable as those who had been afforded more expensive educational opportunities than I had in my own life.

At the start of the program I was a little more reserved, just as I was for the start of the TASP program in the summer of 2013 during my sophomore year of high school. I realize that I presented myself to be a little standoffish for the first two weeks of the TASP program but looking back I only made the program harder for myself. I made the vow to myself that if given a second chance to participate in TASP for the summer of 2014 that I would be friendlier and make an effort to talk to everyone in the house more. I fully expected to be more open but when I saw that there were well over 17 students, I knew I probably bit off a little more than I could chew. After I actually started opening up to my fellow TASPers I really started to enjoy the program. I feel TASP prepared me for any environment. TASP prepared me for college classrooms and my future work field. I am grateful for my Telluride experience; it forced me to step out of my comfort zone in order to make new connections with lifelong friends and great mentors. This summer program gave me an advantage that would be useful for me once I actually started college.

On December 23, 2014, I received an e-mail that impacted my life in ways that 17-year-olds like me never could imagine. "Congratulations, you're in!" When notified I had been admitted into the Comprehensive Studies Program (CSP) at the University of Michigan, I was confused and wondered why I was being admitted into a program that I never applied for. Throughout the duration of the CSP I questioned why I needed summer school when for so long I had been at the top of my class. In fall of 2015, I found myself on the Registrar's Office website analyzing the admission statistics.

The numbers I discovered made me question this university's dedication to diversity, my admission, and my place at this school. Why was I lucky enough to be among the 200 black women admitted into the graduating class of 2019? Of the 6,251 students admitted into my graduating class, why were there only 298 black students? I wondered what percentage of blacks needed the Bridge Program as a prerequisite to attend Michigan. I do not doubt that Bridge is a much-needed program, but I wondered why the students that need the most help come from backgrounds as similar as my own and how I can impact the education world to change these conditions.

My freshman year I decided to take an Intergroup Relations class on Race and Ethnicity. There were not many students of color, and the instructors were around our age and not professors. Being the class was three hours long we had plenty of time for discussions. During one of our class periods, we were talking about our feelings when we found out we were admitted. One of the students shared he felt it was unfair because his friend who applied to the University of Michigan was denied, yet the school saved spots for students who benefited from Affirmative Action to get in with low test scores and less work. As if his uninformed comment was not enough, halfway through the comment he had been making eye contact with me as if I was the only one in the class, and he resented my presence in the class. Many people assume that when I say I earned a full ride to college it's because of financial aid, and not because I actually applied for scholarships and do a lot to maintain my scholarships.

My college experiences make me reflect on my own interracial friendships: I have never had a white friend. This is partly because I have never been in social settings with white people before college. However from summer programs that were big on diversity I have participated in, I have made close friends from different races and ethnicities. I do not feel comfortable around white people. Being the only black person in one of my Michigan classes makes me feel more aware of my blackness than at any other point in my life. I try to pretend they have not noticed I am the only black person in the room, while they probably make an effort to not acknowledge the fact that I am different from everyone else in class. In short, I am still trying to navigate college. While I have learned many valuable lessons, I know there is still so much left for me to learn here at Michigan. I treat every day as an opportunity to apply what I have learned and to learn even more.

Part IV
Upper-Middle Class

NEW YORK, NEW YORK
ROBERT MICHAEL BAKERIAN JR.

I was born to economic privilege. I am very lucky because not many children can live my financially stable worry-free life. Not only is it worry-free, but life was and still is filled with pleasures so many are unable to acquire due to their social class. Class status was something I did not think about as a child because I knew and understood I never had to worry. I did not think about it, because I did not have to.

Young children do not learn about economic classes in kindergarten along with addition and subtraction; it is not another mathematical formula. Sure, you could say privilege is having x number of dollars or living in a y square-foot size home, but that does not capture it all. It's one of those things that just hits you at some point and you finally understand: the grand economic differences existing in our society. I have been shaped in many different ways by my upper-middle-class background. Regardless of the downfalls or benefits, I want to thank my parents, Joanne and Robert Sr., whom I love unconditionally, as they have been there for me through thick and thin.

As Winston Churchill once said: "We make a living by what we get. We make a life by what we give."

I grew up in Whitehouse Station, New Jersey. Never heard of it? Do not worry, no one has. And I do not have any facts to enamor you with other than the town was named after a white building—a tavern—built back in the 1700s: creative I know. The town was small with a gas station accompanied by a few family-owned restaurants, like the pizza place—Sorella's—I have a nighttime delivery job at. I was born into suburbia where all houses were eerily similar looking, perfectly spaced, with nice little pools and picnic areas in the middle of the neighborhood. The complex held a few hundred houses of the same design stacked in neat little rows, which compares with the town you make when playing Monopoly. This beautiful neighborhood consisted of mostly newlyweds and couples with their first child.

My home was about 45 minutes southwest of New York City, perfect distance to grab a train for a New York Rangers Game. Dad works outside of New York City, only about 35 minutes away from our home. I cannot remember much about the house, other than James Taylor CDs my parents played while we sat outside on the patio. Who doesn't love James Taylor? Oh, and Hooch. You are probably thinking I am lying (or crazy), but there was this ginormous deep sea blue peacock that would come out of the woods. He would wobble down the pathway and come right onto the patio. Curious but eager, he probably kept coming back because mom would feed him every time. Saltines, for some reason, were his favorite.

I also remember the Ranger Games. I will talk about my hockey career later, but I know my passion for hockey developed from seeing the Rangers play. "Welcome to Madison Square Garden, the World's most favorite arena," still gives me chills. My family had season tickets, only a few rows behind the glass: perfect seats if you ask me. Dad tells me stories of bringing me to my first game with mom before I could talk, spilling beer on me when he raised me up when the Blueshirts scored. Since we were so close to the ice and tunnel where players would leave, sometimes I got pucks from the players or, even better, a stick. One game, a player on the opposing team got hit in the face with a puck. Blood poured onto the ice as they escorted him off. The arena was dead silent except for one five-year-old who suddenly blurted out: "Excuse me sir, can I have your stick?" Yup, that was me. But even at that age, I was nice and always respectful. I did not get a stick that night.

When mom got pregnant with my little brother, Luke, her third child, my parents decided to look for a bigger home. The first house was small and could not contain three "rugrats" stomping around. Right after my ninth birthday in 2003, we moved into Stanton Ridge Golf and Country Club, walking distance from the second Tee-Box. It was gorgeous. The country club had a gym, pool, driving range, tennis courts, and dining room. It was awesome that I could play golf whenever I wanted! Summer camps were fun; I golfed all day, returned home, and couldn't wait to go back in the morning. I had fun and I was out of the house: a win–win for my parents.

When grade school started, I was an outsider. No one really played hockey and the in-crowd consisted of football players. At recess, I was usually the target of typical grade-school banter and I was never good at comebacks. Sometimes I bragged about the golf course as a comeback, until one time I boasted in front of my parents. They pulled me aside and nicely told me it wasn't acceptable: "Be nice to the other boys." Out of curiosity, I occasionally asked dad about how much money he made, but he wouldn't tell me. This would mark my first cognizant experience with social class. Why couldn't I tell people where I lived? At the time, I didn't know why my parents would tell or not tell me these things. Looking back, it must have been tough to teach kids about economic privilege. But I always learned to treat others nicely no matter what, even if they were not nice. During my elementary school years, Christmas never seemed to disappoint; there was always exactly what I had asked for under that tree. My most powerful memories of social class did not come until high school.

Though my town was off the radar, the regional high school I attended was quite large. Enrollment was around 3,500 and I passed new faces in the halls every day. The school pooled from five different municipalities which created an interesting blend of social class backgrounds. There were groups of students I didn't mesh with not because of different class status, but because I was often in the weight room or on the ice. Languages of all sorts could be heard in classrooms and halls, as certain townships tended to be mostly immigrants. There was a less well-off section of town and many Hispanic Americans lived in that area. I had no interaction with these groups, not because I didn't want to, but because we just did not cross paths. I took a finance class while others took an art class. Some kids attended parties while I played sports. I would have loved the opportunity to make more connections. A good number of students, mostly my friends group, were in the upper-middle class. Hunterdon County was and is on the top 20 list of highest per capita incomes in the country. High school at Central was the first time I noticed my social class and the impact it had on my life: high school class differences hit me in the face.

During my senior year (2013–2014), I drove my own brand new car; I spent spring break at the beach, and did everything a high school–aged kid wanted to do. Obviously, I did not pay for this: my parents were my support structure. If I needed something they could give it to me. But before I continue my social class story I would like to tell you theirs.

My parents both grew up in the lower-middle class in two different New Jersey small towns. Mom was one of six, walked a mile to school every day, and with her siblings slept in a room about the size of an average college dorm room. Her father, a coal miner, was a stern man who expected perfection and her mother was not much different. Mom grew up to become a doctor and only finished paying off her student loans about five years ago. Dad was the son of a vending machine worker. He did well in school, went to a decent college, and started working in the service industry. After a few years, he transitioned to the mortgage industry as a sales person. Call it luck, or being in the right place at the right time, but he and a colleague decided to leave the company to start one of their own. To this day, it is one of the more successful small mortgage companies in New Jersey. My parents always stressed two things: hard work and education. "Work hard and good things will come" was a common phrase in my home. The next most important thing was my grades. These two elements were what allowed me to be successful in my younger years.

I started playing hockey when I was four years old. Hockey was basically all I did. I was studying, traveling to and from school, traveling to the rink, on the ice, or in the weight room. My dream was to throw on that Ranger blue sweater and skate onto Madison Square Garden ice in front of 20,000 New Yorkers. Hockey is probably one of the more expensive sports with ice time around $300/hour and equipment always costing good money. Hockey taught me the most important lesson I think one can learn: "Hard work pays off." If I worked my ass off at practice earlier in the week, I noticed the coach would play me more. If I lifted that extra 5 lb or practiced harder, my legs would feel much better than teammates in the final minute of play.

College hockey was the "realistic" dream. Of course, the National Hockey League is the big one but only 36 kids in the world born in each year will make it there. You just need to be realistic. Boston University, Boston College, Harvard, Michigan, Minnesota were some of the few colleges where I wanted to play. But schools like that did not take students right out of high school; they required players to take 2–3 years after finishing high school to grow and hone your skills. The normal route most kids take is "juniors," which is the general term for any league that restricts age to 21. For the hockey community playing juniors essentially means drop everything and worry about hockey for the next year. No school, no work, just hockey: all day, every day. I was very tempted by this route. But if I got hurt in juniors, without an education, the rest of my life would be in question. But education was priority number one.

So instead of playing juniors, I pursued the option of a postgraduate year or a fifth year at a New England boarding school. Not only I would be playing hockey and developing myself athletically, but I would also challenge myself academically. I considered four different schools, Canterbury, the Kent School, Loomis Chaffe, and finally, the school I ended up attending: Phillips Academy Andover. All schools had tuitions like the more expensive colleges. Without my parents and their hard work, I would've been unable to pursue my dream.

Compared to Hunterdon Central High School, Andover was a whole new world. I felt like I had lived in poverty compared to some of these kids. The occasional Rolex was flashed at the lunch table and those students who went home for break often flew first class. Those who didn't go home would go away. I still picture sitting in calculus class talking about plans for fall break which consists of a Friday off before the usual weekend. I sat there hearing about how a student needed to rush out of class to get home to pack a weekend bag for a ski trip to Vail, Colorado. These students always had the newest fashion, whether that was the new Gucci loafers or a new Canada Goose Parka. The immensity of wealth at Andover was astonishing. But no one acknowledged it. Common place to most people, it was not even referenced. The only time you talked about it was when you described someone. Weird, right? Rather than saying a friend was tall with brown hair and on the hockey team, they'd say something like: "Yeah, he's got money." I am not trying to speak negatively about Andover, but it was interesting to see how social class differences were handled. I loved the school, my teachers, my coaches, and the competitive atmosphere. But the spectrum of wealth was greatly expanded compared to my previous experiences. At the same time, Andover had kids from poverty: talented gifted kids, who were on full scholarship for sports or acting or academics. You could easily pick up on these things. They wouldn't go home over break, or go out to eat as often as others. Overall Andover was great. I was exposed to a very different environment that made me more competitive and aware of social class differences.

This fall of 2017, I will be a junior at the University of Michigan and to be honest I have no idea how the hell I got in. Growing up I never thought I would end up at Michigan: luck maybe or Andover. I would choose the latter. I love the University of Michigan: the football, Ann Arbor, the squirrels, my friends, the architecture. I love it all. It's a pretty sweet little town, lots of shops with a ton to do on campus. But the 45,000 students was and is slightly intimidating. So like jumping right onto the hockey team at Ando-ver, I decided to rush and ultimately pledge a fraternity. I immedi-ately noticed the affluence of some brothers. Spending $200 a night at a bar is common place. Some spend spring breaks in Mexico, Morocco, and on mountains all over America and Europe. Being such a big school you don't notice the money some people have. It is not thrown in your face like it was at a boarding school.

Fraternities get a pretty bad reputation for being "white, wealthy kids who like to party." I take a strong stance against that because I get characterized like that and know it's untrue. My brothers and I have contributed hundreds of thousands to charities including American Cancer Society and Autism Awareness through our phi-lanthropy events. My fraternity is actively looking to reduce num-bers of sexual assaults on campus by going above and beyond the required university-mandatory seminars. We are more than just wealthy kids. I was elected fraternity president in November 2016 and this has allowed me to understand each brother's financial sit-uation. Despite the stigma of wealth behind fraternity houses, many brothers are on payment plans for their dues. You also start to fig-ure out who has money by observing spending habits. Without Sun-day breakfast in our meal plan, many chose to go out to restaurants like Angelo's or Aventura restaurants in their Canada Goose jackets for a nice omelet and mimosa. You think I am joking with the jacket thing. Look up "March of the Canada Goose," on YouTube: it's there. Many are reluctant to go and decide to conjure up what they can from weekly leftovers. You do not have to be the son of a wealthy Green-wich banker to join a fraternity. That does not matter and there are most certainly brothers from a variety of social class backgrounds. I am grateful for it, because it creates a great blend of guys who have different viewpoints: There is always something new to learn.

Aside from my fraternity, I am involved with an investment club and have two off-campus jobs. The investment club is a group of similar individuals who have an interest in stocks. I have always wanted to work on Wall Street. Dad's business had New York Rangers tickets and I attended quite a few over the years. I've been to a few big cities around the country, Los Angeles, Boston, and even Denver. But nothing compares to New York. Nothing comes close. As a kid it had always been a dream of mine to live in the Big Apple: the home to endless potential, an aura of success, and the "big time." Maybe Wall Street won't be for me: I still have a few years to go. But watching dad run his business has given me an entrepreneurial spirit. For the time being, I enjoy my two Ann Arbor jobs that I work while at school. I started bouncing at a local bar named Circus on Friday and Saturday nights. I see all my friends, but still get to make a dollar on the side. When no hours are available there, I shift my focus to Domino's Pizza, which surprisingly pays pretty well now. It's got nothing on New York City pizza though! Or New York bagels. No other location in the country can beat those two out.

Writing this essay has made me realize I hate social class constructs and the stereotypes behind them. In high school I quickly noticed some students would treat me differently because of my class. It bothered me. People would say I was "riding off mommy and daddy." That was the worst and it really got to me. I guess it bothered me because I knew I had an advantage, but I was also working hard. Yes, my parents put me into situations that most kids were not fortunate enough to have, but I worked my tail off when I landed in those situations. When the clock struck 10:30 p.m. and the Zamboni driver came out to clean the ice, he often found one guy remaining: me. He had to beg the kid—me—to get off the ice and go home. Here at Michigan, I am often up at 7:00 a.m. prior to class heading to the gym to pursue a goal of a better body.

Moral? I work hard and I always want more. I always want better, I always want to be stronger, faster, or smarter. Good is not good enough. I think and wonder about all the kids who don't have the opportunities that I have. I am sure they'd be working hard in my shoes. My experiences with social class have pushed me to work to help create a society where I can encourage those around me to be successful: allowing others to have opportunities I had and will be able to choose from.

BEING UPPER-MIDDLE CLASS

OLIVIA BLOOMHUFF

What does it mean to be upper-middle class? Is it simply a numbers game? If you have an income between $100,000 and $249,000, which is a very wide range I might add, are you ultimately upper-middle class or is it more a cultural attitude? Is it being born into the "right" family? Is it the way you are socialized? Is it traveling extensively, owning a boat, driving in a brand-new sports car, living in a large house without a care in the world? Is it the way you treat employees at restaurants? Numerically, I am in the (lower) upper-middle class, but I would argue my socialization, because of the influence of my parents, has given me a life of social class consciousness and self-awareness that I strive to implement day to day. Self-awareness can be lacking from the minds of some upper-middle-class children, but arguably is increasing in my millennial generation. Your judgments of me is up to you, but allow me to tell you more about my class background before you jump to conclusions.

My class awareness stems from the fact that my dad was temporarily unemployed and then underemployed for a few years during high school. My eyes were opened to how stressful and emotionally challenging life can be for those who are without work. There was a day-to-day struggle because of money. This was a huge adjustment for everyone in my family that historically had never struggled to make ends meet. My parents always kept me well informed of our financial standing, which was a stark contrast from my peers, but it was not always an easy position to be in. Every day I went to school hiding the fact my family life was being turned upside down and filled with uncertainty; I didn't want people at my school to look at me differently. I tried to make sure my academic achievement wouldn't be affected by this life change. I tried to keep myself busy with an extracurricular schedule of student government, sports, and volunteering to escape the stress going on in my own home. I was lucky, unlike many other high schoolers in my position, to maintain a strong sense of self, not having to get a job to make ends meet at home. I was blessed during my dad's un/underemployment that I didn't have to worry about my education. I knew I would graduate from my high school, Grosse Pointe North in Grosse Pointe Woods, Michigan, no matter what the future held for us. Though I stressed about how unaffordable college would be, I knew my family, especially my grandparents, would make my dream of attending the University of Michigan in Ann Arbor a reality. My parents and grandparents, Nannie and Dodup, never made me feel like I had to worry about finances, but instead, made sure I was informed so I could better prepare for the future. Everyone always wanted the best for me, as all families want for their children. Without the support of my family and the open-mindedness of my parents I wouldn't be the person I am today.

Since I was little, Nannie and Dodup were always scooping me up and taking me on magical vacations around the world to experience new cultures and places. I was far too young to remember my first plane ride and many of my first vacations, though I am sure I enjoyed myself. Most of my cherished memories are trips from our cottage in northern Michigan to cruises through the Caribbean. These trips exposed me to many different cultures that changed my perspective. My grandparents' influence on my life has been insurmountable. Without them, my life would not at all look like it does right now. Beyond just financial support they have culturally shifted my point of view.

As my mom, Nannie, and I were walking along the narrow, cobblestone streets of San Juan, Puerto Rico, in 2013 we saw a disheveled man and his skinny dog sitting in a doorway. He was weaving a basket made of palm leaves and had multiple other baskets scattered around him. One of these baskets had a few dollars in it. I looked at my mom who responded in her knowing way, that yes, we should buy one these baskets from the man who clearly needed the money more than these palm leaf baskets, when she didn't even know the price. We walked over and motioned that we would like to buy a basket, but he began to only point at the baskets and say numbers in Spanish. He picked up the smallest basket saying "cinco," the middle "ocho" and the largest "diez." Those were basically the only words my mother and I could understand from the sweet man. We could understand his body language as he gestured to the dog allowing me to pet it, but we couldn't properly thank him for making the beautiful basket and tell him how perfectly it would end up looking in our home, where it still sits. My choice to learn Spanish stemmed from this trip to Puerto Rico. I wanted to be able to communicate with that man, who I'm sure was starved for personal communication. Trips with my grandparents were amazing, and breathtaking, but Nannie and Dodup always kept me grounded in what it means to be mindful of others and how privileged I am. I guess this is what people mean when they say: "It takes a village to raise a child."

My parents are my true role models. I am certain I don't say it enough, but the life and perspective they have afforded me is something I will always cherish. Growing up in Grosse Pointe Woods I felt like I fit in—well, most of the time. For those of you who are unfamiliar with Grosse Pointe, it is a suburb in Southeast Michigan, bordering Detroit. But these worlds are financially, culturally, politically, and racially divided. Affectionately coined "the bubble," Grosse Pointe is a community for wealthy businessmen, old money conservatives, entrepreneurs, trust fund babies, and stay-at-home moms who enjoy lives with other people just like them at yacht or country clubs. That may sound harsh, so please allow me to clarify.

Grosse Pointe is an amazing place to grow up in and raise a family for a multitude of reasons—amazing schools, involved public officials such as police and fire services, beautiful homes, and a safe community. Growing up in Grosse Pointe assures high quality of K–12 education. I attended some of the best schools in Michigan and they were right around the block from my house. My school's close proximity allowed me to walk to and from school every day. Additionally, the Grosse Pointe School System offers countless after-school programs and extracurriculars that enhanced my learning environment. Without these programs my parents, both educators, would have had to find alternative child care for me while they were assisting their own students after school. The opportunities I had during my K–12 years magnify the dividing line between Grosse Pointe and Detroit. Lower-income families, without these services, are often forced to sacrifice wages or well-being to accommodate the needs of their children. If I hadn't attended Grosse Pointe schools, there is no guarantee I would be a student at the University of Michigan. But Grosse Pointe does have faults in my eyes: it is homogeneous. There are a lot of white, affluent, conservative, and traditional families that live in a close-knit community and this privilege does not always allow for self-awareness.

I am lucky to have parents who go the extra mile to expose me to other types of people from different backgrounds. My parents both teach in lower-income districts surrounding my neighborhood in metro Detroit. They mindfully exposed me to diversity and those who have less privilege than I have as an upper-middle-class white female. They show me a life far beyond that of Grosse Pointe. I often go to their schools to help, volunteer, and meet their students. While grocery shopping with my mom, I can remember buying food for her to take to her kindergarteners so that they would always have something to eat. She goes above and beyond her job description for her students but also included me in the process when I was young. She showed me how her actions could impact the lives of others and taught me I have that same power inside of me. Our class standing should be used for the betterment of others.

Both my parents embody this ideal and always talked about it in our household.

My dad gives out our address and his phone number to his underprivileged high school students so if there is anything they need they know he is someone who cares about them and their well-being in- and outside the classroom. When I was just seven years old, I heard a knock at our front door. Opening the door, I saw a young man whom I did not recognize. He was dressed in ripped jeans, a tattered jacket, and worn-down sneakers. His hair was long and shaggy. I did not expect to see this 18-year-old boy. I might have expected a delivery man, but not him. He was one of my dad's high school students. He asked to see my dad, talk about what had been going on, and how he was doing in school. He was worried about graduating on time. My dad wasn't home, so my mom and I—already headed out to dinner—invited him to come along. He cautiously obliged.

We ended up at a small casual burger place, nothing fancy. As the waitress took our orders she moved from my mom to me and then to my father's student. He hesitated, whispered his order, barely making eye contact, but still ordered his food. My mom tried to make the most of our conversation with the little chitchat he mustered. Then he said things I will never forget. This was his *first* time at a restaurant: seriously, his first time at a restaurant! This burger joint I had been to dozens of times and thought nothing of? He described how he had gotten to our home walking 23 miles in the rain—just to talk to my dad. You read that correct, he walked 23 miles. My dad had made such an impact on this student that he walked for over 20 miles, one way, just to talk on a Sunday instead of waiting until the next day in class. My dad had made such an impact on this young man with a completely different lifestyle. What if everyone took a moment to be like my dad? What if we took the extra time to relate to someone different than themselves and reach out to those in need?

I remember early mornings in the spring when my parents and I would drive around downtown Detroit, not just to the popular places that had been gentrified, but the real, true heart of Detroit: the side streets and restaurants owned by native Detroiters who didn't always get as much attention as those newly featured in the news media. Going to the Detroit Institute of Arts on Woodward Avenue with my dad always involved a detour to the nearby Charles H. Wright Museum of African American History to recognize struggles of other groups and how my actions and words could influence history. My parents inspired me to look beyond my own perspective and imagine what life is like for other people without luxuries that I have been so fortunately given. They taught me the skills to understand how other people lived and the awareness that not everyone has the same opportunities I have, such as trips with Nannie and Dodup. Honestly, this class-conscious mind-set allows me to better identify with others but also to be more and more appreciative of what I have. This awareness sweetens my experiences. I am more mindful of just how special our trips to Alaska or the Dominican Republic truly were. I feel I have the ability to be more grateful than some of my Grosse Pointe counterparts because I know just how rare opportunities like these are.

Attending the University of Michigan (UM) and graduating with little college debt, in my eyes, are two rare opportunities I am fortunate to have. I am even more fortunate to attend one of the best universities in the nation. I cherish college life each and every day, even when I spend all day working in the undergraduate library (UGLi) or sprinting through the Diag to get to class on time. I know UM tuition is not cheap and I am honored and privileged to be one of the students able to attend. The cost of college and the college atmosphere in Ann Arbor attract a large majority of students from the middle- and upper-middle classes. Additionally, there are first-generation students, who are first their families to attend college, and other students receiving financial aid. Currently, only 13% of undergraduates at UM are first-gens. The diverse cultural upbringing I experienced helps me relate to both. I do not want that last statement to be misconstrued as me saying I know the true struggles facing people in the working class and poverty. I do not. But I know there are fellow students on campus who grew up in different economic circumstances and I aim to recognize their struggles and perseverance. The stresses people in poverty face are immense. I can't imagine the daily hardships, but I know how stressful it was for me when my dad was unemployed. The struggle must be much harder for them.

Being class conscious for the majority of my early life allows me to be a bridge between different social classes. I am able to connect with people on both ends of the spectrum, those who are very well-off and those who have not been as fortunate and worry about money every day. While living in Grosse Pointe I was always crossing this bridge and trying to discover which side I belonged on. Now that I am at UM and interact with so many people, I realized I do not need to pick one side, but rather to invite others to explore both sides with me. One of the most important things I remember is that people on one side of the bridge are just as important as those on the other. Why do we label people—middle class, upper class, lower class? It shouldn't matter. Everyone should be able to develop their talents so they can attend this selective university. Unfortunately, not everyone can attend excellent K–12 schools like I did. But why should social class divide us on this campus? Why should social class determine how we treat others? Students experience a campus culture surrounded by social class inequality. But we can choose how we want to interact with others. I choose not to use social class as a barrier but as a gateway that allows me open and easy conversations between diverse groups of students.

On campus and in classrooms, I have faced the stigma that accompanies being from Grosse Pointe. This stigma is linked to the Grosse Pointe of old money and all white, exclusive, conservative families. Personally, I don't fit into these rigid categories. I am liberal and attend a liberal university. I do not have old money. I wouldn't say my family and I are exclusive. I feel the need to tell people: "I'm from Grosse Pointe, but I'm liberal, middle class, balanced, and cultured." That being said, I love the community I am from and the wonderful opportunities I've had. But I do not agree with the self-entitled ideology that many other Grosse Pointers have. I was exposed to many different cultures, not just the limited views available in some parts of Grosse Pointe. I "popped the bubble" and am now in a new environment that again is opening my eyes to new perspectives. I can blend relationships between social class backgrounds especially between those having a lot of money and those not being as fortunate.

Being part of Greek Life on campus also creates another stigma about my fiscal background. There is a common misconception that sorority women rely on their parents to pay for anything and everything, don't know the value of a dollar, are constantly carrying around a cup of Starbucks coffee with a designer handbag, and don't have ambitious goals. The reality I have experienced here at Michigan, in and outside of my Greek house, is very different. We are hardworking, dedicated, and thoughtful young women. I pay for my own dues and don't just call up my parents or grandparents for money on a whim, nor do I want to. Many women in my sorority work and pay their own dues as well. Of course, there are some sisters who do rely on their parents financially, but college is a time to grow and learn about responsibility in whatever way works best for the individual. College is meant to prepare and educate me for life beyond these few years. My sisters and I do not all fit into a narrow stereotype. We are just students who deserve the same respect as anyone else.

Being in a sorority has honestly changed my college experience as I have met women who have upbringings both similar and very different than mine. Our differences create stimulating conversations. Yet, at the heart of it all, we are united by our values, our devotion to philanthropy, and thoughtful sisterhood. We are not "paying for our friends." It is just the opposite. I feel we are *being paid* in memories with our sisters. I know, this sounds corny and I apologize, but these stereotypes are harmful. They deter women and men from joining fraternal organizations, are restricting, and unfortunately define first impressions of those involved in Greek Life. These students do not want to be labeled this way and therefore do not think joining a Greek organization is the right fit for them. When in reality, they could be missing out on an opportunity to form lifelong friendships and gain potential job opportunities. Greek Life creates a diverse college experience where members interact with each other, value one another, and are granted countless leadership positions. If society stressed these aspects of Greek Life, instead of the incorrect stereotypes, the culture surrounding Greek Life would be changed and it would be more accurately portrayed. These harmful labels are not accurate, at least not for me, my sisters, and Greek Life at the University of Michigan.

Yes, based on my parents' combined income I "qualify" as upper-middle class, but that label does not stay true to the stereotype. I will always be a Grosse Pointer at heart and my social class background will likely always be upper-middle class. But that is not *all* I am. My socialization created my open-minded, liberal perspectives. I recognize and respect others' points of view. I not only acknowledge my privilege, but try to understand and recognize other people's lack of privilege. I seek to counteract discrimination and promote cultural and socioeconomic diversity.

I have many questions. What does it mean to be upper-middle class? What does it mean to be middle- or working class? What does it mean to be *your* class? What perspective has this given you? Would you like to change your perspective of social class? If you do, that's great. If you don't, that's fine too. But what we need to remember is that we are all just people. Without the labels associated with social class, race, and gender, we are just people who deserve honest and kind considerations of others.

"Just Because They Show Money Doesn't Mean They Have Money": Realizing Social Class

Abigail Conway

Mom was rummaging through her bottomless pit of a purse, scavenging for the exact coupon that brought us to this store in the first place. The cashier's impatience mirrored mine and my sister's, Allison, as it felt like hours went by until mom finally found the coupon. In the same moment that I sighed in relief, Allison, just a toddler at the time, blurts out: "Mom, why are you so cheap?" Stunned by her rude comment, mom grabbed our bags of newly purchased uniform clothing and dragged us to the door and out to the car before she had any time to see the cashier's reaction. With that coupon, mom had just saved $1 on a $6 uniform shirt I needed in the upcoming first grade school year.

Allison, even from a very young age, was very outspoken about nearly every thought she had in her mind. I, on the other hand, didn't speak up much and kept many of my thoughts and questions to myself to ponder on before addressing them with mom or dad, or anyone else for that matter. I was painfully nervous for mom's reaction to Allison's comment, and we sat silently as she threw bags in the car, buckled Allison into her car seat, and tossed her purse onto its designated front-seat location. Before she started the car, and as Allison and I waited anxiously for her to say anything, mom whipped her head around and firmly stated: "I am frugal because dad and I choose to send you both to an expensive private school and we value your education. It is inappropriate to bring it up in public, and it will not happen again."

Mom grew up in the solidly working-class, industrial town of Meadville, Pennsylvania. Her parents, John and Sally, were in their early twenties, married, and pregnant with mom's older brother, Joe, when Sally left school and John was finishing up his English degree at Gannon University. Money and the lack thereof were always on the minds of John and Sally. When mom was a baby, John worked his day job as a high school English teacher in an underfunded school district alongside two extra nighttime jobs, including playing drums in a traveling band, and working odd remodeling jobs to bring in some extra income. Every Thursday night, Sally would travel to three separate grocery stores around town searching for the best deals for every essential food product they may need, dozens of coupons neatly organized in Sally's handbag.

* * *

Allison and I attended a private, Catholic K–12 school in Beverly Hills, Michigan, just a few minutes' drive from our comfortable white-sided, two-story colonial home located on the very edge of the city of Royal Oak's vast perimeter. Our schedule was extremely predictable. Mom carpooled Allison and me, along with a couple children who lived closer to school, in the mornings, and the other parent would drop us off after school had ended, while both mom and dad were still at work. They would drive themselves to work each day, arriving home predictably around four or five, just in time for dinner, then soccer and dance practices in the evening. Mom was one of the only mothers at school who worked a full-time job. I never gave it much thought, as mom's working was to be expected, as it had always been. But mom occasionally felt the uneasy guilt of remaining incapable of picking us up from school every day, coupled with her inability to be readily waiting to provide us with elaborate after-school snacks, like many mothers had the luxury to accomplish.

Allison and I were the only children in the neighborhood to attend private school. Every other child attended K–12 at Royal Oak public schools, and most continued on to Royal Oak High School. I had always found it peculiar that we attended a different school than all our neighbors, making me feel, at times, uneasy and unwelcome in the tight-knit friendships the neighbor kids seemed to possess. I made nearly all my childhood friends at my private school. We all felt so alike, dressing in identical uniforms, each child with their own extracurricular activity, parents ready and able to shuttle their children to and from school. What I had not realized, maybe because mom and dad chose not to talk about it or maybe because I was living in a snug, privileged bubble of stability, blissfully unaware of social class differences, was that not every child came from the same comfortable, suburban lifestyle as mine. What I had not realized was that dozens of children, several in my grade, were bussed in every day from Detroit and other underprivileged school districts on full scholarships. No parent picked them up from school every day; they were unable to participate in extracurricular activities and lived in a very different world than my own.

*   *   *

When Uncle Joe came to live with us, I had not yet understood the extent of our social class differences. Joe received English and Communication degrees upon graduating from Gannon University in 1990. From then on, Joe lived a nomadic life, first settling in Los Angeles, working as a freelance writer while working in the restaurant industry to pay the rent. When the magazine he had been sporadically writing for fizzled, Joe moved back into his college fraternity house in Erie, Pennsylvania, until he ultimately hitched a ride with a fraternity brother to Wyoming, where he spent years couch hopping and continuing work as a cook in various local restaurants.

Uncle Joe called mom when he had reached rock bottom. He had no place to live, no money for rent and food, all the while keeping his struggle to himself for so long to avoid facing disappointment from his parents, John and Sally. Mom and dad bought him a bus ticket, which is what they could afford at the time, and Joe, bringing little belongings, moved in with us for nine months. When Uncle Joe moved in, I did not ask many questions. I took it for what it was: Joe needed a place to stay and we had room, and more importantly, he was family. I never quite understood how Uncle Joe found himself in this predicament. He was college educated, an incredibly talented writer, funny, and unique in every way. Why was my family living comfortably, mom and dad with good jobs, Allison and me in private schools, and Uncle Joe, coming from the same family upbringing as mom, couch surfing, living much of his life on the brink of poverty?

Many of the friends I made at my private school seemed to have much more than me, more material belongings, bigger homes, country club memberships, the list seemed to go on and on. In elementary school, mom and dad couldn't afford to hire a babysitter during winter and spring breaks, so while my peers were traveling in large groups to sunny, carefree destinations like Destin and Naples, Florida, some even traveling internationally to exotic Mexican resorts, I spent my time off from school hiding away in mom's office, coloring pictures for her boss and coworkers with a few crayons mom kept in her work desk. I would get frustrated and feel left out, but mom would always remind me, "We sacrifice a lot to send you and Allison to private school." I knew she wanted to take extravagant trips to sunnier climates, but we Conways are savers, not spenders, as I would continue to learn throughout my upbringing.

Mom and dad had both been brought up learning about the value of saving money for the future, especially when it came to our education. In my middle school years, I became increasingly envious of my seemingly wealthy friends whom I'd accompany to their country club pools on 90° Michigan summer days, those who'd invite me for a weekend spent on lakefront property in the rustically, quaint, and often extremely wealthy, communities of Northern Michigan. After keeping my jealous thoughts to myself long enough, I finally asked dad why we didn't belong to a country club, why we didn't have a cottage to retreat to, and why we didn't seem as rich as many of my friends from school. Dad, always logical and collected, firmly responded, "Just because they show money doesn't mean they have money." Little did I know, many families in our community were living extravagant, materialistic lives, while simultaneously drowning in crippling debt.

Dad grew up solidly in the upper-middle class, his family of five moving from place to place as dad's father, Brian, was regularly relocated to manage various banks along the East Coast and Midwest. Although Brian and dad's mother, Barbara, could afford many luxuries using Brian's substantial banking salary, subsidized by Barbara's various teaching positions, they lived a frugal lifestyle, passing the importance and value in saving money for the future down to dad and his siblings. Being raised by a single, immigrant mother after the passing of his father, Brian became the man of his household, supporting his younger siblings starting at the age of 10 years. His early adoption of adult responsibility molded him into an extremely logical and fiscally responsible man, stressing the importance of saving first, spending second. With Brian and Barbara's deliberate prioritization on saving for education and the future in general, dad entered adulthood, and fatherhood, a level-headed saver, caring very little about how our wealthy community may perceive our level of wealth.

For my entire upbringing, I had always considered my family to be solidly middle class, but according to our savings, I slowly came to understand that we were much more so upper-middle class, especially when taking into consideration how much money mom and dad had put aside for my and Allison's college tuitions. Knowing this, I remained conflicted about my class status, especially during high school years. On my 16th birthday, just before I was headed out the door to attend dance practice, mom and dad surprised me with a pearly white, used 2009 Volkswagen Jetta and I was absolutely thrilled. The first school day after receiving the Jetta, I joyfully sped off to my private, Catholic high school in the notoriously wealthy city of Bloomfield, Michigan. My gleaming pride slowly disappeared as I pulled into the school parking lot, an obnoxiously, brand-new black Cadillac SUV parked to my left and a stunning, navy blue BMW sedan to my right, both shimmering in the Michigan spring sunlight. In one moment I was confidently cruising in my cute new ride, and moments later I was embarrassed of my slightly used, seemingly subpar vehicle my parents had graciously purchased for $9,000. Constantly comparing myself with my peers who appeared to be situated in a wealthier class than my own added an overwhelming sense of uncertainty in terms of what social class background I truly belonged to.

*   *   *

Receiving my acceptance letter to the University of Michigan (UM) was a very exciting moment for me and my family. Mom and dad, both proud Purdue University graduates, joked how they dreaded the day they would finally have to come to grips with my attendance at the "wrong" Big 10 School. Their gleaming pride mirrored mine as I prepared for entering the next big chapter in life, never once considering the newest financial responsibility I had committed myself and my family to for the next four years. Mom left Purdue with nine years' worth of student debt, while like my dad, I would leave with no debt; zero financial burden all thanks to mom and dad's careful saving since the day I was born.

My freshman year roommate and I were friends from high school, raised in neighboring cities, and experiencing similar social class backgrounds for most of our lives. We had both expressed the relieving feeling of new beginnings as we moved into our 11 feet × 17 feet dorm room, squeezing as many of our belongings into the cramped space as we could manage. Trading in our plush, comfortable housing in the affluent Oakland County (where Royale Oak is located) bubble for tight, uniform-looking dorm accommodations made us feel as though all of us freshmen were starting on the same playing field, all in the same exciting and uncertain boat, all of us pursuing some version of a fresh start. This whimsical idea that all of us freshmen were in the same exact boat once entering college was instantly crushed the moment our dormitory resident advisor (RA) asked my roommate and me: "How does it make you feel that you are so privileged? Do you think you are better than everyone else?" Stunned and slightly offended, we returned to our tiny room, suddenly much more cognizant of how much our privilege might impact this fresh start we were so ready to embrace.

The reality of how unique various students at the university were in terms of social class set in very early during my freshman year.

After my RA firmly grounded me in my apparent bubble of privilege, I became much more aware of the unique individuals who populated my dorm and various classes I was taking at the time. For much of my freshman year, I surrounded myself almost exclusively with students I knew from home and their new friends they made on campus. This meant I spent my time with students who, like me, probably didn't have to worry about paying off student loans, consider working several jobs to support themselves at school, or thinking twice about participating in expensive commitments like Greek Life or taking luxurious spring break trips to Mexico every spring break.

My place on the UM social class ladder was firmly established in my mind over something as seemingly insignificant as laundry. On the same day as I was unloading my clothes from the communal dormitory dryer, an embarrassed stranger sheepishly asked for a few dollars in order to get her laundry started, as her allotted laundry money had run out and she did not have the funds to get by until she received her next paycheck. I swiftly paid for her laundry, as my laundry funds were replenished regularly, thanks to mom and dad, grabbed my things, and made my way back to my room. In the same moment I was lugging my overwhelming sack of laundry into my dorm room my neighbor was preparing to drop her laundry off at a delivery laundry service that was very active on campus. Unsure of what the service fully entailed, I jumped on my computer and was shocked to learn the service could cost upward of $200 per week for someone to pick up dirty laundry and return it neatly folded and cleaned. In a matter of a few minutes, I faced three very different laundry experiences, supplemented by what appeared to be the astonishingly vast range of social class distinctions that persisted, often unnoticed, on campus and in everyday life.

* * *

I had occasionally strolled through the Ross School of Business before admittance to UM and during my freshman year, but the feeling I received from stepping through the strikingly massive, crystal-clear glass doors and into the bright and airy first-floor area, commonly known as the Ross Winter Garden, for the first time after being admitted to the elite business school was both overwhelming and exhilarating. The architecturally modern design and comfortably elegant student accommodations screamed money and power. I always had that sense, well before my admittance, yet suddenly I felt a part of this prestigious class of students, a sense of elitism which was inherently promoted by the students, faculty, and staff who roamed the halls, all seemingly confident of their belonging.

Once classes began in the fall of my sophomore year, the uneasiness I felt toward my new Ross business student identity increased more each day as I stepped through those impressive glass doors and took my seat in one of eighty $700 classroom chairs that occupied each of the dozens of classrooms and student study rooms all over the building. The day I found out our classroom chairs cost $700 per chair, I returned home to tell my roommates about how ridiculous that fact was, eager to joke with them about the extraordinary opulence I was surrounded by daily. I was the only roommate in Ross and my friends never let me forget it. They'd comment sarcastic remarks like: "You're so much smarter and better than everyone because, you know, you're in Ross," and "Abby is going to be the richest of us all one day because of Ross, of course." I knew deep down that they were proud of my accomplishments, but their perceptions of the person I was becoming by studying business frightened me, and always kept me tiptoeing around the topic of my major, even with some of my closest friends.

I enjoyed the security the business school provided in terms of my time during undergrad and looking to the future. Ross, for many years, has possessed an elite reputation, so overwhelming that top employers in the most innovative and desirable fields have been drawn to the school for recruiting the best and the brightest. Although I had initially felt I had proven myself worthy of such prestige merely through admittance to the selective school, my tendency to compare myself to those who seem better off than me, as I had unforgivingly troubled myself with in my younger years, overtook me, especially during junior year internship recruiting. My peers utilized their parents' social connections, in addition to their academic merit, to capture the most elite internships at powerful banks, selective consulting agencies, and other various Fortune 500 companies around the country. Ever present in my mind was my apparent lack of these types of connections, as mom and dad did not involve themselves in business, mom working as a scientist and dad as an engineer. My self-worth as a business student diminished as I continued to struggle to use purely my academic record to secure an internship, especially as I had struggled to receive high grades in my challenging classes, a problem I had never experienced in my previous schooling.

I had applied and been accepted to study abroad through the Ross exchange program to Buenos Aires, Argentina; this would take place during my second semester of junior year. Unsurprisingly, the process of receiving acceptance to one of nineteen exchange programs was made extremely selective, as Ross staff controlled the decision of which students would be granted this once-in-a-lifetime sort of experience. The process in place, coupled with the multitude of submitted applications, allowed for numerous deferrals and flat-out rejections from the program. Several peers had expressed complaints and worries about their deferrals and rejections, yet one deferral grievance seemed much more somber than the rest. This student confided her troubles to me, explaining the depth to her dismay; how she was paying her way through college, making sacrifices for cheaper housing, taking out several loans to pay for her education, and always dreamt of one day being able to save up enough money to study abroad. Her only option was through the Ross program, as tuition for the program was comparable to UM tuition, and she could not afford any alternative. Instead of the annoyance I felt with other students' complaints, I sensed an immense guilt that I would be able to go abroad and easily afford the experience, while this student would have to come to grips with never fulfilling her dream, even after saving as much money as she could to ultimately have it all fall short.

Going abroad changed my perspective on social class dramatically. I was supporting myself through the four-month experience, using my personal funds for every outing, purchase, and necessity.

I relied heavily on public transportation systems, and exercised mom and dad's frugal attitudes and behaviors when budgeting which activities I could afford. I returned home with a new perspective, one I had never considered obtaining, as to continue my comfortable upper-middle-class lifestyle. All this ultimately changed the way I acknowledged social class differences in the United States.

Back in Ann Arbor for the start of my senior year, I took notice of the variety of city buses that accompanied the UM blue buses that I learned to love over the past four years, in a sense, reminiscing on my use of public transportation back in Argentina. Mom was helping me move into my new home for my final school year when I asked her if there had been an increase to the number of buses in the area since I've been away. A little confused by my random question, she simply answered: "They've always been there. You just haven't noticed them before." Stunned by my ignorance, I felt as though this experience of obliviousness mirrored my previous confrontations with class differences. My newfound awareness of class seemed to have developed over the course of four months spent living in a completely new world from my own, experiencing monetary limitations, lack of social capital and connections, living in a class so unlike the one I had been raised in and had taken advantage of throughout the past few years in college.

The remainder of my senior year was strengthened through both my improved self-awareness and becoming more cognizant of how social class plays a role in a variety of ways in everyday life. It was bewildering, in retrospect, to think back on my frequent run-ins with class and I reminded myself of reactions to those experiences at the time versus how I felt about them. Whether it was studying abroad or enrolling in my very first sociology class at UM, or a combination of various life choices and events, I have reached a point of clarity where I feel much more aware of how social class impacts my life and lives of those around me.

Things Aren't Always as They Seem

Olivia Dworkin

When I was in fifth grade, I had the longest hair in the entire class. I wanted to donate my hair to "Locks of Love," but I was met with resistance from my father. He actually forbade me from cutting my hair. Instead of simply accepting this undesirable decision, I wrapped a fuzzy orange blanket around my neck to mimic a judge's robe, gathered my entire family in the living room, and conducted a court case for why I should be allowed to cut my hair. Although my haircut turned out horribly, I won my very first case. At that moment, I had my sights set on becoming a lawyer. However, at my young age, I never once thought how expensive the process of becoming an attorney would be.

Come to think of it, growing up, I never thought about the expense of anything. Dad was a successful speech scientist in the ears, nose, and throat department at the Detroit Medical Center, so my family was well-off. We soaked up the hot sun in Puerto Rico for spring break in 2003, watched in awe at many Broadway productions, and kept up on the latest fashion trends. In addition, my sisters and I all had the latest laptops, cell phones, and any game console we wanted. Furbies, Barbies, and board games piled up in our basement, and we enjoyed family nights in front of our large TV every Friday. I also played soccer, dabbled in martial arts, took various dance classes, and joined the high school pom-pon team.

I joined whatever activities interested me, and I never considered the cost. I always assumed this was the norm.

Another normal aspect of my life was that mom quit her job as a substitute teacher so that she could stay home with my two older sisters and me. She made us breakfast in the morning, packed lunches for school, and made dinner at night. She always had time to pick us up from school so we did not have to ride the bus, and took us to countless extracurricular activities. She had the liberty and time to sit in front row at all my recitals and performances without ever having work conflicts. I loved how much mom was around. This allowed me to form such a close bond with her and confide in her about anything and everything. I enjoyed her so much that I failed to realize how big a deal it was that she did not have to work for us to still live very comfortably in the upper-middle-class world.

Social class also impacted my school success at a young age. My birthday falls on November 30, the day before the cutoff to be in the grade below me, so I was (and still am) always the youngest person in my grade. I started first grade in 2001 at just four years old, but still surpassed most of my peers in many subjects. This, in part, had to do with factors I never realized were privileges. Dad had a Doctorate, and mom had a master's degree. Growing up with two college-educated parents led me to have lively, intellectual conversations at home, and motivated me to work hard since attending college was never a question. I also grew up attending a well-funded school system with experienced teachers, impressive standardized testing scores, and educational resources galore. I exceeded standard expectations in reading in first grade, and ended up in a special reading group with three other students and just one teacher. We read more advanced books and wrote reports. I still remember being on a plane reading a chapter book when most of my peers still read picture books and the flight attendant did a double take.

"Is she actually reading that?" She asked mom.

School resources provided an opportunity for high levels of success in subjects that influenced my academic achievement, but

I would have never gotten to where I was back then if my parents could not afford to buy me books as well. I walked up and down *Borders'* aisles and picked out whatever my little brain desired, and I would even finish some books before I got home. Books crowded our bookshelves, and computer desks were cluttered with educational computer games I played all the time to help with logical reasoning, spelling, and reading comprehension. These resources helped to skyrocket me to the top in elementary school. What I once attributed to my natural intelligence, I now realize was also influenced by my economic privilege.

I never realized how privileged I was because everyone around me was doing the same. Upper-middle class was extremely normalized where I grew up. Everyone in my class seemed to talk about where they were going for spring break, and boasted about their winnings at various sports competitions or other extracurricular activities. No one ever discussed how they could not afford anything. The similarities even extended to what we wore. Everyone rocked Abercrombie and Hollister every day, Ugg boots, and Hardtail pants. The biggest "scandal" in middle school happened when the whole class found out one girl's Hollister shirt really came from *Plato's Closet,* a hand-me-down store for designer clothing and accessories. Walking down the hallway we heard: "Oh my god, did you hear that she got her shirt from *Plato's Closet*?" and "Wow, I can't believe she can't afford to just go to the mall." We were so confused as to why she did not just go to the store like everyone else, and why she needed hand-me-downs from complete strangers. Looking back, I'm appalled by how naïve I acted about class differences. I cannot believe we made such a big deal about where people got their clothes, and it saddens me people felt they needed to wear designer clothes just to fit in.

It took until junior year of high school for me to get a more accurate sense of different social classes. I remember one day like it was yesterday: I was sitting on my queen-sized bed, bright pink sheets wrapped around me, listening to Ne-Yo on my computer without a care in the world. Mom knocked on my door, but she was not wearing her same sweet, comforting smile as she always did. Then she blurted out what no child ever wants to hear:

"We need to talk."

Nervous, I closed my laptop and sat up in my bed, confused at the situation. My mind started to race about what trouble I had gotten myself into this time, what my most recent teenage episode was or what I had recently fibbed about . . .

"Your dad and I are getting a divorce."

The moments after receiving the news are quite blurry, but I remember waiting for her to tell me she was just kidding. When she kept her straight face, I started to bawl. Dad confirmed the devastating news later that night. By the time he came into my room, I had gone through an entire box of tissues. Looking back at the situation with a clear mind, I could not have predicted this news. I suppose my parents did most of their fighting behind closed doors. Dad moved out in a few short weeks.

I felt as though the world was crumbling around me: everything was changing. Dad took some of my favorite furniture to his new place, loving family pictures no longer decorated walls of the house, and, most of all, class became much more apparent. When dad moved out, he took his doctor's salary with him, leaving me alone with a single, unemployed mom while my sisters studied at college. It sounds horrible to say, but I was truly frustrated and confused with the situation. I went from never having to worry about money to talking about budgeting while mom put herself through school again to renew her paralegal certificate that had expired over the years. I immediately started thinking about law school. Before the divorce, paying for law school was not an issue in my mind. However, we had numerous conversations about how money was tight, and I started to think that law school was not so much of a done deal anymore. I got my first job at a local Coney Island as soon as I was old enough to work in hopes of saving up for my future debt.

Even with my waitressing gig, tension filled the atmosphere at home. I was trying hard to adjust to the new social class I found myself in, but it was not easy. I realize now that I had difficulty adjusting because I grew up largely sheltered from classes other than my own. I was out of my element—I was lost. Mom, to this day, is such an inspirational person in my life for standing strong during this time and being a wonderful example of how to be an independent woman and face adversity with bravery. She never told me to stop working toward law school because we could not afford it anymore, and she continued to encourage me to reach my aspirations. I continued to push for the career I had always dreamt of despite my new financial situation, but that did not shield me from getting into frequent arguments with dad about money.

The court required he pay alimony to my mother and child support for me since I was under 18, but other than that he did not have to give mom any excess money for my two older sisters. He seemed to think this was fair given the fact that he earned the money through his hard work, and his and mom's assets were split in half at the time of the divorce. He did not consider that he still made his same generous salary, and mom had no income despite being left with three girls to support. I imagine now, however, that the divorce probably had a similar impact on him that it did on me. He grew up poor in Brooklyn, New York, and had worked extremely hard to get to the top of the field he was so passionate about. He got used to his large, undivided salary, and now he had to take out a hefty portion every month. It probably felt like he worked so hard just to go back to where he was before. I was suddenly accused of being greedy or ungrateful when I asked for things I would not even have to ask for in the past. It was a sharp turnaround, but in a way, it opened my eyes to class issues. Though I was not getting as much support as I was, I was lucky to get some help from dad at all. I love and respect for him for that.

Social class became much more apparent in college. I was plucked from my bubble of upper-middle-class suburbia and dropped into Ann Arbor, Michigan, in the fall of 2013. I had thought my parents' divorce dropped me down at least three classes, but that was far from the case. Student loans, meal plans, room decorations, and clothes brought out the vast class differences between my peers and me. Back home, almost all my friends had parents that were paying for their undergraduate education. At Michigan the story was drastically different. Right from the get-go I found myself immersed in conversations about student loans where my friends would go back and forth about the this stressful process. They would look at me to contribute to the conversation, and every time I had to awkwardly shy away and tell them I did not have any loans. I was privileged enough to have parents who were paying for my tuition, and even privileged enough to be awarded a small allowance every month so I could focus on school and only have to work in the summer. This made it very simple to keep on track with my pre-law goals since I could focus my time on boosting my grade point average and immersing myself in clubs that would look good on my resume.

Some fellow students in my dorm were even more privileged than me, however. One day, a friend said he was thirsty, but he was too lazy to hop on the bus to get a case of water at the grocery store. Sure enough, the next day there was a box waiting for him in the mail room: his mother had express shipped a case of water bottles all the way from Georgia so he would not have to take the bus. I could not even begin to imagine the cost of shipping such a large package. Another friend would pay for $30 same-day shipping on articles of clothing she did not even need, just so she could have them sooner. Needless to say, while I was living comfortably, I was definitely not in a position to waste money on superfluous materials. Apart from a few social class experiences, it was still semi-hard to gauge exactly where I stood class-wise among peers during freshman year. We were living in required dorms that were the same price and eating the same food that came with our required meal plans. This situation did not lend itself to emphasize class differences too much. I found myself in the middle of my freshman year peers. I was not struggling to pay for school, but I spent money wisely. Sophomore year opened the door to more financial decisions and more class clarity.

Moving out of the dorms and into off-campus housing for the fall of 2014 was a huge indicator of class differences. Trying to find an apartment walking distance from campus, decently priced, and not completely disgusting was nearly impossible. Searching for housing made it clear that I was not at the top of the financial food chain like I was throughout my grade school years. Luxury apartments such as Landmark on South Forrest Avenue were dreamy, but absolutely out of the question. Rent for one person equaled the total rent of my first apartment. My roommate and I were lucky if our front door even worked, and we actually got locked out for more than 10 hours on our first night there. We had to sleep in the hallway.

Even though I found myself tumbling down the class ladder in this category, my childhood privileges still prevailed in other areas such as food. During my first year I had a meal plan, so I never had to worry about grocery shopping. However, sophomore year my roommate and I decided to split groceries. What seemed like such an easy task proved to be amazingly difficult. At home, I was used to name-brand everything. Mom swore by the superior quality of name brand food, and Kroger or Spartan brand items of food never found their way into the pantry. On our first shopping trip, my roommate suggested we buy less expensive, off-brand items. At first, this proposition took me aback. I remember ruminating over the loss of my delicious Kraft cheese slices and the creamy, milky goodness that would melt in my mouth whether I was eating savory grilled cheese or simply enjoying cheese and crackers. The price difference between the name-brand and off-brand items was only a dollar or two, so I did not really understand at first. I missed my tasty General Mills Cereal and Pop Secret Popcorn. Then again, I was still in my comfortable little place in the middle. I was not dropping ridiculous amounts of money on unnecessary items, but I was still unemployed and not really worrying about money. Now, I get anxious whenever mom chooses name-brand food over the less expensive grocery store brands. I learned that saving those couple of dollars per food item really adds up.

During my sophomore year, I had bills for the first time, and an Ann Arbor lifestyle was generally expensive. My parents gave me money every month, but it was a fixed amount and it was tough luck if I ran over. By the end of the year, I was learning how to live quite frugally. I cannot count the number of times I went out of my way to save a few bucks here and there. I even landed another waitressing gig for the summer at the Olive Garden Restaurant in Ann Arbor, and made the decision to continue working there during the next school year. This was the first time I would need to work while simultaneously juggling school demands.

I made this decision because I had to start seriously thinking about my legal career. I thought about it constantly, but my junior year I had to seriously prepare for application season. The Law School Admissions Test (LSAT) is undoubtedly one of the most important pieces of your law school application. If you do not have a decent LSAT score, you can kiss a good law school goodbye: "If you don't get into a good law school, you might as well not go" were words drilled into my head ever since I started college. Graduates from lower ranked law schools have a difficult time in the job market due to the competitive nature of the legal field. Becoming an attorney was my lifelong dream, so I was determined to do everything in my power to get into one of the top schools and pursue a promising legal career. Unfortunately, this required eight months of studying, eight months of stressed out crying sessions, and eight months of paying for overpriced studying tools. Both the private tutor and the *Princeton Review* course totaled over $1,000. Additionally, the books were over $200, and law school applications themselves totaled over $600. That was almost $3,000 just getting into law school alone. I would never have been able to do that on my waitressing salary without financial help from my parents, especially if I was responsible for paying my bills and undergraduate tuition as well. This process truly made me realize how fortunate I was, and how silly I was in high school for being upset at not getting enough spending money from my parents.

My privilege really stood out when observing my friend in a similar situation, except she was studying for the Medical School Admissions Test (MCAT). She worked three jobs to help pay for her courses and books. I struggled to work two shifts a week at one job while trying to study. I remember seeing her so stressed about all that was on her plate and I would ask: "Why don't you just quit one of your jobs so you can focus on studying?" She replied that she could not afford it. Our situation reminded me that not all Michigan students come from the same wealth my childhood friends came from.

It honestly broke my heart to think how many students would not get a decent score on these standardized tests simply because they could not afford the same kind of training, receive financial support, or get time off from work to study. My mental health deteriorated as I studied until the middle of the night. I took practice test after practice test after practice test, hoping and praying I would get my LSAT score up. I kicked myself so many times for not being good enough or not improving fast enough or straying from my strict studying calendar. I did not eat or sleep enough, and when I did get a chance to sleep it would be for half an hour in the library. I could not begin to imagine how much more I would have suffered mentally and emotionally if I could not have relied on my parents to help defray the costs. I would have had to work many more shifts at Olive Garden, and I did not have the time. I asked myself if it was fair for colleges to expect students to spend so much on simply getting in and then ask them for hundreds of thousands of dollars for tuition. Regardless, I ended up taking the LSAT in the fall of 2016, and while I did not get an ideal score, my dream school accepted me—the one and only University of Michigan. Go Blue! Or so I thought.

I have lived quite comfortably during my undergraduate years with my parents' support, but they cannot provide the same support during law school, especially the tuition. Three years of tuition totals about $150,000 minimum, and then I need to factor in the cost of living. Additionally, some law schools prohibit students from working during the first year. This obviously makes law school a huge financial investment. When I was younger, Michigan Law was the only school I ever wanted to attend. Excitement rushed through my veins when I recently got my acceptance e-mail, and I honestly had to give the phone to my boyfriend so he could read it and confirm that it was, in fact, an acceptance e-mail. I could not believe it! I jumped up and down and rushed to call my parents and tell all friends of the exciting news. Then I remembered the full ride I was offered at Indiana University in January 2017.

I started to think of pros and cons of each scenario: "*Indiana ranks lower, but I could go there for free, but my whole life is rooted in Michigan, but I would not have any student loans, but Michigan might open the door for more opportunities in the future.*" My mind raced at a hundred miles per hour to say the least. I put off thinking about finances for a while so I could just enjoy the fact that I was admitted. How was I supposed to think about finances? Contemplating the tremendous debt I would accrue at Michigan tore me apart, but it was such a huge accomplishment to turn down. Though Indiana Law was in the top 25 law schools in the nation, Michigan ranked in the top 10. I can most likely have a better career attending Michigan, but there is always a chance the job market crashes for attorneys and I am left jobless with hundreds of thousands of dollars of debt.

Growing up, I never thought something like this would be an issue. I would get into the law school of my dreams and that would be the end of my story. When my parents divorced, I thought a little more realistically about this, but I was still blind to the reality of debt, student loans, and budgeting. Now I'll have to learn quickly. My immediate struggle forces me to think about those who have undergraduate loans on top of law school loans. They would likely not even have the ability to weigh options, and would need to take the full ride regardless of school prestige. Though I feel somewhat underprivileged in having to think so much about finances, I still run into those awkward conversations every so often when I reveal that I actually do not know how loans work. My class privilege always finds a way to poke its head out, no matter what economic setting I find myself in.

This whole situation helps me to discover where I truly stand on the social class ladder. I recognize that I am extremely privileged and lucky to have had so much support from my parents throughout my undergraduate years, but I am in no position to not have to worry about finances like some of my peers. I find myself somewhere in the middle. No matter how much my social class has fluctuated, I have never strayed from following the goal I have had ever since I tied that fuzzy orange blanket around my neck in fifth grade and won my first case. Regardless of what law school I choose and how much debt I take on, I am going to become a great lawyer. Through all the confusion, frustration, and stress, I have never lost sight of my dreams. I am grateful for my parents and my comfortable life. Although at times I felt underprivileged, my college experiences have opened my eyes to the many classes around me here at Michigan. I am lucky to be right where I am on the social class ladder.

WHY WE ARE THE PEOPLE WE ARE

KATE GRISSIM

As kids we are encouraged to play outside, take in the fresh air, and get our blood pumping and oxygen flowing through our bodies. When I played outside I loved riding my red razor scooter tirelessly up and down the block counting sidewalk stamps like it was my job. What also caught my attention while riding were the numerous houses for sale and the for-sale signs staked into the freshly mowed, well-watered, green grass lawns. These signs often had attached fliers in little clear boxes giving further details about the house. I loved looking at those fliers because of the one piece of information they disclosed: the selling price. The prices always baffled me. I could not grasp the concept of having so much money.

In fifth grade during the 2008–2009 year, it came my family's turn to move and stake the for-sale sign into our freshly mowed, green grass lawn. As you might have expected, the first question I asked was: "Mom, how much are we selling the house for?" Then inevitably came the next question: "Mom, how much did we buy are our new house for?" For some reason, though, mom would not answer these questions. If she answered the question, I would never get the answer I was looking for, and I would be reminded of how it is impolite to ask how much things cost. But why? Why is it rude? Why would mom answer all of my other questions about homework, about why is this or why is that, but not about money? I always wondered, but I was never too worried because I had the type of childhood where you don't have to worry about money. I knew what money was, but not how much it greatly affected me or anyone else in the world. I can specifically remember times when money talk would come up at dinner. What always immediately followed the conversation was my mom remarking: "Oh, but we don't need to tell anyone this. We can just keep this information to ourselves." Thoughts always ran quickly through my mind after this type of conversation. I could not figure out why we weren't allowed to speak of this, and it sometimes frustrated me.

When thinking back to the minimal discussions of money I shared with my parents, I want to think they didn't mean to hide insights from me. For mom it was mostly about appearances and attitudes. She did not want her children to become the rich, snobby, spoiled children that often are found in wealthy families. She also did not want money to be a distraction from fully developing our characters and personalities or for it to prevent us from having a successful future. For these reasons I fully respect her for doing so. Though we had very few conversations about money, the way my parents raised me made me conscious of money because of the restrictions they put on it. My parents didn't throw money around, and I wasn't given an unlimited amount. I even have to pay for part of my phone bill. So in some ways they taught me very important lessons about money and taught me to be conscious of it, yet they did so indirectly since they minimally addressed our social class standing. Now as I see how pervasive money is, while also being so invisible, I think it is something that needs to be considered early in life if we want to make changes.

I now see social class is an issue very rarely touched upon in school and rarely discussed within our society. Class is not something taught to all of us in third or fourth grade history class. Class is also not an issue like race or gender that all of us are aware of and all of us are conscious of in order to avoid situations of racism or sexism. Class is an invisible yet pervasive social construct forming the foundation of our society. But for those who don't have to worry about it, the discovery of social class often does not occur until later in childhood or even into adolescence. This was true for me.

I grew up in a family with four kids and we were very lucky with the situation we were born into. Both my parents went to college, but mom became a stay-at-home mom as soon as my twin sister and I were born. Dad still to this day works in commercial real estate. What really helps to paint the picture of the wealth of my family is the way we spent our summers. Our family went on a vacation every summer because we could afford it. By the time I was 12 in 2011, I had already been on three vacations that involved going on a cruise ship, which is something that many people don't experience until they are adults, if they ever experience it. The town I grew up in, Western Springs, Illinois, is also a big indicator of our economic standing.

Western Springs has been ranked as being one of the safest towns in America. In 2016, *Business Week* ranked it as one of the best places to raise children. My community is home to nearly a dozen parks. Violent crime and property crime are almost nonexistent, with residents having a 0.03% chance of being a victim of a property crime. However, what comes with being such a safe town is a lack of social class diversity. The town has around 13,000 people, yet it is predominantly upper-middle class and white. Since it is such a safe town, everyone wants to raise their kids there, but few can because of the high cost of living. Only the upper-middle class can afford to live in such a town. What are the consequences? Safety is part of this, but children growing up in these types of towns tend to be sheltered and unaware of economic differences. How can one see the invisibility of class ranking when there is no one to compare yourself with? That was the struggle I faced.

On a neurological basis, the human brain is known to prefer symmetry, coherency, and simplicity. Our brains detect patterns instead of allowing randomness to persist. That is what my childhood centered around: uniformity. The education system in general, let alone Western Springs, often does not have to deal with randomness, and is more commonly symmetrical: white walls and white kids, symmetrical and unchanging, no variation. The kids around me in elementary and middle school smothered any chance of perceiving the invisible yet pervasive stratification created by social class. It's not that I went to private schools; I attended excellent public schools, but ones that were in wealthy neighborhoods, which was something very clear if you attended these schools. We were privileged children receiving top education, yet we had no idea of anything different. It wasn't until high school that I saw people from different social class backgrounds, yet knowing details of the differences were hard to come by. I had no idea students could be part of a reduced lunch program or that they were able to get breakfast at school. None of these things were very relevant to me because the majority of my friends fit into the same social class as me, or so I thought.

It wasn't until I started to apply to college when I noticed how some of my best friends did not receive the same privileges as me. When I decided which colleges to apply to, money was not a problem. I applied to schools I thought I could see myself at whether or not tuition cost $20,000, $40,000, or $60,000 per year or were in state rather than out of state. Money had no limiting power over me. One friend's dream school was University of Colorado, Boulder, but out-of-state tuition was $60,000 per year. When it came down to deciding which school to attend, she had to settle for a less expensive school solely because of money issues. I forgot how big of an effect money had on choosing a college because it was never something I had to worry about. A similar situation occurred with my boyfriend. He pays for his own schooling, and so this limited his decisions. Though the school he chose is not notoriously expensive, I will still hear him mention from time to time how much debt he will have after college. I just cannot relate to him about that. All this leaves me feeling guilty, though, because he deserves to attend college and not to bear costs and worries of debt. My friend deserved to go to her dream school just as much as I did. How did I end up getting both of those things, and they got neither? Ultimately, it was hard for me to be so grateful for my situation when I wasn't aware of other people's situations and how different they were from mine.

Most of my childhood friends were well-off compared to the majority of Americans, but I find it odd I didn't know I had significantly more economic privilege. One friend I had known since fourth grade was always in a good economic situation until her parents divorced when she was in high school. She never really liked to open about her situation too much, but when we went on our youth group's annual mission trip she felt safe enough to share. Her mother had full custody of her and her sisters, and her father became distant. Her mom was a teacher for a Chicago charter public school making a small income. This was barely supporting them, and they no longer could afford their house. They moved from one rental house to another, eventually ending up having to live in a family friend's house for about a year and then her aunt's house for another year. Fortunately they have settled into an apartment, but money is still a big problem. She just joined a sorority and started stressing out about the dues she is having to pay. This is a big shock for me as I am also part of a sorority, yet never thought about the related expenses. Her experience has opened my eyes to seeing how different social classes are actually much closer to me than I previously thought.

Throughout high school (2012–2016) I was part of a youth group that encouraged community service. Over spring breaks my group hosted its annual mission trips. We traveled to work with foundations like Habitat for Humanity and Back Bay Mission. Each year we went somewhere different: Louisiana, Mississippi, or South Carolina. Regardless of the place, we were always doing similar tasks. We went off to our work site locations, which were almost always someone's house. Some of these houses were destroyed by Hurricane Katrina, and we were witnesses to the immense repercussions of this storm even 10 years later. Houses had lost all their paint, door knobs and windows were rusting, and mold surrounded the perimeters.

On my first mission trip, seeing the conditions some people were living in was a real shock to me. Our typical tasks included painting houses, hanging drywall, and demolition, but on my most recent trip our task was to clean up an apartment. It was trashed. The carpet was splattered with red liquid, hair balls covered the bathroom floor, and old, moldy dishes piled up in the kitchen sink. The smell burnt our noses. We did not know the full story, but it seemed like the owners fled from the area and left the apartment without gathering their things or tidying up at all. To see someone live this way and then be so suddenly removed from it was truly eye-opening. I had never witnessed such helplessness right in front of me.

At some of the work sites we were lucky enough to meet the homeowners, and that brought me even closer to seeing the real effect of inequality and the large gap between social classes. I was so grateful to have this experience not many people my age have the opportunity to take part in, and I loved thinking how this experience was going to change me for the better. However, I am not going to lie and say I was a changed person when I got back. Once I returned home after the 18-hour bus ride to my small, secluded, wealthy suburb, those social class differences disappeared. It was hard to hold onto those feelings I experienced during the trip. As soon as the break was over, I was once again immersed into my predominantly white, upper-middle-class school. My friends went on this trip too, but it never changed the fact that we all had privilege. Being out of our element it was very easy to think about class, but as soon as we returned home, it dissipated. This is what largely explains why I never really gave too much thought to class until it affected my own friends.

Now that I'm in college at the University of Michigan (UM) I feel like I'm just in a larger version of high school. I understand not everyone here is upper-middle class or owning class, but without consciously doing it, I have surrounded myself with people of the same class. I have joined a sorority here on campus, and never in my life have I ever seen girls have such minimal awareness of money. It seems they have daddy's credit card and never think about how much things cost. They get sushi every Friday night and brunch every Sunday morning. Instead of going out to dinner and spending my money on expensive sushi, I stick to the sometimes boring, dining hall food. It's not even just food, but clothes too. These girls will rarely repeat an outfit they have worn before, but they don't have to. They have an unlimited amount of clothes and an unlimited amount of money to spend on clothes. In my situation, my mom puts money on a debit card for me to buy books and train tickets home, but it's not for fun things like food and clothes. Though it is hard for her to really know what I'm spending it on, I've been taught to not just throw around money willy-nilly, and this is where the money-conscious attitude my parents instilled within me kicks in. I don't see this same idea reflected in some of my sorority sisters. Sometimes their attitudes about money are hard to witness and it can be hard to be a part of such a wealthy group of students that is the Greek system here at Michigan.

Most of these girls tend to be oblivious to many things happening around them. They don't have to worry about poverty and about college debt, so it's easy for them to be superficial. This is something that just happens naturally when you have so much cash at your disposal. Class diversity is all around, yet they suffocate themselves within this college world of wealth. And not until this winter have I ever seen so many Canada Goose jackets in my life. I see flocks of them coming at me from all different directions. No matter where I turn, I see Canada Goose jackets. In case you don't know, they only cost around $900! I don't judge people for wanting to splurge a little when it comes to winter coats, especially when we sometimes live in the polar vortex here in Michigan; however I do not understand the extra benefit coming from this Goose jacket that a $200 or even $300 ones couldn't provide. They seem to represent the epitome of the owning class. The coyote fur hoods and Canada Goose labels scream to the world that students' parents have money and a lot of it. They are the perfect symbol of wealth and excessive consumption.

I'm writing in the winter semester of my first year of college, but I have started to notice affluence all around me. When you go to a school that costs over $50,000 to attend out of state, and a high percentage of the student body population is out of state, it makes sense for most students to be well-off. It's hard to pinpoint what exact aspect of a person demonstrates his or her economic class, especially when someone is just passing by. However, signs of affluence seem to be most present in people's attitudes. Many do not take school seriously. They don't go to lecture, they give minimal effort on homework assignments, and they do the least amount of work as possible. This is not the attitude of the working-class students here at Michigan. They have worked hard to be here and some are often trying to maintain scholarships that helped them get here in the first place. They don't blow off class or don't do homework because they rather go out at night. They take school seriously and it shows. The more affluent kids know they will have money or their parents' connections to fall back on if school doesn't go so well, but working-class students do not have these advantages. They want the best possible future and have to work hard to earn it. Although I may identify with the wealthier students in many ways, I've learned the importance of hard work. Relying on my parents' money is not an option, as I think it would actually hinder me in the end. Working hard is the best way to grow into the person I want to be and find my own success.

The scary thing, now as I have become more aware of social class, is that I still am not 100% sure about where I stand. I'm not positive about the income my father makes. Since my family has always been well-off, the question of how much money he makes never came up. For students in the upper-middle class, finances only come up when we need to fill out forms for testing or for college. For me, it came up for the Free Application for Federal Student Aid (FAFSA) application, yet not even this brought me much insight. During senior year of high school when applying for college, all I ever heard from my counselor was about how important it was to fill out the FAFSA document. I told mom and she simply said: "Oh you don't need to fill that out. We will not be eligible." I told her what my counselor said about filling it out anyway, as an important measure for record keeping or something along those lines. But mom was insistent on the fact there would be no point. That sunk in hard because it seemed like everyone else filled it out. Was I really the only one who was not going to be eligible because my family was too wealthy? The lasting impact from this was that I still have little understanding of my dad's income.

While taking Sociology 295 (The Experience of Social Class in College and the Community), I've been probed about my social class standing and we have been discussing stories about people from all different class backgrounds. Yet I'm not sure if I fall into the upper-middle class or the upper class. Which class should I relate to? But mom and dad have raised me to not really talk about money, so I feel uncomfortable asking them. This is where the problem of our nation lies. We do not talk openly about social class often enough for there to be any real change. Now I can see that and will make sure to openly talk about this with my kids someday. When you have money it is necessary to be humble about it, but being aware is not something you should take away from your children.

College is similar to high school by the fact that I see a lack of money and race diversity. I attended a high school of 4,000 students; with a decent percentage being Hispanic, yet the accelerated classes removed almost all diversity. In Advanced Placement (AP) courses, we all tended to be white and upper-middle class. Diversity of race and class disappeared and courses were very homogenous. Because of this, it was hard to get know people of different classes and racial backgrounds, which may be one of my biggest regrets from high school. The best way to learn about class is through getting to know people from other classes and sharing stories. For me it was hard to develop those relationships unless I purposefully made an effort. Forming those relationships wasn't something that came natural in my school, and I wish I could have had that experience.

Now as I have three years left of college, I hope to find new people to create those important cross-class bonds with. I know that sharing our individual stories is important if we are to understand the large problems at hand and if we one day eventually want to make changes to address class stratification. Though it isn't always easy to cross these invisible boundaries, I look forward to the challenge and experience I will gain.

As for the future, I do not expect to see much change here at Michigan. I know we are starting to implement initiatives to enroll the more talented, low-income students. However, this university is very affluent and I'm sure these new students will have difficulty adjusting or fitting in. As for me, I'm hoping to explore diversity here at Michigan. Unlike my mission trip scenarios where I was immersed in different class cultures, but was immediately brought back to my small town afterward, my life here at Michigan and afterward will be different. I am surrounded by class diversity on campus. I am hoping to take advantage of this and become a stronger person. With these experiences I hope to become more familiar with other people's perspectives and empathize with people who are different. This will all be relevant as I soon begin my journey in the real world, especially if I pursue a career in business (which is my plan as of now), a field commonly known to be filled with high-earning individuals: a world of affluence. Being immersed into this domain I will not forget the experiences of others. I will not disregard their problems solely because they are no longer relevant to me. I will try to stay open to those social class differences and hopefully be able to make changes for the better.

Income inequality is continuing to grow within our nation and is larger now than ever. If we can raise awareness about this issue, we can begin to understand the problem, and then hopefully take steps to actually do something about it. We need to minimize this gap because as it is currently, social class is one of the most pervasive inequalities in the early 21st century. Class shapes life experiences. Wealth often determines the type of education one receives, as well as one's opportunities and lifestyle. Yet social class is something rarely discussed. Too often it remains invisible and a paradox that needs to be addressed. By writing about social class, not only are we coming closer to addressing it and the ethical nature of inequality, but we can also better understand ourselves and appreciate the reasons why we are the people we are.

THE PRIVILEGE OF CERTAINTY: WANT VERSUS NEED

CORINDA LUBIN-KATZ

I was born in Norwalk, Connecticut, in August 1989. My mom was born and raised in Israel, and moved to the United States in her early twenties. My dad grew up in California. When I was three years old, my parents divorced, both remarrying not long after. My dad moved to Hamden, Connecticut, and my mom lived in Oxford, Connecticut, and I went back and forth between the two houses. The divorce was tumultuous, to say the least, but I had everything I needed and then some. Each set of parents loved me dearly and made every effort to make my childhood a wonderful one.

Up until high school, I attended school in Oxford, which is an extremely homogenous town. In grades sixth through eighth, there was one black person, one Asian person, and one Jewish person (me). Essentially everyone else was white and Christian. Though I was never into religion, I loved my Israeli heritage and felt pride in being Jewish, which only heightened as I received a lot of curious questions from friends—mainly of the "Is it true you get *eight* days of presents?!" variety. Even as it was a source of pride to "repre-sent" that facet of my background, I felt homogeneity at my school was odd and limiting. It felt as if I was a source of foreignness—the intrigue of unfamiliar experiences clearly piquing my classmates' curiosity. This was probably the case for the handful of others who fell into an underrepresented identity category. At the time, because it was all seemingly benign and friendly, it never bothered me. I was young and not viewing these social dynamics through particularly conscious or sociological lenses. In retrospect, this dynamic was fleeting insight into the experience of having an identity that was different from the majority—it was brief, minimal, and pleasant, though, and thus was largely inaccurate in reflecting the experiences of others.

I recognized the lack of diversity in racial and religious contexts. Racial, because it was apparent the vast majority of students were white: religious, because I had the firsthand experience of being the only Jew. Social class was less apparent, and thus something I did not consciously think about all that frequently. For the most part, there were no distinct indications of anyone falling outside the general mean—another testimony to the town's overall affluent homogeneity.

Beyond school, the two towns I grew up in were both small and suburban. In Hamden, my dad and stepmom initially lived in a small apartment. She had come to the United States from France when she was 12 years old and later went on to receive her PhD in neuroscience at the Princeton University, ultimately deciding to devote herself for the time being to bringing up the family. My dad attended medical school and worked tirelessly. We eventually moved to a new home, which my parents slowly but surely revamped and enhanced.

Meanwhile, my mom and stepdad, a psychiatrist and psychologist, respectively, lived in Oxford and opened a posttraumatic stress disorder (PTSD) center together in New Haven. They have worked together diligently for years, slowly but surely expanding staff and thoughtfully growing their practice.

In early middle school, my mom, stepdad, and I moved one house over. The new house had been abandoned for years and apparently had been used by a local drug dealer. Today he actually continues to live in the neighborhood and is a very friendly presence. It was a massive, beautiful house, with a stone front, large front yard, and a back pond. However, because of its history and poor inside condition, when the house was reclaimed by the state of Connecticut, there was not much interest in buying it. Its price dropped to much lower than it typically would have cost. My parents took out a mortgage and bought the house, and we moved in. The process of turning house to a home began and continued organically for years.

While I was initially sad to move, I quickly grew to love our new home. I remember feeling a vague discomfort and anxiety about its size and related social class implications. I initially felt hesitant to invite friends over, thinking they would look at this giant house and think I was rich and spoiled—which led me to vaguely wonder: "Am I rich and spoiled?"

One day, the doorbell rang, and I opened the door to find one of my classmates. She told me she used to live here and wanted to see what it looked like now, so I invited her inside. It was a brief and strange visit. We were in the midst of fixing up the house. We stood there straddling before and after, temporarily witnessing a transition, only to turn and go our separate ways. Something about this day imprinted my memory, though I couldn't pinpoint the source of my unease at the time.

I was never spoiled in terms of attitude or expectations. I was always grateful and appreciative and knew not to take any positive element of my life for granted. I had a very privileged upbringing. In both households, I never wanted for clothes, food, school supplies, or toys. As burdensome as my parents' divorce was, I always felt an acute sense of gratitude to not only have two sets of parents who loved me dearly, but who were able to provide essentials and beyond. I was always very appreciative of all my possessions, but was also living in my own context. So the notion this was not every kid's experience was not on my radar, at least not in a consistent way.

I have vague recollections of years of financial stress, but it mostly manifested in my parents' adamancy that we should never take money or privilege for granted. Even as my parents' success increased and things became less financially stressful, they always tried to instill in my siblings and me the importance of not being frivolous with money and knowing to connote money with hard work, not a given or automatic gift. If we ever forgot to the turn the lights off when we left a room, we could expect an earful. On the other hand, the lights were never going to turn off because we couldn't afford to pay them. I never had to carry any burden of monetary stress. I was never in a position where I *had* to get a job, and I was free to focus on school, sports, and social life. There was never a feeling that something I needed would be out of reach and more than that, there was the feeling of access to things beyond necessity.

I attribute the happiness of my childhood first and foremost to the fact I was surrounded by a wonderfully kind and loving family. However, as an adult, I easily recognize many of the wonderful experiences and warm feelings that weave their way throughout my childhood were in fact manifestations of social class privilege. These included: vacations and weekend trips; outings to baseball games, aquariums, zoos, and restaurants; toys, games, and movies; all the recreational sports leagues I wanted to join; piano lessons and gymnastics; new clothes and school supplies every year. When I was 12 in 2001, my parents brought me and my younger brother with them to Australia on a business trip, a place I have yet to establish the financial stability to visit on my own. Over the years, I had the joy of visiting family in Israel many times because my parents are able to afford it. With my dad's side of the family, I traveled to France to visit my stepmom's family. I was always incredibly grateful for these opportunities at the time, but don't know if I understood the extent of my privilege.

It is interesting, humbling, and so important to reflect back on the experiences of my childhood and sift through them with a social class filter. Much of what I experienced was beyond "need" and would be beyond reach for many. These were advantages I did nothing to contribute to, but benefited greatly from them. I wasn't a kid who needed those things to be happy, and yet I know they enriched my childhood tremendously.

Growing up in Connecticut, a state with a vast economic spectrum, was always an interesting intersection of identities, and a somewhat miscellaneous smattering of alternating diversity and uniformity. I lived in two largely middle-class towns. In these contexts, class tended to be a more subtle identity as far as my diversity perception. I was more inclined to notice and think about race. I always hated how little race and religious diversity my middle school had. In high school I moved from being the only Jewish person for years to the majority. Racially, the school was not diverse at all. I could count the people of color on one hand. Thankfully, I immersed in more diverse friend groups outside my school setting. I was more aware of financial privilege in high school, though, because it was an obvious component of simply being able to attend that school.

When it was time for me to attend high school, there was a choice to be made. There was no public high school in Oxford, so we looked to Hamden. There was Hamden High, which most of my other siblings attended, and Hamden Hall, the private country day school with a whopping tuition, a highly rigorous curriculum, and 60 people in each graduating class. My parents debated, and ultimately, I ended up at Hamden Hall.

High school definitely prepared me for college. By the time I arrived at the University of Michigan (UM) in the fall of 2007, I had plenty of experiences with long papers, difficult exams, and other college-level projects. On top of this it was always a given that I would attend college. This was an expectation my parents verbalized casually and often, that ingrained itself in a quiet, habitual way into my subconscious, and was a notion my high school environment adamantly enforced. I honestly think the idea of not attending college ever entered my mind as a possibility. I never had to fear it would be financially impossible, and I had assistance and guidance from four parents who had all attended college and various levels of graduate and professional education. My high school had a college counselor who worked diligently with students, and had plenty of time for customized one-on-one interaction given the school's small size. All of this played a major role in my confidence and ability to attend college and succeed.

My move to college was a fairly easy transition. It's not that I didn't work hard, but the path was laid for me and there were countless resources and people to assist me along the way. I think

I was aware of advantages at the time, but in some ways the ease of the experience neutralized that awareness. As is often the case with economic privilege—and privileges in general—you don't *have* to think about certain issues when they don't affect you.

This lack of awareness was most true for me as far as social class. As a white woman, I obviously benefited (and continue to benefit) from inherent racial privileges. Race and racial issues tended to be on my radar from an early age, whereas while I was always actively appreciative of experiences and opportunities my parents provided that were a product of social class advantage, there were many elements that quietly melted into an overall backdrop of my childhood and adolescence. There were certain things I never worried about and it was easy to accept that as the norm by virtue of simply not thinking about the possibility of it *not* being the norm. This highlights added components of economic privilege, which I perceive as twofold: first, the actual concrete, tangible advantages; and second, the consistent financial peace of mind and freedom from stress. Obviously, each of these elements manifests with many nuances, some of which were obvious to me at the time, and others which again faded into my overall status quo. Having the choice of whether or not to contemplate experiences was a manifestation of privilege I only came to recognize later.

Thinking back to the end of high school, I was immersed in the college application process. There were many factors that helped guide me in shaping my list of schools: location—I wanted to get far enough away to feel a real sense of autonomy, but not so far as to have trips home be a major undertaking; size—after only 60 people in my graduating class, I was ready for a much larger scene. Academics were a priority and basketball was on my radar. Money, though obviously relevant, was not ultimately a deciding factor, and it was not a burden that I would have to shoulder. That was obviously an immense privilege. For countless people that is the main if not sole factor dictating college possibilities.

Now at the other end of college, I am extremely lucky to have graduated without any student loans. My parents paid for what they could, took out and covered loans as needed, and I received a scholarship for part of one semester (significant, but a drop in the bucket, ultimately). Meanwhile, student loans for many others are stressful at an *astronomical* level. I know it is such a gift I do not have to carry that financial worry with me. I have countless friends who shoulder that burden, and who know they will be paying off loans for years. That means the perpetual nag of having a balance owed. The fact that so many young people have to carry heavy educational debt simply for having had a college experience is highly unfair and problematic. I know it's a massive advantage to have attended an out-of-state, extremely expensive university, and to have emerged personally unscathed financially.

During my time at Michigan I began to experience social class as a more definitive component of identity. Sociology certainly helped in perceiving the multiple facets of identity that intersect for each person. I began to compartmentalize elements of my own identity—woman, white, Jewish, upper-middle class, Israeli, etc.— and think about how each one affected my individual and collective experiences. Obviously some identities lent themselves to privilege, others to adversity. As far as social class, my experience was undoubtedly one of privilege.

I remember a moment in college with one of my closest friends. We were in her car, and she was stressed about money. Her family was having a tough time, and she was consistently sending money home to help them—something else I never had to do, and was the opposite of my experiences. My family sent me money. She already had a bunch of her own bills and was feeling anxious and overwhelmed. If she ran out of money, that was it. There was no safety net; there was nothing to fall back on, and no one to ask for help. Of course, her family would have loved to help her, but they simply weren't in a position to do so. As she conveyed her distress to me, we were backing out of a parking lot and she hit a pillar, damaging her car. So life threw yet another expense on the pile of an already burdensome load. I will never forget this moment. We stopped in silence, and I turned to her, unsure of what to say, waiting for her reaction. After a brief pause, she finally started laughing, and said this stuff is inevitable in life so all you could do was stay positive and deal with it. I felt so inspired and impressed by her incredible attitude and perspective. Her amazingly positive outlook and mental fortitude in the face of a challenging situation highlighted yet another realm of my life where I was granted the advantage of financial support. Daily, without meaning to, I took for granted I did not have to worry about money.

This was yet another instance of privilege and how it provides the luxury of a certain mental ease. I had this conversation often with some of my closest friends about race. I developed a really close group of friends, and I happened to be the only white person in the group. We had a lot of conversations about race and what it meant to be a student of color in this predominantly white institution (PWI). For example, we examined the difference in experience for each of us walking into a massive 300+ person lecture at Michigan. Because race was a topic on my mind, I noticed the racial breakdown. After conversations with friends, I became even more aware. I could walk into a room and see a vast majority of people who looked like me. I didn't have to worry when answering a question pertaining to race (or anything, really) that I might be expected—even if only subconsciously—to represent my entire race. I didn't have to deal with the discomfort of entering a room and being the obvious, immediate minority, with any and all (often stereotypical) connotations. My friends did have to deal with this all the time. Their race was overtly apparent to them at all times. As a white person at a PWI, I didn't have to think about race if I didn't want to. What's more, most white people seemed to think of our college as very racially diverse. Yes, many different types of people were represented among Michigan's demographic, but percentage wise, it was vast majority white. The experience of "diversity" was very different depending on whose perspective you took.

This was made even more apparent by the need for safe spaces. Several of my friends joined all-black organizations. In race discussions in classes, sometimes white students would voice opinions that this was reverse racism, or promoting division, or that if there

was a "White Student Union," it would be considered a racist outrage. The obvious rebuttal to this was always there is no need for
a *white* student union, because the student union is already majority white. Whiteness is not only implied, but inherent without need
to carve out a space for it—an implication that is a product of privilege. This is true of all privileged experiences.

In reflecting back on the multitude of student organizations and
clubs at Michigan, many of which were clearly created to serve as
safe spaces, I can't recall ever seeing one centering on social class.
It seems like social class was often the identity that was not overtly
discussed or acknowledged, though it is of course a very significant
one and one that affects many facets of students' lives. Perhaps this
is a result of the notion that discussing money is tacky and inappropriate. Whatever the cause, it is often a largely ignored facet of the
Michigan experience.

Having now entered the real world of post-college life, my relationship with money is different. I live in New York, one of the most
expensive cities in the world, where my monthly rent essentially
eats up an entire paycheck. Of course it's my decision to live here,
because I feel it offers more than it takes. But enjoying most of New
York's offerings requires money as well. As is true with adulthood
generally, the list of miscellaneous bills and expenses has a way
of perpetually accumulating. Rent, electricity, credit card, resid-
ual insurance fees, telephone, Internet, gym membership, taxes,
and the random expenses that life unexpectedly throws at me can
create a lot of stress. As a young adult, the idea of owning a home
feels like a hazy far-off notion. The seemingly endless barrage of
expenses associated with eventually having a kid—or kids—feels
laughably impossible.

The immediate feeling of being overwhelmed at the thought of
supporting a child makes me think about how lucky I was to have
access to so much in my own childhood. I cannot begin to fathom
funding a vacation for someone, let alone college, let alone *multiple*
"someones" if I chose to have more than one kid. I can barely wrap
my head around the idea of spending money to get a quality knife

set in my kitchen. Funding my own life definitely is an experience in contrast to my childhood. At the same time, I also know that I still have that safety net. If I was ever in a real bind, my parents would be there to help. They are able to help along the way even when I'm not in dire life or death situations, but simply finding myself stretched super thin. This is ongoing privilege extending from my family's social class status, something I have had since the day I was born. It is something that, if I choose to have a family, I would want to be able to provide to them as well, and it makes me conscious of what steps would be necessary to get to that place.

Currently, I work at a nonprofit that helps design and launch innovative high schools focused on helping all students succeed regardless of their circumstances. It's a cause I believe in, and a job that allows me to make ends meet in this exceedingly expensive city, which is not always a given for nonprofits. At the same time, my passion ultimately lies in comedy writing. This is a path I've only just begun to pursue, but already find humor a helpful tool in getting through challenges and maintaining perspective—much like my friend in college. It's also another medium through which I can address manifestations of social class. For example, I may be reading about how my long-lost middle school friend is now officially a homeowner, thinking about how I just added water to my hand soap to prolong buying a new one, wallowing in the juxtaposition. But it's likely very possible that I'm at brunch while thinking this. All these experiences are reflections of social class status and I find that humor is a great way to highlight both different and universal life experiences in the context of various identities.

It's hard to tell how my life will play out, but as I describe thoughts and decisions relating to my social class journey, it again becomes apparent how crucial it is to maintain perspective, to be aware of privileges inherent in situations I sometimes find myself stressing over. It highlights to me as well the foundations upon which I've been able to build. Ultimately, every element of my identity is a product of those who came before me. Some of these identities are permanent, others are malleable. There are many people who have to work hard to climb the rungs of the social class ladder (a process that differs in difficulty depending on countless factors). Whatever each generation establishes lays a foundation for those to come. Within the context of my life, social class identity, financial stability, and support were implied. As is the case with any privilege, one must choose to be conscious of it, choose to recognize its multiple manifestations, and choose to understand the many ways it plays out and is advantageous by default. In so doing we widen our perspectives to view and understand the experiences of those around us.

BLACK IN THE BUBBLE
JASMINE MORIGNEY

S tatistics say that upward mobility is rare and, for some, even
impossible. Born in the 1960s, my two black parents managed
to beat the odds. My father was born in inner-city Detroit prior
to White Flight starting in 1967, but his family remained in their
neighborhood to this day. His mother was a homemaker, and his
father was a teacher. He is one of two children. My mother was born
in inner-city Memphis, Tennessee. Her father was a carpenter, and
her mother was a nurse. She is one of seven children. My parents
did not grow up with silver spoons in their mouths. Born to working-class homes they started with humble beginnings. From there,
both went on to become electrical engineers after attending an
HBCU (historically black college or university): Tennessee State
University. By the time I was born, their hard work secured my
place in the upper-middle class.

In Indianapolis, Indiana, I spent the first three years of life in a
sizable house built by my parents from the ground up. I socialized
with other children of engineers of all races: black, white, Asian,
middle eastern, you name it. That is where my little diverse upper-
middle-class bubble started. At age three, just after my little sister
was born, my family moved to Southfield, Michigan, for dad's job.
Southfield is a predominately black middle-class area not far outside of Detroit. However, the daycare I attended was very diverse;
my daycare was located in West Bloomfield, Michigan, where I made

tons of friends. I begged my mom to let me go to elementary school with them. She said since I lived outside the district, I could not go. Then, a woman I didn't know (and still don't) changed my life forever. She told mom about something called Schools of Choice. This program allowed me to attend a school in a wealthier area than those in my district, and ultimately go to school with my daycare friends; a week later I was enrolled. The morning I started at Green School Elementary, mom drove me up to the small brick building and I went in to start my first day of kindergarten. I don't remember much else from that day, except wearing the Bratz T-shirt I had begged my mom to buy for me.

It wasn't until I was 16 years old that I found out what else went on that day. After I went inside the school, my mother sat outside and counted all the black children entering after me. I don't know how many she counted, but it was enough to appease her. I've asked her why she did that and she just said: "I wanted you to see yourself in others." She wanted me to be able to relate to other students on more than just a social class level, but also on a racial one. Her expectation was that since the area was upper-middle class there would be little racial diversity. Thinking about it now, I am so thankful she did that. I honestly don't know how I would have turned out if I had been in a place where everyone didn't look like me. I can only imagine it would have been very lonely, much like how I feel now at the University of Michigan.

At age 10, after being in school for five years, we moved to West Bloomfield, the same town my elementary school was in. It is a predominately white upper-middle-class area adjacent to Bloomfield Hills, Michigan. My house is big, with lots of windows and nestled between two white, Jewish neighbors. On one side, the owners brought me University of Michigan (UM) gear, and on the other, they avoided my family like the plague. They might have been racist, or simply antisocial; either way they aren't very friendly. It is a nice neighborhood with nice enough people and nice schools, but at the time I was living there, I didn't really realize it.

West Bloomfield is—different. It is wealthy no doubt, but it destroys the social class stereotypes set forth by society. It is mostly "white" but that's including Middle Easterners, Jewish people, and Chaldeans. There are also African Americans, Asians, and Hispanics, but in smaller amounts. The schools allow for an upper-middle-class schooling experience for all races and class backgrounds through the School of Choice program I was once a part of. It's referred to by its residents as "the bubble." The diversity combined with its wealthy reputation and low crime rate makes it very unrepresentative of the "outside" world. To be honest, I loved it there, but I know now the world is crueler than that. People are poor, tragedies happen, but I am still a racial minority. In West Bloomfield, it's easy to forget those things.

Social class was not very apparent to me as a child. I knew some places looked nicer than others and that doctors made a lot of money. That was the extent of my socioeconomic analysis. Looking back, I think my first realization that not everyone was in the same class as my family and I was when I was seven. I went to after-school care at a local daycare and one day mom drove my teacher home. I do not know the conversation that took place, but after that it became a weekly occurrence. I did not like driving my teacher home, I did not think she lived in a nice area and it made me afraid. I recall asking my mother over and over why she could not get a car and drive herself. My mom would always reply with the same sentence: "Some people are not as lucky as you." It took me a couple years to truly understand what that meant. I must have made my feelings more apparent than I intended. A year ago, I ran into this teacher and the first thing she said to me was: "Are you still a brat?" I managed to laugh it off, but in the back of my mind I just kept thinking how ungrateful she was. But now I realize, maybe it was how ungrateful I was. Although I was only seven, it must have hurt her to see a child so blind to people outside her social class. I wish I could go back and be more understanding, but can any child who grew up within a privileged social class bubble truly understand?

Either way, I am now truly sorry for how I treated that woman when I was a child.

Little phrases from people began to illustrate the way I looked at my life. People who came to my home such as plumbers or repair men would always ask my parents: "What do you do for a living?" They needed some explanation as to why my black parents lived in a nice house in the middle of a white suburb. Phrases that denied my racial identity because of my class began to bother me the most. My extended family would tell me that I "talked [middle class] white" because I spoke "proper English" and rarely made use of African American vernacular English. I fell outside of what they were used to in their daily lives: working-class black individuals. People at school would say—"I forget that you're black"—as if the way I speak is the sole source of my blackness. Even before college, these things haunted me. I never felt this rejection from my own upper-middle-class black friends, but I felt it from my non-black friends the most. To working-class black people I was one of them, but to my non-black friends, I was not. They held this stereotype in their heads that I and my upper-middle-class vernacular did not match.

For me, that was a very confusing place to be and still is. It all hit its peak in my senior year of high school. My "friends" and I were discussing recent events related to minority groups around the world and one said something in the vein of: "White people are treated as minorities nowadays." As if the struggle of all white people as a whole surmounted the struggle of all minorities. When I took offense to this, she said: "When have you experienced racism? We live in West Bloomfield." She assumed my social class shielded me from everyday racism. I have been very fortunate to never experience overt or violent racism. However, the very threat of it is something firmly engrained in every essence of my being. I do and say everything as a black woman, something white people never really have to consider. I was very lucky to live in West Bloomfield, but even it had its faults. My father, a 6' 1" inch black man with a fondness for black hoodies is routinely followed around in stores in the apparent utopia that is West Bloomfield. This is the same man who was put in handcuffs when he was a teenager for simply being in the area at the time of an alleged assault, with a perpetrator (he later found out) that looked nothing like him. Although these are not my direct experiences, they are things I still have to worry about for myself and those who look like me. At that time I learned no one defines my blackness or my black experience except for me, and I'm honestly still trying to figure out what it means. There is no magic black sign of approval that incorporates all varieties of the black experience.

When college approached, all I could focus on was how proud I was to be admitted to the University of Michigan (UM), the "best" university in the world. I came here with two best friends (one white and one Filipina) and could not be happier; then I got here. I realized I had no close black friends about three weeks after I moved in. I didn't know what to do. I was too scared to venture outside of friends I had grown so accustomed to. However, I also had a level of fear that I would begin to lose myself; and to some degree, I have. I miss relating to people on levels so deep they're unexplainable. There is one other black girl from my high school graduating class here and I barely know her. I lost all connection with those who had a very similar social class and race experiences back in my West Bloomfield bubble. In a recent epiphany, I figured out that all my close black friends went to other universities. Most of them have higher acceptance rates and lower tuition costs; some even choosing to attend HBCUs. I found a comfort in my best friends, both of whom are not black. I neglected to go out and find black friends because they were not the people I happened to interact with on daily basis, since there are so few. My social class helped determine where I went to school and because of that, unfortunately, I feel like I lost a piece of myself in my black friends who went on to other places. With the recent climate, both at Michigan and around the world, I feel the need to be surrounded by black people of all social classes in order to make sense of everything. I have recently begun to make efforts to find black people at this university to connect with. At a PWI (predominately white institution), this is not the easiest thing to do. It is such a large university with so few black faces. Things like the black student union do a great job of trying to bring everyone together, to make it feel less overwhelming. However, when you waited too late to secure those connections, like me, it's hard to recover.

Social class difference at the University of Michigan is outrageous: 36% of the students here have parents who make over $200,000 a year. While I fall into this category, large numbers of people around the country and world do not, and they should be represented at Michigan. The overwhelming number of students from wealthy families, coupled with UM being the most expensive public school in the nation, will always inhibit the university from ever being as diverse as it claims to be. Class inequality at this school has to decrease if it is to consider itself diverse. For reference, black enrollment has never broken 8% and has actually decreased since 2006 (University of Michigan, Office of Registrar). If only I had my mom to count the black faces on my first day. Maybe if social class diversity and race diversity were priorities, then this percentage would be higher. At the end of the day, my social class does not outweigh my race and money is not endless. I had to take out loans and use scholarships to pay my way through college, and my younger sister will have to do the same. I am very blessed, but even that is not enough.

In some aspects, I'm thankful for the marginalized parts of my identity. Being a black woman in today's society has allowed me to be more aware of my privilege in other aspects of my identity; not only in social class but also in my privileged Christian religion. I am able to see a glimpse into how marginalized classes may feel given their standing in our current society. Rhetoric on how the upper-middle class are greedy does not bother me one bit. I have the ability to see this critique as a mobilization by forgotten people and not as a direct attack on me. The issue is that the majority of those with the money and power in America are economically privileged, white, heterosexual males. They are afforded nothing but privilege, and as a result, most cannot sympathize with those of marginalized identities such as the poor and working class. They feel no compulsion to help because they feel a sense of entitlement to what they "earned," however, failing to recognize their paths were shorter and littered with fewer obstacles than those of poor and working classes. I empathize with people of color who fall within these classes. I know the struggle of being black and upper-middle class, where opportunities are already limited by one's race. Corporate America tells us that it can hardly stand the face of a black man, let alone a black woman. African Americans in the poor and working classes must fight even harder to obtain upward mobility. My mother is the only one of her seven siblings to be fully upwardly mobile. She is the only one with a master's degree and also the only one to now be in the upper-middle class. Being upwardly mobile and black with money is hard, imagine being black without it.

Social class in college is something so abstract for me, maybe because people from the working and lower classes have learned to pass, or just because I'm oblivious. One instance when I was touring colleges during my senior year of high school, a student tour leader asked a girl who had completed her application how much she paid. She proceeded to say she had a special code which made all of her college applications free. The tour guide quickly moved on, saying all applications to that college were free. I didn't really think anything about the incident until I got in the car to leave later that day. Mom told me those codes are for people with low incomes who cannot afford the application costs, and that my cousins even had one when applying to colleges. I just remember thinking how stupid I was that this had totally gone over my head. I did not even know that was something colleges do until that day. The only differences I notice are those in higher classes. Unlike before, my focus was on what people had that I didn't. The infamous Canada Goose is my go-to indicator that a person's parents make more than mine, or value different things at the very least. I don't really notice if a person is in a lower class than me. Maybe its America's obsession with the rich that accounts for this difference, but at the end of the day, it doesn't matter. College has taught me to not judge people by where they come from or what they wear like when I was a child. I have met plenty of horrible people from all social classes, and a lot of great ones too.

Recently I was searching the Internet for scholarships while sitting next to one of my roommates, the daughter of a millionaire. She began helping me look. While I sincerely appreciated her assistance, I couldn't help but feel inferior. She doesn't have to look for financial aid; her parents pay for her out-of-state tuition and her brother's private college education with no issue. I couldn't help resenting her just a little, but I could also relate. I find myself falling into "savior" mode when I do meet someone from a lower class. I had a friend who sometimes couldn't afford certain activities like seeing a movie or grabbing dinner off campus. I would offer over and over to pay and I rationalized it by just saying I wanted to hang out with them. In reality I think it's because I could never fathom that their life could be as fulfilling as mine because they had less money. Now I know that I was sorely mistaken.

In some ways, my upper-middle-class upbringing has also made me a bit cold when it comes to my extended family. I know their stories, and all I have to say is that I wish they made different choices. They still live in working-class environments in Memphis, Tennessee: the same ones my mother grew up in. As a result of that, combined with my childhood in an affluent Michigan suburb, I and my cousins are very different. My mother's upward mobility has given her a sense of responsibility to those she "left behind." Trips to her hometown are filled with her paying for everything for everyone. Dinners, groceries, gas, you name it. She even bought my 4-year-old cousin a laptop. I didn't get why she did this when I was a kid, and even less now. My family is well-off and paying for college is no small deed. My family had to make financial sacrifices for my sister and I to attend college; it's hard to get financial aid in the upper-middle class. My parents make too much for any aid but not enough to pay for college out of pocket. Student loans will be a harsh reality for me. Yet my mom still feels an obligation to spend money on everyone else. I can only assume that it's because she wants to create the life for my cousins she wished she had, at least as much as she can. This is where my sense of entitlement comes in. I know I will be okay financially even with college expenses and my mom giving money to her family. However, I don't want to give up my spring break vacations with friends or my $100 pair of leggings. It is a fault of mine, but at this school, it's easier to fit in this way. I have grown accustomed to this lifestyle, and ironically college is the thing that is making this lifestyle even harder. I only hope that my education will breed a life like the one I have, or one that's even better.

College has been a time of reflection and realization. The election of Donald Trump and the increase of police shootings have really opened my eyes. I'm not in my childhood bubble anymore. I have been so lucky, but to some people I will forever be just another nigger. Even families of friends I have known take issue, not with me, but people who look like me. I have been told time and time again by friends that their families are racist, but they take no issue with me. Or, their parents would freak out if they dated black guys, but it's fine that they're friends with me. This makes no sense in my mind. If you have a problem with black people, then you have a problem with me, my mom, my dad, and my sister. I am neither an outlier nor someone who is okay with selective racism. At this time, I like to identify that I am black before I am anything else. I am black before I am a woman, I am black before I am an American, and I am black before I am upper-middle class. I go through college with the painful awareness that no matter how much money my parents or I make, the color of my skin reigns before anything. Honestly, I am okay with that. My social class does not erase my blackness or my experience as a black person in America. It does not lessen my rage against those who voted for Donald Trump, it does not ease the pit in my stomach when I see a confederate flag waving proudly in the southern wind, and it certainly does not soothe the sting of seeing another black man killed by the police. Money does not change my identity; however, it does give me access to a great education. I want to use my social class to educate others. My class has afforded me countless opportunities and I am ready to take them. I want to show people I and my parents are not the exception.

This essay was very hard for me to write. In my life race and class are infinitely linked in my mind. I cannot imagine life with one and not the other. I sat for hours trying to think of an instance when only social class was a factor in a situation; it hasn't. Unlike class, you can see my race. I wear it every day, everywhere I go. My class is something that is somewhat invisible on me as a physical person. Unless you see me leaving my childhood home in that bubble or exiting my brand-new car, you would never know. I am thankful for every single opportunity afforded me because of my social class, all indirectly handed down to me from my parents' hard work: the material things, my education, and my sense of limited safety. This safety is good, but limited because of my race. Since I am doing just fine in one part of life given my social class, my main focus has to be the one that doesn't allow me to lose my temper or truly feel comfortable around a police officer. Take this essay as you will but just remember, money cannot change hundreds of years of fixed thinking and suffering, nor should it. Racism must disappear for money to mean anything to my physical existence.

MATERIAL GIRL
NATSUME ONO

I'm lying on my back in my dorm bed, scrolling through social media on my iPhone. I open Snapchat. Dan Metzler, a guy from my high school forum, has posted a Snapstory. It's long and displays all eight courses of a gourmet meal he's eating while on a date. I shake my head, peeved at the way he throws around money on unnecessary experiences.

*　*　*

In 1996, my parents came to the United States from Tokyo, Japan. Papa had a post-doc position at the National Institute of Health and Mama had left her job as an English teacher. They had very little when they arrived, and Papa's income was limited, so the first home that I knew was a small apartment in Miramont Homes, Rockville, Maryland. Throughout the next seven years, we moved to Bethesda, to Frederick, Maryland, and finally settled in Ann Arbor, Michigan, when Papa was offered a position as an assistant professor at the University of Michigan.

In Frederick, we lived in a small apartment that always vaguely smelled of musty cigarettes. I distinctly remember police cars often entering the neighborhood, but one time, they swarmed our complex blaring sirens. When asking my mother, she told me there was a mix-up involving drug dealers that had resulted in a murder.

Our neighborhood was not only foreigners with lower incomes like my parents, but also working-class, white people.

The next time I was close to anyone who dabbled in drugs was at a summer job in 2016. I was a waitress at a restaurant and had dipped my toes into the lives of working-class people. As I began talking with my coworkers, I learned some of them relied on their meager earnings of mostly tips to pay their bills, and buy food, clothes, and drugs. Thinking about this lifestyle, one where my coworker Dave worked around eight shifts a week to pay for rent and other commodities, I felt they were cutting it very close to the edge. Here I was, buying extra clothes, going out to eat with friends, and watching movies using the money I earned. I was confused when many of them smoked cigarettes or did drugs and complained about never having enough money.

As if cigarettes and drugs were necessary for survival! I thought to myself, raising a brow. I wanted to tell them they'd save more money if they didn't smoke as much or partake in recreational drug use, but I felt they'd think I was on a high horse. Being completely honest, I felt I was wiser than most of them. I, despite being the youngest employee, was on track to become the most successful among the motley crew of servers at Nagomi Sushi Downtown on Liberty Street, in Ann Arbor.

*   *   *

During my junior year of high school, after not thinking about the ACT (American College Testing) at all, Mama suddenly recommended that I take it at least once before the high school administered test.

"Fine," I begrudgingly replied. I would have to wake up at a torturous 7:00 a.m., but I decided it might be worth it. The $50 fee to take the exam was ruled an inevitable cost by my parents, so I went to the exam. Never mind the school exam offered in March 2015 would be administered for free—my parents wanted me to succeed, and so I agreed to be safer than sorry. They were very surprised when my results came back showing two points shy of a perfect score. They composedly realized that if I had scored that well on my first try, I had a chance of getting a perfect score. They were not the types to buy presents for a 4.0 semester or a good test score, but because I had wanted to dye my hair for a while, which my parents had always said was frivolous, I negotiated with them.

"If I get a 36 on the ACT, will you let me dye my hair?"

They agreed, although for what reason I'll never know. Did they doubt my ability to do so, or did they decide this bargain might motivate me to be perfect? To help me, Mama bought me one practice book, and I tried a couple of practice tests. Two months later, after taking the school-administered exam, I was at Aveda Institute in Ann Arbor, asking for copper red streaks in my hair. The dye job cost more than getting a perfect score.

My parents hadn't expected me to have such competitive statistics for college applications. Inevitably, their expectations increasingly grew, and even though I was firmly set on studying architecture, they dropped hints of applying to liberal arts schools as well. Swept up in a group of high-achieving friends, I decided that applying to a couple of Ivys and other prestigious liberal arts schools was not pointless. My parents set one limitation, however. Here was the deal:

> "If after accounting for financial aid or scholarships, the tuition for a school that you are accepted to is not less than the University of Michigan, you'll be going to U of M."

I applied to 10 schools in the fall of 2015. Knowing this was expensive, I felt somewhat guilty when my friend Elonah was upset at our counselor for not filling out her application fee waiver for one school. I never calculated the cost of my applications because Papa just whipped out his credit card for every application I sent in, but I assumed a grand total of about $1,000 is what my parents spent for me to have the luxury to choose a good education. Applying only to Michigan, where I have ended up, would have been free.

* * *

We sat around a dining table at North Quad on State Street, eating poutine (a Canadian dish originally from Quebec made with French fries, cheese curds, and gravy) from the dining hall as Ethan explained to Brandon what it was. All of us eating the same food and having come from the Modern Languages Building together because of our architecture class, it was easy to forget our differences. They continued to chatter about Canada and ski resorts, when the topic switched to the upcoming spring break.

"My mom gave me $1,000 for spring break but I still haven't decided what I want to do," Brandon complained. I looked up from my French fries and tuned into the conversation. "I want to go to Europe, and I know enough people there that I won't have to spend money on hotels," he went on.

1,000? I slowly put down my fork. I was surprised his parents were giving him that much money on a trip solely for fun. If my parents ever gave me $1,000, it was because they believed the money would serve the purpose of academically or culturally educating me. They didn't believe in spending money for the sake of spending money.

My parents felt Interlochen was a worthwhile experience to spend money on. Interlochen Center for the Arts is an arts boarding school near Traverse City, Michigan, that hosts the Interlochen Arts Camp during the summer. Growing up, dance was a major part of my life. During middle school, every dancer is expected to attend summer dance intensives to learn from different instructors and train rigorously for personal improvement. Interlochen offers such a program. In eighth grade, after a nerve-racking audition, I was accepted and attended the camp in June 2012.

At camp, I lay out the required uniforms and dance clothes while unpacking my duffel bag. A girl who had just arrived started to unpack her bags in the shelf next to mine. Perfume bottles after perfume bottles, tubes of lip gloss, a hair straightener, hair curler, hair brush, and many other fashion devices began to line her shelf. She introduced herself as Laney from Chicago, and said that she'd been to Interlochen a couple of times already. I looked at my own sparse collection of objects I had brought. The packing list had said to leave unnecessary objects at home, and Mama and I followed this dutifully. My shelf felt shabby. I realized many of the girls in my cabin would be rich because they could afford this camp, and some were even flying from places like California to experience this well-known arts institution. However, in the end, the rustic setting of the camp and the lack of purchasing power on campus allowed us campers to feel like equals after the first day.

* * *

In late August 2016, I "pulled a Laney" on the first day I moved into my Michigan dorm. Living about 10 minutes away by car, I could bring whatever I wanted, and not wanting to be underprepared, I packed many of my treasured possessions. Although I had talked to my soon-to-be roommate a couple of times via Facebook, I knew relatively little about her. I knew she was coming from New Jersey, so I automatically assumed she was a "rich out-of-state kid." However, when I was mostly done unpacking, she looked at my stuff and said:

"I feel like I seriously under-packed." Shame rose on my cheeks because I hadn't intended to make her feel bad, and truth be told, I hadn't given much thought to what my roommate might think of what I brought. Whenever I hear about anyone attending the University of Michigan from another state, I think they must be many times richer because of the outlandishly expensive out-of-state tuition they pay. Until attending college, I didn't realize I was lucky my state college was such a great institution compared to other state schools that some had decided against attending.

* * *

Especially in the dance world, while growing up, I understood there are few poor girls, because dance classes are a privilege. They cost a lot, and so do costumes, practice clothes, dance shoes, and the additional cost of driving back and forth from dance classes.

Therefore, many dance girls love shopping. Mama always bought $100 pointe shoes when I needed them, leotards and tights when I grew out of old ones, and gifted me with dance bags and warm-up clothes. But we were very careful to never spend more money than we needed to.

Back at Interlochen, I heard some girls talking about how great Yumiko's were. Not sure of what they were, I googled them when I returned home. They were a special brand of customized leotards, and I was quickly sucked into inputting colors and fabrics, sizes, and styles. I looked at the price bar on the right side of the screen. My finished leotard would cost $90! Even though it seemed like a far stretch, I decided to at least ask Mama if I could buy one. She took one look at the price and said:

> "You could buy two very nice leotards for that price. Don't you have enough right now, anyway?" Disappointed but not surprised, I didn't bring them up again.

* * *

"Should we drop Elonah off before you?" Marin turned around in the driver's seat and looked at me.

"Depends on where she lives," I replied. She thought about it for a second, turned to Elonah and said: "I think I'll drop you off first if that's ok with you."

"Of course, whatever works for you," Elonah replied, happy to please. Marin briefly oriented herself and then turned her car around toward Eisenhower Parkway here in Ann Arbor. We drove past a church where I once had done a piano and drove into a neighborhood I had never noticed before. Small apartments lined the street, and Marin eased her shiny Honda Civic into the parking lot near a dumpster. A white car with rust stains around the wheel wells and a duct-taped rearview mirror was all I could see out of the backseat. Elonah got out and waved goodbye to us in her adorable way. I sat, surprised that she lived here, and watching her with her Nike shoes and varsity jacket, I was particularly confused. Then

I remembered she had been struggling to pay for college applications and as I slid into the passenger seat next to Marin, Elonah's financial situation finally clicked in my head—just as my seatbelt clicked into place.

* * *

My parents had sent me to Barnard College for a one-week program before senior year of high school. I loved the city and all the school's events, but being around other girls from places like Long Island, New York, who had mothers with brand-name bags, family yachts, and big white smiles was a little unsettling. My family had two modest cars as our modes of transportation, functioning bags, and our oral hygiene was not excessively based on whitening strips. When talking with Mama after the program about a girl and her mother that Papa and I had met, she laughed and said:

> "I'm imagining that they look like some Bloomfield Hills people" (Bloomfield Hills is a very wealthy area north of Detroit). At a private, liberal arts, women's college, I shouldn't have expected any different, but my experience there was not entirely comfortable. The only thing that saved me was my roommate, a girl from suburban Minnesota, whom I felt comfortable with because of our similar backgrounds.

When I was accepted into Barnard, I tried to sweep this memory into some forgotten corner of my memory bank. My parents wanted me to consider the cost and education of such an expensive school so they decided that we should visit New York City once more. Accepted students' week coincided with spring break, so my parents, brother, and I flew to New York to check out the place once more, and sightsee on the side. At Barnard's reception, I met a girl named Cauria, who had a friendly, talkative mother. She told Mama and me that they didn't have much money, but decided they should check out the schools that she had gotten into. Among them, she listed Brown University and Pomona College, mentioning that she had received a full ride at Brown. She was a first-generation student, named after a small town in Mexico where her father was from. Her mother talked about how it was difficult for them to even afford the plane tickets to visit Barnard. Afterward, Mama and I talked about how she was probably a successful student in a poor community, aided by the college's goals of racial and class diversity. We wondered how much financial aid she had been offered if even a plane ticket was stretching their budget. We had flown to New York mostly on vacation and only fractionally to see a college that I would most likely not be attending in the fall.

*   *   *

"Ethan's a Trump supporter."

God. I looked in disgust at a classmate in the small freshman architecture class I was studying in during the fall of 2016. I tried to be open-minded, but during orientation when he constantly talked about his father's business, and how he's expected to follow suit, and his mother's job as a financial advisor helping him start his own landscaping business, I decided I'd had enough. He reeked of privilege and he didn't hesitate to talk about his advantages because he couldn't realize that not everyone was as lucky. Recently, our architecture studio professor reminded us that any scraps of paper or tape we cut should be cleaned up, instead of being dropped on the floor for the janitors to sweep. He looked annoyed later and asked:

"But isn't that the janitor's job?"

No Ethan, I wanted to scream. *As a decent member of society, you should respect the janitors by cleaning up after yourself.*

In contrast, Dan—from my high school forum's social media—bragged when he photographs himself holding 10 parking tickets and captions it—"Single-handedly bankrolling Ann Arbor"—which shows he is at least aware of his privileged class status. I still scoff though, thinking about how pretentious he is, parking his black BMW wherever he wants because he or his parents can afford to pay off the fees. A couple of days later, he's holding tens of $100 bills saying:

> "'Bout to make an acquisition," I'm annoyed at the seemingly endless amount of money he possesses. The so-called acquisition turns out to be a gold watch: "Small time watch dealer" is what he calls himself—again publicly displaying his wealth.

* * *

We sat in ENVIRON 139 (Taming Nature: Domestication and Conservation) discussing organic food. The verdict was there are some foods that we should always choose organic, like root vegetables that soak up pesticides and berries that are difficult to wash thoroughly. My professor started talking about farmer's markets and whole foods as options for organic food. He added:

> "Plum Market also sells organic food, but it's so expensive that it's not worth it." I smiled awkwardly, thinking of the weekly shopping trips Mama makes to Plum Market, especially when buying lamb for kebabs, because "good meat is important." The food we eat makes up who we are, so in my home, the quality of food is highly valued.

Vera Bradley bags lined the floor of the dressing room at Randazzo Dance Studio. I plop my gray, equally expensive Athleta bag down on the floor next to them. I feel like the odd one out. Mama hates buying stuff when it's trending, so she's decided she dislikes Vera Bradley. This is ironic because she used to buy me their bags when I was six and too young to appreciate such gifts. She valued Vera Bradley bags because they were good quality and lasted a while. She's the type of person who takes pride the fact that she's worn the same shoes for five years and repairs them when the soles wear out. She loves Marie Kondo "The Life-Changing Magic of Tidying Up" because of the emphasis on the need to give love and care for each material possession.

The other day, when I was back home, I pulled out a sample-size facial moisturizer.

"Where'd you get that?"

"It's from the makeup sample kit that I'm subscribed for." I hesitantly reply.

"Wow, you really like to spend money don't you?" She shook her head jokingly but with a hint of reality.

* * *

"Who needs a ride?" The older girls at Salto Dance Company at the University of Michigan looked around and asked after our dance rehearsal. Because the studio we rehearse at is on the far south end of campus, those who have cars often offer to drive us back to our dorms or apartments. And there are a surprisingly large number of girls who have brought their cars to campus. I think about how much it costs to have a parking space and to pay for gas and repairs, and then I think about how much they are paying for tuition. Damn. More proof that the dance world is often teeming with girls who have rich parents.

The vast difference in monetary possessions is very clear on Michigan's campus. In August 2016, I was walking under the covered sidewalk next to the construction site of the $261 million Biological Sciences Building with two other girls I had met during a welcome week event.

"Is anyone else struggling to find a way to pay for college?" It was Annika who had spoken. I looked at her surprised as she explained her dad was recently unemployed and he had to pick his transcripts up from the University of Michigan to apply for new jobs. I was shocked by how open she was about her whole story. Back in sophomore year of high school, when I had finally gotten a cellphone, it was a flip-phone and I was mortified of ever being seen with it. Surrounded by my iPhone-bearing friends, I believed the flip-phone was a sign of being poor. So, when Annika told Jennifer and me the story of how she was financially struggling to pay for college, I stood awkwardly, not sure of how to reply. I had received a generous scholarship, and with my family's income, the rest was not too much to pay for—especially when accounting for the fact my parents were no longer paying for my dance, flute, and piano lessons. I looked at Jennifer, who was attending Michigan from out of state by choice, and recognized she too was probably not struggling to pay for college.

In my English class from winter 2017, we attended performances hosted by the University Musical Society and discuss them. During the first performance, I was seated next to a classmate who introduced himself as Alex. The typical questions came up:

> "What's your major, where are you from, and where do you live?" I told him architecture, Ann Arbor, and Alice Lloyd Hall. He told me biochemistry, Owasso, Michigan, and Mary Markley Hall as a residential advisor (RA). I asked him what made him decide to be an RA; he said he's paying for college on his own.

"Better save money where I can." I sat surprised thinking how some people are paying for their entire education. For a while, as contemporary dancers roll around onstage under a dark blue light, I continue to wonder what kind of place he is coming from.

* * *

I find my parents have trained me to look down on people who buy impulsively or excessively. Especially on a campus like Michigan, I notice when sorority girls have 20 outfits with their Greek letters plastered on them, when students have an abundance of technological gadgets, and when others spend a week on extravagant spring breaks in Cancun, Mexico. At the same time, students complain of the misery of student loans and being a "broke college student." Michigan is a social class segregated campus, and I find myself wandering somewhere on the spectrum, with opposing class indicators like my lack of excess material goods versus lack of student loans. Sometimes I feel the need to prove I am able to afford more, but I've accepted the feeling comes, as Madonna sings: "Because we are living in a material world and I am a material girl."

IF YOU DO THE BEST YOU CAN

EMILY SIEGEL

It is the summer of 2004 and I am nine years old, sitting in the backseat of mom's new blue Toyota Sienna; we are on our way to her cousin's vacation house in Long Beach Island, New Jersey. After a loud honk and a hard break, dad pulls over and another car drives by and stops, its side mirror absent. An agitated woman comes out frantically shouting. Dad's windsurfer has freed itself from our car and struck her mirror, in the luckiest, most safe way possible. After my two brothers and I wait patiently for the police to leave and for my parents to get back in the car, a long silence pervades. Suddenly David, my twin brother, interrupts the silence: "Dad, are we poor?"

*   *   *

When I was three years old, dad gave up his dream home—a house with lots of land, right next door to a farm with a goat named Gertrude—for a house in the suburbs, so that my brothers and I could receive a better education: within the same distinguished Montgomery County, but at an even higher performing school district. Our public schools were ranked among the top 100 in the nation—one only went to private school for athletics or if extra attention was needed from teachers. In Rockville, Maryland, I attended preschool and pre-kindergarten at our synagogue and went to Lakewood Elementary, Robert Frost Middle School, and

Thomas S. Wootton High School. Each school prepared students for the next.

In Miss Shanefelter's second-grade class, a quote hung on the wall: "If you do the best you can, no one can ever ask for more." I always knew that to live to my full potential, college would unquestionably be a part of my plan. If I worked hard, success would follow. At Lakewood, my favorite day of the year was Career Day, when parents from different professions would come in with knickknacks and engaging discussions on what they did. Dad came in with doctors' masks, rubber gloves, and surgeon hats: I was always so proud. While I vaguely remember the dentist, the lawyer, and the astronomer, there was one parent whose speech I can vividly remember—the policeman. I sat in the upper-left corner of the gym bleachers, crowded by my peers, as he discreetly confessed to group of 9- to 11-year-olds that he had not attended college. I promptly crossed policewoman off my endless hypothetical list of career options.

With mom employed as a part-time psychologist and dad co-owning and managing an ear, nose, and throat practice, they worked out their schedules so that someone would be home for us after school each day. Mom worked a full day on Wednesdays—plus working partial days on two other days of the week. Dad took off Wednesdays, always making an event of cooking a big pot of fresh pasta and getting king crab legs from Safeway, something my kosher mom did not eat or cook. Many times we would run into the house from the bus stop with the scent of fresh cookies filling the air. She was also the one to taxi us from soccer to lacrosse to dance to doctors' appointments, haircuts, etc. While many of my friends had stay-at-home mothers or mothers who worked nonstop with nannies functioning as parents, I always thought I had it best: mom was always there for us, but I also knew she worked to help others.

As a little girl, I intermittently dealt with experiences of "separation anxiety," unable to comfortably go to school or camp, or even go to friends' houses. There was a moment in third grade in Ms. Potter's class where I read a sentence in a children's book that read, *the average life expectancy for a human is 77*. As someone growing up with hardly any adversity, the thought of my grandparents, my parents, and most others I knew leaving this earth so soon left me unsettled and fearful. Unable to attend sleepovers or sleep-away camp as the majority of my peers did, mom decided to take me to a therapist. While these few visits provided me with techniques to distract and calm myself, the therapist ultimately told mom I would be okay with time, and I was not introduced to another doctor. She was evidently right, and when both my grandfathers and my great uncle all passed away between my 15th and 16th birthdays, I realized that life goes on after death.

Having a psychologist for a mom and a doctor for a dad gave me access to and knowledge about the health field in a way I thought everyone shared. In addition to the wealth of emotional support I grew up with, having a father as a doctor led to allergy shots and flu shots in the kitchen, strep tests by dad, and diagnoses and treatments for everyday colds, sinus infections, and viruses. All of this without a wait or fee! With no one else to compare to, I overlooked these privileges as normal, everyday life experiences.

Not only did my parents' specialties provide prime access to health care, but they also taught me about the gratifying experience of helping others through their careers. Both mom and dad consistently emphasized the importance of pursuing a career working with people, where you could help others. As a young girl, I wanted to be a veterinarian. When a car hit my dog, Chestnut, and I witnessed him in the hospital with bloody stitches and staples, I decided a route like mom's would be more fitting. My parents emphasized the necessity of an education while downplaying the expense of college and graduate school. They both carried loans into their young adult lives and I was continuously told a story of working hard and living minimally until you can afford more. In fifth grade, dad accompanied me on Wednesday mornings to our school's stock market club, where I learned how to save and invest. Although my parents had money to shower me with excess, they carefully selected when and how to privilege me and when to let me "struggle" ever so slightly, so that I would grow up knowing the value of hard work and money.

As a teenager too anxious to go away to overnight camp with my peers and too old to attend day camp as a camper, I began working as a counselor and babysitter as I came of age. With dad's influence on hard work and saving, I kept some money to spend going out to dinner, to the mall, or seeing movies with my friends. I gave the rest to dad, who put each penny into a savings account he had set up for me when I was younger. Every so often, he would open up the website with our accounts, asking how much money we wanted to invest, and in which stocks. My brothers and I competed for who had accumulated the most. It became clear that this money, one day, would likely go toward graduate school. Never did I question how I would pay for college.

Growing up in Maryland, we always stressed that we lived in Rockville, *not* Potomac. Potomac was where the "Jappy" people lived in bigger homes, driving fancier cars and wearing designer clothes. In stark contrast, a student-government program in high school revealed that some students among us went home to shelters. With a visible and wide range of privilege within our schools, we divided ourselves into cliques based on which neighborhoods we lived in and which clothes we wore. I spent time outside of school with my predominantly white, upper-middle-class peers, but I was friendly with other classmates too—probably more than my "friends." In middle school, I remember sitting in the library and talking to a girl named Diana. She and I had many classes together and although we did not go to each other's houses or sit next to one another at lunch, we worked on assignments together and chatted frequently in classes. She belonged to a 'clique' of girls who were predominantly Latina and referred to my friends and me as "preps," a term I neither identified with nor appreciated. As we sat in the library at a table, she poked fun at how my jeans were probably really expensive. Quickly and defensively, I told her how my parents ridiculed those who bought designer clothing, how they were my only pair of jeans and were from the juniors' section at Nordstrom: $40 at most. She seemed to approve of the cost. I sighed in relief.

In the fall of 2010, my peers and I relocated down the small hill: from middle school to high school. Here, the cliques became stronger and girls became less inclusive. The diversity of wealth became more obvious when cars came into the picture for some, and not for others. We were one of the schools they talk of, where students' cars were nicer than the teachers'. And yet, while my friends showed off their brand new 2014 Jeep Grande Cherokees and Range Rovers, I prided myself on my 2009 Rav4—a safe, yet humble ride. This allowed me to keep my place in the middle of everyone, still poking fun at the more materialistic girls—whom I was guilty of spending most of my time with—while also being someone of wider popularity. Admittedly, I was nominated to be in homecoming court each year.

A crucial part of my life before college began with dancing in middle school and continuing throughout high school. As someone who had trouble understanding the exclusion and self-centeredness displayed by many of my closest friends, I opened up to my ballet teacher, Miss Nadeen, who related to my experiences and was more supportive than any of my friends. While my dance skills were lacking, my work ethic was not, and opportunities arose as I began working as a dance teacher at a local elementary school and running birthday parties with Miss Nadeen. Further, as a camp counselor, I met a family that hired me to babysit quite often and compensated me well. I truly enjoyed this "work" more than the "play" of my peers, so the money I earned mostly went to savings. And, since I had no other expenses, I was able to focus on school and eventually on applying to college. While many teenagers would see this money as freedom to explore and shop, I embodied dad's philosophy: savings are there for when things go wrong. I was able to accumulate a decent amount of money by the time I graduated from high school.

Applying to college definitely required hard work, but I had more support than the typical American teenager. While at the time I did not realize the privilege this was, I had a private college counselor who listened to my interests, aversions, capabilities, weaknesses, and goals. She helped me identify which colleges I should apply to, and worked with me as I took practice ACT (American College Testing) tests—looking over questions I got wrong and teaching me strategies to save time and weed out wrong answers. When I was ready to write my application essay, I utilized my childhood separation anxiety to portray a useful experience, which led to my desire to work with children. My counselor edited my essay, tweaking my wording, thus ensuring grammar and spelling were correct. Looking back, I now realize how much more planning and work I would have had to do without her in order to accomplish the amount I did with her help. And yet, personally, I never saw a bill for her work.

My older brother Justin attended the University of Michigan and after two separate trips, where I visited seven different colleges on the East Coast and in the Midwest, I decided no other school's atmosphere compared. Despite having always thought I would go to "my own" school, and not follow in his footsteps, I could not picture myself in a smaller college town, with less school spirit, or without the prestigious name and expansive alumni network.

When I thought about my future college life, I expected to escape the bubble of Rockville. Girls I knew reached out to camp friends to find the perfect roommate match and brought new, neatly planned out outfits for each round of sorority rush. Instead, I searched for a roommate using a survey about one's cleanliness and expectations and got a lucky match with Nadine. She was a dancer from Colorado studying biomechanical engineering, on track to go to medical school. After speaking for a few days over Facebook about our repugnance toward fake girls and our senior year spring break trips—both to Cancun—we decided it was time to put our names on the housing applications.

The University of Michigan (UM) has two campuses in Ann Arbor, North and Central, where students live in dorms. For freshman year, it is widely known that living on North is undesirable, as one must take a bus to campus where everything is "happening," including classes, restaurants, centrally located libraries, and nightlife. However, since Justin went to Michigan and lived in Baits, the *worst* dorm on North Campus, I expected *and* hoped to be assigned to North. While basking on our warm summer deck with my dog Chestnut, I received a notification saying housing decisions were out. I raced onto Wolverine Access online and saw "Bursley." After a hasty Google search, it was confirmed, I would be living on North Campus! As I excitedly texted Justin, Nadine texted me: "Ughhh we got North Campus." I quickly reassured her it would be for the best.

The night before I moved into the dorms, I anxiously asked mom whether or not I should apply for the sorority rush process. Although she never considered joining a sorority, she encouraged me to apply: *It was only a $25 application fee.* I hesitantly filled out a form with a headshot—*creepy*—and with information of family I had in different sororities—*none.* Is this really something I wanted to be part of? As dad was flying up the next day, I called him with requests for dresses and shoes that I had left in my closet at home, to help adequately prepare me for the rush experience. When my "rho"—a sorority girl in charge of the rush process—called a few weeks later in her peppy voice saying she was "so excited so meet me!" her annoying tone reminded me that I shouldn't be a part of this process, and I quickly asked her to remove me from the list.

While packing for college, friends from home told me how they had multiple suitcases filled with shoes; I boasted how low maintenance I was, with all my shoes fitting into only one small suitcase. There were time slots for moving into the dorms. Nadine and I decided since she was flying and I was driving that I would go for the earlier time slot and then leave, giving her time to move in after me. I made my bed with a new blue and white chevron Urban Outfitters comforter, I hooked up a new stainless steel mini fridge my parents bought me just for our room, and I filled my closet with clothing and shoes. It was only a year or so later that Nadine told me how uncomfortable it made her seeing how much stuff

I had—especially seeing my shoes all lined up at the top of the closet.

While my friends and I were beyond fulfilled without rushing a sorority, we still attended many of the Greek-affiliated tailgates and parties. I clearly *looked* like a sorority girl and got used to being asked: "What sorority are you in?" I'd irately responded, "You don't ask *what* sorority I'm in, you ask *if* I'm in a sorority, and I'm not." Those in Greek Life responded in two different ways to my not being in a sorority: (1) Why not? or (2) You're so lucky.

For my sophomore year, I moved out of the dorms and into the bottom floor of a house with five other girls. Rather than paying for a meal plan, my parents decided it would be fair to give me an allowance equivalent to the cost of a meal plan at Michigan. They also covered the cost of my rent and all utility bills. Still, having to budget for groceries, house necessities, and school supplies for the first time, I began keeping note each week on my phone of how much money I had left for the week, carrying over or subtracting from the following week if I under- or overspent. When I knew my friends' birthdays were coming up or if something big was happening, I made sure to plan ahead and save money for that week. I also had trickling income coming in from being a campus tour guide and babysitting in Ann Arbor every so often. I used this to replenish weeks where I overspent or used it to splurge and order takeout.

It was not until sophomore year that I also learned how my roommates' budgets were different in interesting ways. Lauren was the most interesting case, as she came from a middle-class family on Long Island, New York, where she had a twin sister. While my other roommates and I had our parents send money online for rent, and then we were responsible for writing a check and bringing it to the landlord, Lauren's mom did everything for her. My friends and I also had our own credit cards. While my parents sent me money online and then I managed my own credit and debit cards, Lauren used her parents' credit card. She called her mom for permission each time she wanted to go out to eat, order in food, or buy something online. When it came time for Lauren to study abroad, she found someone to sublet her room. Unsurprisingly, the girl sublet-ting came in confused by how expensive our bills were, as Lauren had no idea and did not correctly inform her. The most interesting thing occurred when I visited Lauren's house on Long Island: it was simple and unfinished. And yet, Lauren had a way of valuing peo-ple by their net worth. Her best friends at school were daughters of a big-time lawyer and a movie producer, respectively. When she sought out boyfriends, she fell in awe with a boy who lived in a pent-house suite in the nicest apartment in Ann Arbor. While she admit-ted he was not the most charming or the cutest, her eyes sparkled when he spoke of his apartment in New York or of his father's fancy company.

Being the only single girls in our house, Lauren and I decided it would be fun to go to Mexico for spring break 2016, like many of our peers who were in Greek Life. My parents, without question, agreed to pay and were excited that I would experience an event-ful spring break. They know how uptight I am and were thrilled when I showed the desire to have this sort of mainstream, uncon-strained fun. Lauren and I went with her more wealthy friends who were unexpectedly more thrifty and conscious of money than Lauren herself. One night, as we all snuggled up in bed, Lauren's friends began to complain nervously about how money created considerable tension for their families and themselves. Both had overspent on their parents' credit cards multiple times, which led to their parents cutting communication with them for weeks. This was a foreign concept to me, to say the least. When her friends left the room, Lauren and I were speechless. These girls appeared to have such close relationships with their par-ents and unlimited access to money, and yet, their parents' lack of communication on limits led to their confusion, anguish, and ultimately to overspending. I realized how lucky I was that my parents never spoiled me to the extent other parents did. I know my parents have money to lavish me more than they do, but their discretion gives me responsibility in budgeting and ultimately allows me to *be* a college student. I am incredibly lucky not to have debt, but I am also extremely grateful that I do not have access to an abundance of wealth.

* * *

When the windsurfer broke free from our minivan, David overheard dad's conversation with the man in the car. He heard him explaining that we would, of course, be responsible for any damage. David thought back to my parents' frugal spending before the accident, as our car had recently broken down. In response to David's concern, mom quickly chimed in: "No David, everything's going to be okay."

* * *

Donald Trump was elected president in the fall of 2016—*sigh*. Lauren, an apathetic political science major interested in pursuing a career where she can wear a fitted suit and fancy heels, voted for him. She decided it would be fun to drink wine and eat snacks while watching the election, and invited her two wealthy friends over to watch. As it became clear what was happening, Lauren sat quietly in her own room—probably roaming Facebook with a grin. Her friends accompanied me in my room as we all sat silently with tears running down our faces. What frustrated me most was when one of her friends, Juju, began to sob, whining of how her mother—a permanent U.S. citizen originally from France—could be deported. Never once did I worry this election would hurt me. Instead, I worried about those whose drive for equality would be neutralized, about those whose families would be broken or whose voices would remain unheard.

Following the election, analyses suggested that rural, conservative, middle- and working-class white people had gained a leader and voice. However, when I spoke to a leader in my Jewish community on campus, she told me about how she was too wealthy to afford Obamacare and too poor to afford health care. I began to wonder, is being a democrat the work of elitism? My liberalism has never derived from my lack of privilege or of access, but rather of the painful stories I have seen—but mostly heard—of others who are less fortunate. I strive to keep an open mind in terms of religious views, sexualities, genders, race, and social class: to ensure that all have the freedom and opportunity in the way that I do. And yet, I am conflicted. If I disregard those who voted for Trump as racist, xenophobic, and sexist, am I helping, or am I standing on my high horse looking down?

Looking back, I realize what has influenced me most in life was not just the message to try my hardest, but more so the message to always question. While I am not particularly religious, I believe this derives from my Jewishness. I have grown up learning to respect authority, but I have also been taught to challenge what I do not believe and also what I *do* believe. As I finish my senior year at the UM, I am confused where I stand. I am lost in a maze of elitism, inequality, differential access, and conflicting values. I am told to do the best I can to reach my full potential, but simultaneously told hard work does not necessarily yield success for everyone. I do not understand how and why Donald Trump became our president. I do, however, understand how I got to where I am. I am encouraged to search for ways to teach others how to address where they stand and to learn how their stance can impact those around them and a wider society.

I am unsure of where my path will lead, but I was recently admitted into UM's Master of Social Work Program for the fall of 2017, the top social work program in the nation. I hope to become more open minded, and more exposed to diversity in the country and to problems of those around me. And ultimately, I hope that somehow I can use my privilege to help those who were born into lives without.

Facts and Feelings of the Upper-Middle Class

Elena Smith

Tension: a relationship between ideas or qualities with conflicting demands or implications.[1] Tension: mental or emotional strain.[2] Tension: something I have felt throughout my entire life and how I would summarize my experience with social class. I would not describe my position in the middle- to upper-middle class as comfortable, as is the common generalization. I would instead describe it as the constant stretches and pulls I feel. From my parents' different social class backgrounds to the extremely disproportionate income distribution at my university, the middle class is somewhere I feel stress, anxiety, and discomfort.

This pervasive tension is rooted in my parents' class backgrounds. My father grew up in urban Philadelphia, Pennsylvania, in a working-class family. He supported his family while he attended college, having to take a semester off to help his mother and siblings after his father died. After graduating college, he helped send his younger sister to college. He is undoubtedly successful—earning a master's degree, completing 20 years in the military, and continuing to work as a civilian. However, his frugal habits adopted early in

1. Oxford Living Dictionaries. (2017). *Tension.* (O. U. Press, Producer) Retrieved March 5, 2017, from https://en.oxforddictionaries.com/definition/tension
2. Oxford Living Dictionaries. (2017). *Tension.* (O. U. Press, Producer) Retrieved March 5, 2017, from https://en.oxforddictionaries.com/definition/tension

his life still dictate how he handles money today. A specific shake of the head—eyes closed, lips pressed tightly, head slightly bowed—often meets questions about money. But, as frugal as dad can be, he did not hesitate to send me on the high school senior trip to Europe, or to pay out-of-state college tuition here at the University of Michigan. This is where my class privilege is tangible, but also confusing. The limits of my privilege—I can use it in some ways, but not in others. It complicates what it means to be part of the upper-middle class and creates a gray area in my class identity.

My mom's childhood was very different from my dad's. She grew up in a middle-class family in Southern California, a family that took frequent vacations and could send her to college without her having to pay for it or her helping to support her family. She continued on to be a lawyer and then a teacher, giving her a solid financial foundation early on in her adult life. Her class background led her to handle money less severely. Extravagant family vacations, new home décor, and new pets were always her ideas. Mom is not irresponsible in terms of handling money; she did not have the same financial restraints growing up as my dad did, and thus she has an easier time spending it.

My parents' different class backgrounds affect how they spend money even today. In tenth grade I joined the Model United Nations club and needed to buy Western business attire for the multiple conferences I would attend. My mom and I ventured to the mall, picking out pieces like dress shirts, blazers, and nice dresses, all of which I needed. As we were shopping, I found other clothes I liked that were not for Model United Nations, but mom bought them for me regardless. I left the mall with my hands full of shopping bags. Just as we turned on our street to go home she said to me: "Don't let your dad see the shopping bags." I nodded, having been through this routine multiple times before. The new clothes were not anything beyond our means, and most of them were necessary for Model United Nations. But because of my dad's frugality and strict budget, I felt guilty. The fact that I had to hold my hands steady so the shopping bags did not rustle as I walked to my room, or vaguely deflect his questions when he noticed I was wearing something new made me feel like I was doing something wrong.

One area that has been an exception to the tension between my parents about money has been my education. My mom left work once I was born and has been primarily a stay-at-home mom, with occasional part-time jobs. She read to me, took me to museums, and organized playgroups. I went to a private pre-school with music, language, art classes. Private elementary, middle, and high school were beyond my family's budget, but I went to good public schools and was involved in many activities; I went to horseback riding camp, played soccer, and participated in Math Bowl. All my summer camps and sports teams were an extra cost, but I was able to do all of them. Once I entered high school, I felt the pressure to excel in school and get into a good college. I went to month-long programs at elite colleges, bought all the standardized test review books, and got an SAT (Scholastic Aptitude Test) tutor. There were never any arguments about these costs. Even now, if I struggle with a course in college, my mom will say: "Elena, we will pay for a tutor if you want one." These are opportunities I enjoy as a member of the upper end of the middle class, with parents who have an income that allows them to save and pay for my education.

Even though the absence of tension is a relief, I feel like there are very high standards set for what I accomplish in and after college. I think it is a common attitude in the middle and upper classes that college is expected and necessary. There are no questions about whether you'll go to college; the questions are whether you want a teaching or research school, a school with a strong school spirit, a public or a private college. My mom started my college fund when I was just a toddler, and until I was in high school, I saw college as something everyone did. My college education was explicitly referred to as an investment, and the fact the investment is so large makes me feel like I need to produce a certain level of returns to make it a good investment. My parents always say "Do your best"; but I want my best to be worth $250,000. College and supportive parents are parts of my social class privilege, but my fears about not being successful enough are part of my discomfort with my class status.

Years ago, I got off the bus and found my place in the Class Nine line on the playground at my elementary school. My friend Jennifer soon walked up, accompanied by her mother, who walked her to school every day. Her mom asked me, a new student at the school: "Elena, where do you live?" I pointed to the houses just on the other side of the fences enclosing the playground and field. These were luxurious, three-story houses; grand staircases, balconies off the bedrooms, a chef's kitchen—easily worth millions of dollars in the real estate market of southern California. Houses like these were the norm in the Seacliff area of Huntington Beach, a small surf town in Orange County. My parents and I moved to Huntington Beach after my father retired from the military and found a job there. We moved from a spacious, four-bedroom house with a yard in the suburbs in Tampa, Florida, to a smaller townhome two blocks from the beach. My friend's mom asked: "Oh, you live right there? Do you walk to school?" I nodded my head yes. This was a complete lie. I was six years old, a first-grader. Was I just being a rambunctious child? Or did I know my house was not as big as the other students? Did I know my dad's car was not the newest model, like the one I carpooled in to gymnastics? Why would I be ashamed of our townhome near the beach? Why would I be ashamed of an older car? At the time, I do not know if this lie was rooted in embarrassment about my upper-middle-class status in this upper-class bubble, but this moment flashed into my mind during my sociology course on social class inequality more than 10 years later. This contrast between having a lot—comfort, security, privilege—and still having doubts and worries about money and status has been a constant tension in my life, since moments like these in my early childhood.

My transition to high school was more dramatic than just moving to a larger school or becoming a lowly freshman. After moving back to Tampa, Florida, when my dad changed jobs, I attended neighborhood elementary and middle schools, both less than five miles away from my house. Students were mostly from middle- and upper-class neighborhoods, with some from the working- and upper classes mixed in. The majority other students were very similar to myself in terms of our family's income, the sizes of our houses, and models of cars. In eighth grade, my mom intro- duced the idea of completing the International Baccalaureate (IB) program, a rigorous curriculum known for its excellent college preparation. However, the nearest IB school was 15 miles away in a lower-income neighborhood. The IB program was part of the school board's efforts to raise the state's grades of low-performing schools by bringing in students from high-performing schools, who would definitely graduate and continue on to college. The IB pro- gram gave me a great education and has made college much easier, but the same commendations cannot be made for the traditional program at the school or the school itself.

When learning about underfunded, failing schools in Detroit in my sociology class, I found a lot of similarities between the con- ditions of those schools and my own high school. The traditional program had much larger class sizes than the IB program, fewer options for classes than traditional high schools, and some of the lowest pass rates on Advanced Placement (AP) and state exams in the county. Besides these educational deficiencies, there were obvious signs of underfunding—I often had to check two or more bathrooms to find one with toilet paper and soap, my homeroom teacher had to change classrooms due to mold spots on the ceiling, and my junior and senior biology classes never got the textbooks we needed. I attended this high school after watching a brand new high school being built right next to my middle school. Most of my friends went to this newer high school, where they had plenty of AP classes and toilet paper. This is another social class tension I felt—a tension between what I had at my high school and what I could have had if I went to the new high school in my neighbor- hood. However, I had a more class-diverse experience at my IB high school, one I did not recognize the value of until I came to college.

In high school I directly witnessed people of different class statuses receive different treatment.

High school had its own tensions within itself between the IB and traditional students. The majority of IB students were from middle- to upper-class families, while the class backgrounds of the traditional students ranged from lower-class and poor to upper class. Despite the inclusion of all class backgrounds in both groups of students, the IB students were generalized as "rich" and traditional students were generalized as "poor." Some of the differences between IB students and traditional students were marked by the cars in the students' parking lot or laptops. There was always underlying discomfort between the two groups, even if it never manifested itself. Aside from our polarizing views of each other, there were other ways beyond our control in which we were divided: different class schedules, few options to take class together, and separate lunches. High school was where I first consciously experienced my class privilege, even if it was as simple as being smiled at by an administrator as I walked down a hall during class, while the traditional student behind me was stopped and asked for his hall pass.

Tampa's class diversity reaches beyond its high schools. Sometimes this diversity was highlighted in a negative way, like poor infrastructure. I was driving to school on a Wednesday morning, running a little late as usual. I had just made it through the slowest part of the trip and was ready to make up some time. I turned onto Waters Avenue, a shortcut I used for its open road. About a minute after turning, my front tire dipped into a deep pothole, jolting everything in the car and making an awful sound. I was worried something was damaged, so I pulled into a gas station to check. Everything was fine with my truck, but I drove more carefully for the rest of my time that morning, navigating around the potholes, debris, and cracked asphalt. I continued to use Waters Avenue to get to school, but throughout the two years I drove to school, the road was never fixed. There was plenty of road construction in other parts of town, but never on Waters Avenue, which was in a lower-income area. Maybe this neglect was intentional, or maybe it did not fit into the budget, but the road conditions became a type of metaphor for the social class of people who lived in the area. Class variety in Tampa presented another tension; the city contains everything from professional athletes' waterfront mansions to suburban developments, from an urban art scene to trailer park communities. There are certain parts of town where I am not allowed to go after a certain hour, but I also have friends who leave their doors unlocked at night. Tampa was a very different city from Huntington Beach, a much smaller town with a mostly middle- and upper-class population.

The social class makeup at the University of Michigan (UM) is different than anywhere I've lived before and is in stark contrast from my parents' class backgrounds. One way I've picked up on this difference is through noticing people's shoes. I'm pretty good at it too, identifying brands and styles with a quick glance from afar. I gained this skill working at a shoe store my senior year of high school. I took this job to pay for the expenses of the last months of high school—grad trips, prom, dresses for awards ceremonies— and to begin saving for college. I worked 10 to 15 hours a week during the school year, and 20 to 25 once I graduated. I was making pretty good, easy money for a 17-year-old with no real financial responsibilities. I felt good about myself and my financial situation. Once I came to the UM, those feelings of stability and disappeared; I was a little shocked by the amount of wealth at this state school. Even without the statistics and comparisons, you can tell how wealthy a majority of students are, just by looking at their shoes. On one extremely dreary football game day at the Big House, I wore my beat up, already-stained Converse since there would be a lot of mud and puddles and I did not want to get any of my nicer shoes dirty. As it continued to drizzle during parties before the game, I found myself constantly looking at the ground to stay clear of the deeper, dirtier puddles. While doing this, I caught a glimpse of the familiar Comme de Garçons heart logo on a pair of muddied white shoes. I almost cringed when I saw this—these were $150 designer shoes being ruined by Ann Arbor dirt and rain. Were these shoes going to be easily replaced with a simple online order? Or were these someone's party shoes, not important enough to be kept nice? Both of these possibilities jarred me, and reflect my perceptions of economic position in the university. That is not to say I am a minority at the university; based on my parents' income; I am in the large majority of Michigan students. So why do I care about nice shoes getting ruined? This is where my values, influenced by my parents' financial decisions, my dad's working-class background, and my own experiences with work and class play into my social class identity.

"What sorority are you in?" is a question I receive often at Michigan. Following my response a second question usually comes: "Oh . . . why didn't you rush?" "I don't know, I just didn't really want to, I didn't think I needed to here," is my typical answer. There is truth in this—I never planned on joining a sorority nor did I rush during the first few weeks of my freshman year. But more importantly than these reasons, I couldn't ask my parents to spend thousands of more dollars on top of out-of-state tuition. The deepest talks my parents and I have had about our family's finances occurred during the college application process; there were many fights and a lot of tears. Despite the tension and negative feelings college finances caused, there was never a question of whether I was going to be able to go to college? My choices of application were never limited by a cap on tuition my parents would pay, and I was not discouraged from applying to all out-of-state schools or declining acceptances from schools that offered me merit aid. I realize how many more opportunities this gave me and this was a freedom of choice many people do not have. However, I still feel the burden of the enormous expense of college, from the pressure to graduate in three years to frequent e-mails from mom about scholarships to apply for. So, while I can attend a top university on my parents' dime and graduate without student debt, I still have a constant ache in the back of my mind about the expensiveness of college. Tension.

Despite knowing the answer to joining a sorority would be "No," I managed to find one of the only other extracurricular activities that would cost thousands of dollars. If you had asked me a year ago what I would see myself doing now, it would not include being a coxswain on the men's rowing team. I was connected to the team through a friend I made at orientation who was joining the team. Next thing I knew, I was offered a spot on the team and given a limited overview of the costs of the team during my freshman year. Men's rowing is a club sport at Michigan, meaning it is mostly student-funded. Of course, I wanted to be on the team, but really only one thing mattered: Could we pay for it? I discussed it with my parents and we agreed on a plan to split the dues. By the end of my second semester, I had run out of the money I saved from my job over the previous summer, and my parents were paying all of my dues and lamenting the steep payments. Once again, I knew my class position allowed me this security of my parents being able to pay when I could not. Still, I felt uncomfortable that rowing was a stretch for my family. In general, rowing is a very expensive sport and attracts many wealthy athletes as a result. This applies to the team at Michigan—families donating thousands to the team, paying for travel and accommodations of the team to some regattas, and even just providing a huge quantity and variety of food at races. I sometimes felt out of place in this environment because of my class status. This was especially discomforting because I was in the group that had more in high school, and I often felt like I had less than those around me. Only recently have I discovered that other teammates pay their own dues too. This is comforting, but does not relieve the stress that the extra cost of crew causes.

Beyond the rowing team, I have found that students at Michigan are generally wealthier than peers I was used to. Even within my own group of close friends, I find myself having to say, "No" to extra meals out or trips to music festivals over the summer. Many students and their families have multiple houses, $1,000 jackets, exotic vacations. I can blend in with these students without trying; yes, I have the $400 coat and the $150 boots, but I purchased both on E-bay for less. No one would know this by looking at me, and it does not change the fact I own these items, but I feel embarrassed by the fact I always check Amazon or E-bay before making an expensive purchase. My friends and family at home were heavily affected by the recession a few years ago, and saving money was always celebrated and "cool." This is not a concern or attitude I feel among friends in college. Another change I have encountered is having to say no so often. "Who wants to get brunch at Sava's on Saturday?" "No, sorry I can't." "I'm going to Urban to get a new shirt for this weekend, do you want to come?" "Sorry, I have to study." This is the most financially independent I have been in my life in terms of day-to-day expenses. It creates disconnects between my daily life and reality: I don't feel the social class comfort I did at home, but I also know I am in a bubble of class privilege at Michigan.

My experience with social class has been dynamic, and my understanding of my position within our society's class system is still changing. I am more aware of the class experiences of others around me, as well as the general class groups in society. I am more aware of my privilege and how it affects my daily life as well as my life as a whole. On the other hand I am also very aware of the amount of privilege the majority of Michigan students have, which skews my perception of my personal class status and of class differences on a national level. This awareness is affecting my education and career plans; I want to maintain or elevate my class status, and I know how much work is required to do that. But I also want to help solve the larger problem of class inequality in our country, or at least not be part of the solution. I am still learning and figuring this out, but I think awareness is better than nothing.

JUXTAPOSITIONS

ASTRID SWENSEN

I grew up in a quaint city on the north shore of Boston: Beverly, Massachusetts. Although it boasted a population of 40,000, Beverly felt like a small town. If running errands or going out to eat, it was almost guaranteed you would see someone you knew. Although we did have sections of the city that were low income, most of my town was middle class. My family is upper-middle class; however, due to school loans and the exuberant amount of money spent on my career as a competitive swimmer, we lived modestly.

My parents, who attended the University of Massachusetts, Amherst, studied natural sciences and revolved in the same social circle. They met 3,000 miles away at Southern California University of Health Sciences, where they were both studying chiropractic. My father approached my mother in the library and said she looked familiar, and asked if they had ever met before. My mother, who I imagine was hours and many cups of coffee into her study session, was annoyed that this boy was bothering her, and quickly replied, "No." Although they had never formally met before, they had many mutual friends and I find too hard to believe that they had never rubbed elbows before at late night parties or stopped at the same coffee shop on campus.

Romantic stories aside, my social class can be drawn back to my parents' education; it both makes me richer and poorer at the same time. Although my grandparents paid for most of my parents' expenses through college, my parents were on their own after they graduated. Four years at chiropractic school started my family off in a deep hole of debt. Even today, when my mother is stressed about financials, her parents' failing health, her aunt whom she takes care of, or her students, she will mutter under her breath: "And we still have to pay off those pesky school loans." Over 30 years of working, and the ridiculous price of education still weighs on my parents.

While growing up, money was not an issue that was often brought up. Aside from comments here and there when times were especially tough, my sisters and I were told that it wasn't our place to worry about money; we would have plenty of time to do that when we were adults. I understand why my parents kept our financial situation from us. My sisters and I all struggled in middle and high school. Between social stresses to fit in, my swimming career, and mental illness, my sisters and I were exposed to a fair share of strain and my parents didn't want to contribute more to it. It isn't as if my parents never discussed money with us, however, because they did. I remember being in elementary school and starting my savings account at our local bank. I filled out the forms, line by line, requesting assistance from my mom when I didn't know what a social security number was. I loved depositing money and checking the account balance. Every few months, my sisters, my mom, and I would empty out my dad's piggy bank and split the coins between us. My parents taught me that it was important to save money, which was easy to do when they insisted on paying for everything. Despite this, my parents taught my sisters and me the worth of a dollar. We all had jobs throughout high school, were encouraged to be thoughtful about purchases, and to always buy things on sale. However, I still feel disconnected when discussing money. I understand I have much more than some people and much less than others, but where does my family fall in that in between?

Until recently, I had no idea what social class my family belonged to. I felt poor when I was hanging out at my friend TC's house. He attended an all-boys private high school: The Prep. He drove a brand new BMW, exclusively wore Vineyard Vines clothing, and had two elephant tusks framing a plush couch in his living room, which I had never seen anyone actually sit in. He lived in the Farms, the wealthiest part of town, down a long windy road. His house was tucked away in the woods, hard to find unless you knew it was there.

On the other hand, I felt rich when I spent time with my friend, Dylan. He dated one of my best friends, Rose, for about a year and a half when we were in high school. He seldom talked about his family, and he often spent the night at a friend's house rather than going home. Did he even have a home? I'm still not sure. A couple weeks ago, he texted me asking if I could buy him a shirt from M Den store here in Ann Arbor and bring it back home the next time I was on break. (He is a huge University of Michigan football fan). He explained that he didn't want to "bother with online shopping" and that there was probably a better selection of shirts in Ann Arbor than on the M Den website, anyway. After reflection, I realized it wasn't that he didn't want to buy something online, but he wasn't able to because he doesn't have a credit card. I went to M Den, picked out a shirt and decided I would mail it to him. I asked him for his address, and he said I could send it to his friend's house. "I just don't have a good spot to drop packages at my house," his text message read. I'm not sure what that really meant, but I sent it to his friend's house anyway.

Dylan and TC are just two examples of the two ends of the spectrum in which I frequently move back and forth from. My friends from school, like Dylan, were mostly middle and working class, and significantly less affluent than my friends from my swim team, like TC. I spent a lot of time in high school moving between these two groups, but I never knew where I fell in between them. I often found myself trying to fit in with my wealthy friends, but finding it hard to. It was much easier to bum around with my public school friends, who found enjoyment in playing music together and sitting around a campfire for hours. Friends from my swim team insisted on getting dressed up and going out to eat in Boston. They liked shopping (they never bought from the sale rack) and Starbucks. They loved name brands.

When I was 11 years old, I was at the Eastern Massachusetts District Swimming Championship when, Rosemarie, a teammate, walked into the locker room wearing an all-white Lululemon track suit. My teammates whispered, "She's wearing Lululemon." I, of course, had no idea what that was, or how much it cost. (I learned later that a pair of pants are $98!) After that day, this brand has been a part of my life as a symbol of wealth and affluence for me.

Toward the end of middle school, Lululemon made reappearance in all the girls' closets on my swim team. They raved about how the clothes were such high quality, how the leggings didn't stretch out like other brands. I lusted for a pair of my own. I can still remember the gasp from my mom after I told her how expensive they were. Still, I searched the website frequently for sales. I constantly felt like I needed to prove myself to my teammates. If I had a pair, I would be accepted.

During a shopping trip to an upscale secondhand store, Second Time Around, I found a pair of Lululemon pants with the tags still on them. They weren't the typical yoga pant or legging style that are most popular, but they were still Lululemon. I had to have them. At only $25, I was practically stealing! I got home and immediately put them on. I wore them around the house, feeling like I was on top of the world. When I wore them to swim practice, however, my attitude quickly changed. I tried to play it off nonchalantly, but I was visibly upset when a teammate made a comment. She asked me, in a condescending tone, why I picked that style over the other and more popular styles. I knew she could see straight through me. She knew I had obtained them in a nontraditional manner; she knew I couldn't afford to pay full price.

Months later, my best friend, Sheehan, said she had surprise for me. Sheehan and I have been inseparable since kindergarten. We used to joke about how we were twins, and when we wore our matching purple shirts to class, our teacher wasn't able to tell us apart. Besides our long blonde hair, Sheehan and I are exact opposites. I have always been a little chubby, with short legs and broad shoulders, while Sheehan is tall and thin. I told her about the incident with my Lululemon pants and she sympathized. She comes from a working-class family, and fell in love with horseback riding, a very affluent sport. One afternoon when she was at the barn mucking stalls, which helped her pay for lessons, she noticed that someone had left behind a pair of Lululemon yoga pants. She took them home, washed them and brought them to me. She explained they were a little too big on her so she thought I would like them, but I know even if they were her size, she would have still given them to me. Almost five years later, they are worn, the colors on the waist band are faded, but they are still one of my favorite items of clothing.

I will admit, I do own my several items from Lululemon today. My teammates were right; they do make high-quality clothing. However, everything I own has been on sale and for special occasions like my birthday or Christmas. Every purchase has also been followed by a flash of guilt every time I put it on. I feel as though I succumbed to social pressure, to my bullies. I wish I could have brushed off the comments my teammates made to me. I wish I would have worn my thrifted and sale-rack clothes with pride in front of them. Instead, as an insecure teenager, I tried to find my place in a sport with so much affluence.

As grateful as I am for the opportunities that swimming has given me, I constantly feel guilty knowing my family would be in a higher social class if I didn't participate in this sport. Between coaching and entry fees, gas money for travel, plane tickets, clothing, equipment, and meet fees, my parents spent thousands of dollars on me since I started swimming at the age of eight. Becoming an elite athlete at the age of 13, I never thought much about the costs. At one point my parents and I had an argument because I wanted to compete at a meet and they told me I couldn't because it was too expensive. I didn't understand how much money I was spending. It wasn't until high school, probably freshman year, that I offered to book my own plane ticket (using my parents' credit card, of course) and realized how much money plane tickets actually cost. I was immediately overwhelmed with worry about the financial strain I was causing on my parents. My mom said that swimming was a down payment for college. Yes, we were spending a lot of money now, but I was bound to get a full scholarship to a prestigious school, and we would end up saving money. As a 13-year-old, who was quickly improving, that answer satisfied me; I assumed I would continue improving at a rapid rate. After Olympic Trials in 2012, however, my relationship with swimming changed drastically. The pressure of being an elite athlete at a young age is great. Coming from a small program, fast swimmers were rare. Leading up to the summer of 2012, I got a lot of press in my town. A local newspaper called the meet "the ultimate test in my blossoming career." I failed that test. The pressure was too much for me. Between a coach who never failed to ask more of me, unsupportive teammates, and friends who supported me, but didn't understand what I was going through, I cracked. My trajectory of improvement quickly declined, as did my love for the sport. When it came to recruiting during my high school junior year, I still desperately wanted a full scholarship. With racing times from seasons ago, I was still a part of the elite group of swimmers; however, I hadn't swum that fast in years.

From the moment I stepped on campus in Ann Arbor in August 2014, I knew I wanted to come to the University of Michigan (UM). After meeting the coaches and the team, I was fully convinced. Because of my upbringing, I didn't even think to look at how expensive tuition was. When it came to talking about scholarship, the coaches at UM offered me a much lower deal than I was expecting. My parents and I had previously discussed that the hopes of a full ride at UM was a little out of reach, but I had around $25,000 saved for college, so the farther I could stretch that money, the better. I was severely disappointed that I couldn't afford to go to my dream school. My mother, who saw how much I struggled to get to that point, cried on the phone to my future coach, asking for more scholarship support. Despite not being able to afford the school, my parents encouraged me to commit here anyway. They said it was my decision and if this was my dream school, then I needed to follow my gut. I signed my National Letter of Intent in my high school's library. My parents brought their camera and took pictures that so many high school students dream of; I was sitting at a table, holding a pen, wearing a UM shirt and hat, and signing the document. Shortly after, I felt nauseous with the knowledge of how much money my parents were about to spend. Many times my senior year, I became upset and cried to my parents about my guilt.

My UM freshman year was very tough. As a fairly independent teenager, I assumed the transition into college would be seamless. Instead, I struggled. I missed my friends, many of whom I had known for over a decade, I missed my sisters whom I am very close with, and I missed the ocean. I felt as if I was throwing away tens of thousands of dollars attending a school I was miserable at. The promise of a high-paying job after graduation motivates many to attend expensive and prestigious school like UM. However, how ironic it is to me, that in order to get rich, you must first be poor due to debt.

In order to pay for my schooling, my parents both took up jobs as college professors. My mother teaches at a community college, a small state school, and a small private school; my father teachers at the same small private school. The difference between the community college and the private college is stark. The community college was filled with adults, many of them with full-time jobs. Some are immigrants who barely speak English.

When my mom arrived home after her class around 10:30 p.m., she often had interesting stories to tell about her students. Most of the women were single moms. Sometimes my mother invited them to bring their children to class because they could not afford child care. She told stories of their resilience, of moving to a foreign land, and leaving their whole life behind. "How terrible it must be," my mother said one night, "to live somewhere so horrible, that you leave everything behind to move here. They don't have anyone they love here." She admired that many spent their little savings on an education. I am sure these students, many of them far past the age of college kids, dreamed of making a life for themselves in the United States.

My mother, throughout many semesters of teaching, noticed patterns in her students. She was able to pick out the particularly bright ones very early on, even if they did not appear to raise their hand the most or get every question correct. After developing a relationship with these students, mom learned that many were nurses, doctors, and technicians in their home countries. *Why did they leave?* I always thought: *If they had a good life, why leave it?* As an upper-middle-class, young white woman I can say that many oppressions women face around the world have not impacted me. I have not had to flee a totalitarian government (not yet at least). I have not been ostracized for being a woman, for wanting an education. However, these women, these people, have. Their lives were so difficult, so dangerous, that they gave everything up to start fresh. The students my mother teaches show resilience on another level each and every day. They go to work all day and attend class until 9 or 10 at night. They offer to stay late and meet outside of class with mom because they know how important it is to succeed and are willing to put the effort in order to do so. It pains me to know that, especially in the state of the United States today, the chances of my mother's students being upwardly mobile as far as social class goes are slim.

At the small private college on scenic Route 127 on the Atlantic coast where mom teaches the buildings are state of the art, thanks to the wealthy alumni base. The campus reminds me of Pacific Coast Academy, the boarding school on the Nickelodeon TV show, *Zoey 101*. The dorms overlook the ocean, there is a huge fountain in the middle of campus, and a beach volleyball court set up on the school's private beach. When my mom came home from her classes, her mood was quite different than her night classes. She was often frustrated that her traditional students did not want to study, complained about homework, and were always trying to talk their way into extra credit. This understandably upset her. These students had everything handed to them—few of them paid for school; they drove new, name brand cars; and, unlike her other students, could actually afford course books, yet refused to even open them. There was such juxtaposition between the two schools: one group of students who were often working during the day, supporting families, and having to borrow my mother's student edition textbooks because they could not buy their own. The second group slept past their alarms, missed their 10:00 a.m. classes, grumbled about 10 pages of reading, and complained after every exam that it was "too hard."

Observing these two groups made me analyze social class in high school, although I didn't think of it as such at the time. The obvious difference between the two schools make me think about Detroit and surrounding affluent areas, and how just like these two schools, rich and poor stand next to each other, yet rarely interact.

My little sister, Mia, visited me during spring break in March 2017. She had been to Ann Arbor twice before, but always with my parents. I was excited for her to spend time in my house and show her around the city. One of my housemates was gone for the weekend and offered me to borrow her car so we could go into Detroit. Mia is an art fanatic, and although I know a lot less than her, we were both excited to visit the Detroit Institute of Arts (DIA) on Woodward Avenue.

The first time I visited Detroit was the fall of my UM freshman year. I grew up in a Roman Catholic family, but drifted away from religion in high school. After a particularly homesick week, one of my teammates convinced me to attend an Athletes in Action (AIA) meeting. AIA is a Christian group of athletes who spread the word of God through their sports and the connections they make through them. After approximately two minutes at the meeting, I remembered why I stopped going to church; however, I ended up signing up for a trip the following weekend into Detroit to learn about a parish that was being built between Indian Village, an extremely wealthy community and a nearby extremely poor community. The parish was aimed toward bringing these two communities together so they could connect and help each other. I was very involved in community service in high school and thought that besides the constant praying, it would be a good use of my Saturday.

When we were driving to Detroit, the leaders of the group briefed me on how Detroit is set up and to prepare myself to see more poverty than I had ever seen before. They reminded me, however, that the people of Detroit, although they live in poverty, are people just the same. "Many people are afraid of Detroit. On the news it is always projected as being scary. Do not be scared of Detroit. You could have grown up there. They did not choose to be poor, they are under terrible circumstances. It is our job, as privileged people, to help them," said one of the leaders. And he was right. From the little I knew about the city, I expected a dark urban landscape and the constant ringing of distant gunshots. However, it didn't look scary, it just looked unloved. As we drove through Detroit on our way to the parish I couldn't help but think that this didn't look like a city at all. There were almost no tall buildings. Many buildings were falling apart and vacant. It appeared that all the buildings were homes rather than businesses. I also remember how quiet it was outside. There weren't very many cars and I saw no one outside, even though it was an absolutely beautiful day. After our day of scheduled activities was over, we took a detour on our way home to see just how close and different Indian Village was to the neighborhood. The difference made my jaw drop. Mere yards away from each other were completely different worlds. One was full of privilege and the other was barely surviving. Even now, over a year later, I frequently think of these stark differences.

After leaving Detroit this first time, I put two and two together. Grosse Point, Michigan, neighborhood where several of my acquaintances at college were from was one of the wealthy sectors of the Detroit Metropolitan Area. Gross point and Detroit sit next to each other, yet never interact or attempt to help one another. I cannot help but chuckle to myself when I see them wearing, "Detroit Vs Everybody" T-shirts. They grew up in affluence, how could they possibly understand the struggle of growing up south of 8 Mile Road?

As Mia and I drove down I94 into Detroit, I told her of this story, and of the inequalities of education and opportunity for people of Detroit I was learning in my sociology class. After we visited the DIA and the nearby Heidelberg Project, we drove back to Ann Arbor and discussed what we had seen at the museum and in the city. She agreed that it was unlike anything she had ever seen before. It feels wrong of me, sometimes, when I go to Detroit. I feel as though I am an outsider looking in at a world I know nothing about. In a way, going to the museum and going to the streets of Detroit are one and the same. During both experiences I was an onlooker. At the DIA, we observed priceless masterpieces and great affluence. In Detroit, we saw empty houses and poverty. At the Heidelberg Project, however, the two worlds combined. Piles of trash were transformed into art at the hands of the artist Tyree Guyton whom I met that day. This convergence of life and art, forgotten and praised, is something that has stuck with me. If only, we could all be more like the Heidelberg Project. If only, the two sides of the spectrum could meet in the middle. Imagine if the community and college students met. What would they learn from each other? If I introduced my working-class and upper-class friends, how would they act? I can guarantee they could bond over a favorite band or TV show. And if we brought the people of Detroit together, if we tried to connect the short physical distance, but very different experiences together, what beautiful things could come from that? I am not convinced that these juxtapositions are the best way. Rather than serving as each other's foils, we should work to meet in the middle, to compromise, rather than ignore each other's similarities and differences.

SITTING ON THE SOCIAL LADDER, LOOKING UP AND DOWN

SACHIKA TOMISHIMA

My dad showed me the physical representation of social class in Shanghai, during a vacation my family spent together. We visited this busy city, stopping at attractions. Among the most famous gourmet there was xiaolongbao, a type of steamed bun with meat inside cooked in traditional bamboo basket. We arrived at the most reputable restaurant located at the middle of some souvenir shop clusters. We saw a huge line before we even reached the door. "Isn't this too packed? Shall we change a place?" We asked, but my dad didn't stop: "So the first floor is for cheap takeout," he calmly explained and walked straight to the entrance, passing the fat line of people waiting in the heat. The sun was generously casting its light down, and the cement was also generously sharing its heat up. The line squeezed under the shade, but the temperature still made people's chat seem louder than it was. We reached the building. "The second floor is a bit expensive," he guided us up the staircase, but did not stop at the second floor, where there were people sitting and eating at their tables. It was air-conditioned, but still nearly packed. "And the third floor charges the most, but they also have the most delicious and most types of food." We sat at a table at the third floor, and the crowd downstairs seemed so unreal. It was quiet and cool; the menu was thick and there was a glass window for us to see through to the kitchen where they made xiaolongbao with great dexterity and speed. Customers were sitting at their tables sparsely throughout the restaurant, and I can still remember that boy who was drinking his coke with a straw. I could never have remembered a person in the huge crowd downstairs. The idea of climbing upstairs and getting better food with higher price remained in my memory more than the exquisite food and the bill we paid that day.

My mom is Japanese and my dad is Chinese, and we live in northern China where dad works as a manager at his eye hospital. My mom's nationality helped us evade the infamous one child China policy. There are three children in my home: me and my two younger brothers. One child is complicated enough to raise, but my mom managed to bring up three of such creatures with her amazing patience and love. Part of the reason was that first, she did not have to work, so she had more time than many other parents to devote her attention to the three of us. My dad is the typical breadwinner of our family, and this fact alone demonstrates his successful preying skills in the modern society. He earned enough so that everything worked out. He is such a skilled hunter that our lives have surpluses, which brings me to the second point: we were able to hire a live-in nanny. All the chores and mess created by three children simply could not be done by only my mom; one child is annoying enough to take care of. My dad kept a nanny at home for about 13 years, until we all grew up and grandma passed away. My mom stressed many times we didn't need a nanny any more. Although I did not know my dad's wage (because he never paid attention to such things and therefore doesn't know), I knew that the nanny's wage was climbing every year, and though nannies were not uncommon in my friends' houses, nobody hired a full-time nanny that lived with them for months—even years like us. The more I think about that, the more I feel that my family is in a privileged class.

In China, nannies are predominantly from rural areas, often daughters of farmers, moving into town for various familial reasons from education to health care. We lived near the center of the province with an upper-middle-class lifestyle. One thing often handled by nannies in our house was cooking, and the first dish requested for that new nanny was fish. There are little tricks to cooking fish, but she did not know that. Her fish was overcooked outside, the skin stuck to the pan and the inside spread out. The flavor was good, but she was not used to cooking fish: "because pork is cheaper than fish . . . we don't usually buy fish, only during new year, perhaps." I was stunned. Because my hometown was inland, distant from seas, and fish, especially fresh ones, were more expensive than pork, but we never restrained our consumption. What we would usually do was compare the price among fish, not between fish and pork. We thought about what we wanted to eat, not the price. She was also overwhelmed by ironing my dad's shirts, and declined the work that was much more demanding than she previously thought, near crying when she left. She had never done like that in her house, because no clothes are required to be ironed. "I'll go find a different place to work—this is just too much for me—I'm sorry." I did not know, and still didn't know what to say.

Although, or because, our family's financial state is like this, never getting into trouble eating and buying things, my mother gave us little pocket money. She told us that children should not take abundance for granted, that parents don't have the obligation to support a child's every single want financially, that children should learn to make choices in limited boundaries, to make clever choices, and learn to endure. So each month, she gave us the amount of money equal to our grades: if I were in seventh grade, I would get 7 yuan (CNY). But compared with other kids' pocket money, it was like placebo. It just wasn't enough. A notebook ranged from 3 to 5 yuan; the cheapest pen was 2 yuan; potato chips were 3.5 yuan and the most popular egg waffle the street vendors sold was 5 yuan. I could not afford most of the soft drinks and popular snacks. I learned to buy refill packets rather than a pen, so that I could get some candy with friends. I learned to save money. I learned to give myself three to five days of buffer and really thinking about if I really wanted something. I learned to compare less with peers, which made life easier for me.

But sometimes I became someone I myself despised, trapped in tiny greed that took up much more of my life than it was supposed to. I craved for Mentos candies for days, and I was sure I wanted it. My heart itched when I walked past the little supermarket, but I didn't have enough money left. I wandered between the racks and made sure the price didn't change—2 yuan. Then I started my life as a magnet. I picked all my pockets and checked behind the bed and inside the drawer, and always kept an eye on the floor—even at school. What often came out was 1 jiao (a tenth of 1 yuan), but that slowly added up and finally reached 2 yuan. I counted the jiaos many times, made sure I had enough, and hurriedly rushed to the store and quickly paid for the candy. I threw that load of coins into the cashier's hand, and skipped out the shop before she finished counting. I heard her loud voice when I shut the door, but I didn't stop my hurried walk of delight. The Mentos was so delicious after days of thirst and being a magnet it was also outstanding how quickly that satisfaction vanished and my blood stopped circulating when I saw 2 jiao left at the corner of my desk. I did not take all the money when I rushed to the store! She was shouting to stop me! I was shocked by myself, becoming careless and numb to the surroundings when obsessed with something, and that obsession was a mere candy bar.

Thinking back, my greed might have also been triggered by my friend who was affluent enough to buy herself three candy bars at a time, Coke sometimes, and Oreo cookies often. The comparison added to a kid's natural want and made up that blind and intense crave. Material objects, especially food for me at that time, meant so much and could sometimes not be suppressed. In hooks's book, that is a required reading for Sociology 295, she states: "Most children experience greed in relation to food—endless longing for sweets" (hooks, 2000). I definitely experienced that as a child longing for candy treats myself and what they represent. I used to look down upon those who compared what they didn't have and what others had, and became obsessed with unimportant things, but two weeks later I was one of them. From this I learned that comparing myself with other kids does nothing good. Saving money according to what was inside my purse is more plausible than endlessly staring at my friends' possessions and the expensive treats that I don't have. But reflection like that was always done afterward, when I had more money flowing in and out of my pocket; when buying Mentos seemed rather trivial and cheap, which was never the case when I was a child.

There were always more affluent people around me as I grew up. The girl who lived next to my neighborhood did not know which bus to take because her mom always picked her up from school and she took taxi on other occasions. Another girl had a Starbucks card, which was a symbol of wealth among high school students. Another boy usually ordered delivery lunch menus two times more expensive than mine. Their families might have not have cared about the amount of money, but our parents brought us up differently. I always looked at prices before I checked the food when I ate out. My parents always made sure I had enough, but did not exceed the needed amount. In other words, I was affluent at home with my parents, but slightly restricted when I was outside with friends. The boundary between need and extravagance constantly popped up in my mom's motto, and she was great at giving us needed money that let us stay above thrift and within need. My friends were also in about the same social class as mine, so we didn't feel any gap when hanging out.

I was appalled by the unimaginable tuition in my college application season. My father told me to not worry about the money and go anywhere I want. "Don't just look at that tuition column. Your dad can afford it," he reassured, "even if it's not enough, we can sell stuff to pay for education." This was half joking and half exaggeration, but was still serious in attitude. Yes, that was both my parents' and my grandparents' motto; that is why all three children of my grandparents went abroad even though it was extremely difficult time for them. They can now harness what they have learned and swim well in the society. This motto reflects extremely respectable words. I was gratefully looking forward to the joy that privilege would give me and I would graduate from the University of Michigan free of tuition debt.

But the first semester at the University of Michigan (UM)—fall 2016—I figured out that not everyone was from the same class. FestiFall events on the Michigan Diag bombarded us with a dazzling amount of club activities and I marched into mass meetings of various clubs. One club offered a dinner outside after the meeting and I walked along with my newly met friends. The topic of expensive tuition and financial aids was brought up, and everyone grumbled. But when we reached a nearby restaurant, one girl didn't order anything. She ordered a cup of water while we lined up to look at the menu, and sat with us and chatted. "It's too expensive, I'll just have water," she said. One, two, and then everyone's meal arrived. Feeling uneasy, I ordered the cheapest noodle dish, but it didn't make anything different. I still got food in front of me. Every dish smelled nice, and the food scent enveloped our table. The table was not that big, so everyone's plates squeezed in and competed for space, making the space in front of her less prominent. "But I feel bad! You are not having anything!" I said. One student looked at her while he moved his fork. "It's alright; I had dinner at the dining hall," she said. I did not get if her first statement was a joke, but her not ordering food when everyone else did remains in my memory. After all, I was not hungry enough to eat at the time. I was just conforming and spending money on what I didn't actually need. I was no longer that girl who enviously watched other children getting snacks every day; now I am on the side of the "haves." Then I quietly multiplied by seven to that bill and thought about how much it cost back at home. I felt more weight about that noodle dish in front of me when I thought about myself five years before, as the girl sipped water beside me. I laboriously ate everything, feeling nauseated when I stood up, trying to bury something stirring in my stomach.

Although I grumble and still feel guilty every month I pull out my father's credit card and vaporize a couple thousand dollars for tuition. I personally do not feel the pain and pressures that college gives me financially. My father is paying everything for me, anything from tuition, to dining and dorm fees, to insurance, and maybe even a car in the future. One U.S. dollar is currently 6.9 Chinese yuan, and that tuition is not a small burden when your father is working in China and the payment multiplies.

I work at a university dining hall. Since I have classes from seven in the morning to nine at night back in high school, no one in my class had a job. Driven both by curiosity and a longing for independence, I marched into the dining hall with my newly given T-shirt as soon as I figured out how to work. But the ultimate motivation was, of course, money: I wanted money. My parents gave me a card and some hundred dollars of cash, but I had to tell them what I spent the money for when I swipe the card and I felt ashamed about that. But at the same time, I didn't stop because of that shame. I was trapped in the consumerist thought. I was spending the cash at a spectacular rate: textbooks were expensive; I wanted to buy UM goods once so I found the M Den store; fashion was different, so I wanted some new clothes to blend in a little more; Amazon Prime was friendly to students, so I wanted to order soft pillows my roommate had; I needed winter shoes that would help me live through Michigan winters. Everything was new in shops and aroused my consuming will. From clothes to food to tools and cosmetics, I wanted to try out everything to feel the same experience as my friends, to catch up with what they were talking about. I didn't know about Nutella and Pop tarts, I never wore leggings and tank tops, and I hated the moments I had to pause and ask what those things were. That urge to pick up everything my friends experienced combined with the shop's sales catchphrases encouraged so much unnecessary spending that did not stop despite the guilt. I knew it was okay to not know the things my friends have and they were always telling me what they were. I knew that those purchases would only bring me temporary, instant gratification, and that I should stop this superficial imitation, but still this lasted for the entire first semester of my freshman year. Consumerism, as it is named, gloomed more like a disease than a pervasive social phenomenon. Cash was running out, but it was so embarrassing to spend so much money and tell my parents. You will run out of money if you are only thrifty, but it's a different story if I make money: that thought drove me into the dining hall.

The working experience was much more pleasant than I expected. I heard: "Hey, you are so good at spreading the sauce! I can never do that so artistically." With warm encouragement like this, Jeff taught me how to make pizza and how to bake it in a hearth, occasionally telling his story. He had been cooking for about 20 years, and has just passed the Michigan Dining Chef test. He cooked basically everything, and it took him only a little more than a week to master how to bake a delicious pizza in a hearth that will never be in someone's house; these chefs are all incredibly talented and friendly. Many workers are black people, and I have some difficulties understanding their speech. When closing, there was a guy who works at the same station with me, and he always nicely offer to cover more jobs than he is supposed to. However, the first time he offered me help, I couldn't get completely what he was saying, and froze while my brain was processing. It took me a second, and he definitely thought I was afraid of him, treating me more politely and making his sentences shorter. It is awkward to reconcile, and we still haven't because I still need time to process his words. Anyhow, this is only a blue-collar, part-time job and the tuition with so many zeros is simply unimaginable.

My roommate, on the other hand, knows she is going to pay for tuition. Although she got a scholarship, and in-state tuition is much less than out-of-state ones, she is paying it back to her mom in the future. That fact alone should be a huge chunk of pressure. But she is so much braver than me. If I were told to pay back my father after graduation, I would be extremely careful and cowardly choosing my major; perhaps turning to something I do not like at all but fits in labor demands in the society. Even now under my father's protection, I am still hesitating in front of history major, concerned about my future job. But my roommate is extremely venturesome. Undecided as well, she is thinking about becoming an art student, because she loves art so much. There are several exquisite paintings in our dorm room showing her talent and work, but that was such a courageous statement, because another tacitly agreed rule in my community is that being an artist, singer, or actor is almost a dead path for most people; such path is not worth gambling. But she is willing to gamble with all that pressure above her! I believe this is more courage than cultural difference.

Other than feeling that realization of social class difference from newly met college friends, I was surprised in my encounter with a high school friend during winter break. Because our breaks were equally short, and the plane ticket back home seemed to cost more than it is worth, we decided to meet in Baltimore; residence halls were closed, and we had to leave anyway. He could drive there, and my cousin studies there, so it made a perfect place to meet. The moment he jumped out of the car, my eyes almost rolled out in astonishment. He lost weight! "What happened?!" Even those who dislike American cuisine would gain some weight, because dining hall food tend to contain more oil than what we used to have at home. He must have undergone an abnormal lifestyle. "I didn't eat in our dining hall," he said, "because it is too expensive." They didn't have an unlimited meal plan, and their dining hall worked like a restaurant. He had to pay for every portion he took, which is far from economical. He thus had to make food himself, and although he is a great cook, college students don't always have time to make every meal and consider the perfect balance; they might also be buying only the cheapest material in the grocery store. His friend who came with him was also in similar situation, calculating gas, insurance, and an additional expense for his lost glasses: "Hey, I can buy a pair of new ones if I had two meals a day from now on!" I have never been driven into a corner of being stingy on meals. Looking at his smaller tummy, I could feel the seriousness of that unrelenting dining hall and the crisis of not having enough money to eat. I never noticed any differences between us back in high school; maybe leaving home exposes the ultimate class condition, when even breathing in this foreign land costs money.

But it might not necessarily be the financial condition of a household; it can rather be the social class differences between parents and children. My cousin, on our way back to his apartment, told me about how he only had two meals as a freshman, because everything loomed so expensive after calculating the dollars into Chinese yuan, although his family is far from being poor and never told him to restrict his spending on food. He too, lost weight, and his mother burst in outrage when he returned home, telling him to eat normally and not worry about money. Even in rather privileged classes, there is a class gap between children and parents. Perhaps the child feels guilty about spending the parents' money, especially after witnessing the amount themselves and having peers who are responsible for their own expenses. Perhaps it is a natural response after they encounter the American way of reduced parental obligation and the change of value inside themselves. Perhaps it is a result of not knowing the parents' financial situation and underestimating the household's viability. But after all, there are such cases where children experience social class disparity from their parents, which is not uncommon in privileged classes as well.

Class difference becomes more salient during breaks, when people have more free time to determine what they do and how much money they would like (and afford) to spend each day. Spring break exploded throughout American colleges, and the ubiquitous Facebook photos told everyone's footprints. "Do you want to go to Orlando with us?" the offer went. "Of course!" I said. "That is the land of wonder and everyone's dream!" This shattered in the face of the plane ticket, hotel expenses, and the attraction tickets that relentlessly added up. I could have gone somewhere if I asked my parents, but that budget simply seemed too much, added to the shame of asking for more money. I knew my father could afford all the expenses to Orlando and would have encouraged me to go, but some force told me it was too much, especially after some quick math converting that amount to how many dining hall shifts I would pick up. I didn't deserve that. The friend who was planning to go also gave up after calculating the money she would need to pay, and we spent our spring break walking around the museum and the Arboretums here in Ann Arbor, which were placid places full of surprise and beauty.

Many of my friends from high school went to Orlando, Florida, someone to Mexico, some to Canada, and others to New York. In one of my courses after the break, our professor asked if anyone went abroad during spring break. Several people raised their hands. Previously I would be taking that as a valid reflection of wealthy people, but now I don't convert that into absolute conclusion. Choosing to travel during breaks does not necessarily mean they are significantly wealthier than those who did not travel; perhaps they have different focus on where to spend money or perhaps many who chose to stay at home experience the situation of the parents being rich and the children feeling poor. Rather, the fact that traveling is a valid option means their families have more surpluses to spend and that option should be examined when thinking about social class issues.

Only after I have attended college, physically displaced from home—witnessing the tuition, withdrawing cash for driving lessons, buying plane tickets and food—have I been more exposed to opportunities that allow direct contact with money. I realize explicit and implicit social class differences around me, as well as class differences within families across generations. As I continue my study at the University of Michigan, I will likely encounter many other people from different countries and different social classes, and that will be an eye-opening, incredible experience. Although class is a "c-word" that is not commonly discussed in this country that promotes free speech, it will be only beneficial if people start acknowledging its existence and start talking about it. I would appreciate if they could tell their stories, and I am more than happy to share mine.

Work Cited

hooks, bell. *Where We Stand: Class Matters*. Routledge, 2000.

Part V

Upper Class

NOT-SO BLISSFUL IGNORANCE: A SELF-EXAMINATION

MAGGIE PAUL

While filling out my first college application in the fall of 2013, I reached the "personal information" section, and confidently began filling in the "white," "female," and "U.S. citizen" bubbles without hesitation. However, when I reached the "family income" section, I was stumped. I was given five options; along the lines of "less than $30,000," "$30,000–$50,000," "$50,000–$100,000," "$100,000–$200,000," and "$250,000 and above." I sat there for a couple of minutes, knowing that I must be in the upper half at least, but unsure what option fit my family income most accurately. I decided to consult my parents, who for my entire 18 years of life had never spoken about money or social class, or given me any specific numbers to refer to. "Mom!" I yelled out, "What bubble should I fill out for family income?" What happened next will forever stay with me as the moment I became brutally aware of my "social class," a phenomenon I had never given much thought to before then. Without a second of hesitation, she took the application, read over the options, and motioned toward the "$250,000 and above" bubble. I cocked my head and looked at her with surprise at how quickly and confidently she was able to answer the question, and she turned and walked away before I could infer anything else. It was almost like it pained her to have to finally tell me, to finally admit to one of her children that she had kept was innocently unaware of our socioeconomic status at the top of the pile.

I think what stuck with me from that moment was her swiftness in answering my question and moving about her day, purposely avoiding further conversation or inquiries on the subject.

I was a member of two country clubs by the time I arrived in this world. My parents drive a Mercedes Benz and a Range Rover, I have lived in Darien, Connecticut, and now reside right outside of Boston, and my family has a summer home on a lake in New Hampshire. We have a ski boat, a jet ski, a hot tub, and enough TVs for every child in the family to watch whatever program or movie they choose each night. My golden retriever is well trained, well groomed, and well fed. I am a vegetarian, and in my kitchen, you will find unlimited fresh fruits and vegetables, various kinds of tofu and tempeh, and only "sprouted grain" bread, because we all know that white stuff has far too much gluten. No one in my family of six has any significant physical, mental, or emotional issues we have not been able to efficiently tackle with a world renowned doctor or psychiatrist with ease. My parents met at Dartmouth College in New Hampshire and have been happily married for 27 years. My older sister attended Phillips Andover Academy, an elite preparatory school in Andover, Massachusetts, where she went onto attend Amherst College and land a job at a top consulting firm in New York City. My younger brother is following in my parents' footsteps and attending Dartmouth College in the fall of 2017, and my younger sister is a sophomore at a private preparatory school in Massachusetts. I attended Middlesex School, a boarding school in Massachusetts with tuition rates comparable to the University of Michigan (UM) out-of-state tuition rates. I have traveled to Europe multiple times, once with my family and once on a student trip where I got the chance to visit Pompeii, Italy, eat a baguette near the Eiffel Tower in Paris, and drink wine on the Italian coast. I have never known anything but privilege and fortune, and although I have been immersed in this world of luxury for the entirety of my life, never deviating from the comfortable life I was born into, my social class is not something that I have given much thought or attention to in my day-to day-life.

Thus far in my young adult life, my socioeconomic status or social class has never felt like a part of my DNA. By that I mean, it's not a personal characteristic of mine or a key part of my identity. It doesn't govern what I like or dislike, what I purchase, or whom I choose to associate with. My perception of my social class doesn't keep me up at night, and it rarely ever crosses my mind. For this, I am privileged. I am lucky enough to fall asleep worrying about things like relationships, homework, my future career, and my life aspirations. I do not wake up in the morning and wonder how and what I am going to eat that day, or how I am going to complete my homework before I start my shift at work. I go to school at a prestigious university, I have a decent amount of homework and daily responsibilities, and there are times I get stressed out about grades and assignments. I also have a job, as a nanny, out of a sheer desire to make extra money to spend on weekends, on nights out drinking, and eating with friends. My life isn't necessarily a "walk in the park." I have my own personal battles just like everyone else, but in the grand scheme of things, life has been relatively flawless. Of course there are times when my social class does cross my mind and I am suddenly made hyper aware of where I stand in comparison to those around me or the world at large. However, that usually only occurs when I deliberately put myself in situations where I am forced to confront the reality of my privilege, in hopes of becoming more educated and more understanding of the world around me.

I am outspoken. I am passionate about criminal justice and issues of race and discrimination in the United States. I am a feminist, and I believe in standing up for women's rights in the workplace, the classroom, and everywhere else. I am fascinated by addiction, and I spend my free time watching documentaries that chronicle those struggling with the crippling disease. I am a political science major, and I spend most of my time in the classroom attempting to tackle real, dire issues in the United States including minimum-wage laws, immigrations laws, and health-care accessibility. I spent a full year volunteering at two local criminal justice facilities in the area, interacting with inmates and patients and helping them cope with the realities of confinement. I volunteered at the University of Michigan Hospital, where I spent weekend nights caring for and entertaining young children whose parents could not afford to take time off work and be with their child while they were receiving cancer treatment. I go out of my way to put myself in situations where I am directly exposed to people who are struggling, who are different than me, and who were dealt a different hand in life. I am also funny, and I approach challenging situations with humor in order to ease tension and calm worry. I am a loyal friend, and an obedient daughter. I didn't break the rules much in high school, and I have always respected my parents and my home even throughout my teenage years. I became a Division 1 NCAA (National Collegiate Athletic Association) lacrosse player at the UM by dedicating nearly all of my weekends and summers to traveling to tournaments, camps, practices, games, and training sessions far from my school. I am disciplined in my daily life; I exercise every day, I eat a balanced diet, I complete my homework, and I study hard for exams. I do not tell you this to gloat; in fact, given my fortune in life, this is all quite frankly the least I can do to give back to society and to my parents. I am attempting to illustrate who I am, on a personal level, so you can get an inside look into my own burning question: Why do I care?

I am a political science major here at UM, and for a while, I was planning to minor in criminal justice. I have always taken classes dealing with social justice issues, because I find them fascinating and sometimes eye-opening. I have taken countless political, sociological, and psychological based classes where I have gained incredible amount of academic insight to the world around me by virtue of books, articles, documentaries, and knowledge professors possess. One class in particular that had the biggest impact on me and my perceptions of my own social class was Psychology 211: Project Outreach. This course allowed students to do something outside of the classroom in the hopes of contributing to the greater good of society, and hopefully gaining knowledge far beyond what a textbook or lecture could offer. I ended up taking the course twice: once as a student and a second time as a student-teacher, where I had my own section of students that I was responsible for grading assignments and managing at our prospective "sites." The first time I took the class, a group of 10 peers and I were assigned to volunteer at Washtenaw County Jail, located just 20 minutes from Ann Arbor. We were told we would be teaching a creative writing class to the inmates for one hour a week, every Wednesday night.

I found myself beginning to get extremely nervous as we pulled up to the jail for our first site visit, and it suddenly began to hit me that I was about to enter a real-life prison, with very little training or preparation. We went through an immense amount of security before we were able to actually enter the facility, and once we did they lead us on a short tour through the jail. As I looked around at the faces that looked back at me from behind bars or class windows, I was breathless. I looked into the eyes of other human beings, some my age, some my parents age, some black, some white, and I saw people who were in such a different place in life. What had they done? I looked into the eyes of a tall black man, close to my age I assumed, and I thought there was no way he could be a criminal. Of course, before we went to our first site visit we had attended lectures, had discussions about disparities in the criminal justice system in the United States, and how certain people or groups of people are more likely to end up behind bars. Much of it came down to race and social class, and very little of it came down to being a "good" or "bad" person. We learned about the "War on Drugs" in the United States, where hundreds of thousands of black men and women were incarcerated for up to 30 years for the possession of drugs like cocaine and oxycodone, drugs that as a 21-year-old college student, I had been exposed to. Why did I have friends and acquaintances at UM that drank under the age of 21, did illegal drugs, stole, lied, and cheated, but they never ended up behind bars? Why, where I am from, do people just get "in trouble" with their parents or their schools, and never have to worry about the harsh realities of ending up in a jail cell?

One night during my senior year of high school, I and my friends were drinking in my best friend Hannah's basement. Hannah's on again, off again boyfriend had stopped by, and he and Hannah began arguing about something or other. As the night progressed, we all kept drinking, and I noticed Hannah's boyfriend, in particular, was drinking vodka straight out of the handle. I didn't think anything of it at the time, until we received a call at 2:00 a.m. informing us that he had wrapped his dad's Mercedes Benz around a tree. We were not aware he was planning to drive himself home that night, or that he had even left Hannah's house; when we got the news of his accident we were terrified for his life.

Fortunately, my friend survived the crash with a minor concussion. After the initial shock of the accident began to settle, we started wondering about legal repercussions; he was blackout drunk, after all. We assumed that he would get a DUI (Driving under the Influence) infraction, would be dropped from the school that he had already been accepted to play lacrosse at the following year, and would have trouble finding a job for the rest of his life. One year later, his record was clean, he was playing lacrosse at the college he had planned to attend, and it seemed like any remnants of that night had disappeared without a trace. Thanks to his father and his success as a lawyer in the state of Massachusetts, he was able to null all charges against his son and pay a large sum of money to wipe his record clean. This was the first time in my life that I had been acutely aware of how much your social class really does affect everything in your life, and how stark the differences are between people who have a higher social class, and people who do not. My friend's boyfriend was able to avoid a lifetime of devastating consequences, after he had put his life and the lives of others in extreme danger, without much of a sweat. This all came back to me as I stood in the Washtenaw County Jail that first night, gazing into eyes of people that looked like they could be my friends, but whose lives had taken a completely different turn. I realized that semester that depending on your social class and your family's financial status, the likelihood of using and selling drugs, of succeeding or failing in school, and of getting caught doing what most all teenagers do at some point in their lives can be drastically different.

Another example of a time where I deliberately put myself in a situation I knew would make me uncomfortable and force me to take an honest look in the mirror was when I decided to volunteer at the University of Michigan Mott's Children's Hospital. It was my junior year, and I had reached a point in my academic and personal life where I felt generally unfulfilled. I thought about joining a campus singing group, or perhaps participating in one of the many intramural sports programs offered to students. But none of those options felt like they would fill this particular void I had been feeling all year long. I needed to do something with my free time to help others, or expand my understanding of the world around me in a meaningful way. I was placed on the "cardiac" floor, meaning I was mostly working around children who had serious heart problems that caused them to stay in the hospital for long periods of time to receive treatment or consistent monitoring by hospital staff. For a period of about four consecutive weeks, my task was to "hang out" with this one little girl who was in the hospital alone most of the time. Her parents, I was eventually informed, could not afford to take off work and travel the distance from their hometown to remain with her in the hospital at all times, and as a result, she was often alone in her dreary, sad hospital room. I played with her dolls, watched movies with her, and tried to entertain her as best as I could in the hopes of distracting her from the harsh realities of what she was going through, and how she wasn't even able to hug her mom or dad in the midst of it.

This experience, similar to my experience at the County Jail, was one that stunned me and completely shifted my perception of the world, and how privileged I was on so many levels. I could not imagine not only dealing with a serious health issue, but on top of that dealing with financial stresses that come along with it. I could not imagine getting extremely sick and needing to spend weeks on end in a hospital bed, and my parents not being able to take time off of work to spend the night with me. I could not believe there were people, not far from where I lived and went to school, who had such significant financial burdens I was so acutely and blissfully unaware of. I think to me and to a lot of people like me getting sick is one of the worst things that could happen in our lifetimes. However, I have never once had to think about how I would be able to afford treatment if something ever did happen, or if my family would be able to spend time with me while I was receiving treatment. This realization has remained poignant in my mind since my experience in the hospital, and it has drastically influenced my perception of my own privilege.

I'm not sure I will know the answer to the question of why I, a white, upper-class girl at a prestigious university, take time and effort to place myself in situations that make me uneasy and make me take a long, hard look in the mirror at my own privileges. What I can say, however, is I think it has something to do with the whole "not being part of my DNA" thing. I have always felt disconnect between my social class and who I am "on the inside"; this influences the way I perceive people around me. I don't look at the teenager in the Washtenaw County Jail as a "bad kid" or a "criminal"; I look at him as someone who was born to a section of our social class hierarchy that puts him at a greater risk of "following the wrong path," or getting caught doing it.

The notion of "social class" is relative to one's environment. As a student at the University of Michigan, I am already constantly surrounded by people who are of similar "social class" to me, and I am rarely confronted with the realities of where I truly stand in relation to the world at large. For example, in my sorority, I am of significantly lower social class than many of my peers. Some of my sorority sisters are children of politicians, celebrities, professional athletes, and Wall Street billionaires. Many of my friends have last names like "Kennedy" and "Romney," while my name does not correlate with any particular sense of financial or social success. While my family is very well-off and we comfortably sit in the upper class, within my sorority I am toward the lower end of the social hierarchy. However, when I drive just 10 minutes down the street to my internship at Big Brothers Big Sisters, I am surrounded by young people whose parents cannot afford to put dinner on the table. Children go to bed hungry. I like to contribute my sense of curiosity and genuine desire to work with and understand those from different social classes than my own to my personal need to feel like I am doing something to give back. Maybe I feel guilty that I have been handed everything in life and feel the only way to ease some of that guilt is to do everything I can do to help those less fortunate. Maybe my urge to go outside my "bubble" and confront serious social and political issues head-on is simply due to my genuine curiosity about those who are different than me. I like to foster that curiosity head-on.

Growing Up Rich, but Not Knowing It

Abigail Siegal

I like numbers. I always have and I probably always will. I like the way numbers quantify things. I like that there is a right answer and a wrong answer when it comes to numbers. When I walked into my sociology class—The Experience of Social Class in the Community and Education —on the first Thursday of the winter 2017 semester, I was excited that our first handout was a chart with numbers. It listed the family yearly income next to each social class. I scanned down the page to find where my family fit in; I stopped when I got to the last and highest number on the page: Upper class: $250,000 or more. That's what this chart says my family is. Throughout this course I learned: that my family is in the top 2% of Americans; that if either of my parents stopped working my family would still be upper-middle class; and that while I have never seen myself as rich, that's how most people would classify me.

To me, rich people are the ones who make seven figures not six. The rich are people like Donald Trump, Bill Gates, or Warren Buffett. Rich people act like the characters in *Gossip Girl*, dropping hundreds of dollars on jeans or being driven around in limousines, at least in my head. The rich have multiple homes and private planes. I think the reason why I have never considered myself rich is because of where I grew up and how I was raised.

I grew up in Beverly Hills, Michigan—a small village in the Detroit Metropolitan area, with an average family adjusted gross income of $195,151; almost quadruple the national average. And if the high average income of my hometown wasn't already enough to blind me from what normal Americans earn, the fact I live in the second richest city in Michigan, sandwiched between the richest and third richest cities, probably didn't present a very eye-opening experience.

So it took me 19½ years to discover my family is rich. I feel like it's necessary to explain why it took this long. I have to go back to before I was born, because social class is determined by the family you're born into and ways you see yourself are determined, at least in part, by how you're raised.

Dad was raised in the lower-middle class, living in a small home in the Detroit suburbs. Having succeeded in high school and scoring very high on his ACT (American College Testing), he was offered a full ride to Wayne State University, in Detroit. He and his siblings were the first in their family to get a high school degree, let alone go to college. As I navigated my college selection process, I listened to my dad explain that since his parents didn't have that much money, despite his desire to attend the University of Michigan (UM), there wasn't a choice. The full ride was the only choice. When he graduated from Wayne State, he took out loans to attend law school at Michigan. He now works as a partner at a top-tier law firm. I've always thought that dad is the type of person that conservatives like to point to as an example that the American Dream is achievable for everyone, but the reality is that he is the exception, not the rule when it comes to upward mobility.

Mom was raised in the upper-middle class. Her parents put her and her two brothers through college, allowing her to graduate without debt. After earning her bachelor's of business administration from the University of Michigan, Ann Arbor, she joined the workforce. After working for eight years, her MBA (Master of Business Administration) from Michigan was paid for by her employer. She worked at banks for a while before shifting to fund-raising and now she works at UM as the Director of Stewardship for the College of Literature, Science, and the Arts. This means, on a fairly regular basis, she's rubbing shoulders with CEOs and owners of sport teams in order to keep them happy and giving to the university.

We never talked about social class in my home, but looking back at some of the things my parents told me, I realize the social classes my parents were raised in are different from the one we live in now. One evening, as we were driving back from eating dinner at a local chain, my dad commented he had read an article about how some intelligence tests were biased against kids with lower socioeconomic status. He explained that there were questions like: "What time is rush hour?" My brother and I both promptly responded 5:00 p.m. to 7:00 p.m. Dad said: "Yes, you know that because that's when mom and I get home from work, because we work white-collar jobs. But," he continued, "kids whose parents don't work white-collar jobs get home at different hours; like I would have said rush hour was around 10:00 p.m. or 11:00 p.m. because that's when my dad got home." His comments were generally a little rawer, talking more about how much money his family had, than my mom's since he had been raised in the lower-middle class rather than the upper-middle class.

Mom would describe how her family vacations were usually road trips, with the occasional cross-country trip. She told me about going to the Pictured Rocks in the Upper Peninsula of Michigan and traveling to Dinosaur National Monument in Utah. And the summer before my sophomore year of high school when my camp takes campers on a five-week hiking trip out west, my mom recalled going when she was in high school. My dad mentioned that his family rarely traveled. When we were on our most recent trip to Walt Disney World, there have been several over the years, he recalled that he had only been to Disney once, before he was an adult.

These simple, offhand comments made me think about all the places I have traveled and how normal it is to me. Many people are surprised when I say I have been to 33 states and 4 countries; both numbers are likely to go up the summer of 2017, but more on that later. Every year my family takes a vacation or two. These trips are often to places like Los Angeles, Cancun, Mexico, and Disney

World. We flew, but never first or business class, always coach. On one of our trips, my parents made the decision to buy a timeshare with Sheraton. With the timeshare, our vacations meant staying in villas with big fluffy beds, Jacuzzi tubs, and infinity pools. Occasionally, the end of summer resulted in a weekend trip up north to Midland or Traverse City, Michigan, but it was clear there were social class differences between the people we encountered at the resorts in exotic locations and the ones we met at the hotels on these weekend trips. The differences weren't obvious in the sense of what they were wearing, although there were differences there as well, but more in what they were doing. On our week-long resort vacations, we'd chat with people about whether they were going swimming with the dolphins that day or what overpriced restaurant they'd be going to that night. On these weekend trips, we watched as bachelorette parties drank wine from plastic cups and kids ran around restaurants.

The main thing I remember from my childhood is there was very little downtime. My family has always been go, go, go, go. My weekends were filled with trips to the Detroit Institute of Arts on Woodward Avenue, roaming the halls looking at hundreds of years of art; visiting the Detroit Science Center, doing any hands-on activity; or attending Detroit Tigers' games, eagerly recording all the statistics flashing on the big screen. This was the norm in my house. I would later learn this type of busy lifestyle is common for upper-middle-class and upper-class families.

If we weren't going to museums, sporting events, or movies, our weekends were spent volunteering in the local community. Many Christmases were spent driving around Detroit delivering presents or hot meals, wishing people I would normally never interact with a Merry Christmas. I'll be honest, this wasn't a huge sacrifice since my family is Jewish, but my parents made it clear that giving back to the community is important. This is something that I have carried with me and why I continue to be involved in my community.

Being Jewish has also been a big part of how I was raised. I attended private, Jewish day school from kindergarten through eighth grade. Dad was never hesitant to remind me that he spent the same amount for a year of kindergarten as he does for college tuition now. While attending day school, I always thought my family had less money than classmates because they wore more expensive clothes, their parents drove nicer cars, and their moms picked them up dressed in Lululemon workout clothes, sipping $5 Starbucks drinks after spending their days doing whatever it is stay-at-home moms do. It's not that I don't respect stay-at-home parents, because I do, but with two working parents, I never really learned what nonworking parents spend their days doing. I later heard that two-thirds of my classmates were on scholarship, a fact that truly shocked me. This amazed me because while I thought it was pretty standard for middle schools to go to Washington D.C., I knew most schools that do make this trip drive on a bus; my class, however, flew. In the seventh grade, my entire class got on a Delta Airlines flight to Washington D.C. We stayed in a nice hotel, visited the White House, and explored museums on the national mall. It was a simple three-day trip, but it was made all the more extravagant by having 45 seventh graders fly to and from the city.

This was not the only trip my class took. In eighth grade, as a culmination of all of our Judaic learning, we took a three-and-a-half-week trip to Israel. Before leaving, my parents sat me down and explained my class probably wouldn't be staying at places as nice as the ones we stay at as a family. I realized how true that was when we arrived at a hostel-esque building which had scratchy blankets on uncomfortable beds and a shower that grossed me out because it was so dirty. This was by far the worst place we stayed, but as the trip went on, the places we stayed got nicer and nicer culminating in a stay at a luxury hotel in downtown Jerusalem. There was, however, some drama on the trip because one of my classmates was so appalled at our accommodations that she called her mother. This resulted in her mother flying to Israel and taking her off the trip. I remember being shocked by the fact her mom could and would drop everything just to fly to Israel to comfort her daughter because she didn't like the hotel. I guess I shouldn't have been surprised since most classmates seemed to live lavish lives and weren't afraid to show it.

The biggest and most obvious example of their extravagant lifestyles is bar and bat mitzvahs. What is supposed to be a coming-of-age events for 12- and 13-year-olds becomes a way to show off how much you have. While the bar or bat mitzvah is actually just a simple service, it has become common to accompany the service with an expensive party. And when I say lavish, I mean *lavish*. My bat mitzvah party was one of the tamer ones. There was a cocktail hour which included a mashed potato bar and pigs in a blanket followed by a buffet style meal for my 300+ guests. My parents hired a disc jockey (DJ), a master of ceremonies, and a few dancers to really hype up the party. We had a picture station where you could have your picture taken in front of a green screen, and at the end of the night, my classmates took home embroidered towels. The decorations included a giant foam board with "Camp Abby" written on it, which now hangs in my garage, a wide variety of balloons, and different camp-themed centerpieces. I say this was a tame bat mitzvah. In comparison, I have attended parties where the DJ was brought in from New York, I walked home with multiple T-shirts and sweatshirts, or the family had purchased Apple products to give away. This was standard for me, which is part of the reason that I lived in a bubble for so long.

When it came time for me to pick where I would attend high school, I looked at both the local private Jewish school and my district public school. My parents and I agreed that it would be best to attend the public school because it would offer a more well-rounded education and more diversity. While the school did offer more racial and religious diversity, social class diversity was nonexistent. There was a small amount of class diversity but it was uncommon for people of different social classes to mix because of the actual classes we were enrolled in. Most students were sorted onto one of three tracks: the honors/Advanced Placement track, the regular track, or the O-TECH (Oakland Technical School) track; not that the school ever acknowledged these tracks, probably for fear of losing its golden status. I was on the honors/AP (Advanced Placement) track taking almost entirely honors or AP classes except when the school didn't offer an honors or AP version of the class. It was rare to spend any time with kids who were on the O-TECH track. The other side of this that shows exactly how privileged my high school was, and still is, is the sheer number of AP classes offered. While many high-achieving students in low-income areas attend schools where there are few or no AP classes, my high school offered APs ranging from calculus to studio art to computer science. There was never a conversation about cutting classes or art programs. In fact, my senior year the orchestra traveled to Rome and the band traveled to London to perform in the London New Year's Parade. These trips were not paid for by the school, but there were plenty of things the school charged our parents for because they knew they would pay. Junior and senior year meant physics, and physics meant a trip to Cedar Point, Ohio. The school charged our parents and almost everyone went. The school charged $75 for a year of parking and people paid for it, myself included, despite living within walking distance of the school. Part of the reason for this, serving as another display of upper–social class status, was that upperclassmen were allowed to go, and commonly went off campus for lunch. This meant spending $10–15 every day at local restaurants or chains like Chipotle. Every day, luxury cars pulled out of the parking lot and students headed off to spend more of their parents' money.

My high school was not the only place I saw a lack of social class diversity. I was heavily involved with BBYO, a Jewish youth group. While the staff loved to claim that "cost should never be a reason for missing a program," there were significant costs, even more so if you wanted to be a leader. Each weekend there were local programs which cost money about half the time. Throughout the year, there were region-wide programs and international programs. Regional programs involved paying about $250 for a weekend. International programming was a little more involved and significantly more expensive. One international program involved flying to another

U.S. city. Baltimore, Atlanta, and Dallas were places I traveled to and my parents paid large fees to attend. This program gave me opportunities to do, see and be a part of incredible things. For example, I have seen B.o.B. and Flo Rida perform, I have heard Michael Jordan's manager speak, and I spoke in front of a 3,000-person crowd.

This organization had a huge impact on me and on my parents from their time in high school, so they make it a priority to support BBYO. I remember picking up a handwritten thank-you note addressed to my parents. It was from one of my friends thanking my parents for her scholarship contribution and how it would allow her to be able to attend a summer leadership program, another expensive experience. I never realized my friend wouldn't be able to have this experience without my parents' contribution. I understood how fortunate I was that my parents had been able to afford eight years of sleepaway and day camps when I was younger, followed by two years of youth group leadership programs. I realized how few people can actually afford to have these opportunities.

When sophomore year of high school rolled around, I began preparing for the ACT (American College Testing) test. My parents hired a tutor to help me achieve my goals of getting a 30 and being admitted to the University of Michigan (UM). I took the $59 test twice as a sophomore and four times, including the state-required edition, as a junior, but I did eventually reach my goal of 30. While I was striving to achieve this, I met someone who was excited her score was above the teens.

At the same time I was living in the lap of luxury and was working a minimum-wage job at a sandwich shop. This was probably the first time I really encountered people who weren't in my social class or at least close to it. On the first day of work, our boss explained if anyone went out back for a smoke, they had to wash their hands before coming back and serving customers. I looked around assuming I would be faced with a bunch of other teens like myself who had no interest in smoking, but instead found a very diverse group of people. I would later learn my coworkers ranged from those who were trying to contribute to their college savings, since community college would be a stretch for them to pay for, to those who were working three minimum-wage food service jobs just to get by. I learned some people had to plan their work schedule around bus schedules and some filled their gas tank only by the amount they hadn't spent on rent and food. While I was there to make a few extra bucks, these people were working for their lives.

They never once made me feel bad for not having to work, but I also found I was uncomfortable mentioning my 30 ACT score or where my family was going on vacation. Our conversations weren't about future plans; rather they involved current music and movies. We ignored class differences and pretended they didn't exist. I internalized these differences without ever realizing it.

By the time I was applying for college, I had no contact with my former coworkers; in fact, they and their struggles left my mind entirely as I thought about beautiful campuses and high admissions standards. After visiting several Midwestern colleges over spring break my junior year, I decided to apply to five: University of Michigan, Michigan State University, DePaul University, Loyola University, and Miami University. I was admitted to all five, accepted into the Honors College for four, and received merit aid at three. I only visited two: Michigan and Miami. Dad made it very clear I shouldn't worry about cost when choosing a college, something that had floated over from the slight resentment he still had about not having a choice in his college education.

In the end I chose the University of Michigan (UM); most people who know me would tell you this was not a surprising decision since I have long loved the Wolverines and Ann Arbor. I surprised myself though. I liked the idea of going out of state and meeting new people and going somewhere where no one knew me. I had some apprehension before the start of school if this was really the right choice. But when I finally moved in with all of my things, so new they still had the price tags on them, I was delighted. I continue to love my experiences on campus, especially as I get more and more involved.

One of the organizations I joined since coming to UM is the Solar Car Team. Since I'm not an engineering student, the first question people often ask is what I am doing on an engineering project team. The answers: I ask companies for money. I spend 10 hours a week in meetings finding and reaching out to businesses, but on top of that, I spend countless hours writing e-mails, making phone calls, and meeting with managing partners and directors of major corporations. When I walked into a meeting with the commercial and engineering directors of a company that grosses $4 billion per year, I was more uncomfortable with the fact I was wearing jeans than I was when I asked them to sponsor our team at $40,000 over two years. That's the thing about coming from a family with money; I'm comfortable with money, I'm comfortable asking people for money, and I'm comfortable speaking with people who earn more money in one month than some people earn in one year.

The lack of social class diversity on Solar Care is another thing I picked up on very soon after joining. The team is predominantly out-of-state or out-of-country students, which means they pay higher tuition. I would also be very surprised if anyone works since there is a huge time commitment. I spend about 15 hours a week and this number is even higher for the engineer students and leadership.

The most expensive part of being a dedicated member of Solar Car is an obvious one. Every other year the team participates in one race: the World Solar Challenge. This race takes place in October and entails members dedicating their spring and summer breaks to work leading up to the race, culminating in a trip to Australia lasting from the end of August to the end of the race. While the team covers flights to and from Australia, members are expected to cover living expenses for the summer and also commit to taking the fall semester off from school, a luxury many people can't afford. On top of that, since team members have already taken a semester off, many spend the rest of what would be fall semester traveling around Oceania or Asia.

Another student organization I have become heavily involved is Michigan Dance Marathon (MDM). This organization also focuses on money, simply by what it is. It raises money for children with disabilities. There is no way to separate money from MDM, but that's not why there a class bias most people might not pick up on. The first barrier is the $40 registration fee that goes toward shirts and food at the main event: VictorThon. Upon arriving at VictorThon, it appears that pretty much everything is sponsored. But I digress; the next barrier is the minimum $300 that needs to be raised to attend. For me this is easy breezy because dad usually shares one or two of my posts on Facebook, and after donating himself, I usually hit the goal. Over my two years in MDM, I have raised over $1,000. I recently realized this is not something that is that easy or simple for people of a lower social class. If you're barely scraping by at school, whom are you going to ask for $300 to support children's therapies? If you didn't grow up around money, would you even be comfortable asking other people for money? If you work every spare minute to pay for school, can you even ask your boss for a weekend off? These were and are questions I wouldn't have even thought to consider a few months ago, but now I understand why I rarely interact with students who are from a different social class.

This also means I generally am not in tune with many issues of students who have less than I do. This year I have served as a member of the Student Campaign Committee, a group of diverse students who represent interests in the current university fund-raising campaign. This has, by far, been the most eye-opening of all of student organizations I am involved with. I have spoken with students who are on scholarships and with donors who wanted to make sure students who receive scholarships have the best possible experience. I learned that even if students have full ride offers, they sometimes have to turn them down because they don't cover living expenses or they can't afford to not work full time. I also learned there are many students who cannot take on leadership roles in student organizations because they are not paid positions. This was something I had never considered previously and why I now take time into account as something I am privileged to have. I have the privilege of making the most of my Michigan experience and leap at every opportunity presented.

My campus activities are not the only place I've noticed social class differences. I see subtle differences within my friends group, in the ways we spend our money, in the activities we are involved in, and the ways we travel. I live off campus in a house with six other girls, five of whom I lived on the same dorm floor with last year. Moving from the dorms into off-campus housing brought social class distinction into focus.

While we rarely discuss where we fall on the social class scale, the differences are still evident. I notice we buy groceries at different stores and some of my friends, more accurately their parents, are willing to shell out for dining plans. When we decide to go out to dinner, our class differences become more evident simply by the places each of us suggests. Even at the most basic levels, each of us pays different amounts in rent and has different necessities when it comes to subletting our rooms for the summer. These invisible lines don't cause boundaries in our friendships, but they do change the ways we experience Michigan, as well as shaping who we are.

I learned that it is more common for upper-middle-class and upper-class families to be more active; this is something I've noticed carries over to college. My friends who are more actively involved on campus are the same ones who suggest expensive restaurants when we go out to eat. Some student organizations involve huge time commitments and travel, others involve purchasing large amounts of expensive clothing, and some involve both. I have friends who have to make decisions if they want to be a part of a group activity, like going to an expensive music festival in Chicago, or if they will spend their money on other things.

The biggest example of this is spring break. While some of us flew down to Florida for the past two years, others stayed at home, or chose travel to nearby places. This causes those invisible lines I mentioned, because there are inside jokes and stories that bond those of us who are able to travel together. The differences are also present with family travel. There is a distinction between families who travel to Europe, who fly within the United States, and who take road trips. There are places my family would fly to, while my friend's family will make the drive instead.

My family has given me certain expectations when it comes to money, which is part of the reason I notice these differences in my friends' social classes. While my parents make the effort to come to campus and take my friends out for dinner, some of my friends' parents come to Ann Arbor and make no indication of wanting to take us out to dinner. I recognize this is another aspect of social class boundaries; I have the expectation while they may not have the means.

We all make choices about what to spend our time and money on. I have friends who constantly complain about not being able to do things due to financial restraint, yet choose to travel internationally and not have jobs. I have friends who choose to participate in group activities and do so because they work two jobs. I notice these differences in summer plans as well. I have friends who take courses, friends who work for money, and friends who don't know what they are doing. The balance between income and interest is something I struggle with when it comes to my summer plans. The number of states and countries I travel to will increase during the summer of 2017. I will be taking an unpaid internship in Poland and traveling to Israel, Greece, Italy, France, Belgium, the Netherlands, Germany, and the Czech Republic, followed by a family trip to Hawaii. I opted to be unpaid this summer, while still spending significant amounts of money on travel. This opportunity is one that is not normal and an option that most people could not even consider.

What I have considered to be normal has changed over the course of this sociology class, but, like I said, I like numbers and there's one that has stuck with me. That number is four. On the second day of class, our professor told us the number of students in our social class category. My family was in the upper class and out of 39 there were 4 in the same boat as me. I remember looking around the room trying to find the other three, but as the course went on I realized it's hard to place people into a defined class by an arbitrary number or their appearances. I learned it's less important what social class each person is in, rather what's important is each person's story.

A Case for
Cross-Class Dialogue
Andrea Tillotson

I step out of a well-kept car. I don't even need to hand my keys to a valet; the chauffeur will park the car I didn't pay for. I am welcomed into the arms of a community I never earned or chose, but that I belong to. I shift my dress—a dress I didn't pay for, but that I *did* go to four separate dress stores to find. I must have tried on no less than 20 dresses, of which the combined prices could pay for a thrifty U.S. family of four's weekly grocery budget 70 times over.[1]

I walk inside, and I admire not the meaning of this event, but the price of it. *How much did they pay for all of this?* At the wedding ceremony, I can barely see through the seven professional photographers and videographers buzzing about, trying to capture every angle for posterity (later, the too-perfect video seemed more like a movie than a memory).

The party afterward is by far the most elaborate part. Everyone is dressed in floor-length, gala-style attire, tailored down to the centimeter with shiny cuff links for the men and dazzling jewelry for the women. My dress—beautiful, beaded, *and expensive*, plucked for its perfection among 19 others—was also tailored just for me. When I went in for the private fitting, I was served hand and foot. Three women helped me take my dress on and off. They offered me

---

1. United States Department of Agriculture, *Official USDA Food Plans: Cost of Food at Home at Four Levels, U.S. Average*, February 2017.

complimentary lattes and teas. They showered me with compliments. Everyone at the wedding dons a seamstress's work, forgetting the seamstress herself.

We're so vain.

My makeup and hair—and I wouldn't doubt most others'—were done professionally and to perfection so that I might focus on enjoyment, indulgence, and celebration instead of on maintaining my appearance throughout the evening. I am, however, careful to not let my stomach poke out because the food and my vanity are limitless, as are the alcohol and desserts.

We are gluttonous, but we revel in our gluttony. ("How many shots can you take?" "How much can you eat?" "How much can you spend?") We are at once proud and envious as we marvel at our own beauty while scrutinizing others who we are secretly afraid look better. We are charitable. Among all those in the room, much wealth has been redistributed through donations and charities, but in Antigua, Guatemala, the same city where we host this glorious celebration, there are many who have no home or live in poverty. I can't donate the self-worth my advantageous upbringing has granted me to those who society has stripped off their dignity. But this, of course, is not on my mind as I dance among and converse with my wealthy and affluent peers. I'm having too much fun to worry about that.

*   *   *

My social class background is more dynamic than just one label, as I believe everyone's social class background is. For the first several years of my life, my father was still in college, receiving his PhD in industrial pharmacy, and, though he was paid to attend, our lifestyle wasn't lavish by any means. We were solidly middle class; emphasis on *middle*. My parents could afford private Catholic elementary schooling, ballet, and tap lessons. We took occasional trips to the aquarium and zoo and afforded trips to Guatemala, which is where my mother is from, but we weren't frivolous.

A couple of years after my dad graduated, we moved to Guatemala where he began a pharmaceutical business with a friend from pharmacy school. Again, I attended private school, though this time at an Austrian Institute that taught in nearly all-German. Thank God this didn't last long (I was *really* bad at German), and we moved back to the United Sates. This time we moved to a small suburb outside of Grand Rapids, Michigan, with a great neighborhood and amazing public schooling. Dad got a job as a pharmaceutical scientist, and we settled into the higher echelons of the middle class.

Since then, we have quickly climbed as my father's rank in his company has risen (he is now the Pharmaceutical Technical Business Director for the Americas). He travels constantly, which has given my family and I the opportunity to go with him at times to France, Italy, California, the Netherlands, and New York. This past year, we moved to the wealthiest neighborhood in our small suburb where all the houses are situated on a beautiful lake and the Homeowner's Association makes sure every house is put together and neat on the exterior. In this part of my life, I am solidly upper-middle class, but class is about more than a family's income.

My mom's side of the family and my Guatemalan roots are imbedded in the owning class of Guatemala. My extended family is full of diplomats, ambassadors, former presidents, lawyers, and doctors. My grandfather was the Chief Justice of the Supreme Court of Guatemala for a time, and he owned and operated the family law firm: the most successful law firm in the country. When he passed, the law firm went to my uncle, and, when my uncle passes, the firm will stay in the family. We are what is considered "old money" in the young country of Guatemala.

Because of all these factors—my privileged upbringing and my endless connections through extended family members and family-friends—I know I have every opportunity I could ever want in my grasp. As a pre-law student, I have a guaranteed internship every year of college and beyond. If I wanted to switch to a pre-med path, it would be no problem! My other uncle owns a chain of diagnostic centers and knows plenty of doctors. If I had an interest in banking, business, or finance, another family member is a higher-up in one of Guatemala's top banks.

My entire family and our status serve as a personal safety net to anything I could ever want to do in my life. Whenever I screw up, I comfort myself with that. I can't imagine a life where a misstep could close the only open door I have because I have endless open doors.

* * *

Even though I'm in college, I still talk to mom almost every day. A typical conversation goes like this:

ME: Love you, bye.
MOM: Hey! I almost forgot. We got you a new car. What color do you want it in?
ME: (Is slightly shocked. Already has brand new 2016 Chevy Malibu in a shimmery, dark purple.) What did you get me?
MOM: A 2017 Malibu. They have it in blue, silver, white, black, dark gray...
ME: (Dislikes blue cars and silver and white are too in-your-face. Black is too basic. Dark gray is kind of cool.) No purple, though?
MOM: No purple
ME: (Disappointed, but dark gray isn't a bad second choice.) Dark gray sounds good.
MOM: Okay.

Now I own a dark gray 2017 Malibu.

* * *

My freshman year of high school, I dated a boy named Peter. As freshmen, our relationship—if it could even be called that—was obviously not serious in any way other than he fell in love with my family.

My family is stable. We eat dinner together every night, my parents are married, and we have plenty of unspoken rules and traditions that allow for smooth cohabitation (pizza every Friday, methods of solving disputes, hierarchy within our home). Peter's life was not like this. With his father, a constantly commuting truck driver, mostly absent from his life and his mother working regularly as a waitress and bartender to keep his family afloat, he was rather lonely. Because of this, Peter had plenty of free time and independence, but, though he attended the same excellent public high school I did, he never engaged with school beyond the eight hours he was mandated to go. It was hard for me to understand, considering the five after-school clubs and extracurriculars I participated in myself (piano, violin lessons, debate club, drama club, and tutoring students in Spanish).

At the time, I thought it was because he was insubordinate and rebellious, barely able to get through a day of school without a passive aggressive—or even forwardly aggressive—comment to a teacher, let alone a few extra hours of after-school activities. In retrospect, however, I believe he opted out of these opportunities because, by high school, the educational system had already failed him. He was very aware of the low chance he would ever succeed within it or benefit from any of the extracurricular activities so heavily dominated by his wealthy and affluent counterparts, of which I was one.

In my family, I think he saw hope. Before, I don't believe he had ever considered himself to be capable of anything more than the hand he was dealt. But, within our home, he was asked about how his day went and how he hoped his future would go. Over time, his answers about future plans began changing from truck driver to high school science teacher, a sparkle returning (or maybe appearing for the first time) to his eye. He loved chemistry.

What struck me most as I got to know him was the color and depth of his person. It seems obvious to me now, but, when surrounded by people with similar identities, you forget that other people are just as dynamic and complex. Peter loved movies, especially from the 1980s. His movement had character to it, and he was very honest, not shy at all about being vulnerable. His ability to joke with my parents showed a level of maturity most people wouldn't have noticed as they wrote him off as a misfit.

Even after we stopped dating, he visited our house every once in a while, looking more rundown with each visit. Eventually, I stopped seeing him around school, though I was never surprised to see him wandering our small town with a buddy and a cigarette. Early one summer, he stopped by, chatting with my parents and me on our porch, catching us up on his life. He had moved on to an alternative high school and was still struggling with classes. He had failed most of them, and he needed to make them up that summer if he had any chance of graduating on time. The classes would cost over a thousand dollars that his parents did not have.

Dad offered to pay the whole amount, and mom offered to drive him. "Thank you Mr. and Mrs. Tillotson. I'll think about it."

He never got back to them, and he never graduated. The last I heard, he had been to juvie (juvenile detention) and then jail multiple times on drug and other charges. I'm friends with him on Facebook, so I see him post about how he's gotten clean every few months and then about how he has relapsed. He thinks he will make it big in the music industry, and I hope that works out for him. But all I can think when I think about him is there is one less spectacular chemistry teacher in the world than there could have been if life had been fairer.

When I first read this part of my class story to a friend, she asked, "How did this impact *you*" because this is, after all, a story of my own class experiences. My answer is that it really didn't at the time. Peter was actually kind of a nuisance to me, someone who kept popping in and out of my life, always needing something and always disappointing me as I knew he could be something better. Now, however, I realize this:

> The first time Peter realized he had value was when some-one valued him. I have always known someone to value me and have thus always valued myself. Because my parents have always affirmed that I have endless opportunities and am capable of much, I am empowered to take up space in

a room, believe in myself, and will myself to succeed. This combined with the fact that my parents can pay for my success (more specifically, my education) has gotten me to where I am: a student at one of the most prestigious universities in the country. I have had advantages over Peter since the moment I was born. I have realized that some amount (likely a large amount) of my accomplishments stem from the fact that I was born higher on the socioeconomic—social class—hierarchy.

I often feel like I could have done more for him. Checked in on him, tutored him, and more than anything believed in his dreams. But, as he told me when I later asked him why he never took up my parents on their offer; "It would have been a waste of money. I couldn't have passed those classes." He didn't feel he was worth it, and he didn't believe in himself. Why would he? Everything in his life had worked against him, systemically. His parents had to work constantly to keep their family afloat, so he never got the attention he needed. In school, he was always singled out as a "problem child"; no one wanted to "deal" with him, so he was shuffled off to the principal's office. No one took the time to tell him they cared about him or believed in him, and, when someone finally did, he seemed to have already internalized what had been told to him, indirectly, for most of his life. I couldn't remedy that for him.

* * *

At the University of Michigan (UM) here in Ann Arbor, the majority of students come from a family with means: economic means, political means, social means, connections of all types. I am one of those students. I've never really wanted for anything. My parents weren't ones to spend money on everything I asked for, but, if I *really* wanted it, they would pay for it. I think my parents were unique in this way: they could have paid for absolutely everything I ever asked to do, but they never presented that as our circumstance. They made sure we were wise about which activities we chose to do. Nevertheless, we had economic means.

I take this for granted often. The way I spend money can be shortsighted, at best. I can't imagine a life where I couldn't afford to buy a latte or cover my friends' dinners every once in a while, and I do these things with frequency and little regard for where this privilege comes from. This describes a lot of Michigan students, in my opinion. With a steady flow of cash from our mothers and fathers who subsidize our lavish lives, why would we ever worry about a five-dollar espresso drink that will satisfy us for maybe five minutes? I forget other students don't have this luxury.

"Those drinks are so expensive." A classmate says to me, nodding at some drink I bought in the café.

"Yeah, I know. It's so annoying." I crinkle my nose when I say this, but I hardly mean it. I mean, sure, it'd be nice if I could have paid half the amount, but it didn't really bust my bank account to buy this drink. This is my first mistake: for me, it's not only barely annoying, but barely noticeable that this drink is so expensive. For others, not being able to afford luxuries like these may be socially detrimental. They can't go out on the frequent coffee dates I might. They bring a water bottle they reuse from home if they absolutely have to go out, but I'm sure it's embarrassing when they get asked why they're not getting something. They have to deal with: buying expensive tickets to events or functions, dinner with friends, missing out on these things or killing yourself working two jobs just to catch up with everyone else.

"Yeah... annoying." She says to me.

"It makes it so hard to budget for the week... they're just so good!" I'm still so oblivious.

"I'm actually really good at budgeting!" She brightens, and I know she must be proud of it.

"I wish I had that skill," I say, "It's actually embarrassing how bad I am at it."

"Yeah, I have to be careful with the $25 my parents give me every month."

My jaw drops. Only $25 a month? I receive twice that every week, and I barely skate by.

"Wow, I could never get by on just $25 a month . . ." is my immediate response, though I know the moment I say it how offensive it must have sounded.

My classmate and friend immediately stiffens, sitting up very straight, her face becoming both blank and cold. "Well, *my* parents can't afford to give me more than that."

I try to recover, mumbling something like, "Yeah, of course. That's very nice of them," but the damage is done. Now she knows I'm wealthier than she is, and I know that she is less privileged than I am.

Socioeconomic divide, in my opinion, is one of the hardest divides to live with in a friendship or relationship of any kind. Because it sits there, existing in every way we live our lives (what we do on vacation, if we even take a vacation, whether we go out once a month or every day, how we dress, how often we see our parents, how we perceive the world), but we have been indoctrinated to believe that it doesn't exist or at least wouldn't if it weren't for others' laziness. In college, this is particularly discomforting because we're all trying, especially the poor and working-class students who are often working while going to school and may have the added stress of being their family's only hope for upward mobility. So the laziness narrative is unraveled at the seams with nothing left to replace it but "that's just the way it is."

Is that really the best we can do?

* * *

As I mentioned before, most of my mother's side of the family lives in Guatemala. There, social class and the nuanced ways it is present in people's lives operate differently, but, in one way, it is much the same: eating. One does not use the salad fork or—*God forbid!*—a dessert fork for the entrée. The bread plate is on one's left. One's water glass is closer to the center than the wine glass. One should always offer to others the last of the bread before taking it for herself. The head of the table is reserved for the host or hostess and the seat to his or her right is for the most important guest. This list goes on and on. I really wish that I could fill the part of my mind dedicated to these rules with information I should have memorized for my economics class, but thus is life.

In any case, the summer before my junior year of high school, I invited my best friend at the time, Allie, to join me in Guatemala for a month. We had a great time, mostly traveling around the country to different tourist spots, but, for a week or so, we found ourselves in Guatemala City.

Every Sunday, my extended family gets together for a fancy brunch, forgetting about any family drama and reconnecting after a week of work, school, and other typical things. When Allie and I walk into the restaurant, I introduce her to the family as we go around the table, greeting each other in the traditional way—a kiss on the cheek. One of my cousins is missing from brunch but his father, my uncle, is there, and he says to my friend; "I should set you up with my son!" Already, I'm mentally rolling my eyes (one of my least favorite things about Latin American culture is the idea that, if you're a girl older than 17, you have to have a boyfriend), but it isn't until later during brunch that I find myself truly floored.

Allie is turned toward me, her hand politely covering her mouth as she answers a question I had asked her while she had been chewing. Seated on her other side, my uncle's mouth turns down in distaste, and his forehead crinkles slightly. "You know, if you're going to meet my son, you better close your mouth when you eat," he says to my unsuspecting friend. She turns to him, her eyes a little wider, and says: "Sorry." My jaw is somewhere on the floor. *Such an unnecessary comment, such an unnecessary show of "superiority."* I've never understood the need to make other people feel bad when they don't follow the specific social code you learned when you grew up. Personally, I've been in inverted situations, where I'm eating pizza with friends and they mock my use of a knife and fork, which is how I was taught to eat pizza. It's not something specific to one social class. It's an interclass problem. It's a lack of understanding for social mores that fall outside one's own, probably because we never make an effort to seek out people different from ourselves.

* * *

At Michigan, students can get a pretty great discount on football tickets. For $200 total (or $25 a ticket), a student can go to all the football games for the season, and, if she can't make it to one of them, it's easy enough to sell the ticket for $25–150. I personally am not a huge fan of football, but I do like cheering like a fool for hours so I got season tickets.

A friend of mine, Nate, had his family coming one weekend to visit him, and he had found tickets for all but one of his sisters. The weekend happened to fall on one of the more popular games, so tickets were selling pretty high. I offered him my ticket—I had other plans that day—for $25: a steal for this particular game and only breaking even for me.

Later that day, he texted me: "How about $20? I know you get an allowance every week. Wouldn't want you to go hungry, though."

The comment came with a sting. It wasn't the first time Nate had made reference to my allowance. Earlier in the semester, we talked about our families and their relation to our college experiences in what I thought had been an open, reflective discussion, but I have regretted it ever since. He now calls me "rich girl" on occasion and teases me when I mention I am stressed or constantly busy. "At least you don't have to work...," he mutters.

He's right. I don't *have* to. But I do. I work two jobs.

I don't pretend the stress of juggling my schedule is equivalent to the stress he told me about in his part of our earlier discussion where he admitted he grew up under a tight budget and graduating with debt scares him. But I think we both could have been more understanding of one another. At the time, I probably could have been less frustrated and tried to understand where his seeming contempt of me stems from. And he could have afforded me the benefit of the doubt.

Ironically, though his treatment of me stemmed from a conversation with social class undertones; I don't believe that the way to reach a higher understanding of others is to end that. Rather, I believe the solution is to facilitate more cross-class dialogue. Without it, how would we ever find the compassion and understanding we should all treat each other with?

*　*　*

I have structured my essay in order of when I was least to most aware of the social class dynamics at play at the time of each story. In the first three stories (the party, the car, and Peter), I was basically oblivious to how different facets of social class were influencing my and others' lives at the time of their occurrence. I attribute this to the fact that, in these stories, social class wasn't having a direct, negative impact on me; the effect was either positive or on someone else. In the last three stories (my friend's allowance, the shaming of Allie, and my football ticket), social class was impacting me more noticeably and negatively. The impact was clear as the realities of my privilege in relation to my friends' became evident.

The adverse effects of social class rarely hit the middle and upper classes, but, when they do, it is often through these ugly realities. I think it is *extremely* important that the middle and upper classes face these moments more often and, with time, with more consciousness. In my experiences, poor and working-class individuals are much more attuned to issues of social class, likely because the most difficult effects of it hit them most directly. This is evident in the abundance of social class writings that come from this perspective. Middle and upper classes have much to learn from them.

I believe—I hope—that cross-class dialogue will send us on a path of greater understanding and awareness, which is the first step of changing any social ill. I am proud to be a part of a project that is dedicated to collecting the stories of *all* social classes, forcing us to confront the different roles we play in this system. I encourage you to do the same, even if it is just for yourself. I'll admit, it is liberating and terrifying. We have so much work to do. But we are all in the place to do something.

Part VI

MIXED CLASS

MUTT: MIXED CLASS AND UPWARDLY MOBILE
IVY AUGUSTINE

prelude

The quickest way to know someone's social class is to look at their shoes. Any upwardly mobile lower-class kid can tell you that. We're class chameleons, experts in the art of passing as upper-middle class or above. We know every last tell. We imitate the gentile dialect, we dance at the same frat parties, we go on spring break trips out west, but we don't have the money to back it up. We don't need it, we'll say. Sometimes we're better at playing rich than the rich are. At least, that's what we tell ourselves late at night when rent money and loan debt make it too hard to sleep.

My story is not unique—just another small-town kid deemed worthy to chase the American Dream by the fairies in the Office of Financial Aid. Before all of that though, before I even considered going the University of Michigan, I knew that social class changes how others see you; hell, it changed how I saw myself.

Fourth Grade: Class in Comparison

"Wow, three bathrooms?!" Jenny squeaked incredulously.

She, Shelby, and I are about 10 years old in 2006 and sit cross-legged on the cool linoleum floor of our small elementary school. Our little heads are bowed around a single piece of scratch paper I'm doodling on. We are talking about our homes, so I decide to sketch a quick floor plan of mine. Their cries of disbelief at my home's three bathrooms (comprised of one full bath, a smaller bathroom with a leaky standing shower off the master bedroom, and a half bath downstairs) fill me with a warm sense of pride that spreads into a smile. I couldn't articulate why at the time, but I can now: schadenfreude, the feeling of one's own place in life being better because of the misery of others in comparison. Didn't *everyone* have three bathrooms in their house?

Until then my family's home, a two-story affair tucked snugly just outside the city limits of Jackson, Michigan, in a picturesque suburb, just one white picket fence shy of the ideal American home, seemed completely normal. We were at the bottom of middle class; there was nothing flashy about us, but my dad's job as an insurance salesman enabled my mom to stay at home and paint artwork or murals for income. We didn't go on fancy vacations or anything, but we weren't hurting either. Judging by their dropped jaws and widened eyes, three bathrooms were some kind of fantasy. Both of them actually lived in the Vandercook Lake school district of Michigan and rode the bus to school past Burger King and the Cozy Manufactured Home Community (or more colloquially, Cozy trailer park) to get here. Shelby lived with her dad, and Jenny with her grandparents in squat, one-bathroom houses next to the bowling alley. The bell rang and we went to our classroom, the satisfied grin stuck fast on my face. Somehow their lack made me feel special. How good it felt, to be privy to something exclusive.

Wholesale Ravioli (2008)

The Great Recession tastes like undercooked cheese ravioli from Gordon Food Service, like Sloppy Joes hastily made after mom's waitressing shift at Daryl's Downtown restaurant, like soggy potato chips covered in crisp shredded cheddar cheese on the top of tuna casserole. After mom left dad in 2008, that was just about all my sister and I had to eat. I can't stand to eat any of it now.

I was 12 and didn't really understand a lot about economics when the effects of the 2008 Recession hit, but I remember the mounting arguments between my parents before mom departed in November. They were always about money. Dad didn't get the raise he said he would. Mom, like many lower-middle-class women looking to advance her status through displays of consumerism, had a shopping habit that was becoming more difficult to manage as dad's clients left town one by one. This, along with other issues, led to her announcing one Wednesday night that she was divorcing our dad, and we were moving out within the next three days, before he returned from his hunting trip. My sister and I dealt with this news differently: she chose to go back to school the next day, but I couldn't bear being seen this upset, so mom called me in sick to help with the move.

What defined the new apartment was a sense of lack. It lacked familiarity. It was cold and blue and small enough that my sister and I would have to share a room for the first time. It lacked material comforts I had taken for granted as essential or expected of a home in my middle-class suburban bubble: a washer and dryer in the house, a garage. We didn't have an Internet connection or Comcast cable for a few months. There was also only one bathroom that we would have to share. Instead of a sprawling backyard lush with grass, there was a gravel parking lot. Above all, it lacked security, both because there was a police shootout outside the liquor store across the street that kept my sister and me up one night, and because mom had an erratic work schedule as she juggled waitressing and working at the YMCA.

Between Homes

After a bitter battle ending in shared custody, I ping-ponged weekly between two worlds: the world of the (then falling, to become working class) middle class and the working poor. The house I returned to when I visited my dad was a bastardized version of the original. Each familiar floor creak reminded me of a time I could not return to, when I hadn't yet inherited money worries from them that left a learned twinge in my stomach with every purchase. He'd replaced all the furniture mom moved out with things gotten from St. Vincent De Paul's or from friends and neighbors. However, his house still maintained the security of middle-class life, even after the second mortgage. His work schedule remained relatively unchanged after the divorce. He'd leave for work at eight, come home for lunch at noon, and return home from work at three to cook dinner. The material comforts I lost in the move with mom were all here, but now I felt a sense of guilt for what I had when I looked at the meat freezer in the garage, or cupboards and refrigerator teeming with food.

Although my grandparent's had bought mom one of those squat houses in Vandercook Lake which we moved into permanently from the apartment, her home was much more unpredictable. Between working 10- to 14-hour days on weekends, she didn't have a lot of time or money to get groceries. She wasn't eligible for WIC (Women, Infants, and Children) or EBT (more commonly known as food stamps) either, on account of her four jobs and owning a car and the child support she got for my sister and me. She had taken on four different part-time jobs to support all of us in addition to child support. Food became an unspoken insecurity that only came about when she nagged me for "eating too much," or the years where I was claimed by dad on tax returns and didn't get free lunch at school. Those weeks I usually just scavenged a bag of chips or whatever I could find in the cupboard for lunch. My middle-class raising made me too proud to ask for food from friends most of the time. When I would fill out parental information forms at the beginning of the school year, arms sticking to the table in our school's unconditioned cafeteria, I always left her work phone number blank. I never knew it and chances were, it would change soon anyway. She was always moving from restaurant to restaurant, desperately trying to find a place with enough tips to justify gas money to get there. Around this time I started to take on the frustration she felt at constantly having to change jobs. Maybe she'd be doing alright but then something would happen—the car broke down, as it often did—and she'd be back to square one.

School Supplies

The band room in my high school was home to a variety of smells. There was first the stale, musty smell of the room itself that greeted you at the metal push-bar doors separating it from the long hallway. It was difficult to say exactly *where* the smell came from, but it was perhaps a mix of 50-year-old carpeting soaked with years upon years of the students' spit, and whatever mold was most certainly growing in the water-soaked ceiling tiles high above. No worries though, the custodians had installed strategically placed five-gallon buckets to catch the droplets that inevitably fell through the roof when the snow melted. Some even sprang for trash bags in the buckets. Then there was the smell of old metal and dust that came from the musical instrument closet, which was more of a mausoleum really. Almost all of the instruments there were broken. It's not like my school had the money to fix them, especially after splurging on rebinding the U.S. history textbooks that stopped at George H. W. Bush Sr.'s presidency in 1993. Of course the most pungent room was the marching band uniform closet. The uniforms were new, one alumnus had told me at the 2013 homecoming game, in 1975.

Concert Band Festival, a competition of sorts between schools where bands were graded by judges on their performance and sight reading abilities, would roll around early March every year. The high school portion was always held at Jackson High School, the largest in our town. Even though we went to Jackson High every year for Festival, the size and quality of the school astounded me each time. It looked like a massive gothic church on the outside, but on the inside it was state of the art: new lockers, massive cafeteria, air-conditioning, the whole deal. It was the first time any of us had seen a classroom equipped with a Smartboard and books that weren't falling to pieces. The band room was spotless, not a bucket in sight. When students would lead us from the warm-up room to the stage, we would all gawk at how different the quality of the school was when we were only a 10-minute bus ride apart.

Maybe that's why we never did well at the festival. How could we compare to the other schools that had double the band students and funds to replace bass drums that had holes in them that actually had a bassoon section because their instruments weren't broken? Maybe after sitting in front of the grand fireplace in the library for the sight reading section for four years in a row, getting the same score every year, we just gave up. I remember the bus ride home from the festival was always the same. We were all quiet, disappointed but unsurprised.

Awards Ceremony

Eighty-nine students sat sweating in their graduation gowns under the hot lights of the Vandercook Lake High School gym, comprising the entirety of the class of 2014. We weren't graduating from high school yet—that would be held at the local community college because we had no auditorium of our own—but rather we were herded into the gym for the awards ceremony where scholarships were announced and cords were received. The guidance counselors had asked us to submit our scholarship awards to be announced a week prior, but I never turned in the slip stating that I'd be getting a scholarship to the University of Michigan in Ann Arbor that amounted to $40,000 over four years. When I received a letter offering me the scholarship a week after confirming my decision to attend Michigan, I couldn't believe it was true. I worried so intensely about how I would pay for college; sure I was going to have to take on crushing federal loan debt. I was so excited that I immediately told my parents, teachers, and friends, but that excitement faded as the year drew closer to the award ceremony. Instead, I started feeling guilty about having gotten such a large scholarship, especially because some of my friends were still waiting to hear back from other colleges or hadn't gotten any word of financial aid. The amount of $40,000 was a lot of money and I started having doubts that I actually deserved it. Sure I was a good student, but I wasn't a valedictorian. I had only gotten a 27 on the ACT (American College Testing), when the University of Michigan average was somewhere around a 30 to a 33. Most of all, I was worried the other students would feel bad if they heard how much money I had been given. So I let the deadline pass without doing anything.

As I sat listening to all of the scholarships my classmates had received, I started wishing I had actually turned in the slip. Not to show anyone up, but because I realized a lot of them were just as fortunate as I was. As if reading my mind, when I was called up for High Honors in English, my favorite teacher, who wrote my letter of recommendation for my college application, announced that I was awarded $40,000 from Michigan. I received a standing ovation for it, and was aglow with pride in all my hard work to get there. It seemed people from the Vandercook Lake community were proud too, because people I didn't even know congratulated me after the ceremony.

However, not everyone was quite so happy. My friend Eric, class valedictorian hopeful to go to Michigan Tech for engineering, was so angry at me for getting a scholarship that he refused to speak to me for the rest of the day. He was $5,000 away from being able to afford to go to Michigan Tech, and in spite of his class standing, was awarded no scholarships or financial aid. The guilt washed over me anew. I wasn't the leader, I wasn't the best, and yet I had been chosen to get most of my tuition paid for at the University of Michigan. And I didn't deserve it.

CSP/AP/IB (Freshman Orientation)

In days leading up to Freshman Orientation I received my scores back for the required aptitude tests: all showed that I scored below average in every category, and recommended I take remedial courses so that I might barely compete with incoming classmates. The undeserving feeling that had been planted at the award ceremony in May bloomed into a fine self-doubt rooted deep into my self-esteem. That self-doubt took hold when mom dropped me off at orientation, and I noticed how cheap my clothes looked compared to all the other freshmen. I sat with a couple people from Troy, and they told me at least 30 people from their class were attending Michigan. Thirty people in my class hadn't even graduated high school. Most people had never heard of Jackson, so I was completely alone. They talked about the stress of taking AP courses, and how rigorous IB was. I never even heard of the Inter-Baccalaureate (IB) program, and Advanced Placement (AP) courses were not offered at my school. I couldn't relate. The loneliness grew after we took the chemistry test (on which I scored below average again), and I overheard two other freshmen discussing how easy it was, especially the questions about how air pressure affects chemical equations. My chemistry class had never even gotten to gas pressure. Looking at all the shiny Mac laptops around me, I had a sinking feeling I did not belong here, that there had been some mistake.

As I and my fellow fresh-faced incoming freshmen were filed into a darkened conference room in the office of the Comprehensive Studies Program (CSP), I felt the twinge of apprehension that had permeated my orientation sharpen into a stomach ache. A prior student of the program gave a presentation, explaining how we were not stupid because we were in CSP, but that *maybe* we needed access to smaller classes with longer class time and free tutoring. They explained that CSP was for students who were "hard-working and determined," a phrase ripped right off the CSP website. That was a red flag to my working-class sensibilities. If no one in an organization can tell you exactly what the objective of the program is without using buzzwords, chances are they can't be trusted; *especially* if they're a bunch of suits. Judging by how the other students were shifting uncomfortably in their seats during the presentation, they were feeling the same way.

Now I understand that "hard-working and determined" is basically code for working-class and first-generation students who didn't have the same quality of education other students enjoyed.

Let me be clear here, I'm certain CSP does great work for the students who use it. However, because the coordinators never openly talked about how social class affects the quality of primary education, I left the meeting feeling singled out and hostile. Though they said I wasn't in this because I was stupid, I felt like I was being told I was stupid. I felt taking CSP courses revealed the truth: that I didn't belong here, that I wasn't good enough to be a Michigan Wolverine. When I finally registered with my CSP advisor, the first and only time I ever saw her, I registered for no CSP courses. This was partly because almost all of them were full, or not what I needed. This was also because I was angry, and my "hard-working and determined" ass was about to prove I deserved to go here by enrolling in regular college classes with everyone else. I was going to earn every dollar of that scholarship.

Ladies of UofM: Buy, Sell, Trade

I was running a little late to our meeting, but I find the girl I'm buying a flannel shirt from seated in the lounge area of the Undergraduate Library (UGLi for short). She looks impeccable, her makeup perfectly complementing her shirt, which coordinate with her belt and shoes. We exchange pleasantries and she pulls out the rust-colored flannel button down shirt for me to try on.

Discovering the FaceBook group "Ladies of UofM: Buy, Sell, Trade" was key to me passing as upper-middle class on a budget. My richer classmates would sell their designer (or at least more desirable brand) clothing, shoes, and makeup at a discount that I could afford, inadvertently helping me to blend in. I bought shirts that would otherwise cost $15 for $5, $20 jeans for $8, and so on. By this time I hadn't shopped at a mall in years. The only thing I bought new were my Chuck Taylors from Kohl's, but new shoes were a necessity to my disguise.

I told her I wanted to buy the flannel and started to pay her through Venmo, a Smartphone app through which people can send money, when she said, "Oh, I'm just selling this because my friends have seen me wear it so many times. You know how it is." I nodded but didn't say anything. If I had said something it would have been: *No, I have no idea how it is. In fact getting rid of clothing simply because I've worn it often is something I can't even fathom. What a nice life you must live, where the worst thing that can happen is your friends noticing you wear things more than once.* But I wasn't about to make her check her privilege. She was selling me a nice thick flannel shirt for $5, after all.

Mrs Degree

"You know, I could've chosen to work at McDonald's for the rest of my life and not contribute anything to society, but instead I decided to become an engineer," says Brian, my then-boyfriend.

My mouth forms into a tight line. He'd just come back from work at his paid internship at a tech company in Palo Alto, California. He flew me out for a week to visit him in the plush apartment the company was paying for. What I had thought would be a relaxing week away from my groundskeeping job I had back in Ann Arbor over the summer to pay rent became an incredibly isolating one. Brian hadn't planned for me to do anything during the week while he was working, and had just expected me to fulfill some sort of domestic role. At least in regard to cooking him dinner in time for when he got back; seeing as he didn't know how to cook, his parents or service was always there to do it for him. The apartment had its own maid service, which I discovered on Sunday when I returned from the pool after finishing the only book I brought. I stumbled upon three Latina women cleaning different parts of the apartment. It filled me with a sense of my personal space being invaded, then shame when I discovered later that one of the maids had put my clothes strewn about the floor neatly back into my suitcase. I should have done that for myself so they didn't see how much of a slob I was. Perhaps the worst feeling was the one I felt more and more recently, which was alienation from people in the working class as I became more integrated into a middle-class college life.

I knew that when the maids saw me, they saw a blond white woman back from the pool, lounging around and feeling sorry for herself while they had to work. I was becoming one of *them*, the upper-middle class that had been a source of disdain for me. I quickly shut the door and ran out to the pool again, hoping that when I returned again they wouldn't be there.

At the same time I never could be one of them, which became more obvious as I tried to conform to college life. When I first met Brian's father and told him I was from Jackson, he snorted and said: "Oh, you're from *West* Michigan," and proceeded to ask me what kind of money I expected to make with a bachelor's in English. The higher I went, I discovered, the more divisions I saw: working class/upper class, uneducated/college educated, East Michigan/West Michigan. They were endless. What was most trying in dating Brian, truthfully, was that he was blind to all of it. He saw no class divisions, only money. Poor people were poor because they were lazy and chose not to educate themselves. We broke up after I visited him in California, and afterward he would admit he had considered breaking up with me before he graduated, so I could find another wealthy college-educated man to "take care of me" because I was poor. What shocked and saddened me more than anything about what he said was that there was no malice to it. He simply believed it.

I looked at him in the eye then, the frustration at his ignorance making me reckless, and said, "People don't *choose* to work at McDonald's, Brian. It's either work at McDonald's or fucking starve."

Homecoming

As a part of the working poor, mom's life involved a lot of trade-offs. When my sister and I lived with her, she had to sacrifice time spent with us to spend time working different jobs so that we had what we needed. Once both my sister and I were gone off to college, and she no longer received child support from dad, these sacrifices only intensified. Because she worked many part-time jobs, she was not eligible for government assistance with food. She was also uninsured, having made $300 too much in 2014 to qualify for Medicaid, and needing to make $1,000 more for the Affordable Health Care's premiums to be $600 cheaper. So she sacrificed income by working less over the summer to become eligible for Medicaid.

In the summer of 2015, I actually had to stop working university grounds a couple weeks into August and move back to mom's house. The lease on the apartment I had shared all freshman year with my sister and her roommate ended because they both graduated, and the lease on my new studio didn't start till September. Originally I wanted to move back to dad's, aware that I would be less of a financial burden to him than to mom for those three weeks. But in a phone call she casually mentioned how she hadn't been to the grocery store for a month or so, and had been living off of whatever was in the cupboards. Mostly popcorn, crackers, and coffee. She complained about being cold and jittery all the time. The doctor said she had an iron deficiency. I knew I had to stay with her, because I had food in the apartment I could give her, and for those three weeks I could take care of groceries with the money I had made.

Even though I promised to take care of food, she still bought me the things she remembered I liked to eat when I was a teenager: Chef Boyardee Ravioli, DiGiorno's Pizza, maple and brown sugar PopTarts. Even made tuna casserole one night. I couldn't eat it though, the processed foods made me sick after a diet of fresh fruits and vegetables in Ann Arbor.

(Re)Construction

Over the next summer I worked at the grounds at the UM Golf Course and biked home every day. I didn't have a car, so it was the only way to get quickly to and from work. Every day at 2:30 p.m. or so I would bike past the Dennison building on campus (now called Weiser), which is being renovated. Because I worked a manual labor job too, the construction workers would be getting off shift when I was. From my safety yellow shirt and khaki shorts covered in dirt and grease, they recognized me as a fellow outdoor worker. We would respectfully nod or give a curt wave to each other as we passed, acknowledging a shared sense of belonging in lines of work that wore tan lines on your skin and made you sweat.

Once the school year started back up in September 2016, I would walk past these same people dressed as a student, backpack slung over one shoulder, and they would do nothing. They regarded me with what I perceived as suspicion or vigilance as I walked past. No nod, no wave. It was as if they looked through me. I got the feeling that I was being seen as one of *them* again. Hell, maybe I was one of *them*, I only worked summer labor jobs and the rest of the year I spent unemployed, studying at a school for the elite. Who was I kidding? I was only playing at being working class.

And as they started to look through me, I found myself looking through them, too.

Literature, Science, and the Arts Scholarship Donor Dinner (2016)

How different it feels to go to a dinner where you know you'll be making a speech. I wipe my hands against my dress in nervous anticipation and join students and donors for cocktail hour. Although I am abuzz with the knowledge I will be addressing all of these people some time tonight, I feel relaxed. Finally, a place I can be authentic. Even though I'm all done up, I can finally talk with other kids who get what it's like to go from some small town to the University of Michigan. I talk with upperclassmen scholarship kids mostly, but we counsel the doe-eyed freshmen about classes and fitting in. This isn't my first Scholarship Donor Dinner, so I know the routine: find your name tag and table number, eat some hors d'oeuvres (which I now pronounce correctly) and chatter pleasantly, but not too much. If anyone didn't know any better, they'd swear we were born into this social circle. Of course, there are always small tells. A girl uses the wrong fork at dinner, for instance. A guy with rumpled slacks laughs too loudly at some joke, drawing attention from a nearby table. But that doesn't matter here. We're all mutts anyway, not quite belonging to any one social class.

As we sit down with our donors for dinner, I muse to myself bitterly about how much money must be in this ballroom. The gross domestic product of, say, Bosnia perhaps? Maybe more? But I catch my inherited scorn for the wealthy, and remind myself that all these people are here because they give working- and lower-class kids a chance. Instead I look at our waiters, the catering service of the Michigan League made up of students on work-study or otherwise working their way through college. I feel the guilt again that seems attached to this scholarship, but it relents into gratitude I am fortunate enough to have it at all. After a couple of courses and speeches from the faculty, punctuated by moments of decision as I linger over the array of silverware in front of me, the knot resting in my stomach tightens as it's my turn to give my speech.

I don't really remember giving the speech itself, but I do remember the reactions afterward. Most donors came and shook my hand, congratulating me and Andrew, the other student speaker whom I sat next to throughout dinner. We each thought the other's speech was better. What interested me most, however, were the few donors who came along and asked me questions about my comment regarding my hometown. I had described Jackson as a "bedroom community that lost its day job when the Recession hit." For these men, this was false. They liked Jackson, thought it was a fine town. I did not disagree with them, but I realized the Jackson they saw and the Jackson I saw were two different places. I realized that as much as these people had done to help out kids who otherwise might not be able to go to Michigan, they could never see, could never feel what it was like to grow up in a place of constant stress about money. Perhaps my class transience allowed me to realize we very much become the places we inhabit.

coda

The quickest way to know someone's class status is to look at their shoes. Any upwardly mobile lower-class kid can tell you that. But shoes aren't enough to tell you how that person got there or who that person is. You aren't really seeing them if you just look at their shoes.

My story is not unique, most certainly not here at the University of Michigan—but it's the listening that changes us. It's the listening that helps us see people for who they are.

A Journey to Stability: Through the Infallible Strength of Family

Sharae Franklin

It is March 7, 2016. There is still a biting chill in the air outside—one that courses through my body as I re-enter the hospital for the fifth and final time. I walk through the now familiar halls of Oakwood Hospital from the parking lot, trying not to fear what is coming. I go to the restroom to try and pull myself together so that I can be strong for my sister and dad; I look in the mirror, take a few deep breaths, and prepare to walk into the inevitable I have to face. I enter the room, and once again, I am welcomed by the steady beat of machines, the smell of antibacterial soap, and the *pish pish* of the respirator. My sister, brother, father, sister-in-law, brother-in-law, and I all take turns saying something to mom. Before long, it is time. They pull the plug, and the EKG monitor loses control. The heartbeat reading goes up and down for what feels like hours until it hits the steady pitch that means mom has officially left this world behind. But just as the machine beeps a rhythm of crescendo to its final decrescendo, I think about how this represents the ups and downs of mom's life, as well as our lives. We had seen victories and failures while navigating barriers built into a society of inequity: a society in which the poor remain impoverished and the rich are able to sustain their wealth. Yet despite an imbalance of access, the woman before me—who has now transitioned out of the Earth—always smiled.

An overwhelming silence overcrowds the room and a warmth fills my body as my mind tries to process the situation. As I stand there, family members, one by one, begin to gather into a circle, all with one hand outstretched toward the middle; then, we sing:

"I love you Lord, and I lift my voice. To worship you, oh my soul—rejoice. Take joy my King in what you hear; and let it be a sweet, sweet sound in your ear."

This is our anthem of praise reverberating air waves around us whenever we enter a family situation that is difficult and incomprehensible. That day, as I left the hospital, I watched the sun shine and the sky dance with grandeur of warm colors. I replayed the last few moments that had just passed, and my understanding of family and community was pristinely present in that moment.

Now, as I glance back at that moment and look deeper into my past, I truly realize how people around me play roles in my understanding of social class and its impact in my life. Growing up in Detroit, I was surrounded by the sound of Rhythm and Blues (R&B), people playing basketball in the streets, the sound of my grandfather's deep laugh, and the feeling of warmth from my father's and mother's hugs; these life remnants remind me of the strength I have found in my community. As I feel the teeter-totter of social class position—always on edge, not quite sure when the scale may turn toward an economic increase or decline—I am reminded of this strength.

While growing up, our house was filled with the laughter of young people and the cries of infant babies still not used to being away from their mothers. In the midst of this cacophony of sound, mom's face radiated with the love she felt for children who came to her in-home daycare: C.A.R.E. Around the Corner Daycare. This vision of providing affordable care for babies, toddlers, and latch-key for school-aged children emerged from needing to take care of my sister and I without the economic strain that comes from paying for daycare services. Dad's income from working as a biomedical technician at the Henry Ford Hospital in downtown Detroit added sufficient support to what mom was earning. We would have been considered lower-middle class based on my parents' incomes. My thoughts were not bombarded by fears of whether I would be able to get uniforms for extracurricular activities, or whether I would have transportation to get to practices, book club meetings, or my engineering program I attended every Saturday with dad. Money was not something I thought about since my priority was to go to school and learn. But soon, elements of our lifestyle changed.

In 2003, dad no longer had his job at the hospital. Instead, he decided to pursue full-time ministry alongside mom, as well as assist with the in-home daycare. Shortly after, we entered the working class. In time, I understood the meaning of FoodStamps,[1] Department of Human Services (DHS),[2] Bridgecard,[3] and government cheese.[4] My parents went through DHS in order to file for government assistance to purchase food and medical care. When they returned home after their DHS visits, their faces were streaked with silhouettes of exhaustion. They would talk about being at DHS for hours and going through piles of paperwork needing approval in order for us to purchase what should be considered a "human right." Food and good health are something everyone should have access to no matter their social standing. However, it is not easily accessible for many poor and working-class families. Oftentimes, dad would look very frustrated because it was never a guarantee after waiting in crowded waiting rooms of the DHS office that they would be hearing "yes" from their caseworker. How can there be so much red tape to give access to a man who helped support this system for 25 years? When the time came for the system to give back, it

1. FoodStamps—government assistance provided for people of low or no income to aid with purchasing food.
2. Department of Human Services (DHS)—provides child and family welfare services.
3. Bridgecard—a card the government provides for low- or no-income families to buy food.
4. Government cheese—big block of processed cheese that is given to people who receive welfare.

closed its hand, shut tight, unyielding and unwilling to relinquish support in return. Fortunately, my parents were finally approved, and we were given our first Bridgecard.

That night, the smell of T-bone steak, potatoes, and green beans permeated the air of our three-story home. We sat around the living room, laughing and sharing stories as a quiet thankfulness flowed from our hearts. I looked around the room, and an immense happiness filled me as I saw a weight lifted off of my family. I ate until I could hardly breathe, then I stretched across our black-and-white loveseat, content and happy. This was a meal of sacrifice, determination, and love because my parents had to endure several obstacles to gain a card that could enable us to purchase food. Although food was easier to pay for, other necessities—that required monthly bill payments —were not always easy to obtain.

When our family needed to discuss something important, my parents would call a meeting. This usually meant everyone would gather in the living room, but in one instance, my sister and I had not been called down. We sat at the top of the stairs listening. "Okay, so we asked to have a family meeting because we have been told that our lights may be shut off in a few days if we do not pay bills that we are behind on. We know that you all have been working hard at your jobs and are trying to save, but we need your help," dad said to my two older brothers and my sister-in-law. They looked around and decided they would help take on the responsibility. I sat closely to the pole of the banister feeling helpless. My eyes were opened to the idea of "social class," although I did not know the term for it.

With everyone chipping in, they pulled together money to pay the bill, but it was too late. On that cool, late Friday afternoon in the winter of 2004, a man from DTE Energy came and shut off our electricity. My parents would not be able to pay until Monday, so we had to make do. Dad purchased some firewood and placed it in our fireplace to make a warm, cozy fire. As we gathered around, we prayed, told stories, and shared in the comfort of one another's laughter and presence. I thought it was fun to be able to have a camping experience indoors, but I was not as attuned to the rules and regulations of handling late bills. I could not fathom how most organizations look at their companies from perspectives of numbers and dollars instead of human lives. Still, even without electricity, we had one another to lean on.

The next year, 2005, my sister and I decided we needed to figure out a way to help take on some of the family responsibility for bills and expenses. It was a hot summer day with the sound of children's laughter and the *tick tick tick tick* of our neighbor's sprinklers. The sound rode the waves of warm breezes, blowing through the air as we set up our table and poster listing an array of foods we would be selling. I was only eight years old at the time, but I was just as determined as my sister, who was 11, to do something that would alleviate some of the financial burdens our family was facing. School was starting soon, and both of us attended an elementary school requiring us to wear uniforms. This meant we needed to buy clothes for the new year.

Our plan was to purchase uniforms and give whatever was left over to our parents. I wanted to give back to them just as they had always given to us. I put on my biggest smile and walked the block of our street. "Excuse me, would you like to buy a hot dog, bag of chips, candy, or Kool-Aid popsicles? I and my sister are selling food in front of our house down there if you would like to buy something." My sister handled the money exchange and had great customer service. Our partnership attracted the attention of our closest neighbor and family friend. He told us he would buy whatever was left at the end of the day. I was elated: we had accomplished our goal. I finally felt like I was able to help in this struggle against a system I had yet to identify or be fully aware of. Despite the fact that the system had oftentimes failed us, our family came together to work toward the same goal. We had each other to fall back on, and for that, I have always been eternally grateful.

As I grew up, I watched how hard my parents worked to make sure we were fed and insured. Because they were pastors, they also had people who were under their leadership and whom they were constantly checking in on. Even when my parents did not have much, a portion of the little we did have was given to others out of the abundance of their hearts to make sure the people were supported. My parents would always tell us: "We cannot live our life in fear, always anxious about what is to come. We have to walk by faith and not by sight knowing that as we follow in the footsteps that the Lord has paved for us. He has promised that He will never leave us nor forsake us." These words of wisdom were a testament to what I had experienced. From these moments, I knew I had to push myself to do my best in school. I would need to get an education that would help me bring balance to this seesaw of life experiences our family had endured despite their unwavering faith. Never again did I want to feel helpless and unequipped to join in the fight. Education was my strategy to bring my family to a level of stability.

I attended public schools in Detroit for 11 years, and spent three years at a charter school in Redford, Michigan. As a senior in high school, I filled out the FAFSA (Free Application for Federal Student Aid) which would help me find out how much federal assistance I could get to help pay for college. "Mom, what's our family income?" I asked. "About $20,000," she said. I looked at the drop tab to search for the dollar amount. We were the last income range on the list. This is when I became more aware we were a part of the working class or working poor and that scholarships would be essential to help get through college with the least amount of debt. I had a goal. I would not add a financial burden to my parents now that it was just my older sister and I at home.

Before departing for the University of Michigan in the fall of 2014, I was already anticipating some expenses I would have and how I would pay for them. My siblings seemed to sense the lines of deep thought and worry that were sketched on my face. "Hey, now we all talked about it, and we think that before you take out any loans or worry about having too many jobs, we want to help you. We know that doing well is important to you, and we do not want you to be up there stressed out ok?" I looked into the faces surrounding me. I smiled, and we rounded into a group hug. *How did*

I end up so blessed? I stood in comfort and strength that surrounded me, and I knew I would be able to make it through. Their advice seemed very reasonable since I was burnt out from high school, and I would need time to transition from living away from home. But as I entered a new social environment where I was surrounded by people from every place within the spectrum of America's socioeconomic ladder, I oftentimes struggled to keep up.

During my freshman year, I did not work at a part-time job. I solely lived off money my parents and family could put into my bank so that I could buy snacks, toiletries, or extra materials for school. Because FAFSA did not calculate in-living expenses, there was usually a monetary contribution my family would have to make toward my school bill. The award summary the university provided shifted to make me still owe money no matter the amount of outside scholarships I received. My parents and older siblings all helped me to get a payment plan and would put money toward my bill each month, but as a first-year student, I was surrounded by the bustle and sound of new opportunities and experiences. I was enticed by the idea of entering new spaces and meeting new people, but that usually required money I may not have had or held tightly onto in case of emergencies or the unexpected.

There were always popular events that should be attended or the restaurant that just opened on State Street that everyone had to try. My friends group began to expand, and soon I understood the differences between social classes that can be all but subtle for one person and completely invisible to another. "Hey, do you want to go try that new restaurant, Tropical Smoothie? We should grab coffee at Starbucks or Expresso sometime and catch up! Oh, how about you just grab an Uber (a car service similar to that of a taxi) to get there." These were comments I often heard from friends I could not openly share the struggles that came with being a part of the working class. They had parents who could easily support them financially whether they were working or not. In this way, eating out, calling an Uber, or buying coffee seemed like something casual and spontaneous. When hearing these comments over the phone or seeing them through text, my heart sped up and an internal conflict arose. I frantically checked my bank account to consider if it was possible. "If I go, will I overdraft and have to ask mom and dad to put money in my account?" I was frustrated, and my heart was conflicted between realizing the difference in our class positions, their obliviousness to that difference, and my pride in not being able to let go of an opportunity to socialize despite the binds I put myself in. I questioned myself and tangoed with trying to find balance. "How could I ask for money to go to the new hotspots on campus when my family was already offering so much to help me even be able to stay enrolled in school? At the same time, a person only experiences undergrad once in their life." I wanted to live with no regrets: "but wouldn't it be selfish to ask for help from back home when they had to work hard to sustain themselves?" I have struggled throughout college with internal pulls that are energized by outside barriers continuously pushing me into a social class corner.

During my freshman and sophomore years, class differences became more and more apparent as I entered new circles of people, attended dialogues, and joined organizations. Spring breaks and holiday breaks were times when invisible veils of social divides became acutely visible.

I am sitting with a group of people at an event. Everyone is discussing their upcoming plans for spring break. "I am going to Cancun. I am going to Barcelona, and I will probably do some traveling to other places nearby. I am going on a cruise with my family." The question usually asked to lead into this is: "Where are you traveling for the break?" Although asked innocently, I realize being able to travel during a break seems like the norm for many people that sit throughout the room. I sit in silence just listening and starting to see how easy it is for some to travel to these places as if it is a universal expectation. They have not yet come to see this is a privilege that usually accompanies families from higher social class backgrounds and smaller family sizes. I have not even experienced my first plane ride until the age of 18, while those who sit around me have traveled with their families for a greater portion of their lives.

As I enter more of these spaces, and become more aware of my own changing identity and a young adult, I begin to figure out ways to obtain a financial balance.

*   *   *

Due to the financial strain my freshman year, I decided to work during my second year since I felt more acclimated to campus life. I obtained a job as a student leader in my learning community, the Michigan Community Scholars Program, as well as an intern position in the Office of Student Affairs, School of Education. Both jobs had flexible hours outside of mandatory meetings and events, and they allowed me to work with people passionate about education, social identities, and bringing people together from diverse backgrounds. The money I received from these positions allowed me to hang out with friends without being as anxious as I was my first year. It was easier to be more social and have money to go out. By my junior year, I had saved some money over the summer and felt more financially secure and less dependent on my family. I worked toward getting more scholarships and working a campus job to have a source of income. I also began to see the strength in suggesting free, fun activities. There was even more enjoyment in socializing when I was able to do it without the hesitancy of thinking about whether or not it was worth spending money. I was beginning to understand my social class in more ways and although many of my experiences were different from my peers, I began to not see them as something to be ashamed of. It may take me more steps and more time to reach the same goals others are striving for, but the most valuable lessons have been learned through that process. I experienced this when I looked for housing that could provide my own personal space so that I would not have to share a room.

Because I am a first-generation college student and all my older siblings lived at home when they commuted to the universities they attended, I did not have that many people around me directly who could give me advice about housing in relation to Michigan's campus. Once I started looking into options, I was reminded once again of my childhood, and the difficulties of trying to maintain a place that is comfortable and has all the necessities. As a junior, I wanted to finally have my own space within the dorms, so a single dorm room seemed like the best option. I had not realized this luxury was not for working-class students. The extra $2,000 for an additional small span of square feet, just to have personal space, was not something easily attainable for me. An extra fee hung heavy over my head, always in the back of my mind. I promised myself that the following year, I would have an apartment where I could have the space I needed in order to be at peace.

I began searching for such a place and started to understand what it truly meant to have economic privilege. For months, my future roommates and I searched for apartments on Central Campus, hopeful we could find something within our budget that was still of good quality and had a suitable location. As we went on tours and made phone calls to real estate agencies, it was always the same: they had requirements set in place that hindered us from being able to confidently fill out an application and sign a lease. There were application fees, 1.5 times the rent as a down payment, some amenities were not included, and sometimes the places would be highly priced and low quality. My peers with upper-middle-class parents were able to go through with these transactions while I sat meticulously calculating trying to figure out ways to make it work. I often heard: "You cannot find anything? There is plenty of affordable housing on Central." What they did not know was that yes, there were places that did not have expensive rent, but before even reaching that point, there were prohibitive costs. Unlike many of the more privileged students, I did not have the option of asking my parents for that amount of money. This was something I needed to plan for a year in advance, yet I had not known the year before.

On the last day of trying to view places, I was sitting with my two roommates in the back of the realtor's van riding to the last place. The guy was nice, told jokes, and was very honest about differences in apartments and what his previous tenants had said about their experiences. We arrived, and I felt like this could finally be it. We walked in, and the building seemed quiet. The walls of the hallway were an off-shade of pink providing a peaceful and calm feel. The apartment had two floors, a patio, and a nice sized living room that would be perfect for small house gatherings. The living room and bedrooms were floored with soft carpet that would make coming "home" restful and relaxing. We looked in rooms and checked out the furniture and appliances. We went upstairs, and I was welcomed by sunlight peeking through the window and door leading to a patio. As I walked out, I thought about days I could lounge on a chair, my face kissed by the sun, while reading or journaling. Aesthetically, the apartment seemed like a perfect fit, but as we began to talk about logistics of the place and how much it would cost us, reality began to sit in. "We can put you all on a payment plan, and you would not have to pay it all at once." To me, this simply meant another bill would loom over me. I was still trying to pay off my current semester charges, and I could not afford to add more expenses. That night, I was walking with a friend on East Liberty. As the cool night air made me slightly shiver, I sent the text declining the offer. As the evening breeze blew past my body, so did my hope of living on Central Campus.

I reluctantly let go of this expectation, but was reminded this location was not set up to adequately support students from the lower-middle class, working class, or working poor. The place we all could afford was an apartment on North Campus. Although it was further from where we were used to living, we would make it work. Central Campus supported those from economic privilege while isolating others to the geographical margins. I could not wholeheartedly call upon my family to help pay for the apartment. I would sacrifice a mere distance in location for a chance to stabilize my economic standing. I was tired of all the money I worked for and scholarships I applied for being continuously snatched away by bills that shifted unexpectedly. It was time to be in control, better understand this system, and figure out ways to navigate it. I no longer wanted to face the endless motions of the unknown, the fears of having to take out loans, or constantly thinking: "Will I be able to register for classes next semester?" But even in these moments of doubt and imbalance, I found peace within the storm. I saw my mother's smile, and I was reminded of her strength. I was reminded of my childhood days watching my family endure loss and lack, but also witnessing how much we gained and achieved when we worked together.

When I am most alone and feel like I am part of an environment that hinders some of my capabilities because of my identities and social class, I remember the family always standing next to me, ready to tackle obstacles that may come my way. Together, we will not only complete our journey to stability, but we will thrive. It takes a great deal of humility to realize that oftentimes our goals cannot be accomplished alone. There will be barriers and roadblocks making it seem difficult and unattainable, but with the help of others, especially family, those obstacles seem less intimidating.

A Transnational Dilemma:
A Mixed-Class Paradox
Anonymous

Eight thousand two hundred eighteen miles away in a remote village in Africa, the smiles of my neighbors and the rays of the everlasting sun tranquilize my thoughts. As I commute back to my temporary house, while the sun sets over the mountain, I submerge myself onto cascades of glimmering colors shining over the village. Every morning and night, my host family waits for me to start dinner. They share all they can and attempt to have conversations, despite the language barrier. I am calm and joyful, and for the first time ever, I have a sense of belonging. My cortisol levels are replaced with serotonin and euphoria. For the first time in a long time, I am actually happy. There are no levels of social class since it is an agrarian society, which means the economy is entirely based on producing and maintaining crops and farmland. In Malawi, Africa, the residents are happy and free.

The town of San Ignacio, Mexico, my hometown, is perfect for two things: vanity and imprinting deep colonial religious roots. Women are judged for their looks and dream of winning the title "Senorita Region De Los Altos," a prosperous beauty competition that ensures a husband and life full of lavish luxuries. Men assume the roles of the providers, since it is a traditional Catholic town. My mother, one of eight children, grew up in a house that made ends meet. Although she did not finish high school, she never had to work to help provide for the household. During her youth, she

MIXED CLASS | 479

decided to run for the everlasting beauty title due to pressure from her parents. My mother, now a pageant contestant, at the age of 18 competed to be the town beauty queen. This unofficial rite of passage in the 1970s led to the marriage of my parents.

I vividly remember growing up in a small town in the middle of Jalisco, Mexico. Known for its prosperous tequila production and brick manufacturing, San Ignacio Cerro Gordo was the place where I spent most of my childhood before coming to America. I never realized the privileges I had growing up in Mexico. I attended a private Catholic school because my mom was too ashamed to put her child in a public school. Completely oblivious of my social class position, I played, laughed, cried, and watched television with local kids. Although we were from the same neighborhood, my mother did not allow me to hang out with them for long periods of time. Instead, she would send me to my family's milk production farm, so that I could learn some tangible skills. Everything I did as a child had to have a meaning. After playing for no more than a few hours a week, I was sent to the cow factory to learn about manual labor. As a child from a prominent family in the bourgeois town of San Ignacio, fun was not an option.

In elementary school, my class went on a trip to the city of Guadalajara to visit a magical place that was a mix of a theme park, waterpark, and zoo! The cost was only around $80 and, of course, I had to go. For me, it was never a question of affordability; rather it was a question of asking permission and doing chores that held incentive value. It never crossed my mind whether or not other children had access to go on the field trip because I assumed everyone had a similar social class standing to my own. I was wrong. Even in my idyllic, homogenous town, there were families who could not afford to send their children on this magical trip. I assumed those who couldn't go simply did not want to go, and I honestly did not care. I was going to a theme park with some of my closest friends, and that was all that mattered.

When my family first obtained residency status to come to the United States I was in second grade in 2004. In order to obtain the status as a resident "the right way," as Donald Trump suggests, you need to have at least $10,000 to spend on a great lawyer who will help with your case. After four or five years and a pretty penny, residency status is usually given and you are free to come to the United States.

For my sisters and me, our future was set in the United States without question. As soon as I was born, my father hired the best lawyer in town. My parents envisioned a life for me that included going to the best schools America had to offer, at least for college. Without hesitation, we boarded the first plane to Detroit and bought the first house my father deemed appropriate for us in Detroit. In order to understand why my family chose to reside in Detroit, you need to take migration patterns into account. As I mentioned before, we are from a small town in Jalisco. It just so happens that about 40% of the immigrants from San Ignacio choose to reside in Detroit. A place where friends and relatives resided was perfect, regardless of the stereotypes. For others who are born in the city, Detroit is their only option. The luxury of choosing where to live is not something all Americans share, but we had that luxury and we chose Detroit despite its notorious reputation.

Being a Detroit resident made me see a lot of unpleasant things. I constantly saw homeless people roaming the streets, neighborhoods that were abandoned as a result of urban flight—when people who lived in Detroit moved to the suburbs—and entire complexes were filled with graffiti asserting negative connotations or gang-related phrases. At night, sirens turned into everyone's lullaby and the smell of a burning house reminded you of a warm summer night. Unlike the Malawians, Detroit residents knew of the riches, as well as inequality, in America. They knew they were in a powerless position and could do little to nothing to change this fact. They were constantly reminded of their failure. They repeatedly heard about a broken, bankrupt, impoverished city. This oppressive system was perpetuated and the citizens were in constant battles with themselves. Unable to reach their full potential, they ended up in a classless status, unable to buy basic necessities. As a child from a well-off family, I was completely oblivious to the economic struggles of others.

So, there I was, sitting on a carpet in my third grade classroom at Neinas Elementary School, reciting vowels and adjectives without knowing a single word of English. Back home I was doing long division. I practiced my vowel sounds and went around the room trying to learn nouns. Soon enough, I learned English. By the fifth grade in 2007, I was placed on the "Advanced Proficient" scale on the Michigan standardized test. My parents did not allow me to hang out with any of my peers. Since I went to a Detroit Public School, my mother assumed these "friendships" were of no use to me and she could not be bothered to set up playdates, take us to the movies, or go roller-skating. My only job was to go to school and obtain the best grades possible. Every time I would bring home a friend after school she would greet them, but was never very welcoming. She would always tell me, "We brought you to the United States, so that you can get the best education possible. We did not bring you to make friends or to go to the movies." I don't think my parents ever understood how a child should live.

When it was time to choose a high school we had two options: a private Catholic school and a Detroit Public School. After being adjusted to public school, I felt most comfortable there. Besides, I was always number one in my class and going to a private school again would be too challenging. Not only would I be judged for being a citizen of Detroit, but I would also be behind academically. Public schools obtain funding from property taxes, but due to the location of most Detroit schools, they receive very miniscule amounts of revenue because residents pay lower property taxes. My mother, with her primitive instincts, insisted I should attend the Catholic school, despite all of my public school friends. Going back to that system—a mere reminder of what I left behind—symbolized my hometown in Mexico. I fought, argued, and ended up staying in Detroit schools.

Entering Western International High School brought a few challenges. For starters, the food choices were extremely unhealthy.

We were fed processed, unfulfilling, prison-like food. As a result, I had to make my own food at home and bring it to school. Daily lunches consisted of a Chobani yogurt with granola, blueberries, and pecans. I also had bananas and sometimes baguettes with my favorite organic butter. The food I ate illustrated an idea of who everyone assumed I was, a spoiled daddy's boy.

During my high school years, I got a job as an assistant manager at Starbucks. I switched from buying at low-income stores, like H&M and Hollister, and switched to designer stores, like Nordstrom, Barneys, and Bloomingdales. This came with a price. Apart from friends in my classes, the general population bullied me and assumed the worst of me. They did not understand that I worked for everything I owned. For every 20 hours I worked, I was able to buy a scarf from Yves Saint Laurent. At work, I was the student who worked to support a lifestyle that was outside his own reach. In my mind, every new piece of clothing, every dollar spent on a new cuisine, and every weekend vacation to Toronto illustrated a new class I was so desperately trying to portray. I wanted to experience the feelings I had in Mexico. In America, I would attend college and work for what I have. In Mexico, I have access to family savings and revenue from the company. I was addicted to this culture of consumerism and I hated it. Unfortunately, I couldn't stop, for stopping meant realizing we live in a world full of inequalities. I assumed I was going to end up in the same position as my high school peers l, some of whom did not graduate from high school. I needed something to differentiate myself from my environment. Everything I ate, everything I bought, every single weekend retreat planned with my best friends reassured me that I was different. Living in Detroit came with a price. I've seen things that a child can never forget: a mother weeping at the sight of her child dying in front of her eyes, a teenager burning himself due to unforeseen mental illness right in front of my high school, and even a drive-by shooting of a high school party.

Throughout high school years in 2012 through 2016, I was able to go to New York and Africa, as well as take multiple college classes through my local community college. Although some might say these privileges resonate with that of my other private high school option, Western International provided various opportunities to those who showed any form of potential. My friends in the Advanced Placement (AP) classes always had first picks on schedules, never needed a bathroom pass, and were allowed to skip class and go out for lunch without any questions asked. Some even took trips to Spain and lavish spring break trips to Cancun, Mexico, during the school year and still graduated with honors. Western International was where social standards were of the most important.

The first impressions your teachers had of you foreshadowed grades that you received and opportunities given. If you were a nice kid, who used polite language and said good morning every day, you were more likely to pass than a kid who had "ghetto" tendencies. Students like myself and others are benefited from everything Detroit Public Schools had to offer. Similar to manifest destiny, we took and conquered any resource given to us because we felt like we earned the right to do so. Teachers and administrators told us we were the best and the brightest. As a consequence, other students were often neglected and shunned. In some sense, Western International was an example of society and capitalism. Like capitalism, those who show the greatest amount of potential and we were on top. Honors and AP students were in the core and the general population was on the margins. High school in Detroit is not a place of equal opportunity; rather high school is a direct reflection of social class inequality in the real world. We are born into a certain class standing, essentially unable to change our surroundings and the outcomes of our lives. We become products of our environments, and as a result, many students fail. The correlation between classism and success in high school is exemplified in Western International. Some students whom I knew had to quit in order to make ends meet, while others were allowed to skip school and go on luxurious vacations or hire tutors for the ACT (American College Testing).

My mother did not end up winning the beauty competition, but she did marry my father. After 10 years of living in America, he sold his portion of the milk factory in Mexico to my uncle. Figuring out my social class has always been a challenge. I live in one of the poorest cities in America and went to Detroit Public Schools, but I will also have inheritance when my parents pass away. Sitting in a drawer in our office back home, a document gives me rights to three properties. When I turn on the news, I am constantly bombarded by insidious news stories that Fox 2 News chooses to illustrate about Detroit. When my sister dropped out of high school recently, she was rewarded with an all-expense paid trip to Cancun because my parents claimed she was "depressed," while I was rewarded with a pat on the back after getting accepted to the University of Michigan.

Every now and then my family goes back to our home in San Ignacio. We pause our life and escape Michigan, the world surrounded by poverty and inequality. In San Ignacio, my family name has power, prestige, and liquid assets readily available to satisfy our deepest desires. My father returns to his role of an alcoholic who assumes that goods with monetary value equate to a fatherly role. My mother continues to be self-centered, focusing on her vanity as if it is her only child. As for myself, I continue my life, oblivious to my parents' demands, looking for something real, something complete. I continue to struggle with consumerism, but I now understand this struggle will never change anything. The Malawians have something right that we will never accomplish in America: happiness.

MOVING THROUGH CLASSES
JIANELLA MACALINO

When I was three years old, my parents took a big risk and moved our family from the Philippines to the United States. It was a move my parents had strived to make ever since they began working and had me; they had the same mind-set most immigrants have about moving to the States—sacrifice everything you have in your home country and move to the richest country in the world in order to give yourself and your family a better life. The American Dream was so enticing at the time my family and I packed our whole lives up and left the small island we had known for a shot at that dream.

As a child, I remember not feeling like any place was really home. The three years before I started kindergarten was a whirlwind of change and large life events. My mother got pregnant right before our move and our first year in the States involved living in California with my grandparents in their small, three-bedroom townhouse until my brother was born. We didn't have insurance; we didn't even have our own home yet. Luckily, my brother was the easiest of my mother's three pregnancies and with only the essential doctor visits and the support of my aunts and grandparents who had already lived in the States for a few years, my brother was born without complications. After six more months, we were preparing for another move. My father was on a work visa, and the company that had petitioned for him was located in Michigan. At the time, all of our family lived in either California or Kentucky, so moving to Michigan meant leaving the comfort and support of my grandparents and the majority of our extended family for a new, unfamiliar state. A family friend so generously allowed us to live in his home in West Bloomfield, Michigan, until we could afford our own place. The four of us lived in a single tiny bedroom for two years. West Bloomfield is a small, Metro-Detroit suburb with an upper-middle class population; my immigrant family lived on a working-class salary and I never overtly noticed the difference when I was younger until I looked back in retrospect.

I met my first best friend the first day of kindergarten and we were inseparable throughout elementary school. She was quick to invite me to her house for playdates almost every week, but I never invited her to mine, because my family didn't have a house, we had a bedroom we paid rent for. I didn't mind; her house had a pool and a game room and her family was always welcoming and kind, understanding the situation my family was in after our parents met. They always let me stay for dinner whenever my dad couldn't pick me up because he was working late hours, or offered to drive me to classmates' birthday parties if my dad was working and my family only had one car. Their kindness alleviated the stress that came with my family moving to a new state with no family around.

After about a year, we were able to move out of our family friend's home and into a two-bedroom apartment just around the corner. I began to realize the strong sense of community amongst immigrants when my parents allowed my mom's cousin and a family friend to rent out one of the two rooms in our apartment after also getting petitioned to move from the Philippines to Michigan on work visas. My parents' hospitality meant another two years of my family of four living in a single room.

After my father had been working at the same company for about four years, he began to move up and began receiving a larger salary; enough of a salary for us to move once again, this time to our own four-bedroom, two-story house. Although, there was a catch this time, the house we would be moving to was half an hour away in Pontiac, Michigan, a lower-class city in Metro-Detroit. The neighborhood was relatively new, and just on the border of Pontiac and Waterford, a majority white, middle-class town. The common conception of Pontiac is that it is made up of the working class and working poor and followed the same downward economic trends as Detroit. Long story short, it is far from the friendly, upper-middle class suburban dream of nearby West Bloomfield. It was a much larger change in economic environment than I had been aware of at the time; my family went from earning much less than our neighbors to eventually earning more in our new neighborhood.

Although I was moving to another school district, West Bloomfield's School of Choice program allowed me to continue going to school in West Bloomfield; much to my parents' relief since Pontiac is a widely known underfunded district. So, from then on, I lived in juxtaposition with my home life and school life. I went grocery shopping and to restaurants amongst lower-middle-class and working-class people, but my best friends from school and my peers were all a part of the upper-middle class.

Eventually, my brother was fortunate enough to attend the same school district through School of Choice as well and with both kids out of the house, my mother began her own job hunt. At the same time, my father left his job at the company he had moved to Michigan for to a job more closely associated with the field he wanted to work in. His new salary was enough to get us by; my parents were able to pay the mortgage, afford two cars, and put food on the table. But raising two children is expensive. My mother began working part-time as an office manager for a family friend and the extra money was extremely helpful.

Middle school rapidly approached, and I had gotten used to the 30-minute drive to and from school. My best friend from elementary school had chosen not to go to one of the public middle schools in the district, and instead, her parents enrolled her in a Christian private school. I remember begging my parents to let me go with her, not wanting to be separated from the girl I've been attached at the hip with since the moment we met. Obviously, my family did not have the means to give me a private education, so we went our separate ways, and I continued with public education.

Throughout the years, I've grown extremely appreciative of everything my parents have given me and my siblings. I was like any other young teenage girl. I wanted the latest trends my friends had, even though my parents were making significantly less money than my friends' parents. I refer to my mother as the "queen of sales"; we coincidentally lived 10 minutes from a huge outlet mall, and my mother knew how to shop smart. She'd know which stores would change their sales on which days, she became friends with the workers who would give her the in on when their stores were about to have big sales and she'd always buy winter clothes in summer and summer clothes in winter since they were always on sale then. She'd be able to buy a week's worth of outfits for under $50. So, when I'd go to the mall with friends and they'd talk about how a single $20 sweater was a good deal or how they had to have those $100 leggings, I never understood. My mother could buy me almost the exact replica of those clothes, for half the price. Trips to the mall with my friends became solely to spend time with them, since I refrained from buying things with them, when I could go with my mother and spend significantly less money. Yet, because my mother was so smart when it came to shopping, no one ever found out about my family's lower social class through my appearance. Once, in high school, a classmate found out that I lived in Pontiac, and said: "Oh, I didn't know that, but I know you're not poor because you dress nicely." With that statement, he proved that the negative connotations about those who live in Pontiac were strongly believed amongst the surrounding, richer suburbs. Granted, my family is nowhere near poor, but we did earn less than most of my classmates' families; my appearance throughout middle and high schools did a good job hiding that.

My mother ended up getting pregnant again in 2009, and it was as though my parents were starting over with raising children. When my sister was born, I was 13 and my brother was almost 9; my parents had long outgrown their "new parent" days, but they found themselves faced with the financial burden of raising three children instead of two. When my sister was about a year old, my father was fortunate enough to receive a job offer at another company. The increased salary sustained our new family of five, my mother was able to work part-time from home instead of full time in order to take care of their new child, and he was happier working there than he had been at other companies. From receiving a job offer around the same time as the birth of my sister, to receiving an even better one when I was diving head first into student loans a few years later, my father's hard work coincidentally paralleled large life events my family experienced that changed our family's financial stability. Every time our family faced a significant event, my father took an opportunity to change jobs with an increased salary; we were lucky that when we were faced with a situation that required more money, the chance for my father to make more money was there.

I often think about how different my childhood was compared to my younger sister's. My family was struggling with immigration, moves, and money throughout my early development. I lived through my family's upward mobility, but my sister will only see the tail end of it. We now live a very comfortable lifestyle in comparison to the lifestyle we lived when I was her age, and her experiences and outlook on life may differ from my own because of it.

High school came and soon enough I was turning 16 and getting my driver's license. The parking lot of my high school was filled with brand-new BMWs and Jeeps, nice cars my parents didn't even drive. Since my mother was working from home and taking care of my sister, she didn't have many places to go during the day so I was able to use dad's 2005 Toyota Corolla. He used the mini-van to drive my brother to middle school and then himself to work, and in the afternoon, I took my brother and home after school.

For any teenager, having a license is a rite of passage and having a car brings about a newfound freedom. Once my friends and I all had our licenses, it was nonstop trips to the mall, to the movies, to dinner, to away football games, anywhere. All these trips also meant I was spending a large amount of money I wasn't spending when I was younger, not only to buy clothes, food, and tickets, but also a large chunk went to gas. Living 30 minutes away from friends and my school meant I spent a large majority of my life driving back and forth between home and the rest of my life in West Bloomfield.

Some days during my senior year I would drive to school, go home early, drive back at the end of my brother's school day, drive him home, then drive back to West Bloomfield to hang out with friends, just to drive back home later that night. I would spend upward of three hours in the car on a daily basis. Every time I asked my parents about plans I had, the one question would always be asked: "Do you have enough gas?" I wasn't working and my parents gave me an allowance every two weeks when my dad received his paycheck. All that money I used to have a social life in high school, to drive to my friends (since they weren't going to go to Pontiac—it's too dangerous at night), to eat with them, and shop with them. My friends never had to think about the amount of money they were spending or pick and choose between certain costly activities, while I had to and I didn't want to miss out on those times with them so I never really saved my allowance; I used it to keep up with my friends.

Senior year brought about a whole new chapter of my life—college. Growing up in my school district, there were no discussions about whether or not to go to college—everyone went to college. Even more, an extremely large chunk of the graduating class each year goes to Michigan State University or the University of Michigan, Ann Arbor, the two most prestigious schools in the state, and also the most expensive. I applied to and was accepted at four schools: Wayne State University in Detroit, Central Michigan University, Michigan State University, and the University of Michigan (UM). Once I officially received admittance to all four, a series of many discussions with my parents about where I would be headed in the fall of 2015 started. I knew where my heart was truly set the second I was admitted: the University of Michigan. The catch was that it was also the most expensive school I applied to, and I hadn't received any scholarships from them. When I was accepted to UM I had already been admitted to both Wayne State and Central's Honors Colleges with almost full-tuition scholarships. Although there was really no debate in my eyes, it took time to convince my parents that a University of Michigan education and experience outweighs the financial support Wayne State and Central was offering. My mother's vote was Wayne State because, apart from the money, I would also be able to live at home and commute for classes. This was common for college-goers in the Philippines, but I wanted the full American college experience—cramped dorms, dining halls, spirited student life, the whole package, and I knew UM would give me that. Eventually, I convinced them, the prestige of a University of Michigan education and diploma to show for it was the most redeeming factor.

After finally committing to the university of my dreams, my family had to focus on the next step—paying for it. I filed for the FAFSA (Free Application for Federal Student Aid) and received a grant from the university as well as a few government loans, which I accepted, but it still was not enough. We ended up needing a private loan that has paid for the part of my tuition and housing that the university didn't cover for the past two years in college. I knew they were worried, I was too; the negative feedback in the media about student loans and getting into debt before even starting a career has haunted me since the second I was approved for the loans. My father, who has always been one of my biggest supporters, assured me that he would support my schooling and continue working for as long as he needed to if I still needed assistance in paying these loans. After all, they did move to America in order for my siblings and me to live successful, prosperous lives. The conversation grew my appreciation for the sacrifices my parents have made for me.

As I prepared for the new chapter of my life, I got my first job the summer before my freshman year as a host at a restaurant in Ann Arbor. I got my first taste of the city I was going to live in for the next four years and I fell in love even more. But once I started classes, the restaurant proved to be a stark contrast compared to actual campus life. From the perspective of the customer service workers I got to know, UM was filled with snotty smart rich kids who could afford $14 ramen and $15 sushi rolls the restaurant offered. Except for me, of course, I was different they would say, but was I really? I had grown up in demographics so eerily similar to the university, and had fallen comfortable into that lifestyle. Yet, I still knew where they were coming from having experienced my family's own financial struggles living in a working-class city.

Starting my college life was an easy transition, I was rooming with one of my best friends from high school and my other best friend was a short bus ride away. I knew at least 50 people from my high school's graduating class alone and I was only an hour away from my family. My roommate and I did what our orientation advisors told us; we kept our door open to meet as many people as possible. We quickly developed a group of friends from our hall and it didn't take long to be comfortable talking about anything and everything. Through getting to know each other, I realized that many came from much wealthier families, especially the ones out of state. It took a long time for me to even notice the difference in social class, but when one of my friends casually brought up her parents' house in Switzerland that she'd be spending spring break in or when another one turned to me at a football game and told me it was her 17th Michigan homecoming game because her parents flew their family in every year, social class differences were brought to the foreground. With such a large population of the university in the middle- and upper-middle class, I realized that I hadn't really met anyone who wasn't in the middle- to upper-class category, and I still haven't met anyone else after almost two years. Or at least I haven't gotten close enough to anyone where they opened up about their social class.

Freshmen year came and went and I applied for another loan for tuition and housing. I decided to spend my summer back at home and work at the local outlet mall. I was immersed in the culture of my working-class home environment more than ever before. One of my managers was always vocal about how she detested higher education and how it wasn't worth the money. And here I was already in thousands of dollars of debt after just one year of school. Another time that summer, a new coworker who had only overheard conversations about my housing situation in Ann Arbor assumed that I was heading back to Eastern Michigan University in the fall: a smaller, less prestigious college in Ypsilanti, about 15 minutes east of UM. Another coworker was quick to correct him before I even could because I was hesitant. It wasn't that I was ashamed of my school; I am so proud of getting into one of the top public universities in the nation. But I knew what people thought about students that go to UM through my other job, and I knew the area I was in was even more susceptible to believe those opinions and ideas of what Michigan students are like. I also knew that it was a reasonable assumption because there aren't many people from Pontiac who end up at the University of Michigan, as the under-funding of their public school districts guarantee that. I was fortu-nate enough to go to a school district that not only emphasized the importance of a college education, but also provided the resources to achieve that goal.

As my second year began, I was faced with the issue of having too much on my plate. I went back to working at the restaurant but classes I were taking proved to be much more difficult than anticipated and I quickly became overwhelmed. My parents and I decided it'd be best for me to leave work permanently to focus on my studies, but I was extremely hesitant. I had spent my first year away from home extremely independent when it came to spending money on everyday things. I was able to purchase at least half of my own books and I never had to ask them for money—I made enough to sustain my own lifestyle at that point. Unfortunately, I wasn't going into thousands of dollars in debt to value a part-time job over the education I so badly wanted. I resigned, focused on my school-ing, and my mother transferred money to my account whenever she'd see it dip low. I felt bad, but I worked hard in school for the chance to make it up to them some day.

At the end of my first semester of sophomore year, my father received exciting news. He was offered another job at a company of one of his colleagues, and they were offering him much more than he was currently earning. My father was absolutely in love with his job, with his company, and with his coworkers, so it was a very difficult decision. With myself in college planning on going to grad school, my brother in high school a year away from getting his driver's license, and my sister in elementary school wanting to do every extracurricular, my parents have learned long ago that raising three kids wouldn't be easy or cheap. So dad did what he felt was right and moved on to the next company. After about two weeks, we received another blessing in that his previous company realized his worth, and wanted him back. They made a counter-offer, and offered him the position he had wanted since his first day there. I remember hearing the relief in mom's voice when she explained the situation to me over the phone as I was walking to class. My father, at 45 years old, finally had his dream job, and the salary allowed my family of five to live and grow up comfortably.

I have always been aware of my family's financial struggles. I grew up hunting for sales, wearing hand-me-downs, and moving from place to place. I also knew how our family grew more comfortable paralleling my own growth. My brother's childhood experience is different, and my sister's is different than both of ours because of the hard work my parents dedicated their lives to in order for us to have a good life. My upward mobility has only inspired me to continue to move forward, to make sure my parents' sacrifices and work are not taken for granted. Some social scientists argue you are born into a social class and stay there, but my parents and I moved into one and my parents spent their time in America moving out of it. They left the comfort and home of the Philippines in order to give us a better life and they used America's tradition of working hard to achieve success in order to do so.

The Problem with Compartmentalizing

Sarah Volk

It's easy for me to place every event in my life into two categories. There is a before and there is an after: the line sometimes blurs. I had already been in college for a year when dad passed away, but for the most part I am easily able to characterize my pre-college life as life with dad—a time characterized by parents from two different classes who experienced downward mobility instead of upward. It would make sense for me to experience my most serious economic hardships after the death of a parent, but it's been exactly the opposite.

When mom's dad died in the winter of my freshman year of college, it was easy for my grandma to joke that he had always wanted to be buried on the side of Crown Hill Cemetery that's south of 38th Street, where prominent Indiana politicians, President Benjamin Harrison, and poet James Whitcomb Riley were laid. The north side of 38th Street was a less exclusive extension of the cemetery, where demand for plots was scarcer and there was less name recognition. My grandpa was laid to rest on the south side of Crown Hill, just as he and my grandma had always planned, and my grandma easily purchased her plot alongside him. At the head of the plots is a stately headstone, probably close to two feet tall. Large enough that you can easily see the last name from afar, but nothing that would make you look twice when compared to the neighboring obelisks and mausoleums. Overall, an appropriate tribute to my grandpa, a man who, after finishing his time in the navy, started a limestone drilling company that allowed him and my grandma to live an upper-middle-class lifestyle easily—the true American Dream. On important holidays, namely Memorial Day, we still go to my grandpa's favorite donut shop and lean a donut on his headstone.

A few yards back and to the right, you come across Eric Andrew Volk's headstone lying in the shade of a centuries-old oak tree, a tree that I posted a picture of on the first Father's Day after his death. The tree was bright green when I saw it the second time around—*too green*. *It was too green and too bright and too springy for the occasion*, I remember thinking to myself—pretty inconsiderate of the tree. The headstone below the tree is flat to the ground with just a full name and two years; noticeably simple. I can remember sitting in a conference room with mom and grandma picking out the size and the shade of granite for my dad's headstone. Thinking, *this shade of gray is really pretty, but we're already spending this much for the shape that's slanted, so we could go with this lighter gray and spend less*, and knowing on the inside that when my grandpa has passed six months before, my mom's mom was comfortably able to choose whatever shape and color she thought did my grandpa justice. Now my grandma was offering to assist in paying for her son-in-law's headstone, which was already so much less grandiose than her husband's.

Before dad's passing, there was always a subtle tension between what my parents and I did not have and what the rest of my mom's family did have. I can remember crying to my mom one day when I was in middle school because my cousins, the daughters of successful entrepreneurs, had drawers and drawers of bright colored papers and markers. They drew and painted anywhere and anytime; their house decorated with their work. I would come home with a feeling of disappointment. As an only child, my small ranch house was a block south of the friendlier, suburban neighborhoods. I was surrounded by retired people and bachelors, along with the occasional married couple looking for a starter home. My neighborhood was by no means unsafe, but it also did not have the vibrancy and community that I always thought I deserved, characterized by streets with sidewalks for biking with friends, and homes that used coasters on every surface because their furniture pieces were *investments*.

* * *

My freshman year of college at the University of Michigan, Ann Arbor, I came home to Indianapolis for winter break to spend time with my family. This was before my father's death, but after four months at a wealthy, out-of-state university, I was already feeling a little holier-than-thou. One day, I opened up my phone to see three classmates from high school posting from the same event. It appeared to be some sort of cotillion practice. I remember being confused—we all took cotillion in sixth grade from the same instructor who had taught my mom and many other parents years ago; why are they learning how to waltz now? These social media posts continued throughout the week, and my curiosity finally got the best of me. Texting one of the friends who had been posting, I asked him what he was up to. He replied he was at practice for the Dramatic Club, some organization his parents and grandparents were making him join. A quick Internet search revealed that the Dramatic Club was Indianapolis's version of a debutante coming out ceremony: the sons and daughters of Indianapolis's seemingly elite were presented to society.

To say I was jealous would be an understatement, although looking back I'm not quite sure of just *what* I was jealous of. Probably the status and the ability to post about something like Dramatic Club on my own Snapchat story, because in reality, I hate spending money and dressing up. I immediately confronted my mom about the group. She told me that Dramatic Club was for "old money Indy," or the wealthy families who had been established in Indianapolis generations ago, and that she remembers feeling exactly as I did when she was my age. *Old money Indy?* I thought to myself. Mom's side of the family, the side that was native to Indianapolis, had been here for decades. The entire family (aside from my parents and me) sat comfortably middle- to upper-middle class, just as my Dramatic Club friends. What was my family missing?

I struggled with Dramatic Club for most of winter break. To me, growing up and watching the two generations immediately above me, it appeared that my family *was* old money Indy. My mom grew up in a large brick house with enormous white pillars in front, and my grandparents were easily able to pay for all four kids' college education without taking loans. This idea of how my mom lived, compared to our current two-bedroom ranch house and the mountain of student loans I knew I had ahead, unsurprisingly set me up to think that my mom's side *was* Indianapolis royalty compared to what I personally had.

Grandma tells a great story about going to retrieve her wool coat at a black tie event, and not being able to find it amongst all of the furs. She and grandpa had the connections and were in the right circles which allowed them to attend such an event, yet there was still some sort of differentiation between them and others. At times I thought this family history—even the culture of my family that my cousins and I experience—meant that we were less than: that we clearly had less money than other people, despite our obvious privileges compared to the entire income spectrum. In reality, we did have this privilege. It just showed itself differently.

Wealth can manifest itself in a variety of ways: it can be the obvious, attention-grabbing amount of money that seemed (and still seems) so foreign, so out of reach to me. However, wealth can come in another form—a subtle, unspoken stability that slips past without being noticed. Living in a gated community, but you don't live on the closed-off street where former National Basketball Association (NBA) basketball players live. Encouraging your children to be financially independent, but having the ability to assist when tragedy strikes. Two households' financial assets can be exactly the same while appearing to be in two completely different social classes.

If I noticed anything growing up around my mom's side of the family, it was that financial security, although sometimes more under the radar than one's physical possessions can make you feel just as out of place. Whereas my parents would struggle to pay for any of my undergraduate education, my grandparents on my mom's side were able to create a savings account for each grand-child. I grew up watching my grandparents and my cousins live comfortably in the upper-middle class, and never felt like I related.

* * *

I've done a lot of talking about my mom's side of my family, likely because I grew up around them in Indianapolis and was constantly reminded of our differences. For a complete understanding of my social class background, however, you have to look at both my parents. My dad by no means grew up poor; I would call his side solidly middle class (although I'll admit I really am not sure to this day). My grandma was a high school English teacher and grandpa, who immigrated from Germany, was a manager of an engineering and manufacturing firm.

My dad's class background affected my class background to say the least. He was a fierce entrepreneur, who left a job in sales to go into financial advising, which he felt had more income potential. What followed was a series of not successes, but also by no means failures: financial advising, then helping my mom open a retail store that was closed after the recession in 2008, then back to financial advising, and then working as an independent Medicaid enrollment representative. My mom, reflecting on these times, tells me my dad likely felt guilt about doing better than his own father. He did not want to overshadow where he came from, and my mom says she believes he subconsciously held back so as to not pass the threshold where my grandparents lived. At times, my dad's various careers did not do enough to cover our family expenses, and he picked up second jobs. For a time, he was working night shifts at the FedEx shipping center at our airport. Other times, in between ventures, he would work as a substitute teacher at the school district one over from mine.

My first time coming to class consciousness that I can vividly remember was school picture day in fifth grade. My family was down to one car and my parents both had to get to work and take me to school. I sat in the back of our car as my mom drove my dad to the high school for his substitute teaching job. Then, we were off to my school, which was easily a half an hour away. I was swiftly dropped off at the front of the building, but my class wasn't in our room when I got there; students had already been taken to the room where pictures were being taken. I got there just in time, being handed a comb so that 10-year-old me could ensure her hair looked fine.

It was at that moment that I realized other people didn't have to be late to school because they were down to one car and both parents had to be at work. Granted, I was in one of those "gifted and talented" elementary school classes—so comparatively, my classmates were likely more privileged than most. But when you're 10 years old you don't exactly have great perspective on this sort of stuff; to me, I just knew I was somehow less than them. I didn't see kids coming to school by bus or by foot. You only are able to recognize what is right in front of you, and what was in front of me was my entire fifth grade class, who were all on time to school pictures because they seemingly had parents with plenty of cars to ensure punctuality.

My family was never in *trouble* financially. I can remember plenty of times when my dad would tell me to "just hang on until September," and then September would come and we would just have to wait until October, and so on. It wasn't that we were forgoing utilities or food, but we were forgoing things that, in my opinion, I was entitled to after seeing my cousins and mom's side easily purchase them: new school uniform shirts, new art supplies, new bikes. We were safe and we were generally comfortable, but growing up surrounded by family that was better off, I felt like no matter how much I had, I always had less.

*   *   *

My junior year of high school, everyone had a car. Very few got a Mercedes Benz for their 16th, but everyone had someone's old used Camry. Except for me.

Now of course, looking back, not everyone had a car. Tons of kids in my grade rode the bus, or carpooled, or walked. Some took the city bus. But I, a student in all Advanced Placement (AP) classes, only saw what was around me: dozens of kids who had gone to private schools before high school, who got cars for their 16th birthday.

I would fight *vehemently* with my parents over not having a car. On days my mom needed her car and I couldn't take it, I would be embarrassed to be dropped off. On days when my dad had to pick me up, I made him wait until the traffic rush was over right after school so I could just hop in and not be seen. I was embarrassed, and I cringe thinking about how bad I likely made them feel.

One time, the summer before senior year, the car my mom and I shared stalled out when I needed to get to an event with friends. I *panicked*; I cried. And I was so afraid of texting someone and asking them for a ride. Letting on to the fact that my parents weren't well-off enough to get me a used car was the end of the world to 17-year-old me. I had carefully led everyone to believe that the 1999 Chevy Trailblazer was mine, and that there was some ambiguously nicer car that belonged to my mom.

* * *

It's no secret that the University of Michigan comes with a steep price tag, especially for out-of-state students. Coming from Indiana, I did not find myself relating to others from out of state. In contrast to those who were able to afford the tuition, the only reason I was here was because the Office of Financial Aid had been incredibly generous. More than generous: I had to appeal to get more aid before I was able to consider coming here at all, as my parents would be paying for essentially none of my tuition.

Despite the university's generosity, I still had to make the decision to take on thousands in student loans. My parents made it clear that as I would be the one paying them back, I had to be the one to decide if I was going to take them on. We were in an incredibly unstable place, and after many serious talks, my dad concluded that he and mom likely would not be able to contribute anything to my college tuition. We had never discussed a financial plan to afford college before, but I was shocked and furious, that my parents seemingly hadn't bothered to put any money away for me. I cringe thinking about how I thought the world worked back then; why wouldn't my parents pay for most of my higher education? Why wouldn't they get me that Toyota Camry?

Despite the fact I would be taking on a mountain of debt, I was also an eager 18-year-old who *really* wanted to get out of Indiana. I chose the UM, and I chose to take on loans. I chose to go to an institution whose average student financially looks nothing like mine.

*   *   *

I came home after my first semester at Michigan feeling pretty great, to say the least. I lived in a dorm with a ton of new friends, I had just joined a social sorority, and we were constantly told we were the *Leaders and Best*. No one had it better than me, a freshman at an elite institution, right? I finally felt like I was living the life I was meant to live—the life as a financially stable WASP (white Anglo Saxon Protestant) that mom always wanted us to live. I felt like my environment finally matched my insides, the version of me I felt like I couldn't act on due to financial constraints; the version of me that fit in with all of my cousins and mom's side of the family.

I have found it incredibly easy to fake being upper-middle class at Michigan. My financial aid package has allowed me to live in a safe, nice apartment building, and the money covers things like books and room and board. I realize how lucky I am to be on the receiving end of this package—trust me. It allows me to feel more financially secure than I *ever* did growing up.

Faking class status is especially key for me, as I decided to join a social sorority freshman year. My mom was in one, and before her, my grandma. Mom and grandma were both in the same sorority, and they were *really* gunning for me to join one as well, as I was a "double legacy." I didn't join, and I'm sure somewhere, someone in the Indianapolis Dramatic Club scoffed at my choice. Despite choosing not to carry on the family legacy, I have found that social class is just as significant as I forge my own path. I'll *never* forget my freshman year, when my parents couldn't pay my sorority dues on time; once I got an e-mail threatening expulsion from the organization. Extremely sisterly of them, right? To be fair, I didn't exactly tell the treasurer I was struggling—it was my deepest secret. I now know that if I had, she would've worked with me. I was too ashamed to do so, however.

The precise moment I recognized that my upper-middle-class act wasn't going to last was during my sophomore year, when I was living in our sorority chapter house. One of our officers planned a Valentine's Day secret admirer activity where we were paired up with another girl to make valentines and give gifts to each other. I believe the guidelines said something along the lines: "You don't need to spend much. Just like $20." I remember thinking to myself: *Hmm. There go my meals this weekend.* I was being facetious (or just dramatic, take your pick), but I was still shocked some girls truly did not see an issue with requiring a multitude of people to spend $20 at the drop of a hat. Yes, I had the ability if necessary to spend that money, but did it take a chunk out of my personal finances? Absolutely. It certainly wasn't money to throw around.

The upper-middle-class act is one I'm still keeping up every day. When asked why I am not studying abroad during my undergraduate career, I say that I don't have time in my course load to take a semester off. In reality, the plane tickets, gourmet meals, and other overseas expenses immediately riddle me with anxiety. My Ann Arbor life is comfortable enough, so why fix something that isn't broken? I can't afford that chance.

Over my nearly three years at the University of Michigan, I've boiled down how to appear upper-middle class to one key possession: a winter coat. Or, at least, my freshman year self certainly used this as criteria. As I've come into social class consciousness, I have realized how much more complicated it is than what brand of parka you own. However, when I was a freshman, I easily figured out if I was to perceive someone as a *more than* (they weren't on financial aid, perhaps wouldn't have to repay loans after college, and perhaps came from a neighborhood with sidewalks) based on if they owned a Canada Goose winter coat—the long black kind with the fur on the hood.

I remember exactly where I was when I naively pulled the Nordstrom website up on my phone, because I was curious as to how much these coats cost. (Side note: Another side effect I've determined that comes from feeling *less than* is the constant curiosity about how much others' possessions cost.) It was November, and I was eagerly looking forward to Thanksgiving break because grandma had promised she would buy me a new parka. My old coat was by no means inadequate, but it had feathers falling out of seams that had been loosened and I had already identified having a good, long parka as an essential for a sorority member.

I was walking away from the Chemistry Building and toward the main bus stop on Central Campus, near the C.C. Little Building. I have no clue where I was coming from or where I was headed, but it was cold. It was gray and it was cold. The area I was passing through is completely concrete, and I'm sure it was overcast. Everything was gray, and I was cold, and I just wanted a nice new coat.

$900.

Nine hundred dollars was the price listed under "The Coat" on the Nordstrom website: I *immediately* texted mom with my shock, and she responded, equally shocked. I had never seen one of these coats before coming to the UM, and now they were everywhere, and they were $900. A lot of the importance I placed on *the Coat* had to do with my own increasing class consciousness, but *the Coat* was truly *everywhere*. Look up the YouTube video "March of the Canada Goose" and you'll get an idea of just how common this damn coat is; people make *videos* about its prevalence. The videos go *viral*.

I do not own a Canada Goose, and I do not think I will ever purchase a Canada Goose. I will always be envious of those who do own one, which is where my bitter tone is likely coming from. It's hard to put into words that I am not judging people with more money for spending this much, when in reality it's *their* money, and a coat is a ridiculously practical thing to spend money on. It's easy enough to say that I'm likely upwardly mobile due to the prestige of my undergraduate university, but I will still never own a Canada Goose during my undergraduate career. And when will I ever see this many parkas again? It will never matter to me as much as it mattered when I was 18 years old.

* * *

I think somewhere along the line, I learned how to keep this act up from mom. She and I talked a *lot* about what I would write in this essay. People would read it. People who maybe only knew my mom from my wealthier grandparents or from the Indianapolis Children's Museum Guild (a sort of philanthropic and social club she is a member of). When she lost her retail store to the 2008 recession and dad had to start picking up extra work, it was so secretive: any secret is to some degree perceived as something bad, because why else would we be keeping it a secret? My family was going through these big financial changes during my most formative years, so of course I took my own parents' behavior to heart. Money and social class status were so important that they would hide whole aspects of our lives from others to preserve some twisted image of stability.

I cannot even begin to describe how often I thought about money growing up and how it has affected my college experiences. I pick up on *everything*; guessing how much everything costs, and automatically putting people in boxes if I think they are wealthier than me or not.

These habits have remained even after dad's death. After he passed away, mom and I received a lot of help from grandma. I initially was ridden with guilt when this began, but came to terms with it when my grandma told me it's what my grandpa would have wanted: for us to not be burdened with the cost of living or paying for a funeral for that matter. This assistance, paired with generous UM financial aid, has allowed me to be better off than I could have ever fathomed growing up. But I still notice the money I'm spending regardless. My situation may change, but I would be shocked if my mentality surrounding social class ever does.

On the first day of Sociology 295, Professor Lang asked us to write down on an anonymous piece of scrap paper what our class backgrounds were. We had been handed a chart listing the various income levels and their corresponding classes (working poor, working, middle, upper-middle, etc.). I looked at this chart and realized I had no idea what class I came from. Income-wise, my parents probably made the equivalent of the working class or perhaps the lower end of middle class in our best moments. With dad gone, mom and I likely made enough combined to maybe reach the threshold between working poor and working class. However, did I feel like I grew up in the working class? Absolutely not. I was afforded outside resources, such as support from extended family, that allowed me to live in a social class that was really not my own. I felt and occasionally continue to feel like an imposter. But social class is not static. I will not likely remain in one social class and I do not even have to define myself as belonging to any one class.

There is a before and there is an after, but the lines blur, just as my social class fluctuates.

AFTERWORD: REFLECTIONS ON TEACHING SOCIAL CLASS

AUBREY SCHIAVONE

As a writing teacher and coeditor of this collection of student writing, my social class identity creates both connections and tensions with students. Like many of the students whose narratives appear in this anthology, I am a first-generation college student, and I come from a working-class family and home community. My earliest teaching experiences came attached to my work as a graduate student, first as a master's student and then at the University of Michigan (UM) as a doctoral student. My teaching positions paid my tuition and provided stipends to help pay my bills and the many expenses that graduate study entails. As such, during my time at Michigan, my social class identity was in flux, similar to many of the undergraduate students who describe their experiences in this anthology. The many resources for graduate students at UM helped me to inch upward toward lower-middle-class status. Now that I have left Michigan to start my new faculty position as a Teaching Assistant Professor at the University of Denver, I am decidedly middle class—still fluctuating somewhere between lower-middle and upper-middle class. My social class status is still in flux while I am working to pay down the mountains of student loan debt, both federal and private, that have enabled me to pursue and successfully complete my undergraduate and graduate education.

Not surprisingly, I often find it easy to relate to students who describe experiences similar to my own, students who talk and

write about places and people who are familiar to me: their working mothers and fathers; their extended family members who have
lived with them in their homes on and off over the years; the varied
and numerous workplaces they have populated as working teenagers; their high school teachers who have inspired them to pursue
college; and their aspirations to pursue careers that allow them to
serve their home communities. Often, these students are working
class; sometimes they are middle class. I learn from these students
and their stories readily and often, and have felt welcome and confident in sharing my own stories with them.

When I transitioned to my role as a writing instructor at UM,
these connections with my students were under siege. In this elite
institutional context with its more affluent student population,
I have found that students' reactions to assigned course readings,
contributions to class discussions, comments in office hours,
and written narratives—including many of those housed in this
anthology—often describe settings and experiences that are unfamiliar to me. These students describe vacationing or volunteering
abroad; pursuing expensive extracurricular experiences in elite
music programs and competitive team sports in and out of school;
and unpaid internships at prestigious companies where their
families have connections. These students often tell narratives in
which they recognize their own privileged familial, educational,
and extracurricular experiences. While in conversation with them
as they drafted their essays, I communicated my genuine interest
and empathy for all their experiences—especially those that differ from my own. They have helped to broaden my perspectives
on social class privilege in college and in the broader community.
While I remain interested and empathetic toward all student experiences, I have at times felt other-ed by advantages described in
these narratives and by privileges that students have described in
their writing and contributions to classroom discussions in the
writing courses I teach.

Faced with these moments of tension, I began reflecting—often
in conversation with other teachers like Dwight or with my fellow

UM graduate student instructors. I reflected on my experiences as a working-class graduate and undergraduate student, on the campus social climate, on my goals for teaching writing, and on my goals for teaching this population of mostly affluent students. I asked myself, are there working poor and working-class college students in my writing courses who, like me, feel invisible? Is my silence perpetuating their silence? How can I best serve this population of mostly privileged students while also recognizing the experiences of less affluent students? How can I honor the experiences of students from all social class backgrounds? How can I create conversations about social class between students with different class identities? Through these reflections, I balanced my trepidation about my own social class identity with concern for meeting all students' needs and respecting their experiences and narratives.

I encourage you to meet these student narratives with the same attitude of reflection. Ask questions of those narratives that seem different from your own as well as those that resonate with your own experiences. Leave room in your reflections on these essays to celebrate the great risk these undergraduate students have taken in writing about such a controversial issue as social class. Try to appreciate the grace and effort behind descriptions of their families, high schools, friends, and experiences before and during college.

It is our hope that as a reader of this anthology you will even be inspired to do a bit of writing or speaking out about your own social class experiences and identity. As Dwight highlights in the introductory section of this anthology, collections like these can assist colleges across the country to more effectively address social class disparities on campuses. Both in college and broader communities that we participate in, collective reflection and social action can change the unjust effects of social class stratification in America. We hope these students' reflections will inspire you to take similar reflective actions in your own lives.

Editors

Dwight Lang is Lecturer in the Department of Sociology at the University of Michigan, Ann Arbor and Professor Emeritus at Madonna University, of Livonia, Michigan. He is Faculty Advisor to *First Generation College Students@ Michigan,* an undergraduate group for University of Michigan students who are first in their families to attend college. His publications include: "The Social Construction of a Working Class Academic," in *This Fine Place So Far From Home: Voices of Academics from the Working Class*, C.L. Barney Dews and Carolyn Leste Law (eds), Temple University Press, 1995; "Those of Us from Rio Linda," in *Class Lives: Stories from Across Our Economic Divide*, Chuck Collins, et. al. (eds), Cornell University Press, 2014; "Singing the First-Generation Blues," *Diversity in Academe: The Chronicle of Higher*

Education, Volume LXI, Number 36, May 22, 2015, P. A18-A19; "Witnessing Social Class in the Academy," in *Working in Class: Recognizing How Social Class Shapes Our Academic Work*, Allison Hurst and Sandi Kawecka Nenga (eds), Rowman & Littlefield, 2016. Dwight likes to watch sunsets over Lake Michigan, read cartoons in *The New Yorker*, and drink coffee at Espresso Royale on State Street in Ann Arbor. Dwight wonders how social class inequality is a moral issue in early twenty-first-century America?

Aubrey Schiavone completed her Doctorate in the University of Michigan's Joint Program in English and Education in May 2017. In September of 2017, she joined the faculty at University of Denver as a Teaching Assistant Professor in the University Writing Program. She is a first-generation college student who comes from a working class background, but given her advanced higher education, now moves back and forth between lower-middle and upper-middle class status. Her research interests focus on first-generation college students' speaking and writing practices as well as writing instruction for all students in college. While at the University of Michigan, Aubrey conducted her dissertation research—a qualitative interview study with fifteen first-generation college students. Findings indicate

the many strengths first-gens bring with them to college and thus resist a typical deficit model approach to serving these students. She also co-authored the chapter "Pedagogy at the Crossroads: Intersections Between Instructor and Student Identities Across Institutional Contexts" in the edited collection *Class in the Composition Classroom: Pedagogy and the Working Class*. In addition to her publications and research, Aubrey taught several writing courses in the English Department Writing Program at University of Michigan including first-year writing, upper-level academic argumentation, and professional writing.

Contributors

Vianney Flores is a third-year student at the University of Michigan studying Sociology. She grew up on the south side of Chicago, Illinois. She identifies as a Mexican American woman and a first-generation college student. She hopes to one day make a positive multigenerational impact on urban education, specifically providing equal educational opportunities for students of color and low socioeconomic status. In her spare time, she enjoys teaching Zumba and making desserts. After taking The Experience of Social Class in College and the Community (Sociology 295), Vianney feels better equipped to discuss class and its role in education.

Eduardo Gutierrez is a second-year student at the University of Michigan, studying Computer Science. He grew up in Detroit, Michigan, and is currently active in his neighborhood. Eduardo hopes to someday find a career that mentors future scholars in his neighborhood. After taking The Experience of Social Class in College and the Community (Sociology 295), Eduardo asks: Why does social class have to be a component when dealing with college admissions?

Yadah Ramirez is a Mexican American, first-time creative nonfiction author who questions the intersectionality of race, class, and cultural values. She graduated from the University of Michigan in April 2017 with a BA in Behavioral, Cognition, and Neuroscience, Gender, and Health, Latina/o Studies, and Religion. Currently, she is living in her hometown of Holland, Michigan, where she cares for her parents. Yadah aspires to build a career in the biomedical research field and continues to involve herself in equal education initiatives.

Sean Dajour Smith graduated from the University of Michigan in December 2016. He majored in Sociology and minored in Community Action and Social Change. He enjoys taking walks, trying new tea and maintaining close relationships with his peers and childhood friends. After taking The Experience of Social Class in College and The Community (Sociology 295), Sean asks: Why aren't college outreach teams observing the intersection of race and class in their recruiting efforts?

Nathanael Boorsma majored in Psychology and has strong interests in educational studies and first-generation community college students. In the fall of 2015, he transferred to Michigan from Grand Rapids Community College, where he discovered passions for psychology, education, and mentoring other students. He is enthusiastic about studying the various strengths of community college students, how they might view education differently, and how institutions can help them grow and succeed. Nathanael is enrolled in a master's program in Higher Education at the University of Michigan. Following graduate school, he plans to return to a community college and serve students through a role in administration, counseling, or

program development. In his free time, Nate enjoys the outdoors, fitness, ATVs, cars, and hanging out with friends. Regardless of his career, he hopes to be involved in the development of a community college that effectively serves diverse communities while helping students understand and fulfill their dreams. After taking The Experience of Social Class in College and the Community (Sociology 295), Nate asks: How can colleges and universities increase the representation of working-class perspectives on their campuses?

Candyce Hill earned a bachelor's degree in History and Judaic Studies from the University of Michigan in 2012. After completing her undergraduate experience at Michigan, she was accepted to Teach for America and taught Pre-K in Tulsa, Oklahoma (2012–2014). Candyce returned to Ann Arbor following her teaching experience and worked as a career adviser in U of M's Career Center. She went on to complete a master's degree in Student Affairs Administration at Michigan State University (MSU) and now works as an academic advisor for students in the College of Engineering at MSU.

Ryann Oomen is in her third year at the University of Michigan, double majoring in Sociology and Philosophy, with a subplan in Law, Justice, and Social Change. She eventually plans to pursue a law degree. Ryann works on a Title IX research project where she codes data and participates in data collection. She graduated from a small, rural, northwest Michigan public high school where many of her peers are not pursuing four-year degrees. An important aspect to Ryann's identity is the fact she is the first in her family to attend college—a first-generation college student. Ryann serves on the First-Generation College Students@Michigan executive board as Communications Chair allowing her to pursue her passion for first-gen issues. In free time, she enjoys spending time with friends and family and playing with her dogs. She hopes to pursue opportunities that allow her to continue making her family proud, as well as being a role model for her little sister. After taking The Experience of Social Class in College and the Community (Sociology 295), Ryann asks: How can we combat the negative impacts of social class on children in lower income communities, such as lack of access to higher education?

Lauren Schandevel is a third-year student at the University of Michigan, studying Public Policy with a minor in Community Action and Social Change. She grew up in Warren, Michigan, and remains politically active there, currently serving on its cultural commission. Lauren hopes to someday find a career that combines her policy knowledge with community organizing to enact legislation that combats institutional inequities. In her spare time, she enjoys petting dogs and drinking coffee. After taking The Experience of Social Class in College and the Community, Lauren asks: Why don't we talk about class?

Zach Tingley is a junior at the University of Michigan and majors in Political Science with a minor in the Environment. He is from Stryker, Ohio. Zach hopes to work in a government-related career where he can combat social class inequalities through policy and social justice initiatives. He enjoys visiting new coffee shops, spending too much time in the campus library, and attending Michigan football games. Zach would like to thank Ashley Bishel at Michigan's Sweetland Center for Writing for helping him organize his essay ideas. After taking The Experience of Social Class in College and the Community (Sociology 295), Zach asks: What does the future of social class look like in America?

Ryan Vennard is a third-year student at the University of Michigan, studying Sociology and Political Science. He grew up in West Alex, Ohio, and currently lives in Richland, Michigan. Ryan plans to someday become a representative in the government, focusing on education and class inequality. In his spare time, he enjoys playing guitar and watching comedies. After taking The Experience of Social Class in College and the Community (Sociology 295), Ryan wants to know: Why don't we have equal education opportunities for all children?

Rebecca Wren graduated from the University of Michigan with a bachelor's degree in Sociology and a sub-plan in Law, Justice, and Social Change, with a minor in Applied Statistics. Her senior honors thesis on low-income, first-generation college students at the University of Michigan explores how they navigate a particularly elite public university. She is inspired by her own position as a working-class, first-generation college student and hopes to one day be first in her family to earn a PhD. She aspires to have an academic career, to become a professor of Sociology, and continue to do research on social class and higher education. She has a strong belief in the power of education, but recognizes there are many needed changes to make it accessible, inclusive, and equitable for all students. After taking The Experience of Social Class in College and the Community (Sociology 295), Rebecca asks: Is it truly possible to provide an elite education without being elitist?

Stefan Bergman graduated from the University of Michigan in April 2017 with a degree in Health and Fitness. This concluded four years as a student-athlete on the Men's Lacrosse team and spanned an era of personal and global transitions. Since graduating from LaSalle College High School in Philadelphia, Pennsylvania, in 2013, he experienced campus dorm renovations (West and South Quads), the

leap from a Brady Hoke football era to the Jim Harbaugh frenzy, and most recently, the transition from the Barack Obama era to a Donald Trump presidency. Throughout these transitions, Stefan utilized his studies in sociology to better understand how and why particular components of society are structured. This self-reflection is most inspired when he relates his passion for music, particularly rap and hip-hop, to his shared experiences with and observations of social class. His experiences would not have been possible without his family: Keith, Karen, and Chelsea Bergman. After taking The Experience of Social Class in College and the Community (Sociology 295), Stefan asks: How can we foster communities that promote self-inspired change that positively impact how we coexist with one another? Where do peace, love, and positivity rank among our priorities? Are our daily behaviors conducive to producing changes we desire in the world?

John Carvill is a second-year student at the University of Michigan and is undeclared at the School of Engineering. He grew up in Evansville, Indiana, Grayslake, Illinois, and Saline, Michigan, moving every five years or so. He hopes to gain insight into the way the world works in addition to actually deciding on a major and a rewarding career. In his spare time, John enjoys reading, and regrets being unable to do more of it in college. He would like to say thanks to Areeba Haider for her help in reviewing the essay, and helping it to gain perspective. After taking The Experience of Social Class in College and the Community (Sociology 295), John asks: What is the smallest tell of social class that you notice, day to day?

Chris Crowder is a senior at the University of Michigan. He is majoring in Communications with a minor in Writing. He loves to write and is a columnist and senior sports editor at the U of M's student newspaper—*The Michigan Daily*. In his free time, he likes to write books and play sports. After taking The Experience of Social Class in College and the Community (Sociology 295), Chris asks: How can we make the American Dream possible for everyone?

Charlotte Feldman is a third-year student at the University of Michigan. She is pursuing a Bachelor of the Arts with a concentration in Graphic Design and a minor in the Ross School of Business in Marketing and Sales. She grew up in Newton, Massachusetts. Charlotte wants to combine her graphic design work, her love for interacting with people, and her passion for cause marketing to become a graphic designer.

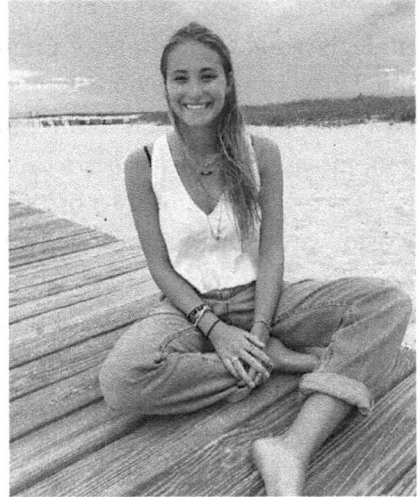

She loves to cook as well as travel. After taking The Experience of Social Class in College and the Community (Sociology 295), Charlotte asks: Is it easier to attain wealth when you have prestige or to attain prestige when you have wealth?

Benjamin Frey graduated from the University of Michigan in April 2016. He majored in Sociology and Spanish with a sub-concentration of Intergroup Relations. His senior honors thesis examined the beliefs, mentalities, and behaviors regarding sex and sexuality of heterosexual men in fraternities and cooperative living communities. Ben completed yoga instruction certification in June 2017, while engaging in other personal explorations of thought, lifestyles, and learning. Along with exercising, being outdoors, writing, and spending time with friends and family, Ben is seeking teaching positions or work opportunities in South America in order to solidify his knowledge of the Spanish language. This goal coincides with explorations of graduate school in Physical Therapy, Education, or Political Science. After taking The Experience of Social Class in College and the Community (Sociology 295), Ben asks: Will poverty ever truly be a thing of the past? How can interpersonal understanding and compassion play a part in reducing stratification that exists in our present socioeconomic framework?

Mya Haynes is a junior at the University of Michigan, majoring in Sociology with a sub-plan in Law, Justice, and Social Change. She grew up in Chicago, Illinois, but recently relocated to New Orleans, Louisiana. Mya is passionate about understanding the inequities impacting minority students, especially educational inequalities. She hopes to someday combine her interest in research and social change with a career academia. In her spare time, she enjoys reading, listening to music, and playing with her dog, Rocky. After taking The Experience of Social Class in College and the Community (Sociology 295), Mya asks: How does the intersectionality between race and social class impact students and their potential to be successful in today's society?

Michele Laarman is a Sociology major from Grand Rapids, Michigan. She works at the University of Michigan library and does alumni relations for the Inter-Cooperative Council. Michele likes cooking with friends, chasing after stray cats, and talking about co-ops. After taking The Experience of Social Class in College and the Community (Sociology 295), she asks why classism receives so little attention.

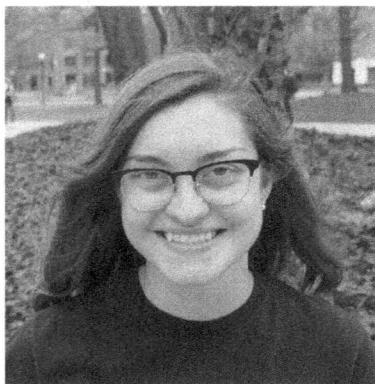

Brittany Lowell graduated from the University of Michigan in April 2017 with a major in Psychology and a minor in the LGBTQ+ concentration of the Women Studies Department. She grew up in Laingsburg, Michigan. Brittany plans to attend graduate school for Master of Social Work (MSW) and pursue a career combining her psychology knowledge with her MSW studies. She hopes to enact social class awareness and bring about reforms to social systems limited by class and money (e.g., foster care system). In her spare time, she enjoys reading and going for walks. After taking The Experience of Social Class in College and the Community (Sociology 295), Brittany asks: Why must social class inequalities limit us in almost every aspect of life?

Coline Michelucci was a French exchange student who studied at the University of Michigan during the 2016–2017 academic year. Her major area of study is political science. She grew up in Saint-Chamas, in the South of France. Coline hopes to find a career that combines international relations and traveling. In her spare time, she enjoys playing basketball and laying on the beach reading on sunny days. After taking The Experience of Social Class in College and the Community (Sociology 295) Coline asks: How are French and American perspectives on social class different?

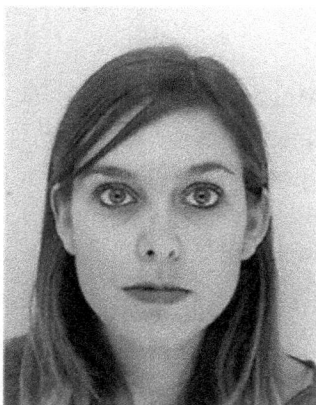

Candice Miller is a senior at the University of Michigan majoring in Neuroscience. She has been involved with the Michigan Community Scholars Program, the Gifts of Kindness Student Advisory Board, and the Comprehensive Studies Program as a mentor for incoming first-year students. Candice worked as a 2017 summer research assistant and hopes to take a gap year before applying to medical school. When Candice is not busy with school, she enjoys reading poetry and exploring different U.S. cities. She hopes her story in the anthology will reach students from mixed and lower class backgrounds—inspiring them to keep pushing forward despite hardships they may encounter. After taking The Experience of Social Class is College and the Community (Sociology 295), Candice asks: How can we better bridge the gap between people with different social class backgrounds in our hometowns? Should parents and teachers start teaching about social class earlier than college?

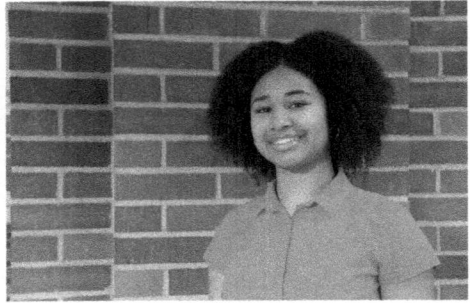

Megan Taylor graduated from the University of Michigan in April 2017 where she majored in Philosophy, Politics, and Economics with a minor in Gender, Race, and Nation. She works for the University of Michigan—Office of Academic Innovation. She is studying the integration of digital technology with college outreach and

preparatory programs to make these programs accessible for all students. Megan wrote her senior honors thesis on the relationship between rurality and higher education. Her research explored how rural environments shape student perceptions of higher education and student pathways to attaining college degrees. After taking The Experience of Social Class in College and the Community (Sociology 295), Megan asks: How can we reimagine education to serve all children equally and fight systematic poverty?

Kim Truong is a senior studying sociology at Michigan and has plans for a career in educational reform. She is currently exploring career options through educational and political non-profit summer internships and is enrolled in a semester long internship and research program in Washington, D.C. Outside of classes, she fills her schedule with music, student organizations, and policy writing groups. She served as the Treasurer of Michigan's First-Generation College Student group, the student group closest to her heart. Besides her academic and professional life, her ultimate goal is to adopt several dogs, cats, and rabbits to compensate for not having a childhood pet. After taking The Experience of Social Class in College and the Community (Sociology 295), Kim asks: Will humans ever be able to live in a world without poverty?

Caycee Turczyn is a third-year student at the University of Michigan, studying Business Administration with a concentration in Finance. She was adopted from South Korea and raised in Lapeer, Michigan. Caycee hopes to someday find a career that combines her two passions: people and learning. When she is not eating her way through Ann Arbor, she enjoys petting dogs and spending time with her large family. After taking The Experience of Social Class in College and the Community (Sociology 295), Caycee poses the question: Why don't we ever talk about class especially in the business world?

Raenell Williams is a senior at the University of Michigan majoring in secondary education with a primary focus on social studies. She is passionate about improving conditions of urban education and has volunteered in Detroit Public Schools since middle school years. Raenell mentors local high school students through Peace Neighborhood Center and is a volunteer for literacy through the Ginsberg Center at the University of Michigan. She also tutors

at the Ozone House, a residential shelter offering youth and family services to Washtenaw County residents. Raenell loves to highlight the intrinsic beauty of black culture and pride using mediums such as poetry, photography, and writing. She seeks to improve her community and have a positive impact on the world by making a mark that will never be erased. After taking The Experience of Social Class in College and the Community (Sociology 295), Raenell asks: What lessons will you teach in order to inspire, encourage, and impact following generations?

Robert Bakerian is senior majoring in Economics and has strong interests in the global economy and stock markets. After completing four years at Hunterdon Central Regional High School in New Jersey, he decided to take a postgraduate year at Phillips Academy in Andover, Massachusetts. It was at Andover where he continued his passion for hockey and unfortunately—due to injury—was forced to hang up his skates. Andover served as a transition to college which sparked his interest in the ways global economies are interconnected. Robert plans to work in the financial field after graduating or continue with his education to earn an MBA. Robert enjoys the outdoors, surfing, and lifting weights. He listens to music in his free time and some of his favorites are Led Zeppelin, The Doors, and The Grateful Dead. After taking The Experience of Social Class in College and the Community (Sociology 295), Robert asks: How can we improve social class inequality through ethical business practices?

Olivia Bloomhuff is a second-year student at the University of Michigan in Ann Arbor, studying Sociology with a sub-plan in Law, Justice, and Social Change. She grew up in Grosse Pointe Woods, Michigan. Olivia hopes to pursue a career in law and political activism combating social inequalities in America. Most of all, she wants to be happy and travel in years to come. In her spare time, Olivia enjoys reading, yoga, volunteering, and walking her dog. After taking The Experience of Social Class in College and the Community (Sociology 295), Olivia asks: What can you do every day to challenge the rigid system of socioeconomic class inequality?

Abigail Conway graduated from the University of Michigan in April 2017 studying Business Administration at the Ross School of Business. She grew up in Royal Oak, Michigan, and intends on moving back to the area to pursue a career in corporate finance. Abigail cares very deeply for her friends and family, and feels as though acknowledging social class differences has had a positive impact on each of her relationships. After taking The Experience of Social Class in College and the Community (Sociology 295), Abigail asks: How can I help others realize class?

Olivia Dworkin majored in psychology at Michigan and has future plans for a career in corporate litigation. She has decided to become a double Wolverine by pursuing her legal career at the one and only University of Michigan Law School. Go Blue! In furtherance of her love of the law, she has spent her undergraduate summers interning at local courthouses as well as Ann Arbor's Office of Public Defender. She also participated in various student organizations at Michigan, including the Mock Trial Team where she served as Team Captain and Assistant Vice President of Finance, and Central Student Government's Health and Safety Commission. When she is not studying, she enjoys spending time with friends and family, watching scary movies, and obsessing over her perfect dogs. After taking The Experience of Social Class in College and the Community (Sociology 295), Olivia asks: Will law school tuition ever be reduced?

Kate Grissim is a second-year student at the University of Michigan. She hopes to study business and recently applied to Michigan's Ross School of Business. She was born and raised in Western Springs, Illinois, a suburb of Chicago. In her spare time, she enjoys going down to the city, playing soccer, and relaxing with her friends and family. After taking The Experience of Social Class in College and the Community (Sociology 295), Kate asks: How can we begin to talk about social class?

Corinda Lubin-Katz majored in sociology at the University of Michigan, where she graduated in 2011 and then moved to New York. She continues to live in Brooklyn, and works at a nonprofit organization in Manhattan that partners with school districts and networks to design innovative, student-centered schools focused on helping all young people succeed. In her free time, Corinda plays in three basketball leagues, participates in a mentor program, and takes classes on sketch comedy writing, resulting in not a lot of free time. In whatever time remains, she enjoys reading, eating, discussing food, exploring, and spending time with friends and family. Ultimately, she wants to pursue a career path in comedy. Studying sociology has helped her become more aware of the many ways in which context and the intersection of identities shape people's life experiences. Since taking The Experience of Social Class in College and the Community (Sociology 295), Corinda wonders: How will social class evolve among our future generations?

Jasmine Morigney is a third-year student at the University of Michigan. She is studying Biopsychology, Cognition, and Neuroscience (BCN). Jasmine was raised in West Bloomfield, Michigan, where she still frequently visits family and friends. She hopes to one day channel her love of cognition and research into a career in the world of sports. In her spare time, she likes

to listen to music and watch movies. Since taking The Experience of Social Class in College and the Community (Sociology 295), Jasmine asks: Is modern day racism a result of classism?

Natsume Ono is a sophomore at the University of Michigan studying architecture in the Taubman College of Architecture and Urban Planning, with a minor in Urban Studies. She was born in Rockville, Maryland, and grew up in Ann Arbor, where she continues to attend college. She would like to incorporate ideas of social class in the future when designing buildings, shelters, and cities. Learning about social class helped her understand some of her first-year experiences through a sociological viewpoint. After taking The Experience of Social Class in College and the Community (Sociology 295), Natsume asks: What defines class?

Emily Siegel graduated in April 2017 with a double major in Sociology and Psychology. Throughout her three years at Michigan she worked as a prospective student tour guide, a research assistant in the Emotion and Self-Control Lab, and served as President for the Chabad Student Government. Currently enrolled in the University of Michigan's Master of Social Work degree program, Emily has plans to work with children and their families. After seeing firsthand the disparity of access to therapy for children with special needs—between her hometown and

a low-income area in Detroit—she hopes to work to find a way to bridge the gap. When Emily is not occupied with thoughts of how to end poverty and create world peace, she enjoys taking naps, watching Netflix, and googling images of puppies online. After taking The Experience of Social Class in College and the Community (Sociology 295), Emily asks: How can we get Americans from different backgrounds and identities to empathize with one another?

Elena Smith is a second-year student at the University of Michigan. She is interested in studying Public Policy with a minor in Spanish. She grew up in Tampa, Florida, but has also lived in California and Arizona due to her father's military service. Her career aspirations include working on international policies regarding human rights and human trafficking. After taking The Experience of Social Class in College and the Community (Sociology 295), Elena asks: How have we let this problem get so bad?

Astrid Swensen is a third-year student at the University of Michigan, studying Movement Science. She grew up in Beverly, Massachusetts, where she spent every sunny day at the beach by her house. She is a member of the University of Michigan Varsity Women's Swimming and Diving Team, competing in the butterfly and individual medley events. Astrid aspires to have a flourishing garden when she is older. After taking The Experience of Social Class in College and the Community (Sociology 295), Astrid asks: Why is talking about money so taboo?

Sachika Tomishima is a second-year student at the University of Michigan, with an intended International Studies major. She was raised in China, but occasionally visits Japan to meet her grandparents. She has worked to make Chinese subtitles for Japanese videos. She plays with cats and draws pictures in her leisure time. After taking The Experience of Social Class in College and the Community (Sociology 295), Sachika asks: Are race problems more important than social class issues?

Margaret Paul graduated from the University of Michigan in April 2017, majoring in Political Science. She is from Weston, Massachusetts. Margaret has three siblings, a golden retriever, and enjoys running and hiking. She lives in New York City and is starting a career in business. After taking The Experience of Social Class in College and the Community (Sociology 295), Margaret asks: Will our University ever reach a point where all students, no matter their social class, feel welcome and able to succeed both socially and academically?

Abigail Siegal is a junior at the University of Michigan, studying Economics with a minor in Computer Science. She grew up in Beverly Hills, Michigan, and remains involved in the Jewish community there. Abigail is a member of the University of Michigan Solar Car Team and is actively involved in Dance Marathon. She enjoys traveling and spending time with friends. After taking The Experience of Social Class in College and the Community (Sociology 295), Abigail asks: Why do we accept inequality in education?

Andrea Tillotson is a second-year student at the University of Michigan where she plans to study Philosophy, Politics, and Economics (PPE), with a minor in English. She grew up in Hudsonville, Michigan, during school years and Guatemala City, Guatemala, during summers. Andrea plans on attending law school after completing her undergraduate education and would like to study International Law with a focus on human rights law. She is an avid coffee drinker and Netflix watcher. After taking The Experience of Social Class in College and the Community (Sociology 295), Andrea wonders: What could we accomplish if we allowed ourselves to be uncomfortable—instead of complicit—with social class inequality?

Ivy Augustine will graduate from the University of Michigan in April 2018 majoring in English Language and Literature and German. She is from Jackson, Michigan, just forty minutes west of Ann Arbor. Ivy would like to further pursue graduate education and eventually become an English professor. When not doing classwork, Ivy is active in the nerdfighter community on Michigan's campus and puts on theatrical productions with her friends. After taking The Experience of Social Class in College and the Community (Sociology 295), Ivy suggests we engage with people different from us, and actively listen and empathize with them.

Sharae Franklin is a senior majoring in Elementary Education with a focus on Mathematics. She is interested in working abroad to gain a global perspective on approaches to teaching and learning, so as to better develop her practice in the United States. She seeks to create spaces for people on campus to engage in dialogic conversations and build community across differences using the arts as a form of self-expression. Through her classroom work and with community organizations, she encourages people to find their voices and passions. Sharae hopes to attend graduate school to study Educational Administration and Policy with a long-term goal of opening an elementary school that provides holistic approaches to teaching and equitable access for low-income communities. In her free time, Sharae enjoys trying diverse cuisines, traveling, ballroom dancing, singing, and watching television dramas in different languages. After taking The Experience of Social

Class in College and Community (Sociology 295), Sharae asks: Is it truly possible to effectively provide equitable access to education if our society is built on the perpetuation of poverty?

Jianella Macalino is a third-year student at the University of Michigan majoring in International Studies and Environment. She was born in Iloilo, Philippines, and immigrated to the United States with her parents at age three. Apart from school, she spends her time hanging out with friends and taking walks in Ann Arbor's Arboretum. The Experience of Social Class in College and the Community (Sociology 295) allowed her to perceive life experiences in a different, unexpected light. She asks: How do immigrants perceive and fit into America's social classes?

Sarah Volk is a senior majoring in Economics at the University of Michigan in Ann Arbor. Originally from Indianapolis, Indiana, she attributes all her success thus far to strong public education. Sarah hopes to pursue a career in education policy and work toward an equitable school system for students of all social classes and income levels. Additionally, she is interested in higher education and is involved with Michigan's Panhellenic Association and college Greek life. After taking The Experience of Social Class in College and the Community (Sociology 295), Sarah asks: How can we cultivate social change when inequality starts so early in life?

Appendix: Social Class Essay Guidelines

Dr. Dwight Lang

Sociological Creative Nonfiction Essay

This essay provides an opportunity to explore social forces shaping your life and changing identity, as they're located in America's social class structure. You'll reflect on selected aspects of your family, education (K–12) or community. You'll also write about important social class experiences here at Michigan. Keep in mind we're not simply products of our personal experiences. How we define ourselves and places in society we've been randomly born into are largely—but not totally—products of shifting social forces and conditions beyond our control. In this way we are socially constructed. You'll explore important social forces/conditions related to social class.

Think about selected aspects of your personal experiences and history. How, for example, have social class conditions and differences existing before you were born and persisting in the present—thus separate from you—shaped various aspects of your life? All people, whether in their twenties or seventies, are influenced by social class. Middle class 18- to 21-year-olds have just as much to reflect on as young adults born to poverty or the working class. We're often aware of these influences and sometimes we're not, so spend time thinking about the complexity of these relationships. Personal experiences and history are part of broader forces related to social class.

If you participate in the social class anthology, you'll be writing a history others will read later in the 21st century or at the University of Michigan's Tricentennial—2117. The title is: Social Class Voices: Student Stories from the University of Michigan Bicentennial. When people read your essay, what impressions will they take away from your words? What is your story speaking from the early 21st century?

Essay Structure

The essay should be 10–15 pages double-spaced. Try not to go over the 15-page mark. This is 2,500 words to 3,800 words.

One-half of your essay will consider selected social class experiences prior to attending the University of Michigan—in family (nuclear or extended), K–12 years, or the community where you grew up (5–7 pages). You can't write about everything from those first 17–18 years of life, so choose the most compelling experiences.

The other half of your essay (5–7 pages) will focus on key social class experiences you've had at the University of Michigan: for example, that first year, your roommates, events in classrooms/ dorms, visiting a professor's office, athletic events, studying in the library, or just in and around campus and Ann Arbor. Of course, there may be other memorable experiences. You're free to choose.

(1) One essay option is to devote the first half of your essay to pre-college life and the second half to college experiences. (2) Or you can move back and forth between the past and present as you tell your story. Again, you're free to choose.

Things to Consider as You Write

You'll be familiar with essay assignments in Sociology 295— especially in *Class Lives: Stories from across Our Economic Divide* by Chuck Collins et al. and *Where We Stand: Class Matters* by bell hooks. These essays are first-person narrative and in the general area of creative nonfiction. But they're also sociological in the sense they're acutely aware of wider social forces—beyond the individual's control—that have shaped personal experiences. In *Where We Stand*, hooks talks about social class, race, and gender influencing her life: in family (very patriarchal), community in Kentucky (sections of her hometown divided by class and race), during undergraduate years (freshman year at a woman's college where nearly all students are white and middle class/later at Stanford where virtually all African American students are middle/upper-middle class), and in post-college years working in academia. hooks says in her memoir *Black Bone* that creative nonfiction is an effort to "recover the past."

Notice how authors we read choose crucial incidents to explore social class. Do the same—building your essay around events, antidotes, or stories that make your experiences concrete for readers. Show how you have gained knowledge from these experiences by connecting them to larger issues of importance to individuals or groups.

As you write, the first priority is to capture key sociological aspects of experiences before and during your college years: how has social class shaped and influenced you. In this sense, you'll be examining how your world and identity have changed over time. This time in your life is probably filled with thoughts of transition from childhood home to young adulthood. Any types of personal or social changes are also filled with emotions. Writing about these elements—as related to social class—enables you to consider the relationship between the personal and social—a key sociological insight.

Remember you only have 10–15 pages so choose structures/experiences accordingly. You can do this in different ways—exploring experiences from a variety of angles. Below I identify possible ways to develop your essay. You can decide which approaches you're most comfortable with, but you don't have to use all of them. You may have other ideas too.

- Discuss the relationship between your personal experiences and public issues/concerns related to social class (e.g., family,

K–12 and college, community, even religion, politics, economics or work—if you'd like). We'll talk about this during class and look closely at bell hooks, Richard Rodriguez (*On Becoming a Chicano*), for example, and authors in *Class Lives* to see how they address these relationships.

- Consider examining your life in historical context, recognizing how social class conditions (e.g., economic affluence, poverty) and people who've come before you (e.g., parents, grandparents, aunts/uncles) have shaped your life experiences—as related to social class.

- Address elements of your personal experiences intimately linked to public issues you have little or no control over (e.g., K–12 educational funding based on property taxes allowing some students to attend the best/wealthiest schools and sending others to low-achieving, underfunded schools; acceptable rates of unemployment—set at 5% by government and financial institutions—that leave millions of families in financial need over long periods of time; college cultures/structures that often reinforce social class differences; public and private displays of classism).

- Explore how the realities of social class have made you the kind of person you are today. Discuss how you've been advantaged and/or disadvantaged by social class structures you essentially have no control over. Consider how you've dealt with, confronted, or embraced these social class differences.

- Feel free to include aspects of gender and race differences and inequalities, but remember the essay's focus is social class differences.

Techniques of Creative Nonfiction

Creative nonfiction (CN) has been described as memory- or fact-based writing: it includes your life with an eye toward the lives of others. Personal and public histories are recognized using memory and observation. As you write, report on the world as it is experienced.

CN refers to what actually happens—what is simply, succinctly, and accurately happening. To the best of your ability describe what has occurred or what is occurring. Describe real people and events in a compelling and vivid manner. Readers are fascinated by honesty and accuracy—imagining they're actually present at places and events you describe.

I've chosen to assign this narrative assignment because I value your experiences and identities and how experiences inform our understanding of social class differences. As you write, include details related to specific places, years, people, and contexts. With more detail, the reliability of your experiences will shine through and effectively engage readers.

Scenes are the foundation of creative nonfiction. Scenes stand out in the reader's mind and are the building blocks of messages you seek to send. In *Class Lives* ("Those of Us from Rio Linda"), for example, I describe scenes of visiting my father's body in a refrigerated room at the funeral home and later slowly driving through my hometown—Rio Linda—hearing the conservative radio commentator—Rush Limbaugh—denigrate working-class people. In *Singing the First Generation Blues* in the Chronicle of Higher Education (see reader), I begin with two scenes: a student in my office and the same student hearing a professor talk in the classroom. Clearly described scenes—at or near the beginning of the essay and strategically placed throughout—help you to catch the reader's attention and connect with larger audiences that may not be familiar with your experiences.

Using scenes to communicate represents the difference between showing and telling. Writing that only tells the reader about subjects, places, or persons feels remote and misses opportunities to connect with readers in immediate and understandable ways. Good CN writing vividly shows people, situations, and places—unforgettable and detailed—in action and dialogue.

As you describe scenes consider using a bit of dialogue or simple statements—in quotes. Don't overdo this. A short quote can easily illustrate (showing) a general principle you are trying to explain, without using numerous words to remotely describe that principle (telling). For example, when I quote the University of Michigan professor—in *Singing the First Generation Blues*—complaining about people who work with their hands cleaning university buildings and grounds, I plainly illustrate classism (showing) without clarifying at length (telling) the existence of classism at the University of Michigan. This allows the reader to engage, interpret, and imagine.

Another useful CN technique is being indirect in how you describe a scene or interactions. What you don't say can be as important as what you say and this again taps into the reader's imagination. For example, in "Those of Us from Rio Linda," I quote Rush Limbaugh mocking working-class Rio Lindans without directly stating he is hopelessly classist. I let his words and the scene illustrate classist tendencies and how those tendencies affect people who are being ridiculed. I ask readers to imagine a conservative radio commentator insulting lower-income people on a regular/daily basis and how they might react to those insults. Readers can imagine Limbaugh talking in his radio studio and what might motivate him to speak in insensitive ways.

Bring your writing alive by describing in a scene what you are seeing, smelling, tasting, hearing, and touching (five senses). Readers can imagine and identify with what you're experiencing when you describe "the kitchen filled with gentle evening sunlight and welcome aromas of mom's home cooking." They can use their own memories of being at home with a parent and feeling the security of that place. Play around with words—not too many—that reflect what naturally happens within important experiences.

Careful/selective use of colors, sounds, temperatures, places (cities, states, neighborhoods, street names), and feelings/emotions (e.g., joy, sadness, success, failure, anger) also help build images and scenes. A simple quote, for example, can easily portray intense joy or anger. What are people wearing and what do they look/sound like? In "Those of Us From Rio Linda"—when I visit my dad's body at the funeral home in Rio Linda after flying from Michigan (*places*)—I describe *colors* (the white sheet covering his body, the maroon rented Ford), *feelings* (being alone, anxious to leave, terrified, disturbing feelings in the presence of a dead parent), *temperatures* (cold room, Sacramento heat), *smelling* (pungent odors from chemicals helping to preserve my dad's appearance), *hearing/sounds* (absolute quiet of the room where his body lies), and *seeing* (his gaunt face with closed eyes seemingly ready to open up; imagining the autopsy that tested for asbestos in his lungs, and his sewed up chest under the sheet just beyond touch).

Always try to orient the reader to a clear sense of time—past, present, or even future. Feel free to use dates and years. This helps bring your story alive.

Essay Construction and Progress

You'll start outlining/writing your essay as you read various creative nonfiction essays during the first two months of the semester. Use these essays as models for what you choose to write about. We'll talk about these essays in class each week as a way to plan and share ideas. During class, you will also work in pairs for short periods of time—sharing writing approaches, etc. I also encourage you to meet outside class time to talk about ideas. Sharing drafts can provide useful feedback.

To receive feedback from someone not taking Sociology 295 also consider making use of resources at the Sweetland Center for Writing. You may have heard about or used various Sweetland Centers around campus. You can drop into a Peer Writing Center and talk/work with a trained undergraduate peer tutor—first-come, first-served. Or you can ask to have the same tutor over time as the revision process proceeds. Show the tutor these Social Class Essay Guidelines.

www.ingramcontent.com/pod-product-compliance
Lightning Source LLC
Chambersburg PA
CBHW050327270326
41926CB00016B/3351